WRITING IN THE ACADEMIC DISCIPLINES

WRITING IN THE ACADEMIC DISCIPLINES

A Curricular History

Second Edition

DAVID R. RUSSELL

With a Foreword by Elaine P. Maimon

SOUTHERN ILLINOIS UNIVERSITY PRESS
Carbondale and Edwardsville

Library of Congress Cataloging-in-Publication Data

Russell, David R., 1951–
    Writing in the academic disciplines : a curricular history / David R. Russell ;
    foreword by Elaine P. Maimon. —2nd ed.
    p. cm.
    Includes bibliographic references and index.
    1. English language—Rhetoric—Study and teaching—United States—
History. 2. English language—Study and teaching (Secondary)—United States—
History. 3. Interdisciplinary approach in education—United States—History.
4. Academic writing—Study and teaching—United States—History. I. Title.

    PE1405.U6 R8 2002
    808'.042'071'273—dc21
    ISBN 0-8093-2467-9 (paper : alk. paper)   2002022818

Reprinted from the original 1991 edition.

Printed on recycled paper. ♻

The paper used in this publication meets the minimum requirements of
American National Standard for Information Sciences—Permanence of Paper
for Printed Library Materials, ANSI Z39.48-1992. ⊚

for Joyce, still

CONTENTS

II.
The Search For Community
Writing and General Education

III.
The Postwar Era

FOREWORD

As someone who has devoted a major portion of her professional life to the current movement called *writing across the
curriculum* (WAC), I find that reading David Russell's *Writing
in the Academic Disciplines* is like studying an intellectual family
tree. By tracing the genealogy of writing in the disciplines, Russell
creates a context in which to understand contemporary educational conflicts. Is writing a set of discrete mechanical skills or a
function of maturing thought? Should students be able to general-
ize instruction in writing to a variety of situations, or do students
need help in discerning the requirements imposed by different
contexts? Should writing be regarded as transparent (an intrinsic
skill), or should writing be highlighted as a powerful means of
learning? Is writing something that the chosen few learn to do
without being taught, or should writing instruction provide mo-
bility within a democratic society? Russell makes clear that we
did not invent these issues in the last quarter of the twentieth
century. They have a history.

Reading this history in Russell's intelligent, honest, and lucid
account is remarkably instructive. Seen through the prism of
writing in the disciplines, Russell's retelling of U.S. educational
history illuminates the general story, clarifying recurring themes:
excellence and access; general education and specialized study;
teaching and research. Like the writing-across-the-curriculum
movement itself, this book is fundamentally an exploration of

the meaning and purpose of liberal education in a democratic society.

The historical context presented in *Writing in the Academic Disciplines* has immediate pragmatic functions as well. Opponents of writing across the curriculum often attack the movement as ephemeral, a fad equivalent to audiovisual aids in the classroom. Russell's narrative demonstrates that WAC has strong roots in American intellectual life. At the same time, Russell provides the possibility of rational response to naysayers who possess the proverbially dangerous little bit of knowledge. Faculty natterers often claim that writing across the curriculum is nothing more than the Dalton Plan or progressive education—or something else already old under the sun—in a new guise. "We tried that already and it didn't work," they claim wearily, secretly gleeful at bursting the bubble of innovation. Russell allows us to counter these reductive responses by placing past educational movements in an instructive context.

This creation of a meaningful context reflects a profound understanding of what writing across the curriculum is all about: the recognition that meaning changes as the stance of the reader and writer change from situation to situation. Contextual variability is not an easy concept to understand. Yet, American education has until recently assumed that this idea—like writing itself—was transient, something for someone else to teach. Russell argues convincingly against the myth that distinctions among contexts and academic disciplines do not exist. He presents that myth as the greatest obstacle to translating and transforming disciplinary differences within the academic conversation.

Russell's scholarship also reflects the tenets of writing across the curriculum. He draws on social history, sociology, history of education, philosophy of science, and anthropology to create a multi-disciplinary text that invariably enlightens, avoiding muddle. While affirming the existence of disciplinary distinctions, Russell himself manages to translate and transform them.

From a personal perspective, I am pleased that a book-length work of rigorous scholarship is not available to explain the strong foundation of writing across the curriculum in educational psychology and in theories of learning. This book should be required reading for writing program administrators, deans, and all others committed to educational reform. In 1981, my coauthors and I published *Writing in the Arts and Sciences,* a textbook that we hoped would allow instructors and students to work explicitly with writing in the disciplines. Now, a decade later, I am grateful to David Russell for the prodigious research and clear articulation of the history and principles that inform the writing-across-the-curriculum movement.

Not only does Russell tell the story of where we have been and how we got where we are, he illuminates the road ahead for future generations. If writing across the curriculum lasts as an educational reform, it will be, in part, because of Russell's skillful cartography and genealogy.

Elaine P. Maimon

PREFACE TO THE SECOND EDITION

I have been very gratified that many faculty and writing-across-the-curriculum program coordinators from around North America have told me over the last ten years that they found the first edition of this book interesting and, at times, useful. That response shows me that they feel the need for a sense of history as they work to help students learn to write and write to learn. But the last ten years have also impressed upon me the immense variety and scope of WAC—and thus how incomplete this book is. I have often wished that I could thoroughly revise and expand it, to give a more complete account. Yet others have gone a long way in doing that, in many ways relieving me of the task.

In the last decade, there has been some excellent research on the history of WAC, which fills in important gaps. A few examples: The role of WAC in historically black colleges has been traced by Zaluda; community college WAC was researched by Ambron; and efforts to teach professional writing have been chronicled by several, most notably Adams.

Of course there have been myriad efforts to improve students' communication across the curriculum that have not yet been researched, and I hope that historical research will expand, as it provides an important perspective on current efforts and new visions for future efforts. For example, there is much pioneering and important work in WAC during the 1970s and 1980s that deserves historical treatment: high school WAC dissemination efforts such as that of Volusha County and the McCauley School; microthemes at Montana State University; the Baltimore area WAC coalition; the first WAC journal, *Fforum;* WAC in the California State University system; the Northern Virginia Writing Project and the formation of the National Network of WAC Programs; the Chicago Conferences in the 1970s; the Ivy League WAC consortium; the annual Wildacres Conferences; the New York City efforts inspired by Mina Shaughnessy's work; WAC at MIT from the 1960s on; and many others. Fortunately, others are carrying on that work now. And a collection of historical essays is being prepared by Susan McLeod that treats most of these.

Thus, the new material in this second edition focuses only on WAC in the 1990s. The new final chapter is an attempt to tell that story, though history written from such a close perspective can often sound polemical. And I must plead guilty to that. My work in the WAC movement over the last decade, on my own campus and in workshops in the U.S. and abroad, has made me an unashamed (though not uncritical) advocate. And I hope this chapter will add another voice to the important debates going on about the future of WAC and of American education broadly.

ACKNOWLEDGMENTS

A National Endowment for the Humanities summer seminar in rhetoric and public address gave me the impetus to undertake this project. I am deeply grateful to the director, Edward P. J. Corbett, and to my fellow seminarians for their encouragement. Indiana University–Purdue University at Fort Wayne and Iowa State University also provided grants of time and funds for research for the first edition. Special thanks are due to the John S. Knight Institute for Writing in the Disciplines at Cornell University, which provided me with a semester to work on the second edition.

Portions of this study benefited greatly from criticism, at various stages, by Wallace W. Douglas, Richard N. Ramsey, James E. Porter, Michael Feehan, Anne Ruggles Gere, Toby Fulwiler, Tori Haring-Smith, Michael Mendelson, Dorothy Grimes, Michael Flanigan, Elaine P. Maimon, Avon Crismore, and Christopher Thaiss. I am especially indebted to James A. Berlin, Sharon Crowley, Charles Bazerman, David B. Owen, and to the three anonymous reviewers from Southern Illinois University Press for their comments on earlier versions of the manuscript. They are deserving of much praise but of course share none of the blame for what is infelicitous, inaccurate, or downright wrong in this account.

ACKNOWLEDGEMENTS

My thanks to my many friends and colleagues who answered and raised so many questions and provided or pointed me toward materials from so many disciplines. Special thanks to Jonathan Kistler and Ralph Rader, who made archival documents at Colgate University and the University of California at Berkeley available to me. Special thanks also to the archivists and their staffs at Iowa State University, Harvard University, Columbia University, University of Chicago, University of Kansas, University of Missouri, University of Michigan, University of Minnesota, Ohio State University, Central College in Iowa, MIT, and Radcliffe University, whose knowledge, patience, and hospitality were invaluable, and to my research assistant from engineering, Jill Hodgson. My editors, Kenny Withers for the first edition and Karl Kageff for the second, and the rest of the staff at Southern Illinois University Press were unfailingly helpful in this project.

Parts of chapters 1, 4, 5, 6, and 8 appeared in earlier versions in *College English* (Jan. 1990); *Rhetoric and Ideology: Compositions and Criticisms of Power* (Arlington, TX: Rhetoric Society of America, 1989); *Research in the Teaching of English* (Dec. 1989); *Rhetoric Review* (Spring 1988); and *College Composition and Communication* (May 1987).

I

THE TRIUMPH
OF SPECIALIZATION

1

INTRODUCTION
The Myth of Transience

Writing in the Academic Disciplines is a history of writing instruction outside general-composition courses in American secondary and higher education, from the founding of the public secondary school system and research universities in the 1870s through the spread of the writing-across-the-curriculum movement in the 1980s. The vexed history of general-composition courses, especially freshman composition, has been told often and well by James A. Berlin, Wallace W. Douglas, Albert R. Kitzhaber, Robert J. Connors, and many others upon whom I often draw in this account. But my task here is to examine the ways writing has been taught—directly or indirectly—in the wider curriculum or, to be more precise, in the myriad curricula that make up the differentiated structure of secondary and higher education in modern America.

As surprising as it may seem to us today, there was no systematic writing instruction per se past the elementary school in America until the advent of mass education and the formation of discrete academic disciplines in the last third of the nineteenth century. Advanced instruction in vernacular language dates from antiquity, of course, and from the eighteenth century American colleges and preparatory academies taught rhetoric in the vernacular. But before the 1870s, writing was ancillary to speaking. Because the whole curriculum and much of the extracurriculum was based on public speaking (recitation, declamation, oratory, debate), there was little need for systematic writing instruction.

For a speaker, writing was merely an aid to memory; for a reader, it was merely a substitute for a present speaker (private oral reading was still common well into the nineteenth century). The leadership roles which graduates of the old college commonly assumed—"the pulpit, the senate, and the bar"—also made writing ancillary to public speaking. Thus, formal writing instruction essentially amounted to training in handwriting, the mechanical process of transcribing sound to visual form. Literacy meant knowing one's ABCs. Once these orthographic conventions were mastered, "correct" writing was an ordinary outcome of being raised a gentleman or gentlewoman who spoke "correct" English, which is to say the language of the upper class. As Susan Miller has persuasively argued, writing was so embedded in the everyday orally based practices of that class that it was largely transparent and required little or no instruction beyond the elementary school.[1]

By the 1870s, however, the role of writing in education and in the wider culture had begun to shift in subtle but profound ways. America created a host of new professions whose members communicated primarily through texts that were never meant merely to be substitutes for oral communication: the myriad reports, memoranda, specifications, scholarly articles, and so on, which modern society developed. Professionals in and out of academia now used writing to manipulate texts as objects, to be silently studied, critiqued, compared, appreciated, and evaluated. With the revolution in print technology (the modern pen, Linotype, vastly improved presses, typewriter, duplicating machines, vertical files, etc.) and the parallel revolutions in industry (systematic management of far-flung enterprises) and in academia (disciplinary specialization), writing became central to organizing production and creating new knowledge.[2] Writing was now embedded in a whole array of complex and highly differentiated social practices carried on without face-to-face communication. The new professionals (academic or otherwise) increasingly wrote not for a general reader (that is, for any member of the educated class) but rather for specialized audiences of colleagues who were united not primarily by ties of class but by the shared activities, the goals, and—this is crucial—the unique written conventions of a profession or discipline. With this enormous expansion of specialized knowledge and discourse, writing became, as Miller puts it, "a way of thinking, not just a way of preserving thinking for speech" (64).

Unfortunately, the new mass-education system America created to train this cadre of professionals failed to adjust its concept of writing to account for the fact that both writing and education had been transformed. In the new print-centered, compartmentalized secondary and higher-education system, writing was no longer a single, generalizable skill learned once and for all at an early age; rather it was a complex and continuously developing response to specialized text-based discourse communities, highly embedded in the differentiated practices of those communities. Nor was academia any longer a single discourse community but a collection of discrete communities, an aggregate of competing professional disciplines, each with its own specialized written discourse. Moreover, the system of secondary and higher education, once confined to the preparatory academy and the liberal arts college, now widened to include a whole spectrum of differentiated institutions (land-grant universities, technical institutes, public high schools, business schools, trade schools, etc.) preparing and credentialing students for a host of social roles. Each discipline, each kind of institution, developed its own "literacy," its own tacit expectations about how its members (and its students) should write.[3] Despite these profound changes, the mass-education system tenaciously clung to the outmoded conception of writing as transcribed speech and to the vanishing ideal of a single academic community, united by common values, goals, and standards of discourse. Operating together, these misconceptions had profound consequences for writing instruction.

One important result was a conceptual split between "content" and "expression," learning and writing. If writing was an elementary, mechanical skill, then it had no direct relation to the goals of instruction and could be relegated to the margins of a course, a curriculum, an institution. Knowledge and its expression could be conceived of as separate activities, with written expression of the "material" of the course a kind of adjunct to the "real" business of education, the teaching of factual knowledge. From very early in the history of mass education, writing was primarily thought of as a way to examine students, not to teach them, as a means of demonstrating knowledge rather than of acquiring it. Though a few reformers struggled to overcome this false distinction, they never had widespread success, and academia never made writing a central part of teaching in the disciplines.

Another, more visible result of these misconceptions is a 120-year tradition of complaint about student writing (which Harvey Daniels has amusingly chronicled in *Famous Last Words*).[4] Because academics and other professionals assumed that writing was a generalizable, elementary skill and that academia held a universal, immutable standard of literacy, they were constantly disappointed when student writing failed to measure up to the local, and largely tacit, standards of a particular social class, institution, discipline, or profession by which they were in fact judging that writing. Educators produced report after report lamenting the "crisis" in student writing, secure in their assumption that writing was simply a form of talking rather than a complex and developing response to a community's discourse—a mode of learning, in other words. In 1892 one of the first Harvard committees charged with the task of "solving" the "writing problem" thought it "a little less than absurd to suggest that any human being who can be taught to talk cannot likewise be taught to compose. Writing is merely the habit of talking with the pen instead of the tongue."[5] Over the next century, committees of faculty and business leaders repeatedly expressed similar frustration that students had not "learned to write" by the time they reached high school or college or graduate school or career. But the complaints rarely addressed the central issue: standards of literacy were no longer stable; they were rising and, more importantly, multiplying. Thus, Miller concludes,

our natural tendency to inform contemporary education with this still-active aspect of an oral residue is also an implicit source for laments for what is curiously always thought of as the recently lost excellence of student discourse. But such nostalgia does not acknowledge . . . [that] literacy must, because of multiplied fields of writing, be relearned in new contexts throughout educational processes and later. We never get

6

"beyond" writing to oratory as the ancients did in their educational sequence, nor can we stabilize writing's conventions and merely reapply school writing in new settings [66].

The assumption that writing was "talking with the pen," an elementary transcription skill, mistakenly led educators to look for a single solution to a specific educational problem when they actually needed a whole new conception of the role of writing in learning, one that would take into account the modern organization of knowledge through written communication. They persisted in holding on to what Mike Rose has called the "myth of transience." "Despite the accretion of crisis reports, the belief persists in the American university that if we can just do *x,* or *y,* the problem [of poor student writing] will be solved—in five years, ten years, or a generation—and higher education will be able to return to its real work."[6] Because writing seemed to be independent of content learning, the many solutions proposed over the years tended to marginalize writing instruction and reinforce the myth of transience by masking the complexities of the task.

The first and most common "solution" was a general-composition course. When late-nineteenth-century educators cast about for ways to solve the "problem" of students' writing, they eventually settled on a single freshman course of about fifteen or thirty weeks (successor to a very different rhetoric course in the old liberal curriculum). Though it was taught in many ways to students of every kind, freshman composition almost always treated writing as a generalizable elementary skill, independent of disciplinary content. The course focused on mechanical skills: correct grammar, spelling, and usage necessary for transcribing preexisting, fully formed speech or thought into correct written form. The teaching of rhetoric, so central to the old oratorical tradition, gradually faded, though not without a fight, to be replaced by general composition. Writing instruction was denied disciplinary status, compartmentalized into freshman composition, and housed in English departments, where it competed (unsuccessfully) with the new professional discipline of literary study. In time, freshman English became ubiquitous, nearly always the only institutionwide requirement for writing instruction (or writing) in higher education. And with systematic writing instruction thus marginalized, there arose an implicit assumption that general-composition courses should teach students from any background to write correct and coherent expository prose for any purpose in any social or disciplinary context—and that a student's failure to do so was evidence of the need for more elementary training or *remediation,* as it came to be called.

When general-composition courses did not succeed in this impossible task (despite countless experiments and reforms), institutions sometimes tried curriculumwide schemes. Though the phrase *writing across the curriculum* is relatively new, dating from the mid 1970s, the idea of sharing responsibility for writing instruction forms a recurrent theme throughout the history of American secondary and higher education. Like so many other educational reform movements, cross-curricular writing instruction was accepted in principle ("Every teacher should teach writing" is one of the oldest saws in American education), but in practice, reforms were absorbed and transmuted by the system they resisted. In this way reformers' ideas lost their power for change and instead merely reinforced the myth of transience, a process educational historians have long noted in other areas.[7]

There have been literally hundreds of cross-curricular writing programs since the turn of the century at institutions of every type. Indeed, each generation has produced its own versions of cross-curricular writing programs, yet none, except perhaps the last, has made a permanent impact on the modern university curriculum or on literacy in America. Sooner or later these programs were marginalized for many of the same reasons general-composition courses were. Because administrators and faculty did not perceive the central role of writing in modern academic disciplines and professional work, they tended to make writing instruction an adjunct to a course or program rather than an integral part of it. When they did require writing as part of regular courses in the disciplines, that writing was less likely to be integrated into the activity of the course or program and more likely to be seen merely as a favor to the English department or the institution, as a way of enforcing standards of correctness or reinforcing general-composition courses, or as a means of evaluation.[8] The most mechanical aspects of writing received the most attention: "grammar across the curriculum," as C. W. Knoblauch and Lil Brannon have termed it.[9] Even disciplines that took responsibility for writing instruction tended to marginalize writing in special departmental writing courses (e.g., business writing, agricultural writing). Thus, the conceptual split between content and expression found its curricular embodiment not only in remedial or general-composition courses but also in discipline-specific writing courses taught by those outside the discipline (usually trained in English departments).

In the rush to find a single comprehensive solution, academia never systematically examined the nature of writing or its potential for improving learning. The myth of transience masked deep conflicts in the mass-education system over the nature of writing and learning: what is academic writing and how is it learned? What is an academic community and who should be admitted? America has never come to terms with the submerged conflicts that underlie its attitudes and approaches to advanced literacy. And this continuing failure to confront those conflicts kept writing instruction on the margins of the curriculum rather than at its center. As Rose concludes, "Wide-ranging change will occur only if the academy redefines writing for itself, changes the terms of the argument, [and] sees instruction in writing as one of its central concerns" (359).

These deep conflicts emerge as themes in my account of America's century-long flirtation with writing instruction in the disciplines. And in this chapter I outline four of these conflicts as a framework for the story which follows. The first two have to do with the nature of writing and its acquisition: writing as a single elementary skill, a transparent recording of speech or thought or physical reality, versus writing as a complex rhetorical activity, embedded in the differentiated practices of academic discourse communities; and writing acquisition as remediation of deficiencies in skill versus writing acquisition as a continuously developing intellectual and social attainment tied to disciplinary learning. The second two conflicts center on the relation between language and the structure of mass education: academia as a single discourse community versus academia as many competing discourse communities; and disciplinary excellence versus social equity as the goal of writing instruction. By bringing these long-submerged conflicts into the light of historical analysis, it may be easier to see the enormity and complexity of the task that American mass education set for itself in teaching students "to write."

Academic Writing: Transparent Recording or Visible Rhetoric?

Because late-nineteenth-century academics failed to shift from the old oral conception of writing as transcription to a new conception that took into account writing's vastly expanded functions, the role of writing in academia—both research and teaching—remained largely transparent, unexamined. Faculty thought of their writing not as persuasive discourse, subject to the same rhetorical and stylistic analysis as a sermon or campaign speech, but rather as an unproblematic rendering of the fruits of research, untainted (when done properly) by rhetorical and stylistic concerns. Historians of both rhetoric and science have pointed to important ideological factors that reinforced (some would say created) this blindness to the rhetorical nature of academic writing. The naive view of language as transparent recorder of thought or physical reality grew up with the scientific method in the eighteenth and nineteenth centuries. It underlay the Scottish Common Sense rhetorical theory of Hugh Blair and George Campbell, which Americans imported in the early nineteenth century and applied fully in the new composition textbooks of the 1880s. James Berlin describes the view:

When the individual is freed from the biases of language, society, or history, the senses provide the mental faculties with a clear and distinct image of the world. The world readily surrenders its meaning to anyone who observes properly, and no operation of the mind—logical or otherwise—is needed to arrive at truth. To communicate, the speaker or writer—both now included—need only provide the language which corresponds either to the objects in the external world or to the ideas in his or her own mind—both are essentially the same—in such a way that it reproduces the objects and the experience of them in the minds of the hearers.[10]

This naive view of language supported an ethic of scientific objectivity associated with an emerging positivism in academia, an ethic which reinforced the high status accorded science in modern industrial society. "Truth is to be discovered outside the rhetorical enterprise," Berlin continues, "through the method, usually the scientific method, of the appropriate discipline, or, as in poetry and oratory, through genius" (770). The ethic of scientific objectivity led academics to downplay the role of persuasion in their enterprise and to view their disciplines as vehicles for discovering the bare facts and immutable laws of nature. Scientists and scholars maintained that the old oral, persuasive rhetoric in the classical tradition (increasingly identified with emotional or grandiloquent oratory) should have nothing to do with intellectual inquiry, that good academic writing must therefore be an objective rendering of reality.

Operating together with these ideological barriers were powerful institutional barriers to seeing the differentiated and rhetorical nature of academic writing. The naive view of language supported the wider organizational structure of the new university by confining discourse to discipline-specific forums. Faculty engaged in written discourse primarily within a discipline, not among disciplines, and expected their students to do the same. In both the new departmentalized university and the new professionalized society, there were powerful reasons why scientists and scholars should *not* step outside their respective symbolic universes. It was the ever-increasing specialization of knowledge (and, with it, of discourse) that allowed modern academia to create new knowledge so effectively and rapidly. Persuading many people from many communities to understand and value one's productions is immensely difficult and time-consuming, often impossible. As various disciplines became accepted into academia, their role within the institution and the wider society allowed that responsibility to shift from individual scholars to the discipline, through its professional associations, or to the institution itself, through its public-relations channels. Though efforts to disseminate and popularize discipline-specific knowledge and to promote disciplines' public images continued, these were largely separate from the increasingly more specialized scholarly dialogues going on within disciplines. And of course dissemination is lower in status than specialized research; it is often left to specialists of a different sort—those in journalism and public relations. On a broader level, widespread dissemination of expert knowledge sometimes constituted a threat to professional communities, whose social role involved commodifying that knowledge in specialized written language to maintain professional jurisdiction over certain social functions (the legal profession is the most obvious example).[11]

Thus, the transparency of rhetoric in academic disciplines is in many ways a function of specialization. As the disciplines became separated from one another and from the wider culture, persuasion became so limited, so bound up with the genres (and activities) of a specific community's discourse, that it could be taken for granted by members of the community. Scholars saw little need to enter other symbolic worlds, little benefit in making their own discourse accessible to outsiders, little reason to translate their knowledge into the genres of other communities and thus reconcile their activities and conventions of discourse with those of other disciplines.

Yet the naive, mechanical conception of writing which specialization fostered contradicted the actual practice of academics, for whom writing was a very human thing, a complex social activity involving a whole range of rhetorical choices, intellectual, professional, and political, as recent research into the social basis of writing has shown.[12] As a social activity, writing is inevitably embedded in and conditioned by a community. By its very nature it is local, context specific, dependent on a community for its existence and its meaning. *Literacy* is thus a function of the specific community in which certain kinds of reading and writing activities take place. Standards of acceptable discourse vary among social and disciplinary groups, a fact that we implicitly recognize in our daily affairs. As Brazilian sociolinguist Terezinha Carraher notes, a professor may, without irony, express pleasure that her maid is "literate" because she can barely decode recipes and take down phone messages, but complain that her students are "illiterate" because they do not yet understand the conventions of written discourse in her discipline.[13]

This social perspective on writing embeds each text in a context of human behaviors. Genre becomes, in Carolyn Miller's formulation, "typified rhetorical actions based in recurrent situations."[14] Those recurrent situations, the habits of a community, give rise to repeated formal elements in texts: conventions of argument, evidence, diction, style, organization, and documentation which allow those familiar with the conventions to recognize and understand the writing of a particular community. Cooperative human activities (to borrow Lev Vygotski's phrase) organize themselves through language. In the activities of modern mass education and disciplinary inquiry, the language that counts most is written—but written in ways characteristic of the various cooperative activities, the various communities and subcommunities that make up the system. As Arthur N. Applebee says of the symbolic universes of the disciplines (*paradigms* as he calls them, following Thomas Kuhn), "These paradigms provide tacit guidelines about proper lines of evidence and modes of argument. Though rarely made explicit, their influence is pervasive; they determine what will be seen as interesting, what as obvious, and what as needing elaboration."[15]

One can understand the writing of a community, as Charles Bazerman has pointed out, only in terms of the community's activities: the issues it addresses, the purposes it serves, the concrete objects it manipulates, the questions it has excluded or already answered to the satisfaction of the community, the things that can be left unsaid because of the community's history and activity, or the things that might be said to accomplish its objectives. To read and write meaningfully, one must, in other words, understand how the community interprets its texts, those shared understandings (Bazerman's term) which connect text to context. Using the conventions of a genre without understanding (tacitly or explicitly) how those conventions operate within the community is as meaningless as learning how pieces move in a chess game without knowing the conditions under which one piece may capture another or knowing that the object is to checkmate the opposing king.[16]

Over the past two decades, scholars have just begun to study the rhetoric of academic disciplines and other professional communities on a case-by-case basis, to analyze the interactional rules, tacit and explicit, which govern the knowledge-making and communicating activities of various discourse communities and subcommunities. These scholars do not attempt, as did earlier critics of academic specialization, to banish specialized vocabularies, arcane "rhetoric," in order to restore some universal clarity to the academic Babel. Rather than seek to overcome modern complexity, they study the ways modern complexity is reflected in and created by writing. Their goal is to advance the activities of specialized communities, not to transcend specialization. Studies by Donald McCloskey (economics), Greg Myers (biology), Charles Bazerman (the experimental article in various disciplines), Glenn Broadhead and Richard C. Freed (business consulting), Hayden White (history), James Boyd White (law), JoAnne Yates (industrial management), along with many studies of knowledge making in science, explore the institutional as well as the intellectual and material settings in which writing takes place.[17]

Such analysis is a complex undertaking within any one community or subcommunity, for each is made up of members who play many and often-shifting roles; the rules of the game constantly change in response to a wide range of intellectual, material, and political forces within and outside the community. Moreover, these studies have often met with considerable resistance from mainline scholars. But only such sociorhetorical analysis, discipline by discipline, will provide a foundation on which to construct meaningful generalizations about how writing works—and how students learn to make it work.

Writing Instruction: Remediation or Development?

The transparency of writing (and rhetoric) within the academic disciplines had profound effects on writing instruction. As I noted, modern mass education carried over a premodern view of writing as a single, generalizable skill, learned once and forever. Students whose writing did not conform to a particular community's standards were thought to exhibit some deficit, which had to be remedied *before* they could be admitted to the community. Thus, systematic writing instruction beyond elementary school was often classed as remedial and relegated to the margins of the system. The systematic teaching of rhetoric as public discourse—the heart of the classical liberal arts curriculum for centuries—almost passed out of the curriculum entirely, as academia increasingly valued the pursuit of specialized knowledge on matters of disciplinary import over the teaching of persuasive discourse on matters of broad civic import.[18]

But if one sees writing (and rhetoric) as deeply embedded in the differentiated practices of disciplines, not as a single elementary skill, one must reconceive in profound ways the process of learning to write. Fred Newton Scott, Gertrude Buck, Sterling Andrus Leonard, and other Deweyan reformers in the early years of this century created an alternative approach to writing instruction, one that saw language acquisition as a socially conditioned, developmental process; but only in the last three decades has a social perspective received widespread attention.[19] Viewed from a developmental rather than a remedial perspective, learning to write becomes, as recent research has demonstrated, a process of socialization or acculturation, analogous to a young child learning to speak. Theories of first-language acquisition (such as Vygotski's) illuminate the process of acquiring advanced literacy in an academic or professional community. The neophyte gradually acquires the community's shared knowledge not only by listening and reading but also by experimenting with verbal formulations, orally, as with children, and later in writing, through situations embedded in the life of the neophyte's community, whether the family or the discipline. Like adults talking to babbling children, the more skilled members of the disciplinary community, instructors, supervisors, or more experienced peers, recast the neophyte's utterances in a form suitable to the community until, as Bazerman says, "the beginner produces an utterance recognized as bearing meaning within the socially shared system" (304).

During this process of linguistic initiation, the community often applies more tolerant standards to the verbal performances of neophytes than to the performances of those it recognizes as fully socialized members. It is crucial to note that this gradual and often-subtle process of observation, modeling, and intervention requires the neophyte to use the language of the community *while* participating in its activity not *before* participating, as the remedial view would have it. Through participation students learn to connect verbal formulations to the meanings with which the community invests them. Through participation students learn not only the community's terms and categories but also when and how to apply them: the interactional rules (304).

In the process of acquiring discipline-specific literacy, the adept's intervention during a student's apprenticeship often comes about through written forms which recognize the neophyte's status: textbook experiments to be performed and written up, standard questions to answer, or model cases to argue. These activities produce a scaffolding, "a framework of meaning into which the neophytes' impulses, behaviors and language can shape themselves."[20] This scaffolding is gradually incorporated into her own behavior, until the instructions of the adept become internalized as self-instructions and she develops what Vygotski calls "an internal language."[21] Eventually, the neophyte so thoroughly internalizes the discourse of the community and, with it, the community's perceptions, assumptions, and behaviors, that she begins to think and act—and write—like a member of the community. By the time she is accepted as an adept, she has at least tacitly understood and accepted the community's values and goals, its rules and sanctions; she has developed an allegiance to the community, an identity and role within it.

This theory of writing acquisition helps explain why writing in the academic disciplines has been so little studied or systematically taught. Because apprentices in a discipline very gradually learn its written conventions as an active and integral part of their socialization in a community, the process of learning to write seems transparent. Scholars and researchers come to view the particular genres that the disciplinary community has evolved (and each member of it has internalized) not as rhetorical strategies, conventional—but gradually changing—means of persuasion; instead, the community's genres and conventions appear to be unproblematic renderings of the fruits of research. Persuasion, as Bazerman argues, "is at the heart of science [and, I might add, of all academic disciplines], not at the unrespectable fringe" (321). But the symbolic universe that a scholar grows to inhabit denies rhetoric while nevertheless depending on it. A researcher is likely to see his writing practices not as rhetorical choices but as business as usual or "simply good science" (321).

The kinds of evidence accepted, the style deemed appropriate, the familiar turns of phrase—these are learned as part of the *common sense* of the discipline, as anthropologist Clifford Geertz uses the term: "not what the mind cleared of cant spontaneously apprehends [but] what the mind filled with presuppositions . . . concludes."[22] Disciplines never acquired a conscious knowledge of the rhetorical conventions they used daily and expected their students to use, for these conventions were so bound up with the activity of the discipline and were acquired so subtly in the learning of the discipline itself that they were rarely thought of as writing instruction. To students bound for a career, as well as to the faculty who prepared them for one, writing was something acquired as a matter of course, part of the apprenticeship in the discipline which formal schooling provided (and the apprentice system was, after all, the method of the German university which the American university adopted in certain respects during its formative years).

The transparency of rhetoric in the academic disciplines also helps explain why writing instruction has so often been marginalized. At the curricular level, if professionals are not aware of the role rhetoric plays in their own discipline, then they will see little need to teach it. From the time the modern academic disciplines emerged as discrete communities in the mid and late nineteenth century, they have rarely integrated systematic writing instruction into their curricula to initiate the neophytes consciously into the written conventions of a particular field. Instead, they have required separate courses, usually general composition. At the most advanced levels of instruction, usually in graduate school, some departments have offered courses in research methods which treat discipline-specific writing conventions. But these have affected only a tiny fraction of students in secondary and higher education; the great majority of students have had no conscious, systematic, discipline-specific writing instruction.

The transparency of rhetoric in the disciplines makes it much more difficult for faculty to see and intervene in the students' socialization into the discipline, though that transparency at the same time encourages complaints. Because the development of discipline-specific writing skill is gradual and subtle, bound up with the activity of the discipline, faculty have tended to mistake the inevitable struggles of students to acquire the rhetorical conventions of a discipline for poor writing or sheer ignorance. As Applebee points out, "When we move beyond remedial or 'basic' English, problems in managing this [discipline-specific rhetorical] aspect of text are the cause of much that we call poor writing."[23] But the students' struggles to comprehend the new symbolic universe and operate within it are often misinterpreted by the instructor, who has been so gradually and thoroughly socialized into the symbolic universe of the discipline that he often cannot see or understand why others, who are writing about the same "content," do not "make sense." Though the students may understand the "facts," they may not understand the essential rhetorical structures: specialized lines of argument, vocabulary, and organizational conventions, the tacit understandings about what must be stated and what assumed—in short, the culture of the discipline that gives meaning to the "facts." Only through a long process of acculturation—participating in the activities of the discipline—will they acquire those shared understandings that allow their writing to "make sense."[24] Because the rhetoric of the discipline appears not to be taught, efforts to teach it may require those in a discipline first to become conscious of rhetoric's role in their activities and, second, to make a conscious effort to teach it. But given the transparency of rhetoric for faculty, the usual tendency has been to complain about poor student writing and locate the problem elsewhere, thus reinforcing the myth of transience.

Yet students have nevertheless learned to write in many ways and places. Despite periodic alarms about the pernicious effects of Americans' poor writing, the nation's secondary- and higher-education systems, its vast industrial plant, cultural activities, and governmental structures have never been crippled by poor writing; indeed, for the last half century America has been the cultural, educational, and scientific center of the world, as well as the dominant world power. Somehow, enough Americans learned to write in the ways they needed to in order to carry on, and rather well at that. The experience of other industrialized nations (few of whom have composition courses in higher education) would suggest that students can and do learn to write as a regular part of their education or of their work in a discipline or a profession.[25] Despite the misconceptions about the nature of writing, despite the marginalization of systematic instruction, America has evolved several tacit traditions of student writing: the notebook, the research paper, the laboratory report, the case study, the essay examination, and so on, through which faculty have taught students the writing of the discipline, though perhaps less consciously or less rapidly or less effectively than with direct instruction.

However, these venues for writing instruction are difficult to locate and study. In modern America, the most complex print (and electronic) culture in history, writing is enormously varied, embedded in countless social activities, and performs myriad functions. Even within the educational sector, students write (and acquire competence in writing) as a part of daily work at all levels, from the most rudimentary activities (a student filling in a blank on a preprinted worksheet) to the most sophisticated knowledge making (writing a scholarly article, for example).

Despite the complexity and transparency of these tacit, unsystematic venues for writing acquisition, they nevertheless form an important part of the story of writing in the academic disciplines. Unfortunately, these tacit traditions of student writing have rarely been studied, much less from a historical perspective. In this study I view the various kinds of student writing as genres, typified responses to the activity of a particular institution, discipline, or profession, which have changed along with the educational and professional environments of which they are a part. The Chemistry 101 lab report is a reflection, however dim, of scientific articles in academic journals or of reports written in corporate research and development labs. The sociology class' case study echoes the social worker's case history, the sophomore's Shakespeare paper the literary critic's journal article. To tease these traditions out of the pedagogical and institutional fabric into which they are woven, I looked to a variety of sources: textbooks, curricula, syllabi, examinations, student papers, surveys of teaching practices. But these sources are inevitably piecemeal and often ambiguous. I have slighted many curricula, subdisciplines, and indeed whole disciplines in this account. I can only hope that those who are interested in the role of writing in disciplinary communities will fill in this very crude sketch, a project that has already begun as the current writing-across-the-curriculum movement (WAC) explores the differences in the rhetoric and teaching of academic disciplines, as I discuss in chapter 9. This exploration of discipline-specific conventions is already yielding much information on the ways disciplines constitute themselves through written discourse. Such study is essential if we are to understand how disciplines perpetuate themselves by initiating new members into the discourse of their communities.

Academic Discourse: Community or Communities?

The complex origins of mass education in America made it difficult for academia to view learning to write as an initiation into a discourse community, a process of gradually coming to use language in a certain way to become accepted, "literate," or, as is often the case in modern American higher education, credentialed in some profession. Before the advent of the modern university in the 1870s, academia was indeed a single discourse community. Institutions of higher learning built an intellectual and social community by selecting students primarily on the basis of social class (less than 1 percent of the population was admitted), which guaranteed linguistic homogeneity, and by initiating them intellectually through a series of highly language dependent methods—the traditional recitation, disputation, debate, and oral examination of the old liberal curriculum. Equally important, most students shared common values (Christian, often sectarian) with their teachers (primarily ministers). They pursued a uniform course of study and were then duly welcomed as full members of the nation's governing elite.[26]

The modern university changed all that. It provided the specialized knowledge that drove the new urban-industrial economy and a new class of specialized *professionals* (the term came into use during the period) who managed that economy, with its secular rationale and complex bureaucratic organization—what Burton J. Bledstein has aptly called "the culture of professionalism." Beginning with the land-grant colleges of the late nineteenth century and continuing with the rise of the modern university on the German model, the academic discourse community became fragmented. Numbers swelled, with enrollments tripling as a percentage of the population between 1900 and 1925 alone. Students from previously excluded social groups were admitted, destroying linguistic homogeneity. The new elective curriculum was introduced to prepare students for a host of emerging professional careers in the new industrial society. The elective curriculum compartmentalized knowledge and broke one relatively stable academic discourse community into many fluctuating ones. And the active, personal, language-dependent instructional methods of the old curriculum were replaced by passive, rather impersonal methods borrowed from Germany or, later, from scientific management: lecture, objective testing, and the like. Ultimately, the professional faculty who replaced the gentlemen scholars and divines of the old curriculum came to see secondary and undergraduate education as only one of several competing responsibilities (along with graduate teaching, research, and professional service). And the teaching of writing—initiating the neophytes into a discourse community—suffered accordingly.

Because it is tempting to recall academia's very different past and hope for a very different future, the term *academic community* has powerful spiritual and political connotations, but today academia is a *discourse* community only in a context so broad as to have little meaning in terms of shared linguistic forms, either for the advancement of knowledge (which now goes on in disciplinary communities and subcommunities) or for the initiation of new members (who are initiated into a specific community's discourse). Thus, to speak of the academic community as if its members shared a single set of linguistic conventions and traditions of inquiry is to make a categorical mistake. In the aggregate of all the tightly knit, turf-conscious disciplines and departments, each of its own discourse community, the modern university consists. Many have wished it otherwise.

Despite these profound changes, American educators have continued to think of the academic community as holding out a single compositional norm, which would speak intelligently about the multiform new knowledge to a "general reader." In their complaints about student writing, academics hark back nostalgically to a golden age of academic community where Johnny could both read and write the "plain English" that purists enshrine. But that golden age never existed in the modern university (and writing per se was not valued or even evaluated in the old college). As Daniel P. and Lauren B. Resnick have observed, "There is little to go back to in terms of pedagogical method, curriculum, or school organization. The old tried and true approaches, which nostalgia today prompts us to believe might solve current problems, were designed neither to achieve the literacy standards sought today nor to assure successful literacy for everyone . . . there is no simple past to which we can return."[27] Though academia held onto a generalized ideal of an academic community sharing a single advanced literacy, there was never any consensus in the modern university about the nature of that community or its language. Academic discourse, like academia itself, continued its drive toward increasing specialization. The university became an aggregate of competing discourse communities; it was not a single community. But the myth of a single academic discourse community—and a golden age of student writing—endured.

American academia today (and for the last hundred years or so) is a community primarily in a broad institutional sense, a collection of people going about a vast enterprise, in much the same way that we speak of the "business community" as a sector of national life. The academic disciplines are in one sense united through their common missions: teaching, research, and service. But disciplines have been so diverse, so independent, and so bound up with professional communities outside academia that they require no common language or even shared values and methods within the university in order to pursue those missions. Those genres and conventions of writing that are shared by all academic disciplines are also shared by professional communities outside academia. And within academia, the conventions (and beyond them the assumptions and methodologies) of the various disciplines are characterized more by their differences than by their similarities. The various disciplines have grown to constitute the modern university through accretion, as Gerald Graff has forcefully argued, and through their relevance to concerns in the wider society, not through their logical relation to each other— so much so that "interdisciplinary" study is always a notable (and often suspect) exception.[28] Indeed, an academic is likely to have more linguistic common ground with a fellow professional in the corporate sector than with another academic in an unrelated field, except in regard to purely institutional matters (governance, academic freedom, teaching loads, etc.). As a leading sociologist of higher education, Burton Clark, puts it, academia is made up of "small worlds, different worlds."[29]

The problematic nature of the modern academic discourse community in large part explains the survival of the myth of transience and the American university's century-long flirtation with cross-curricular writing programs. Since the turn of the century, the whole structure of higher education has depended on what Laurence R. Veysey calls the "patterned isolation of its component parts." This isolation "required that people continually talk past each other, failing to listen to what others were really saying."[30] Because the modern university served so many conflicting interests—students, teachers, parents, administrators, industry, and government, as well as a host of competing disciplines with their own agendas—it required "barriers to frank dialogue which are stylized into courtesy," or in rhetorical terms, discipline-specific conventions operating independently under an umbrella of god-terms whose meanings were not shared or even examined too deeply: research and service most prominently, but also general education, humanism, and science. "Tacitly obeying the need to fail to communicate," Veysey goes on, "each academic group normally refrained from too rude or brutal an unmasking of the rest. And in this manner, without major economic incentives and without a genuine sharing of ideals, [academics] labored together in what became a diverse but fundamentally stable institution" (337). Conscious, systematic, curriculumwide writing instruction was an unfortunate victim of the need for stability.

The modern university's compartmentalized, additive organization of knowledge was made possible—or at least made more efficient—by the transparency of rhetoric and the marginalization of writing instruction. The lack of student writing freed the faculty from much paper grading and interaction with students, leaving more time to pursue those two new ideals which redefined the university in the late nineteenth century: discipline-specific research and utilitarian service. But in a deeper sense, the lack of student writing allowed faculty to ignore other disciplines. Conscientious writing instruction forces a teacher to explain (and to some extent conceptualize) the rhetorical conventions of her discipline and—more difficult still—occasionally to describe how the conventions she requires for, say, a history paper, are different from the conventions a student is wrestling with for a chemistry or literature paper in another class. Ignoring writing instruction in the disciplines made it much easier for higher education to proceed in neat compartments, without confronting messy questions about the relationships between disciplines or, messier still, questions about the ways students should be capable of using language when they enter the broader society. Because faculty rarely asked their students to struggle with the complexities of entering a specific discourse community through writing, they could more easily maintain the illusion that the university was still one discourse community, that such terms as *reason, the generally educated person,* or *the humanities* referred to single, unitary concepts, independent of the new organization of knowledge and the new mass society that created it. Thus, it was in the interest of the university to view writing as a *Ding an sich,* a separate and independent technique, something that should have been learned elsewhere, taught by someone else—in high school or in a freshman "service" course. Chapters 2 through 4 trace these effects of increasing specialization on writing instruction. Chapter 2 examines the transition from the old liberal curriculum to the new differentiated curriculum of secondary and higher education. Chapters 3 and 4 examine the ways the two new ideals of academic life, research and utilitarian service, shaped writing instruction into its modern forms.

Almost from the beginning of the modern university, however, there were critics who attacked academic specialization and the narrow compartmentalization of writing instruction. But instead of accepting or confronting specialization, with its thorny rhetorical and political problems, they ignored or sought to transcend it. Reformers from both the left and the right attempted to reestablish an academic community where students and faculty shared a common language and, in many cases, a set of values.[31] "General education" was the single rallying cry of reformers from irreconcilably opposed camps. Predictably, the reformers did not succeed in building a unified academic discourse community, but they did reinforce the myth of transience by nurturing the assumption that the linguistic millennium would soon come, if only academia would adopt some particular form of general education.

Chapters 5 through 7 treat the history of general-education reforms as they affected writing instruction. I have roughly divided the reform efforts into three strands, although they do often intersect in complex ways. First, the "social efficiency" movement of the "administrative progressives" (Lawrence Cremin's terms) applied the industrial model to education in an attempt to forge a unified society through bureaucratic organization (chapter 5). Its solution to the writing problem was remedial writing courses and programs. Second, the genteel tradition (or "liberal culture," as Veysey calls it) defended the humanities against the onslaught of scientific specialization, commercial philistinism, and the diluting of "standards of taste," which they blamed on immigration and industrialization (chapter 6). It resisted systematic writing instruction and trusted that the reading and discussion of the "great books" would improve students' writing. Third, the Deweyan progressives sought to unify the sciences and arts, manual and liberal education, in a new rational democratic state (chapter 7). The Deweyan progressives promoted cross-curricular writing instruction as part of a broader "correlation" movement, which attempted to unify subjects around social concerns. None of the three established a tradition of successfully integrating writing instruction into the curriculum. Through each wave of reform, the myth of transience persisted; and in the post-World War II era, these efforts to restore linguistic consensus continued to animate reforms in writing and general education, despite the almost complete triumph of specialization in academia. Even today some manifestations of the latest interdisciplinary effort, the WAC movement, still seek to reunite academia into a coherent discourse community and solve, once and for all, the problem of poor student writing and, in the same stroke, the troubling incoherence of modern education. In part three (chapters 8 and 9) I take up these postwar developments.

The Goals of Writing Instruction: Equity or Excellence?

Efforts to initiate students into the discourses of specialized disciplines have continually been marginalized by another fundamental conflict within academia. As Burton Clark has pointed out, modern mass-education systems throughout the world must accommodate the competing claims of "equity" and "excellence," as he terms them or, more broadly, of inclusion and exclusion. Pressure from excluded groups to widen access almost inevitably conflicts with pressure from various sources to maintain or raise standards. Every industrialized nation has these conflicts. In the Soviet Union, for example, the conflict has traditionally been between admitting students to specialized professional training on the basis of competitive examinations or on the basis of their class origins, with workers' children receiving preference. In every nation, excluded groups have at times succeeded, through political pressure, in temporarily forcing educational systems to promote equity. However, such victories are, as Clark points out, likely to be hard won and impermanent, for the differentiated, agonistic structure of disciplines, which organizes postelementary education in the modern world, tends to value exclusionary standards of excellence over equity.[32] Writing instruction is part of that conflict. To teach students the discourse of a professional elite is often a crucial part of initiating them into the profession; to exclude them from such discourse is to make that initiation more difficult, if not impossible. By relegating systematic writing instruction to the margins of academic work, outside the specific disciplinary contexts where students are taught to enter coveted professional roles, institutions preserve standards of excellence and reduce social equity.

However, American mass education has managed to accommodate both values by institutionalizing ambiguity in many ways through its approach to writing and its teaching. General-composition courses have in one sense been a means of widening access by helping to "prepare" students for college work. But to the extent that those courses were treated as remedial or purgatorial, they also performed a "gatekeeping" function by keeping students on the margins of the institution. For much of this century, many institutions have used freshman composition as a way of weeding out those considered unfit for college work *before* they had the opportunity to enter specialized studies.[33] Through this gatekeeping function, general-composition courses have offered the mass-education system a means of dealing with the successive waves of previously excluded students who have continually flocked into the higher-education system since the late nineteenth century.

As Rose has argued, the myth of transience allows this ambiguity to go unexamined. It blinds academics to the effects of widening access and the shifting nature of literacy in the mass-education system. Thus it reinforces the status quo.

Like any golden age or utopian myth, the myth of transience assures its believers that the past was better or that the future will be. The turmoil they are currently in will pass. The source of the problem is elsewhere; thus it can be ignored or temporarily dealt with until the tutors or academies or grammar schools or high schools or families make the changes they must make. The myth, then, serves to keep certain fundamental recognitions and thus certain changes at bay [336].

Rose is referring to general-composition courses here and their marginalization as remedial or preparatory adjuncts to the "real" work of the academy. But another of those institutional ambiguities which the myth of transience reinforces is the split between conscious, systematic attempts to improve writing in general-composition courses and the transparent, unconscious writing acquisition in the specialized disciplines. By relegating conscious, systematic writing instruction (and evaluation) to general-composition courses, faculty in the disciplines have rarely had to address the relationship between writing and excellence, between language and equity, in terms of their own disciplines and professions. Faculty are rarely held formally responsible by institutions for initiating students into the discourse of their disciplines (and therefore of the professional roles tied to them). And, thus, disciplines have found it easy to ignore the role that writing plays in students' preparation for and admission to the professions.

In the absence of conscious, discipline-specific writing instruction, students whose language backgrounds allowed them to learn the discourse of a discipline without such instruction were more likely to enter successfully the professions associated with it; those students whose backgrounds made conscious, discipline-specific language instruction necessary were much less likely to succeed. And because the function of language in this sorting was thought to be generalized, transparent—a matter of prior instruction, aptitude, intelligence, or dedication rather than of conscious, discipline-specific teaching—faculty rarely felt responsible for addressing the issue of language and access to professional roles. Though there were occasional skirmishes over responsibility for poor student writing, these were a small price to pay compared to the full-scale political battles that occurred in nations where students were consciously and overtly selected and tracked on the basis of their written performances on externally graded papers and essay examinations.

At such times when America perceived a shortage of professionals in some field, academics in that field widened access and paid more attention to teaching—initiating—students, including their writing. The times of greatest interest in laboratory writing, for example, came when scientists were in greater demand after World War I and after Sputnik (see chapters 3 and 8); and the current writing-across-the-curriculum movement in large part began as a response to pressure from minorities for greater access to higher education and thus professional roles (see chapter 9).

But in the absence of external pressures for widening access, disciplines typically exert pressure for higher standards and greater exclusion. They are agonistically structured enterprises, both within and among themselves. Disciplines compete among themselves for institutional and social status, with the attendant rewards. Maintaining high standards—"excellence," to use Clark's term—helps to raise the status of a discipline. Thus, it is sometimes in the interest of a discipline to restrict access. High standards are also in the interest of an individual institution to the extent that prestige comes from perceived excellence in research. And valuing disciplinary excellence serves the interests of society at large to the extent that it encourages professions to produce (or conserve) knowledge and provide services considered important to society as a whole. Moreover, scholars within each community compete with each other for professional accomplishment and status. In doing so, they advance the work of the community enterprise. A discipline is structured as a series of hurdles, many of them primarily written—examinations, theses, refereed publications, applications, tenure and promotion cases, and so on—designed to promote and reward the production (or conservation) of knowledge.

The transparency of writing masks that the rules of the game are, in many ways, rhetorical; written discourse plays an important (at some points crucial) role in professional advancement. And the whole system depends upon disciplinary boundaries that are, in varying degrees, established and maintained rhetorically through the unique discursive activity of each community. Thus, conscious, systematic, discipline-specific writing instruction involves trade-offs. Time and resources spent teaching writing may reduce time and resources available for intramural activities, such as conducting research or providing professional services—the century-old conflict between teaching and research. And in a deeper sense, consciously translating the discipline's rhetorical universe into language that students at lower levels could understand may be seen as trivializing or watering down the very knowledge the discipline is charged with upholding. Initiating greater numbers into its ranks may thus pose a threat to the status of a discipline. Attempts at creating well-articulated secondary and undergraduate curricula incorporating writing have been largely unsuccessful in part because they were perceived as lowering standards. A discipline might improve its work by becoming conscious of its sociorhetorical structures, if only because it could more effectively train neophytes—or train more of them. But, unless spurred by external pressures, disciplines have not found it necessary to examine, much less improve, the way students are initiated into their respective symbolic universes. Given the lack of incentives operating within the differentiated and agonistic structure of the disciplines, writing instruction in the disciplines has tended to remain an informal and largely unconscious dimension of the regular activity of each community, a transparent part of business as usual.

By confining formal writing instruction to general-composition courses, academia was able to serve the values of equity without threatening the disciplines' pursuit of excellence. Disciplines were free to set rhetorically based standards tacitly. At the same time they could deny (or leave unexamined) the rhetorical nature of their work and thus the responsibility to articulate or systematically teach their discourse. In this way, the peculiar role that writing instruction played in American mass education reinforced the differentiated curricular and institutional structure. The myth of transience is adaptive, for it helps to mediate within the institution the deep value conflicts between equity and excellence, but it does so at the expense of a genuine examination of the ways that writing influences higher learning—and access to the professions which depend on that learning.

Beyond the Myth of Transience: Some Notes on Scope and Methods

Because my subject is so broad, reaching into every discipline and almost every educational setting, I have omitted much and condensed more to produce a one-volume study of efforts to teach writing across the curriculum. Nevertheless, I attempt, through occasional case studies, to demonstrate how some specific disciplines and institutions have approached the problem of training their students to write. But this history does not do justice to the diversity of writing instruction within subdisciplines and fields or to the enviable variety of educational institutions America has built. I pass over a whole tradition in departments of journalism, for example, and do little more than mention the long traditions of advanced courses in composition and rhetoric within English and speech departments. As current research into the role of writing and writing pedagogies in individual disciplines continues, the story of writing instruction in various disciplines will be told in greater depth and detail than is possible in this overview. And that research, both synchronic and diachronic, will allow historians to offer richer perspectives and make more informed generalizations than those I tentatively posit here.

In the same way, the institutional perspective I bring to this study is also limited, but it offers an alternative to the common approaches to the history of writing instruction. Historians of rhetoric in academia have almost always taken as their subject freshman composition. They have examined it through the lens of the English department or through the lens of cultural and rhetorical history. My method is at once broader and narrower. I look at writing from the perspective of academic institutions, especially their disciplinary structure, rather than from the perspective of a single department or of broad cultural and rhetorical categories.

One focus of historians has been on the evolution of general-composition courses, particularly the ways that evolution has shaped current pedagogical practices in English departments. This focus is logical: the most visible efforts to teach writing and to reform its teaching have centered in English departments. Yet the writing that students do in general-composition courses forms only a small part (though perhaps a more important part) of the writing that they do in their schooling. And the pedagogical practices in general-composition courses may differ from or even conflict with the writing practices in other courses.[34] To understand the ways that students learn to write, one must go beyond the small and all-too-often marginalized component of the curriculum which treats writing explicitly and look at the broader, though largely tacit traditions that students encounter in the whole curriculum. Thus, I discuss general-composition courses only in the context of writing in other disciplines, and the English department only in its wider institutional context (e.g., writing in "great books" general-education programs).

In the end, a narrow focus on the history of composition courses may actually reinforce the myth of transience, since it may credit freshman English with a larger or more cohesive effect than it has ever had. In the process, we may lose the institutional perspective that would see composition courses as one of many ways students learn (or fail to learn) written discourse of many kinds, and the English department as only one site of conflict in the long struggle to reform writing instruction. Simply reforming freshman English (again) will not adequately address the deeper issues of writing acquisition: the nature of academic writing, its relation to disciplinary formation and perpetuation, and its relation to students' access to professional communities.

A second focus of historians has been the relationship between composition courses and broader cultural and intellectual forces—for example, Richard Ohmann's radical critique of freshman composition and the values of the military-industrial complex, or Berlin's study of freshman composition and the development of rhetorical theory in America.[35] My approach owes much to this cultural analysis. These and other radical critiques of composition courses in academia have pointedly revealed the shallowness of historical analysis that ignores the social and political contexts of education. Writing instruction is indeed "always related to the plurality of competing ideologies," as Berlin argues in *Rhetoric and Reality* (5). But those ideological conflicts are rarely debated explicitly in academic institutions, for they are mediated by the compartmentalized structure of knowledge and of labor, by the separation of departments, disciplines, and subdisciplines. The ideological and political conflicts within the English department, or any other, are carried on within immediate institutional contexts, as well as within broader cultural ones. By looking at writing in the context of the organizational structures and attitudes of academia, I tell the story of writing instruction from an institutional perspective, in hopes that such a perspective can illuminate the reasons why specific traditions have grown up and specific reforms have succeeded or failed within academic institutions.

As I trust this history demonstrates, it has been too easy for Americans of all ideological camps to forget that specialization, like the perceived illiteracy which was one of its manifestations, is not a temporary aberration, to be corrected with some new program or philosophy; it is the fundamental organizing principle of modern education and, behind that, of modern knowledge itself. Divisions are not only inevitable but also, if we understand them correctly, invaluable as a means of constructing curricula and writing pedagogies that are responsive to the nuances and complexities of modern knowledge and social organization. And where divisions dictate exclusions (as they must), a conscious understanding of the way language operates to differentiate knowledge and labor may help us to create a more equitable means of apportioning educational resources and social roles, as well as more effective means of teaching students the specialized discourses that are bound up with those roles in our postmodern Babel.

The many critics of education who today, as in decades past, complain that academia is hopelessly fragmented are in one sense correct. Barring some dramatic shift to a single cultural ideal (a frighteningly coercive prospect) we must live with these divisions and exclusions, communities and elites. Language (and knowledge) in a pluralistic society, like language in any but the most isolated culture, stubbornly resists the kind of regimentation that the "plain English" advocates enshrine. There will be no academic Esperanto. But there is certainly no reason to despair.

The present divisions are not the only possible ones (as the many past reforms of writing instruction illustrate). And the greatest obstacle to reshaping and rearranging our current divisions may well be the myth that they do not really exist or that they would soon disappear if only everyone would learn to write properly (or naturally or critically or what you will). Only when academia confronts its confusion of tongues and its myth of transience can the slow work of translation and transformation begin.

Bringing these different rhetorical and pedagogical traditions into the light of historical and rhetorical analysis will mean thinking of writing and its instruction as part of a larger debate about who will learn—and do—what in the postmodern culture(s) we are creating. For as we approach the end of another century, it is sobering to remember that modern society was "revolutionized" not only by positivist philosophy and industrial technology but also by managers, scientists, and bureaucrats wielding the new technologies of the word: the typewriter, the Linotype, the mimeograph, as well as the pedagogical and analytical tools to cement their position through writing. And the new postindustrial society is being formed through another "revolution" in writing: the electronic office and factory and school. Now we must consider how traditions of writing instruction will shape (and be shaped by) the society that they create.

2

NINETEENTH-CENTURY
BACKGROUNDS

From the Liberal Curriculum to Mass Education

Until the last third of the nineteenth century, writing instruction beyond the elementary school was largely unnecessary, for writing was ancillary to speaking. In our modern print culture, it is difficult to imagine a time when education, indeed public life, was so dominantly oral. But this face-to-face, oral character of preprofessional society explains, more than any other factor, the place of writing instruction within its educational institutions and the dramatic changes writing and its pedagogy underwent.[1]

In antebellum society, postelementary education was by modern standards extraordinarily homogeneous, guaranteeing a linguistic common ground. Almost all postelementary schools were unapologetically elitist and sectarian. Students and faculty were of the same sex, race, religion, and, for the most part, of the same social class. Students and faculty lived together, often in the same quarters sharing the same food. The faculty were mainly clergymen, twice-daily chapel was required, and revival meetings were frequent on college campuses. While there was considerable variation among institutions, from old colonial-era colleges of the Northeast and South to tiny new academies that followed the westward expansion, each was a community to itself, with standards of inclusion and exclusion that ensured a fundamental uniformity even without taking into account an intellectual common ground—"academic community" in the modern sense.

The academic community of the nineteenth century was consciously and deliberately an extension of the family and church.

Classmates commonly looked on one another as brothers (there were no social fraternities); the institution was literally *alma mater;* the president was both minister and surrogate father (a legal as well as psychological relationship through the in loco parentis doctrine). With these fundamentally oral, face-to-face social institutions as its model, it is not surprising that the old college maintained a relatively untroubled *discourse* community. Students routinely rebelled, sometimes with a violence that makes modern student uprisings seem playful by comparison (a few faculty were shot, more were beaten). And America's upwardly mobile mercantile class increasingly challenged the relevance of the college as other avenues to wealth and influence opened that did not require knowledge of classical languages or skill in formal oral discourse. But nothing seriously challenged the linguistic homogeneity of the college or its smug assurance that it educated a governing elite to take the reins of power in rural and small-town antebellum society. The system produced, as Edmund Wilson later wrote, "a caste of trained 'college men' who were to preside over the arts and the professions."[2] And the primary marks of caste were linguistic. The old college clung to the oratorical tradition of public discourse, on the ancient classical model, as preparation for the pulpit, the senate, the bar.[3]

In the old college, then, *discipline* did not refer to an organizational structure, a way of *dividing* knowledge and activity as it does today. Instead, it had two very different meanings, both of which referred to the unifying aims of the institution, not to its organization. The first was moral and religious discipline, the duty of the college to instill in its young charges a code of Christian conduct and virtue. Faculty enforced (or failed to enforce) complex schemes for regulating behavior; there were points given and taken for "deportment," with class rankings based on them. The second discipline was mental. Pedagogical methods, particularly after reforms in the 1820s, were justified on the theory of "mental discipline," which the American college borrowed from Scottish faculty psychology and educational practice. The goal of education was to train, through drill and exercise, the various "faculties" of the mind: memory, judgment, will, and so on. Educators saw in the study of classical languages, with their complex but codified structure, the most fitting means of disciplining the mind. But, whether moral or mental, discipline in the old college sought unity and stability, though by mid century the old college found itself plagued by unpopularity and uncertainty of purpose in a society that increasingly defined itself through diversity and change.

The Old Curriculum

The liberal curriculum, along with its pedagogy, reinforced the linguistic homogeneity of the college and, by giving standard training to future leaders, of the social class and religious sects it supported. Rather than a series of elective courses, it was, first of all, a single *required* course of study, identical for all students regardless of abilities, interests, or career plans. The young men (and, in a few cases, young women) moved together through yearlong segments of the single four-year course, not through individual courses. The prescribed course emphasized the traditional subjects: Latin, Greek, mathematics, and rhetoric. Less prominent was "moral philosophy," a course that went by a variety of names and included an even wider variety of subject matter. The president usually taught this "capstone course" to the upper classmen, and whatever the philosophical, theological, political, scientific, or economic subjects he broached, his goal was almost always to affirm the truths of Protestant Christianity against its detractors.

Ordinarily the faculty employed no specialists, in the sense that we use the term today, though some of the better schools had at one time or another chairs of political economy, natural history, natural philosophy, and political science—all connected to the teaching of moral philosophy—and Harvard had its Boylston professor of rhetoric and oratory. The goals and organization of the curriculum did not need specialists. Because almost all faculty were themselves trained in the same liberal curriculum, a single faculty member might teach several or all subjects.[4]

The central curricular activity was language study in the oratorical tradition of Cicero, Quintilian, and the Renaissance humanists.[5] As Walter Ong has pointed out, this emphasis strengthened linguistic homogeneity because the classical languages were far more fixed than were the vernacular, and while there were scholarly and scientific works being written in Latin well into the twentieth century, the curriculum was insulated for the most part against the advances in specialized knowledge, which since the eighteenth century had spread primarily in the vernaculars (112–15). Moreover, knowledge of classical languages, however fragmentary, marked the well educated from the hoi polloi (as the classical lardings of much nineteenth-century prose attest) and strengthened the unity of the "educated class."

Writing and Pedagogy in the Old Curriculum

Within the old liberal curriculum, students learned to read and speak and write the classical languages through the infamous recitation method, the standard pedagogy for all subjects, and through the public oratorical performances (rhetoricals) central to the life of the college community—debates, orations, declamations, and so forth. Though recitation and the rhetoricals were almost always oral, they necessitated much writing as preparation for speaking. Even in the early eighteenth century, Harvard students had to present to the college president or tutor a "fairly written" copy of each declamation to be delivered.[6] From this modest beginning, formal collegewide writing requirements expanded as the role of written discourse grew with the rise of literacy and curricular specialization. But the process was gradual, extending into the early years of the twentieth century.

Recitation has been widely (and in many ways justly) condemned by critics of the system as rigid, mindless, demeaning, and downright foolish.[7] Those critics were mainly former students or advocates of the lecture method or student-centered progressive approaches, which won the day at the beginning of the twentieth century. It is worth noting that the victorious pedagogical practices also have had their share of critics over the last century (students today make the same charges against the lecture method). Without mounting a defense of recitation, I nevertheless explore the ways the method taught language across the whole curriculum, so that I may place modern pedagogies in perspective. Let us visit a typical Yale classroom in the late 1860s as described by a former student, Lyman H. Bagg, himself a critic of recitation.

In a Latin or Greek recitation one [pupil] may be asked to read or scan a short passage, another to translate it, a third to answer questions as to its construction, and so on; or all this and more may be required of the same individual. The reciter is expected simply to answer the questions which are put to him, but not to ask any of his instructor, or dispute his assertions. If he has any inquiries to make, or controversy to carry on, it must be done informally, after the division has been dismissed. Sometimes, when a wrong translation has been made or a wrong answer given, the instructor makes no sign, though if the failure be almost complete he may call upon another to go over the ground again. Perhaps after the lesson has been recited the instructor may translate it, comment upon it, point out the mistakes which may have been made, and so on. The "advance" [lesson] of one day is always the "review" of the next, and a more perfect recitation is always expected on the second occasion;—a remark which is not confined to the languages but applies equally well to all the studies of the course.[8]

We in this post-Deweyan age may share Bagg's feeling that recitation was, overall, rigid and dull. But it must also strike us that the nineteenth-century classroom was a performance-centered, interactive place by comparison with the modern lecture classroom. The hour was taken up with students speaking, so much so that faculty complained that they had too little time for their own pronouncements.[9]

Course materials and student class notes from the early and mid nineteenth century show how extensively writing entered the recitation method. Professors prepared (or borrowed from textbooks) lists of questions for students to answer in recitation. Notebooks (and commonplace books) contain students' written answers, to be memorized for oral presentation in class or on written examinations, which came into wide use in the 1860s. For example, seven five-by-seven-inch notebooks belonging to

Harvard freshman George Wiles contain short responses to both handwritten and printed questions in Greek, Latin, geometry, physics, and history.[10]

If much of the speaking and writing in recitation classes was highly structured, it was at least structured to include many kinds of activities: oral reading, note-taking on spoken and written material, translation, paraphrase, historical and philosophical commentary. Students not only manipulated language (and languages) they did so in progressively more sophisticated ways throughout their schooling, leading up to full-blown public speaking and debate. In the 1870s recitation would suffer wide attack for its sterility, routine, and lack of motivation. But in the hands of skillful teachers (and there were some), recitation was a flexible instrument for gradually developing the linguistic and, with it, intellectual facility that students needed to enter positions of authority in an oral, face-to-face culture.

The second site of writing in the liberal curriculum was the *rhetorical*, a public oral exhibition of rhetorical skill. Bagg's description of recitation leads one to wonder what inquiries or controversies the students carried on with the instructor after the division had been dismissed. Behind the rationale of mental discipline and the overlay of Scottish realism, recitation echoed the ancient *progymnasmata*, or standard rhetorical exercises, in that it was systematic training for public oratorical performances. Students, as Bagg implies, did indeed regularly spend time with their instructors *outside* class. They were preparing and practicing for orations, declamations, debates, essays, compositions, and forensics (to use the terms found frequently in catalogs), which they performed for the assembled college community. During every term of his residence, each student performed regularly at daily (or weekly) exercises, and there were also formal end-of-term "exhibitions" or oral "examinations" to which the wider community was invited. Although these rhetoricals were oral, they were ordinarily first written out and often critiqued beforehand by the professor in charge of the exercises, either in conference with the student or in written comments on the draft.[11]

Often these rhetoricals were held in conjunction with daily

chapel or on special Friday exercises when the whole faculty and student body assembled; elsewhere only the particular class (juniors, for example) assembled for routine rhetoricals. Rhetoricals were a mandated part of the curriculum; and specific, often detailed requirements appear in the first catalogs that colleges printed.[12] Kansas University's announcement is typical: "Each member of the Freshman, Sophomore, and Junior classes appears at least twice each year at the morning exercises in the Hall [immediately after required chapel]. Freshmen and Sophomores with declamations, and the Juniors with original essays and orations." Seniors practiced their commencement orations on Fridays.[13] The order of rhetoricals reflects the fundamental shape of the classical *progymnasmata*. Younger students began with declamation: memorized, paraphrased, or summarized performances of familiar material (often set pieces of prose or verse being studied in the curriculum); older students progressed to "original" composition: argumentation, debate, and oratory, which called for more sophisticated manipulation of materials. Indeed, college freshmen typically took no rhetoric course but instead concentrated on language study—translation and memorization of important texts—to provide them with a fund of material for rhetoricals.[14]

Rhetoricals were often under the direction of a professor of rhetoric (or English, or English language, or modern language—titles varied extensively). But because professors of rhetoric were rarely specialists in English literature in the modern sense (Harvard's Francis James Child in the 1870s might perhaps lay claim to being the first), faculty with training in many fields, most commonly the ministry, taught rhetoric. Indeed, when departments began to be recognized in colleges during the 1830s and 1840s, rhetoric or English was variously combined with moral philosophy, history, logic, or metaphysics, as well as with modern and classical languages. Faculty moved from one "department" or chair to another with an ease unheard of in the modern university.[15]

As S. Michael Halloran's recent research of student diaries of the early nineteenth century suggests, the tedium, formality, and authority of the recitation could give way to a more relaxed and collegial atmosphere when faculty coached students for these performances (in part because the faculty themselves sometimes had to perform as well). And students were often more enthusiastic and serious about these performances than about the daily recitations, as one might imagine.[16] Faculty recognized the importance of rhetoricals in providing motivation. The University of Missouri catalog notes that "enthusiasm is awakened by requiring all efforts to be made before the whole body of students."[17] Through critiques, rehearsals, and conferences faculty had frequent opportunities to guide students individually.[18] As noted, faculty often critiqued the written or oral version of a composition before it was performed, affording students the opportunity (and sometimes the obligation) to revise the work. At the University of Missouri, for example, the 1870 catalog specifically informs prospective students that "essays and orations are examined and carefully criticized by the professor before they are delivered. Declamations may be rehearsed privately before the professor by all who wish." And in his resignation letter of 1869, a Yale professor complained of the burden of "*hearing* so many compositions" in conferences with students (italics mine). The rhetorical system thus forced students and faculty to attend to composition in very direct, immediate ways.[19]

These oral performances also served as examinations—in the daily classroom discipline, in the twice-yearly schoolwide examinations, and in the final oral examinations before graduation. (Written examinations were rare in American colleges until after the Civil War.) Moreover, commencement ceremonies largely consisted of formal declamations, orations, and debates. Students composed and memorized speeches on standard topics then delivered them before the assembled students, faculty, parents, and dignitaries.[20]

The subjects of rhetorical exercises reflected the whole range of studies in the curriculum—no great feat since that range was quite limited. Though subjects of student rhetoricals ranged from classical to modern literature, morals, philosophy, grammar, and natural history, they were all drawn from a common *public* store of knowledge and received ideas, a shared tradition. As Robert

J. Connors has argued (following Albert R. Kitzhaber), compositions were overwhelmingly "unconcerned with personal expression of personal experience."[21] "An Incident from My Summer
Vacation" and other now-standard personal topics began ap-
pearing only in the 1870s and became dominant in composition
courses (though not in other courses) only in the 1880s.[22] In the
liberal curriculum, heuristics involved searching through the fund
of anecdotes, tales, wise sayings, and pithy quotations ("gems of
literature") stored in the student's memory, rhetoric textbook,
notes, and commonplace book. These became material for developing—or merely larding—compositions on standard topics,
usually such abstractions as "Time," "Luxury," "Evanescence of
Pleasure," "Hoping There Will Be as Great Improvements in the
Future as There Have Been in the Past."[23] Though compositions
in the liberal curriculum were, as Connors says, "overwhelmingly
impersonal" and far from the later personal-experience assignments which came to dominate composition courses, my reading
of pedagogical materials and student writing from the old curriculum suggests that this "impersonality" is equally far from the
scholarly impersonality that the new university came to expect
in writing done outside composition courses: an objective, distanced, critical handling of sources to produce an analysis or
interpretation unique to the student—a research paper, in other
words.[24] As a dominantly oral medium, the rhetoricals drew on
common knowledge, received ideas—"commonplaces," in the
traditional rhetorical sense of the term. Students were not expected to analyze sources critically, to compare them rigorously,
to interpret them in the context of a growing body of disciplinary
knowledge, as later scholarship would dictate. Indeed, such critical distance is almost impossible in oral discourse, with its time-
bound immediacy which precludes exacting, text-bound analysis.
Expression and persuasion were the goals, confirmation of shared
values the method—not the discovery of new truth through critical scholarly methods. Moreover, the moral and religious climate
discouraged "originality" in its modern sense: the overturning
or modifying of previously accepted knowledge, values, forms.
Originality simply meant that the student had composed his
own synthesis from an accepted body of texts. Viewed from the

perspective not of composition courses in the new university but from the perspective of courses in the disciplines, this is the most significant difference between student discourse in the old college and the new curriculum.[25]

Writing and Pedagogy in the Extracurriculum

As in postelementary education today, students in the old curriculum devoted much of their time and energy to the extracurriculum and found it more satisfying overall than their classroom studies, to judge by their reminiscences. Writing was important in the extracurriculum as well as in the regular curriculum, though again it was ancillary to speaking. The old college had none of the social fraternities, intercollegiate athletics, or student professional associations which quickly came to dominate the extracurriculum of the new university in the last decades of the nineteenth century. Instead, the extracurriculum centered around the literary, or "cleosophic," societies, organized and run solely by students (though faculty were sometimes invited to attend and participate). Almost all of the societies' activities involved speaking and writing about intellectual and artistic concerns, philosophical, literary, political. The societies brought lecturers to campus, sponsored debates, held public readings of their own and others' work, mounted theatrical productions, and generally maintained the intellectual life of the campus outside the classrooms. They kept their own libraries, stocked with general works to provide material for speeches on a broad range of subjects. In fact, the literary societies often had libraries larger than those of the colleges, and the societies' books were usually more available to students than the college library's. To many students the literary societies represented the greatest contribution of the college to their education.[26] And historians have long noted the societies' contribution to the cultural climate of the antebellum period. Many of the greatest speakers of the age found an important forum in the societies. Indeed, literary societies invited Emerson, Ingersoll, and noted abolitionists to speak when colleges refused to allow them on campus.[27]

Among the major functions of the literary societies was "as-

signing and critiquing compositions."[28] As with class-related performances, students usually wrote the orations, debates, declamations, disputations, humorous dialogues, plays, essays, poems,
stories, and satires which they performed and critiqued at their
weekly or biweekly meetings. Societies typically elected a member
to the office of official critic, to read in advance and respond to
members' contributions. In large societies, a meeting might have
as many as ten or twenty declamations and compositions (with
criticism), followed by a debate with five students on a side.
Elaborate records were kept, with summaries of speeches and
debates, lists of "wise sayings" to use in speeches, and the usual
doodles and personal notes of students everywhere. Outside their
meetings, societies competed with each other for coveted prizes
in oratory, declamation, and debate; they organized programs of
oratory at "exhibitions" and commencements, and even edited
the campus newspaper or published works presented at meetings.[29] The college faculty and administration considered the
societies an important part of the students' education, particularly in developing students' "powers of expression."[30] Colleges
typically provided the societies with well-furnished meeting
rooms, gave them time in the packed class schedule, and in some
cases allowed students to substitute performances at meetings for
required rhetoricals. The societies clearly played a central role in
the education of students, and they did so by giving them a more
creative and socially relevant outlet for the speaking and writing
skills they were exercising in a less satisfying way in the curriculum. Though required rhetoricals may often have been about dull
abstractions, the students assigned themselves topics of great
political and social relevance in the societies.[31] Students were
energetically and voluntarily using the knowledge and rhetorical
methods they learned in class. In sum, though the curriculum and
extracurriculum played different roles, they both centered on the
active use of language, spoken and written. It was, however, the
language of a single class and a narrow intellectual community.
And after the Civil War, the tradition-bound liberal college was
caught in a rapidly changing nation, wedded to a fundamentally
oral, face-to-face cultural model in an increasingly pluralistic,
print-driven culture.

From Discipline to Disciplines: Writing and the New University

How, then, did higher education move from regular, college-mandated writing and speaking on a wide range of public matters for all students in all undergraduate years to the modern system of individual-faculty responsibility for requiring writing (on specific disciplinary topics rather than on general public matters) with no universitywide writing and speaking requirement beyond freshman composition (where private experience was the primary focus of assignments)? How did higher education give up its mechanisms for guided revision, public presentation to the academic community, and extracurricular reinforcement in favor of a system with no formal means of guiding revision, no formal cooperation among faculty, and few opportunities for public presentation or extracurricular reinforcement? The answers lie in the broad changes that swept education in the decade after the Civil War. The old college and its liberal curriculum seemed painfully inadequate to Americans. Though enrollments were gradually increasing, the number of college-age men was increasing at twice the rate. College was not required for entering any career, though advancement to the highest levels often depended on it—as a matter of social fact, not of legal certification. A chorus of voices from around the nation cried out for colleges and academies to become "more practical," to give up their rigid classicism and elitism. In the years before the war, financiers and captains of industry had founded scientific and technical schools such as the Massachusetts Institute of Technology (MIT), or separate scientific schools within traditional colleges, such as Sheffield at Yale and Lawrence at Harvard. In 1862, Congress had passed the Morrill Land-Grant College Act to create "colleges of the people"—with frankly practical aims. And in the decade following the Civil War, as the economy expanded rapidly in the North and West, colleges responded to the utilitarian chorus and began the dramatic changes that would create the modern university and define its role in the new rationalized, urban-industrial society of modern America.[32]

Among the many changes, the one that affected writing instruction most profoundly was the rapid move toward an elective curriculum based on specialized departments—an innovation championed by Harvard President Charles W. Eliot when he began his long tenure in 1869. Though classical learning still had a large following, particularly among the old college's traditional clientele, the reorganized university drew students from a far-wider segment of society, then taught and credentialed them to enter a far-wider array of professions. The overriding curricular principle became division, not unity; accretion, not synthesis.

Other deep structural changes in higher education and industrial society had profound effects on writing in academia, effects that reinforced linguistic diversity. The university took on two new roles, research and service, which transformed writing instruction more thoroughly than did composition courses (which were themselves a response to these broader changes). The university hired and promoted faculty to carry out specialized research and service to society in specific ways for practical ends. For most faculty, teaching became but another way of serving the discipline, through educating professionals to play specific roles in the new industrial order. The department became the organizing unit of the institution, "the discipline" the organizing principle of knowledge. A faculty member was primarily loyal to the discipline (the profession, the research, the department, the majors) and only secondarily to the institution—as presidents quickly discovered when other universities began luring faculty away with inducements of smaller teaching loads and greater funding for research.

As the modern academic disciplines gradually organized themselves out of the inchoate mass of post–Civil War educational ferment, conventions of discourse grew up within each, marking off one from another. Each had its own professional meetings, seminars, journals, books, and all the now-familiar forums of scholarly discourse. So also, each developed its own terminology, methods, rules of evidence, standards of scholarly presentation and documentation. Significantly, those discipline-specific conventions and, indeed, the whole new enterprise of research and service, depended upon print for their growth and influence, subordinating the oral component almost completely. Publication became the vehicle for professional advancement, specialization the mark of a scholar's or a discipline's growth. Even at professional gatherings, scholars read their "papers" verbatim, despite complaints and poor attendance at the sessions. Oratorical culture had become largely irrelevant to the new enterprise. The hallmark of higher learning was that specialization of discourse which is only possible in writing and only capable of being widely distributed in print. In this new economy of knowledge, the institution, as well as its faculty, increasingly had to publish or perish.

Students, too, felt the influence of specialized research and utilitarian service. On the whole, faculty had less time for undergraduate teaching as they devoted more time to their new roles in research and service. For many faculty, the new graduate programs provided the only intensive contact with students. In some ways, Americans built their new research universities on the German model, where faculty supervised apprentice researchers in the discipline. But in America, those apprenticeships came to be reserved primarily for graduate students, who would in theory receive an intensive form of writing instruction—*mentoring*, to use today's term—as they pursued research.

Finally, the elective curriculum affected writing by restructuring the examination system. Instead of the campuswide oral and written examinations, graded collectively by the faculty or by outside examiners, the elective curriculum brought course-specific written examinations, graded individually by each instructor. Moreover, there was ordinarily no final examination or performance required for graduation, as there had been in the old college. Students had little reason to retain and synthesize their learning in preparation for a final performance. For their part, faculty had few opportunities to observe students' verbal performance collectively and systematically much less to gauge its development over time. In a system where each instructor was entirely responsible for evaluating only his own students for a single term, faculty had little reason to discuss standards for judging their students' speaking and writing. The grading system made the question of students' verbal facility moot. And when, in the early twentieth century, "objective testing" was proposed as a more efficient means of grading, many faculty found the argument convincing (see chapter 5). Typically, only the graduate students had to prepare a final performance, the German dissertation, replete with the most rarefied conventions of print: footnotes and bibliography.

The elective curriculum quickly produced the most visible change in writing instruction: composition courses. In response to a chorus of complaint about poor student writing, Eliot began college-level composition courses in 1872 by appointing to the faculty a journalist, Adams Sherman Hill, to "familiarize the pupil with the principles that underlie good composition."[33] For pedagogical reformers like Eliot and Hill, rhetoric—for centuries the center of the old curriculum—represented all that was bad in higher education: it stifled student interest through dry recitation and meaningless, formulaic speeches on "vague generalities," while the students *wrote* English no better (or even worse) than before. Hill responded approvingly to the criticisms of student writing that had begun to appear in the popular press of 1870s: "Within a short time, people have opened their eyes to the defects of a system which crams without training, which spends its strength on the petty or the useless, and neglects that without which knowledge is but sounding brass and tinkling cymbal."[34] The reformers stressed a practical and elementary knowledge of the *written* "mother tongue." Students must learn to write "a simple English sentence" *before* opening a Latin grammar, they argued. Writing was viewed primarily as an elementary skill (as it had been in the dominantly oral university). Writing amounted to correct transcription of fully formed thought or speech, not the process of engagement with a subject or communication with a reader. The oral emphasis of the old college was beginning to fade as writing became dominant, but it left in its wake "the opinion that 'reading and writing' can or should be completely mastered before the main business of education begins," as Susan Miller says (65).

The reformers' new stress on the written forms in language training is most visible in the entrance examination. Before 1872, the Harvard examination only required *oral* reading, from such authors as Shakespeare and Milton. The following year, the catalog warns: "Correct spelling, punctuation, and expression, as well as legible handwriting, are expected of all candidates for admission." In 1873–74, a separate written exam in English was first required, and grammatical and mechanical correctness was the *only* criterion mentioned for its evaluation. Written correctness, not communicative competence, became the focus of composition instruction.[35]

Like the elective curriculum itself, writing training in the new university was "practical"—not tied to classical study. Hill insisted that students must write about what they know and understand before proceeding. And like the elective curriculum, motivation for writing came through the student focusing on what he knew well and was interested in—thus the growing use of personal assignments in general-composition courses (students knew their own experiences, if nothing else) and the drive to put a general-composition course in the freshman year (before, not after, Latin and Greek).[36] Writing was not part of the process of learning a subject but rather a separate accomplishment, independent of content. It was one course among many, albeit an important one. Eliot wrote in 1879, "I may as well abruptly avow, as a result of my reading and observation in the matters of education, that I recognized but one mental acquisition as an essential part of the education of a lady or a gentleman—namely, an accurate and refined use of the mother tongue."[37] In 1900, almost three decades after composition instruction began, Harvard made Eliot's observation curricular fact: freshman composition became the only required course in the college.[38] And that course, English A, had already become the model for required freshman-composition courses around the country, just as Harvard became the model of the new comprehensive research university.

Many historians of rhetoric and composition have told the story of English A, but they have told it from the point of view of the English department. They have, therefore, emphasized the course's importance for modern traditions of general-composition instruction and the marginalization of composition in relation to instruction in literature.[39] But here I examine the rise of composition instruction in the context of the writing that students did within the *whole* curriculum. From the perspective of future developments in English departments, Harvard's freshman requirement was, as historians have viewed it, the great watershed that marked the beginning of the modern era in writing instruction.[40] But the curricular records at Harvard and elsewhere suggest that the transition from the oratorical tradition to the modern practice of a single freshman requirement was actually a long and complex negotiation among departments, students, administrators, and alumni overseers, a process that from its outset envisioned freshman composition, English A, as part of a comprehensive and, in some ways, interdisciplinary writing program. Historians have sometimes briefly noted that there were other writing requirements at Harvard (and elsewhere) from the 1870s to the 1910s, but these requirements (and their relation to freshman composition) have never been systematically discussed in relation to the wider curriculum.[41]

In fact, the reformers originally saw the freshman course as merely the beginning of a four-year program for developing students' writing, a program that retained the essential shape of the traditional rhetorical training. As Hill wrote in 1878, "Gradually [the student] should be led from the skillful use of materials provided by others to the discovery and arrangement of materials for himself, from the practice of clothing another's thoughts in his own language to the presentation of his own thoughts or fancies in appropriate language" (237). To accomplish this goal, Harvard and many other universities tried for three decades to adapt the old practice of required rhetoricals to the demands of the new university, with its elective curriculum and departmentalized written knowledge.

The Forensic System

Harvard, like the great majority of colleges, recognized the need for writing by all students in all four years; and after the elective curriculum was instituted in 1869, the college began modifying the old oral rhetoricals into the *forensic system*—various collegewide writing requirements from entrance to graduation, which endured in the curriculum until 1900 at Harvard and elsewhere into the 1920s. As its name implies, the forensic system continued the old tradition of debate in the final years of the curriculum, but it was a *written* adaptation of oral debate. During the 1870s, students attended lectures and recitation on rhetoric in the last three years (freshmen took elocution), but the catalog also specifically prescribed "themes once every four weeks" for sophomores, "once every three weeks" for juniors, and "four forensics" for seniors. Sophomore and junior themes were analogous to the old oral declamations; senior forensics were ordinarily argumentative essays on some controversial topic, corresponding to the old oral debates. At least in their inception, the requirements were thus a kind of written continuation of the ancient tradition of rhetoricals.[42]

But the transition from oral to written requirements was not easy to make, for the new university was no longer a single discourse community with a single curriculum. Even in the early 1870s, the struggle to find a place for writing in an increasingly elective and departmentalized curriculum was already in evidence. Shortly after Eliot became president, students were no longer required to read their compositions aloud. In 1872 senior "honors" candidates were allowed to "substitute for these Forensics an equal number of Theses in their special departments, provided such substitution is permitted by the professors in those departments."[43] This provision reflects the growing tendency of departmental faculty to assign extended writing in elective courses—"course theses," as they were called, or what came to be called "term papers" in the early twentieth century (see chapter 3). For example, during his last three undergraduate years (1868–70), Frederick H. Viaux wrote 88-page and 63-page theses for history courses, a 30-page thesis for an English literature course, as well as his twenty required themes and forensics.[44]

When Hill became chair of a reorganized English department in 1876, he began the forensic system. Hill hoped to create a system that would lead the student systematically and gradually from less complicated to more complicated kinds of writing, "care being taken," Hill wrote, "to provide, at each stage in his education, subjects suited to his powers and attractive to his tastes at the time."[45] Beginning students would concentrate on description and narration, with subjects drawn mainly from personal experience. Later in their education, students would write expository and, finally, argumentative texts, with subjects drawn from their academic interests.

In 1878, Harvard dropped the junior and senior rhetoric courses (leaving sophomore rhetoric the only composition course) and instead prescribed "certain written exercises only." Significantly, these themes and forensics were supervised by a professor of philosophy (George Herbert Palmer) and a professor of Christian morals (Francis Greenwood Peabody); English faculty continued to teach sophomore rhetoric. The importance of the requirement is indicated by the fact that students could test out of sophomore rhetoric but not out of themes and forensics, though honors students could still substitute course theses with approval. The system was frankly meritocratic: students were tracked; the best were placed in small sections "to enable the teacher to read each theme either with its author or aloud to a section of the division, and thus to make the criticism more searching and the revision more thorough than is possible under any system of notes on the margin," as the large middle and lower sections had to be content with. The English department also began its tradition of composition electives for the best students: "Advanced Course in Rhetoric and Themes" and an elective for selected seniors, "Oral Discussion," which would later become an interdisciplinary course organized around classroom debates, where history and philosophy faculty members cooperated with the elocution instructor to set topics, guide research, and critique performances. This course represents Harvard's last attempt at formal, interdisciplinary cooperation in oral language instruction.[46]

In 1885, after almost ten years of lobbying, Hill managed to get sophomore rhetoric moved to the freshman year and dubbed it English A, clearly a significant development in the history of composition instruction. But that change was only part of a collegewide reform of composition instruction. Students had for some years been complaining that the topics for the required themes and forensics were irrelevant to their studies.[47] In 1883, faculty from other disciplines were again called in: LeBaron Briggs from Greek for sophomore themes (a future dean), and

Josiah Royce for junior and senior forensics (soon to be a leading member of a distinguished philosophy department).[48] Eliot commissioned Royce to collect 250 topics "with the cooperation of instructors in nearly all departments" from which students were to choose and write only two forensics. At least one of the forensics was "a thesis in forensic form [that is, an argument] on a subject that demands a fuller and more elaborate treatment" and that discusses "subjects that have a direct bearing upon their chosen studies." Thus, Eliot's report goes on, "Elective work and forensic work will be brought into close relation with one another, to their mutual advantage."[49] In 1885, the year English A became a freshman requirement, junior themes became a required sophomore course (English B) and juniors and seniors wrote five forensics (English C).

In essence, the English B and C courses were merely the writing requirement, though the instructors offered twice-weekly lectures on writing for ten weeks, attendance optional. By 1890 the list of topics had become a pamphlet, *Specimen Briefs,* with models and advice to guide students in writing the five required forensics. Initially, students prepared one "brief," or sentence outline, of a "masterpiece" of rhetoric (a last vestige of the extensive study of rhetorical models in the old curriculum). For each of the five forensics (of fifteen hundred to two thousand words), students prepared a brief, which was turned in two weeks before the final draft was due. Faculty who supervised English C kept regular office hours for consultations with students, and students in both English B and C were often required to revise their themes and forensics—sometimes extensively.[50]

The surviving English B themes are primarily expository. The forensics, however, differed from themes in that they "should be matters of debate," with both sides of the issue "acceptable of good argumentative treatment," thus maintaining the development from simpler to more complex forms that Hill had envisioned when he began the system in 1878. Forensic topics were drawn from the approved list of several hundred questions, arranged by discipline: ancient languages, modern literature and fine arts, philosophy, political economy, history, and natural sciences (e.g., "Antigone Is Wholly Right," "Members of the

Cabinet Ought to Be Given Seats in the House of Representatives," "The Execution of Postumus Was Ordered by Livia, Not Tiberius").

But the distinction between forensics and "course theses" (papers written for other courses) became increasingly difficult to draw and became more so as faculty in more and more disciplines began requiring extended writing. The forensics, the pamphlet warns, should "not call merely for compilation of research" and "should not be minutely technical."[51] Nevertheless, English C faculty frequently reached the limits of their expertise, especially in the natural sciences. For example, when senior Ralph Clinton Larrabee (a future medical researcher) wrote his first forensic on a controversy over "the algo-fungal theory of lichens," the instructor's comments betray insecurity: "Grade A—I find no difficulty in following your argument, which considering the technicality of the subject is from a layman no small praise." And after a criticism in the margin: "all this with the diffidence of a layman." On future forensics Larrabee stuck to political topics.[52] Despite Harvard's use of faculty from several disciplines, the composition program felt the effects of the "knowledge gap" which has become so pronounced in the modern university. The English C faculty could not teach, evaluate, or, in some cases, even understand the arguments of students from so many specialized disciplines, each with its own vocabulary, issues, and conventions, its own criteria for evaluating evidence and arguments.

In the late 1890s the forensic system began to fade. Part of the cause lay in the tension between general college-mandated writing requirements and writing in specific departmental courses. English B and C were reduced to half-courses in 1897, with only three forensics required (and the third one was waived if the student's grade was an A or a B on the first two). More importantly, the students could substitute "written work done in an elective course" or a senior honors thesis for the required themes and forensics, "with the consent of the instructors in English B and C."[53] The compartmentalized, additive structure of the modern university, with its specialized disciplinary communities organized by written discourse, had outgrown the forensic system it inherited from the oral, face-to-face community of the old college.

Two years later, Harvard dropped the forensic system, substituting instead three remedial courses for students who did poorly in English A. This change marked the end of collegewide writing requirements for the students' whole undergraduate program and the end of organized attempts to integrate systematically the content of other disciplines into the writing program.[54] Comprehensive writing requirements for all students were gone, and the familiar modern pattern became firmly entrenched: freshman composition for all and additional remedial courses for some, augmented by research papers at the discretion of individual faculty, with no formal mechanisms for revision or for evaluation beyond the specific course.

Though Harvard's forensic system was the most visible and influential program of its kind, other colleges and universities found their own ways of adapting the old rhetoricals to the new curricula. In addition to required rhetoric and, later, composition courses, almost all colleges and universities in the last half of the nineteenth century had additional composition requirements for all students throughout the undergraduate years, but these requirements declined steadily as writing supplanted oral performance and as specialization increased. John Michael Wozniack's survey of catalogs at thirty-seven eastern colleges shows that these colleges required "compositions, themes, essays" for a mean total of 6.7 semesters (out of eight total possible) during the period from 1850 to 1859. Moreover, fifteen of the thirty-seven colleges required compositions all eight semesters. Over the next three decades, that figure steadily declined, to 3.7 semesters in 1890–99, with only two, Dickinson College and Rutgers University, requiring writing all eight semesters. During the last decade of the nineteenth century, Wozniack concludes, "the time-honored requirement of extra compositions, themes, and essays was still the most extensive way in which composition was taught" (122). But in the first decade of the new century, the mean requirement dropped to 0.67 semesters.[55]

However, the mere fact that colleges and universities required writing outside composition courses says little about the roles such writing played in the curriculum (or how and why the requirements declined). There were wide differences not only in the amount but also in the shape and role of these writing requirements. Various models emerged as faculty struggled to find solutions to local needs, from the required writing of Latin verse in the liberal arts *ratio studiorum* of Jesuit colleges to required undergraduate "dissertations" in land-grant technical colleges.

Small, private liberal arts colleges tended to cling to comprehensive writing and speaking requirements longer than research universities but for varying reasons. Some retained the tradition of junior exhibitions and senior commencement orations. In 1910, for example, Bucknell University had a junior and senior course in "movements of thought in the nineteenth century" (successor to the old moral philosophy course), where students prepared exhibitions and commencements. Others emphasized personal contact with faculty through writing conferences, as at Wesleyan University in the 1910s, where faculty in all departments conferred with sophomores as they wrote six required essays.[56] Catholic colleges, particularly Jesuit ones (Fordham, Villanova, Georgetown Universities), consciously preserved and defended the sequenced writing and speaking of the *ratio studiorum,* from sophomore oratory (speeches from Shakespeare served as models) and practice in writing verse in imitation of English and Latin poets, through scholastic debate during the last two years as part of the study of Aristotle and Aquinas.[57]

Rapidly expanding research universities had much greater difficulties in retaining writing requirements. Columbia College made an early attempt at assigning the responsibility for writing to specific departments. From 1865 to 1870, the college specified not only monthly compositions from freshmen as part of their rhetoric course but also monthly compositions on historical subjects from sophomores, monthly original declamations from juniors (in English literature) and weekly philosophical essays from seniors in the moral philosophy course. For the sophomores, at least, compositions were "corrected in private interview with [the] student." But by the 1880s, writing was no longer specifically prescribed by the college in any course, though two years of rhetoric were required until 1919, when general education-courses reduced (and later eliminated) all required composition courses (see chapter 6).[58]

The land-grant universities of the Midwest evolved a range of very different solutions to the problems of teaching writing in the face of rapidly rising enrollment and professional specialization. In 1891, Ohio State University hired a young composition expert, Joseph Villiers Denney, to help the only professor in the department of rhetoric—a failed minister—with the increasing work load. They taught the required yearlong rhetoric course, which was supplemented by another year of English literature, taught by the separate department of English literature. In addition, students "took part by turns" in weekly rhetorical exercises, original "speeches and essays" delivered orally—a holdover from the old liberal curriculum. The university president and faculty from various departments (geology, military science, and history, as well as from rhetoric) were responsible for "giving help in their preparation in the way of references, etc., revising them when handed in, and criticism of them when read or delivered." After becoming chair of the rhetoric department the next year, Denney hired an elocutionist to help with the exercises and in 1895 discontinued the exercises entirely, creating instead a group of differentiated composition courses, which taught both writing and, as he put it, "oral composition."[59]

Denney introduced materials from various departments into the required freshman rhetoric course. During the late nineties he gradually added discipline-specific advanced rhetoric courses, taught by English instructors, for the arts, premedical, prelaw ("Brief-making"), and technical courses.[60] Denney attacked such institutions as Princeton University that abolished rhetoric courses in favor of extensive reading of English classics in small classes. In such programs, he said, "composition work is in theory the business of everybody, and in reality the business of nobody."[61] In an increasingly large and differentiated institution like Ohio State, the Princeton model was impractical. During the 1890s enrollment increased from 493 to 1,465. And the number of departments offering majors quadrupled. Differentiated composition courses within the English department were still a workable option, but even these faded with further institutional growth. When Denney retired as chair of the English department in 1932, enrollment was 10,488, a twentyfold increase in thirty years. Oral work was relegated to a new speech department, housed in an entirely different college in the university, and specialized writing courses gradually faded from the English department's offerings.[62]

Iowa State College, another midwestern land-grant university, represents the most thoroughgoing attempt to give departments responsibility for teaching writing. From its opening in 1869, this agricultural and mechanical college had required all students (in addition to requiring the usual freshman course, "Applied Rhetoric") to deliver original orations before weekly college assemblies, with the best students called on to perform at commencement ceremonies. These compositions and performances were supervised by the professor of rhetoric as part of his regular duties.[63]

In 1879, Iowa State began requiring seniors to write a "graduating thesis": "neatly written upon unruled paper, of a size designated by the faculty; after acceptance and formal reading, it shall become the property of the college, and shall be deposited in the Library. . . . Each thesis shall be supervised by the Professor giving instruction in the branch of learning upon which it treats, and such Professor will be responsible to the Faculty for its supervision and correction."[64] Yet the oral presentation continued; all theses were "read before an open session of the Trustees and Faculty," the ten best on commencement day. But significantly, the focus had begun to shift to the written version: a physical product, on paper of a certain size, to be bound and preserved. Equally important, faculty in the disciplines now had charge of the writing. The catalog goes on to require that the ten commencement-day theses be chosen by the departments, "each special Faculty selecting its quota."[65] Now each disciplinary community, not the whole community, set the standards for writing.

That same year, the college also required juniors and seniors to write four "dissertations" (brief research papers) "upon topics embraced in the studies they are pursuing, and approved by the professors and Faculties having charge of such studies. The professor shall have entire supervision of the dissertation so written, being sole judge of its fitness for reading and shall report its completion to the President."[66] The individual professor, as disciplinary specialist, was sole mentor and judge, answerable only to the departmental faculty in these matters.

For a decade the best of these dissertations were both read at student-faculty assemblies and neatly bound for the library along with the graduation theses, combining oral performance with respect for the written product. But in the late 1880s, the requirements shifted further away from oral performance and toward text-based, discipline-specific scholarship under the direction of an individual professor. The dissertation requirement was reduced from four to two in 1887, and more stringent guidelines were laid down, perhaps to decrease abuses. The length was specified, and the student was required to read it to the professor only, not to a public gathering, "at least four weeks before the end of the term," so that the student would have time to make changes and prepare "a neat, final, ink copy" for binding.[67]

A year later, the dissertation requirement was quietly dropped, and English literature was required of all juniors. There is some evidence from course descriptions that faculty required researched writing in individual courses, but it was never again mandated by college policy. Student writing outside composition courses was entirely at the discretion of the individual professor.[68]

Some universities never made an attempt to prescribe writing outside the English department. The University of Missouri gave the English professor responsibility for rhetoricals from the 1840s and simply continued that tradition by making required writing and speaking part of the requirements for English courses, without any involvement from other faculty beyond attending the weekly exercises and end-of-term exhibitions. Until the 1920s, the catalog systematically lists "essays" as part of the work only in required English courses. This was perhaps a function of the early division of the university into specialized professional schools and the active but independent role the literary societies played on campus.

Some of the new universities clung to oral, community rhetorical performance long after they began offering technical and professional studies. Kansas University, organized in 1866 under the Morrill Land-Grant College Act, retained until 1887 daily rhetorical exercises immediately after required morning chapel, with each student speaking at least twice a year. When the faculty dropped rhetoricals in 1887, it adopted a Harvard-style system of freshman rhetoric with required themes and forensics the other three years. But five years later, in 1892, the faculty voted to reinstate "the old system of 'Chapel Rhetoricals'," with juniors and seniors required to "deliver orations from the chapel platform." However, this system lasted only two more years, when elective elocution courses replaced the oral rhetoricals and the faculty voted that "correction of expression either oral or written be considered part of the work in all courses; deficiencies in English to be reported for general consideration."[69]

Like Harvard, Kansas found it difficult to negotiate writing requirements between English and other disciplines both because of increasing enrollment and increasing specialization. When the forensic system began in 1887, students were allowed to substitute papers written in other departments "with written permission of the head of that department," as long as the paper had been given "a stated grade for its substance." But in 1890 the English department refused to accept papers on topics it had not approved in advance to prevent conflicts over its competence to evaluate technical material in highly discipline-specific fields. In 1894 the department found it necessary to publish the "English Department Bulletin," stating that bibliographies and outlines must be deposited with the English department to prevent plagiarism, and the organizational complexity grew immense as enrollments skyrocketed. In 1899 the "English Department Bulletin" began, "The English Department receives each year from 1,100 students about 45,000 pages of manuscript aggregating nine million words, requiring for critical reading and correction the equivalent of four years' labor by a single reader working four hours per day, which is the limit of endurance for such work." Three years later the department unsuccessfully petitioned to drop forensics, and in 1905 the faculty reluctantly agreed but substituted a four-hour junior rhetoric course, which was in turn dropped for lack of staff.[70]

Wozniack suggests that higher education dropped collegewide writing requirements because of "ample provision for advanced elective work" in composition at most colleges, and indeed almost all colleges offered such electives by the 1900s (131). But while English electives might explain why English departments resisted responsibility for collegewide requirements, it begs the question of why the colleges themselves dropped requirements. Most students never took advanced elective composition courses, and even within English departments these represented an ever-shrinking percentage of courses offered.[71] Thus, students were left without any college-mandated training beyond the freshman year. Charles H. Grandgent suggests that Harvard dropped the required upper-level themes and forensics because, "like other things outlived, they were made superfluous by the great amount of writing called for in the various courses. Indeed, there was (and perhaps is [1930]) cause to fear that constant scribbling may do more harm than good."[72] Whether most students at Harvard (and elsewhere) actually had extensive writing practice within the various disciplines is a question I turn to in the next chapter. But the fundamental reasons for the decline of collegewide writing requirements beyond freshman composition transcend the specific practices of English departments or individual courses and instead lie in the dramatic growth in the organizational complexity of the American university and the shifts in values as its mission and clientele changed. As Berlin points out (following Kitzhaber), enrollments increased dramatically in the period 1880–1910, as did the teaching load for composition teachers—and the complaints from administrators about the cost of composition instruction (60–61). But these increases must be seen in their institutional context. In fact, the student to faculty ratio in American postsecondary education remained essentially the same from 1880 to 1910 (ten to one).[73] What had changed was the institution's values. The new missions of research, graduate teaching, and scientific and professional instruction drew resources away from the central task of the old college: undergraduate teaching in the liberal arts, including rhetoric. The elective curriculum and departmental organization made a specific place for composition courses where there had been none before but no place for collegewide writing requirements outside the course structure. As writing became one more subject among many, it ceased being a central part of all of them. Despite pious pronouncements about every teacher being an English teacher, responsibility gradually shifted from the whole faculty to the English department. But even the English departments' values increasingly lay elsewhere, in literary teaching and scholarship, so the burden actually fell on the junior faculty and, more commonly, teaching assistants or part-timers within the department.[74]

The story of how composition instruction remained on the fringes of the department, without disciplinary status, has been well told by others.[75] But here I note that this shift in responsibility without a corresponding increase in status had a chilling effect on writing instruction across the curriculum. Faculty had a license to complain about poor student writing but an institutionally sanctioned excuse for not devoting time to their undergraduates' writing. As early as 1879, Hill complained that the new university professor, "absorbed in his specialty, contented himself with requiring at recitations and examinations knowledge of the subject-matter, however ill-digested and ill-expressed," and thus could not be relied on to improve students' writing.[76] By 1910, the focus had shifted toward enacting reforms in composition courses rather than improving students' writing universitywide. And those reforms increasingly adopted the remedial model which lay behind the birth of composition courses in the 1870s. With each new cycle of complaint and reform, the myth of transience became more entrenched. And in the new political structure of the university, composition lacked disciplinary or departmental status—and thus the wherewithal to compete for resources to enact meaningful reforms. Faculty in the disciplines, competing for excellence in specialized research, could not reconceptualize writing instruction because writing was so embedded in the professional activities of their disciplinary communities that it was largely transparent. And the new English departments, pursuing their own specialized teaching and research agendas in philology and·belles lettres (not composition), rarely had the means or the will to push successfully for collegewide writing requirements.

The Great Compromise: Writing in the Secondary Schools

From the beginning of their rise after the Civil War, through the triumph of the comprehensive junior and senior high schools in the 1930s, the public secondary schools faced an even more difficult conflict between the competing claims of specialization and community, disciplinary excellence and social equity, than did the universities. Secondary schools looked up to the new universities for their disciplinary structure but down to the common school for their democratic orientation and open admissions—unlike the old preparatory academies, which looked only to the college. Secondary-school faculty and administrators were primarily trained in normal schools or separate education departments, which were oriented toward public schools (schools that other departments kept at a distance). Yet secondary schools were expected to prepare an increasingly large percentage of their students for some form of higher education.[77] On the one hand, students were not expected to specialize in a single discipline during secondary school (as they were in other industrialized nations); on the other hand, there was no consensus about what a general education should include, since students came from and would enter all walks of life. This need for schools to be all things to all students, for teachers to serve both specialized disciplines and broad social ends, made secondary-school writing instruction dauntingly complex.

The first national attempt to tackle the problem of writing instruction in differentiated schools came from the Committee of Ten, a blue-ribbon commission (chaired by Charles W. Eliot) formed in 1892 to shape curriculum for the burgeoning secondary schools. Its proceedings illustrate the obstacles that writing instruction faced as disciplines struggled to define themselves and stake out their curricular turf. The Committee of Ten's English subcommittee, the English Conference, was divided over the role their newly formed discipline should play in language instruction. The subcommittee chair, Samuel Thurber of Boston, strenuously denied that high-school and college English teachers had a unique responsibility to teach composition, since any "respectable" teacher could and should correct his students' grammatical and mechanical errors.[78]

While the subcommittee eventually rejected Thurber's extreme position and made English primarily responsible for writing instruction, it agreed that such instruction should be clearly subordinate to instruction in literature, the new discipline's chief concern. The English Conference recommended that composition take up only 30 percent of the new English curriculum and that it be taught mainly through analysis of literature (which also made up another 60 percent). The conference grudgingly allowed rhetoric, the mainstay of language instruction in the old liberal curriculum, to occupy a mere 5 percent, grammar another 5 percent.[79] Like the other disciplines, English was asserting its identity and value as a specialized component of the curriculum, not its eagerness to cooperate in language instruction. And differentiation would prevail, despite attempts by administrators and other disciplines to cast English in the role of "service department" in language instruction. Critics like Homer E. Woodbridge lamented, "Our modern schools, like our modern battleships, are made up of watertight compartments."[80] But the power and efficiency of the new structure ensured its success.

When the Committee of Ten instituted national college entrance examinations in composition, based on the Harvard model, which required students to write only on vernacular literary classics, the secondary curriculum was forced to adopt the perspective of the eastern colleges and teach composition as analysis of literature—"infant criticism," as its detractors called the approach.[81] But secondary-school teachers and administrators with a common school perspective chafed at the college domination and eventually staged a successful rebellion in the 1910s. They were to some extent influenced by Deweyan progressive ideas: education should prepare students for democratic life by involving them in meaningful activities appropriate to their stage of development, activities "integrated" or "correlated" with students' life needs. But more importantly, secondary curriculum was shaped by the demands of "social efficiency"—the effort to administer economically a burgeoning system which included more and more students who would not attend college but, unlike most students in other nations, who would attend secondary school (see chapter 5).

The National Education Association's (NEA) influential *Cardinal Principles of Secondary Education* (1918) forged a compromise between the claims of academic discipline and the demands for greater access to secondary schools.[82] The schools would have both Deweyan integration and curricular differentiation, "education for life" but within a disciplinary structure. The NEA commission defined seven broad areas of curricular focus: health, command of fundamental processes, worthy home-membership, vocation, citizenship, worthy use of leisure, and ethical character. This "general education" would provide social equity (and social control) in the system. But each of the traditional disciplines would reorganize itself to accomplish these within each school or track. In the next few years, the major disciplines produced a "reorganization report" outlining a plan for reconciling disciplinary values with the values of a far more inclusive secondary-school system. For example, history, geography, and political science became the new field of *social studies* and set about training Americans for citizenship (though in different ways in different schools and tracks). Secondary English also redefined itself in terms of social goals rather than a literary canon (though in fact the canon remained intact, both in the National Council of Teachers of English's [NCTE] seminal reorganization report of 1917 and in most secondary curricula).[83]

Significantly, that crucial compromise left writing instruction dangling. All of the disciplines were theoretically responsible for teaching this "fundamental process," but only English did so systematically, and even that instruction was a relatively minor part of its overall task. More importantly, the compromise also severed the connection between academic writing—the genres of specialized disciplinary discourse as practiced in the university—and the goals of secondary education. Most American secondary schools, unlike their selective European counterparts, were not primarily in the business of preparing students for specific professions or institutions of higher education, so the writing of those professions and disciplines was not considered crucial. As the distance between secondary school and university widened, universities gradually did away with essay examinations for admission, the strongest link between the two curricula and, not coincidentally, the chief target of secondary-school reformers.

Thus, secondary teachers, unlike elementary teachers, were representatives of a discipline, but they were not full members of it, at least from the point of view of university faculty. And few had written extensively as part of their disciplinary training. They were responsible for upholding the standards of the discipline but not for initiating neophytes into it. Given the ambiguous position of secondary teachers, it is not surprising that many saw writing primarily as a means of *testing* content mastery, not as a means of attaining it. Students wrote to show learning, not to learn.

Moreover, secondary-school teaching methods evolved away from formal recitation, with students rising from their seats to answer formal questions, to the "socialized recitation," a mixture of lecture, informal questioning, and discussion.[84] Socialized recitation was still rigidly teacher centered, but it was stripped of the curricular and extracurricular reinforcement that formal performance gave writing in the old preparatory academy. Fewer and fewer students were required to keep commonplace books or formal notebooks, to prepare answers to questions in writing, or to engage in extracurricular forensic performances, as in the old curriculum.

If secondary teachers gave up many of the old pedagogical traditions that provided meaningful verbal interaction, often written, they did not adopt Deweyan progressive methods to provide new places for writing. In his history of twentieth-century American teaching practices, Larry Cuban has shown that secondary teachers were much less likely than elementary teachers to adopt progressive or student-centered teaching methods, such as flexible arrangement of classroom space, a preponderance of student over teacher talk, small-group or individual (rather than whole-class) instruction, and student participation in curricular planning. As Cuban argues, secondary teachers were much less free to adopt student-centered methods than elementary schools not only because the differentiated curricular structure gave teachers five times as many students as elementary teachers but also because "subject matter drives methodology in the class-room" (248). More than their elementary-school counterparts, secondary teachers faced external pressures from higher educa-tion, potential employers, and accrediting associations to teach content first and foremost. But it was all too often content stripped of its disciplinary meaning, facts divorced from the ques-tions and theories and activities that drove the disciplines and demanded extended writing. Some writing-dependent activities common in the old extracurriculum found their way into the new secondary classroom as a means of loosening the formalism of recitation, such as book reports and debates. But these were, as Cuban concludes, "scattered and isolated," not integral parts of a rigidly content-centered curriculum (136). The one tradition of writing that secondary schools borrowed from the university, the term paper, was also a curricular appendage which served the ends of content mastery and evaluation rather than initiation into the discourse community of a discipline (see the next chapter).

Had secondary schools specialized more thoroughly and artic-ulated their curriculum with higher education, as in Europe, secondary teachers might have learned and taught discipline-specific writing as an integral part of specific curricula, gradually initiating students into a disciplinary community. Or if secondary schools had thrown off disciplinary organization entirely, as some progressives wished (see chapter 8), teachers might have adopted progressive methods and developed traditions of integrating writ-ing instruction into student-centered general-education activities. But the great compromise between the claims of elementary and higher education, general education and discipline, social equity and disciplinary excellence, left secondary education without in-stitutional structures and pedagogical traditions to incorporate meaningful extended writing into the curriculum.

The transformation of schooling from the old liberal curricu-lum to the mass-education system mirrored the vast change in American society from the old face-to-face rural and small-town culture of the nineteenth century to the print-driven urban-indus-trial America of the twentieth. The education system, along with the wider society, became conscious of writing as a subject—a school subject, certainly, but also a matter of educational policy and, in the broadest sense, a subject of social concern. For the first time in America, the term *writing instruction* meant more than teaching handwriting. But despite the new interest in composition, educators never fully grasped that their old ways of thinking about written communication were no longer adequate, that the division of knowledge and work into disciplines and professions had permanently shattered the centuries-old concept of writing as ancillary to speaking, of readers as a general audience to which all writers could appeal. And the organization of the mass-education system around discrete disciplines kept educators from realizing that this fundamental change had taken place. Writing remained transparent, and the myth of transience grew more firmly entrenched with each new round of complaint and reform.

In sum, the differentiated organization of curriculum and instruction increased the distance between faculty and student. Shortly after the turn of the century, students began to complain of alienation, detachment. In the absence of the old communal structures—chapel, rhetoricals, literary societies, exhibitions, and commencements—they found community in the new social rituals of undergraduate life, fraternities, athletics, and the like, or by identifying with a career goal and thus a department.[85] The academic community had ceased to be a community in the sense that those raised in the oral, face-to-face culture of rural and small-town America understood the term. The college had become divided, rationalized, efficient, with knowledge committed to specialized writing, though students had no clear means of mastering those written conventions. In short, it had become modern.

3

WRITING AND THE

IDEAL OF RESEARCH

Some Tacit Traditions

Despite many efforts to adapt the old oral rhetoricals to the new mass-education system, the burgeoning universities and comprehensive secondary schools could not maintain formal, institutionwide curricular and pedagogical structures to develop students' writing, apart from general-composition courses. The desiccation of the oral tradition, the triumph of the elective curriculum, the departmentalization and secularization of the old academic community, the sheer growth in numbers—all thwarted educators' attempts to adapt the rhetorical tradition of the old liberal curriculum to a more differentiated, more democratic institution. But adaptation of the old rhetoricals was not the only option available. Because the overall student-faculty ratio remained about ten to one from 1860 to 1985, despite a 240-fold increase in enrollment, other options were available.[1] America might have developed an Oxbridge-style faculty tutorial arrangement, a German-style privatdocent system for supervising individual and small-group undergraduate study with graduate students, or even adapted the native tradition of the literary societies to create a writing-rich extracurriculum. But significantly, the new organization of knowledge by specialized disciplines gave academia responsibility for specialized research as well as for teaching. America imported a new ideal of research scholarship from Germany, along with certain pedagogical forms for inculcating students with that ideal. Of course, this new faculty responsibility took time away from undergraduate teaching, and the time- and energy-consuming activity of writing instruction was doubtless a frequent victim (the pain of paper grading was a common lament among faculty).[2] However, the research ideal not only competed with teaching but also molded student writing into its modern genres and curricular sites. Thus, to understand why certain forms of student writing endured and others faded, or why certain pedagogies included writing and others did not, one must look to the character of the research ideal and the ways it interacted with writing in the new mass-education system, most visibly at the graduate and undergraduate levels but also in the secondary curriculum which was also organized by academic disciplines. In this chapter I examine three new pedagogical sites for writing that America imported from German higher education during the late nineteenth century—lecture course, seminar, and laboratory—and the three genres of student writing associated with them: reading notes, research paper, and laboratory report.

In one sense, the ideal of research "contributed to a decline in supervision of undergraduates," as Veysey has shown (138, 143–45). The German-inspired ethic of free scientific research looked with disdain on the paternalistic moral discipline of the old college: taking attendance before class, preaching moral virtue during class, and policing student conduct outside class. Research-oriented faculty upheld the ideal of unfettered inquiry as the institution's fundamental reason for being, a positive good, which sensible students would willingly, independently pursue (as the faculty had and did). Faculty chafed at the old formulaic rhetorical exercises, at reading or hearing endless themes, at correcting students' grammar and punctuation. "If investigation was the principal aim of the university," Veysey says, "then giving one's energy to immature and frequently mediocre students could easily seem an irritating irrelevance" (144). The researcher's model was the oral, master-apprentice relationship, best expressed in the new, more informal pedagogies of lecture, seminar, and laboratory, not in the recitation hall with its formally structured questions and answers or in the agonistic oral performances of the old college rhetoricals. Today the researcher's neglect of undergraduate teaching has become an educational cliché. But in an-

71

other sense, the ideal of research began with a genuine regard for an ideal of inquiry that encouraged serious study, intimate contact with students, and precise, if not always elegant, writing. The research ideal first resisted what it saw as the intellectual flabbiness of the old curriculum, but as research took on greater importance, the ideal began to conflict with the democratic values of the vocationally oriented university, where undergraduates did not always share the researcher's respect for specialized, "disciplined" inquiry and the genres that embodied that inquiry. Nevertheless, research-oriented faculty held to the assumption— the hope—that students could and should find interesting questions about which to write, discover an appropriate methodology for investigating them, and report the results using the conventions of a discipline—all without the formal, often routine instruction of the old curriculum. This assumption was all too frequently unrealistic, a vain hope, given the nature of the mass-education system, but the disappointment was nevertheless real.

The ideal of research not only distanced the faculty from lower-level instruction but it also narrowed the focus of instruction to the content and issues addressed by research and thus narrowed the range of genres acceptable in academia. Student writing increasingly became *researched* writing, an imitation of the writing that the institution valued most: the documented or "research" paper and, to a lesser extent, the laboratory or experimental report. Early in the history of modern universities, the research ideal came to be bound up with a narrow view of the production of written knowledge, and faculty carried that perspective into the classroom, where it permeated writing instruction, consciously and unconsciously, throughout the curriculum.

The academic researcher of the late nineteenth century, Veysey points out, "prided himself more on the discovery of truth than on its pursuit. His goal was certainty—not a labyrinth of tentative opinions or opinions true only for the people of one time and place" (145). His was the old Enlightenment project: the progressive accumulation of facts, painstakingly but firmly wrested from nature, revealing immutable, universal laws. It was also, one must remember, a *written* project, where only that knowledge which appeared in the acceptable written forums was valued and preserved to become another "brick in the temple of wisdom," as a common metaphor had it. The research ideal derived its tacit understanding of the nature of written communication from John Locke, that preeminent Enlightenment philosopher: language is merely a conduit for transmitting preexisting, preformed truth. "The academic researcher," Veysey goes on to say, "believed he was dealing with reality, not expressing transient attitudes" (148). Expository prose, like the science it communicated, was not the site of a rhetorical struggle among shifting interests for impermanent victories, it was objective and fixed. Those who shaped writing in the curriculum held an abiding faith in the power of written knowledge to defeat ignorance and error and bring permanent progress. Truth would triumph without rhetoric—or in spite of it.

This dogmatic and, by current standards, epistemologically naive approach to research and writing endured for decades without serious challenge, largely because, as Veysey says, "the dominant characteristic of the new American universities was their ability to shelter specialized departments of knowledge." For the most part, researchers stayed within the bounds of established theory and found no reason to leave their various disciplinary universes. The ethic of objective, distanced inquiry obliged faculty to "maintain an air of politeness about their work which kept the intellectual tensions within the system under control" (142). With the decline of the old collegewide forums for intellectual discourse, students and faculty had no curricular mechanism for seeing the differences in the ways disciplines pursued and represented truth, or, in rhetorical terms, their different heuristics and conventions. Not surprisingly, discussions of student-researched writing were few and predictable; they assumed researched writing in academia was essentially uniform: an unproblematic recording of the facts in correct language.

Moreover, the positivist ethic of research limited dialogue not only between academic disciplines but between disciplines and the wider society. Though late-nineteenth-century academics held opinions on politics and religion and all manner of controversial topics, they learned to speak publicly, *ex academia,* only in their areas of expertise, and then only in acceptable forums. In the next century, this respect for specialization and appropriate occasion would become a tacit condition for academic freedom in modern society. The research ideal thus narrowed the possibilities for written discourse in the modern curriculum by casting suspicion on genres that were not "academic," which is to say research oriented. Modern academics could not be content with the classical notion that student writing was preparation for public speaking on matters of general civic import. Nor did they ever take to heart the Deweyan progressive notion that students should sometimes write in nonacademic genres, for nonacademic audiences, as a necessary part of their developing understanding of disciplinary activities and discourses. In short, student writing was conceived in the image of faculty writing.

The "undisciplined" gropings of student prose were of course far from the research ideal held up by the disciplines. As faculty never tired of pointing out, student papers were replete with ignorance and error of all sorts, which could seemingly never be entirely eradicated. Because faculty tended to regard poor writing as evidence of poor thinking, not as evidence of a student's incomplete assimilation into a disciplinary community, faculty sensed that the discipline's "store of knowledge," acquired at great sacrifice, was "tarnished" by poor writing. The metaphors are revealing; knowledge is conceived of in physical terms, as a precious commodity discovered and protected from corruption, not as a changing and socially negotiated understanding. "Scouring" student writing for "mistakes of fact and expression" became the goal, and writing instruction "professional scullery."[3] And because academics focused on the "discovery" of truth rather than on the social process involved in its pursuit—the final, fixed product rather than the activity and method of the discipline—student writing remained for many faculty uninteresting at best, and at worst, disgraceful. What counted was new knowledge, new truth; and when students could not "produce" (or appropriately reproduce) "original contributions" in their writing, faculty either had to find other (and from their perspective much less valuable) purposes for writing or give up asking students to write. The resulting discontentment fed the tradition of complaint that I noted in chapter 1 and contributed to the marginalization of writing instruction. Lured by the myth of transience, faculty vainly searched outside their own classrooms and disciplines for a single solution to a problem that was in fact as complex as modern education itself. In the positivist temple of wisdom, there was little room for student writing—and almost none for rhetoric.

From Recitation to Lecture: Learning from Notes

The German import that had perhaps the greatest impact on pedagogy was the lecture. Before the Civil War, lecture was the usual classroom method only in the few scientific courses offered. In the decades following the war, European-educated Americans brought back not only the German research ideal but also the German pedagogical model—large lectures for most college instruction, with laboratory work and seminars for the few advanced students—and adapted it to the demands of a rapidly growing and diversifying institution. As enrollments and research boomed in the 1880s and 1890s, lecture eventually replaced recitation as the standard undergraduate classroom method in almost all areas.[4] Eliot and other reformers argued that lecture, unlike recitation, could reflect and communicate disciplinary values, the "mental toughness" and "intellectual freedom" they prized.[5] Reformers wanted to replace what they considered routine, uncritical memorization or paraphrase from one or two "dry compilations" with a classroom where students listened to lectures based on the professor's critical reading of many sources, including primary ones. "While the power of accurate re-statement of a thing learned is valuable to the student," wrote a Harvard history professor, "the common sense of most [educators] has concluded that the time spent by an educated man in listening to such repetition is an actual loss to science, and that the brighter students of a class can employ themselves very much more profitably than in hearing the mistakes of their duller mates."[6] "Branches of study" were to be pursued "by topics rather than by chapter and verse," the mind conceived of "not as a storehouse for certain facts and theories but as a workroom, well equipped with tools," according to the 1878 Kansas University catalog. Faculty who were trained in the new critical methods of research, with a newfound professional identity in a discipline, could no longer bear to "merely hear recitations, keeping the finger on the place in the text-book, and only asking the questions conveniently printed for them in the margin or the back of the book."[7] They needed to inspire the research ideal.

Moreover, as printed materials (other than textbooks) became more available and as libraries became more accessible to students (and faculty), memorization came to be seen as unnecessary. Class time formerly spent on recitation was freed for lectures, which could do more than merely recount facts available in a single textbook.[8] Faculty sent the students to several parallel or collateral readings on the topics of lectures, readings that required of students a new level of synthesis and critical analysis to yield their fruits. The lecture would be "a skeleton ready to be clothed from [the students'] own reading."[9] According to advocates of this new "scientific" approach to pedagogy, "what the laboratory is to the physical sciences, the library must be to the moral sciences."[10] When Henry Adams was hired to teach history at Harvard, he fought to have study tables put in the library so that he could begin to do "real teaching."[11] The performance-centered, interactive classroom of the old college, where students constantly used language, rapidly gave way to a classroom pedagogy based on solo performance, which required students to be passive auditors—a role they willingly accepted. And reading became not an active preparation for public, community performance in recitation or rhetoricals but a passive, private activity.

Advocates of the lecture method, however, did not ignore student discourse; they merely substituted private sites and written genres for the old public oral ones. The most common was the notebook. Instead of a commonplace book or notes for preparing recitations, students were expected to keep a notebook of lectures and, significantly, of notes on "parallel reading." The notebook would, in theory, lead the students to make connections between readings and lectures, "to oblige the student to think, to see the relation of one part of [the subject] to another," as a Harvard history professor put it.[12] Beginning in the 1880s, faculty sometimes provided students with suggestions for note-taking, syllabi and outlines of lectures and readings, and questions or suggestions to guide note-taking, "arranged so as to call for a little original thinking." Brief written answers to questions were sometimes used in class to illustrate points or to spur discussion, a practice resembling the "microthemes" of today's WAC movement.[13] To "keep students to their own work," there were quizzes and of course final essay examinations.[14] Sometimes instructors collected and graded notebooks, but ordinarily the students had the same freedom in note-taking as the researcher.[15]

Notebooks from the late nineteenth century show that for some students the lecture–parallel-reading notebook encouraged the "independent judgement" that was so dear to the research ideal.[16] In contrast to the copied or paraphrased answers to textbook-recitation questions common in notebooks from the 1850s and 1860s, notebooks from the late 1870s and beyond sometimes contain extensive outlines of the lectures and detailed summaries or outlines of the collateral readings, often arranged in parallel columns to show the relationship between the lecture and the reading. Careful students made extensive notebooks—in some cases a hundred or more longhand pages for a single course.[17]

However, after the initial enthusiasm settled into routine, faculty found that the lecture–parallel-reading method encouraged no fewer abuses than had the old recitation system. Many students did not keep careful notebooks or use them profitably. Because performance was measured primarily by final essay examinations, enterprising students produced and sold what Harvard faculty called "unauthorized professional tutors' outlines": concise responses to questions or topics contained in the syllabi or old examinations of large lecture courses. A year after Henry Adams printed a syllabus for his history course, two students anonymously printed a twelve-page booklet, "An Attempt To Answer the Syllabus in History II," which contained an examination-length response to each syllabus topic, complete with references to lectures and parallel readings. "The compilers believe the above answers to be tolerably full and entirely accurate," the booklet concluded, and "when lack of space has forbidden as full an answer as might be desired, the rest would be suggested to the reader somewhat familiar with the ground."[18]

Just after the turn of the century, the Harvard faculty took steps to curb these abuses. Unauthorized notes were suppressed, and A. Lawrence Lowell, then head of the freshman history program, led an effort to "stiffen up" notoriously easy lecture courses and to prevent students from taking only elementary courses (55 percent of the 1898 graduating class had taken no advanced courses).[19] When Lowell became president in 1909, he modified Eliot's elective system, strengthened the honors program, and instituted comprehensive examinations in some departments (with a tutorial system to help students prepare for them). But despite these steps to encourage intellectual rigor, the "gentleman's C" remained a Harvard tradition, and the lecture model could not prevent passive learning for students not fired with the research ideal.

From Rhetorical to Research Paper

One genre has defined extended student writing in mass secondary and higher education: the documented essay (or research paper or term paper). Significantly, the genre sprang from the new research ideal and has been maintained by it, even in contexts largely devoid of faculty research, such as in secondary schools. Although students sometimes have written in other genres as part of their class work (diaries, poems, speeches, stories, interviews, editorials, case studies, advertisements, brochures, etc.), this genre has come to be ubiquitous, relatively uniform, and almost synonymous with extended school writing.

The term paper has been much criticized by teachers and reformers of every stripe (and of course by students), yet it endures as the primary site of extended writing. However, the term paper has rarely been studied and even more rarely studied as a genre worthy of historical analysis. In treating it generically, as a typified rhetorical action based in a recurring situation, I view it in its social and institutional context and trace some of the roles it played in the activity of mass education.

The term paper is a species of ephemera: widely assigned and written but rarely preserved. Though the genre is an academic fact of life in America, with its own lore and traditions, its own extensive how-to literature dating from the 1910s, little is known about it. The only comprehensive bibliography of articles on research-paper instruction lists but 210 articles published in eighty years—only forty-one if one excludes articles on plagiarism, library use, and suggestions for specific assignments. As the bibliography's compilers point out, there are no experts on student research papers, even among composition teachers, who have for at least seven decades taught "the research paper" as a "service" to other departments.[20] Constructing a picture of the genre is therefore difficult. Fortunately, many course materials, examples of student writing, and comments by faculty and students indicate at least the outlines of its development.

How did the tradition of requiring an extended documented essay begin in the American university? The research paper, like the American university itself, is a grafting of certain German traditions onto what was originally a British system of college education. In the British-inspired liberal curriculum of the eighteenth- and early-nineteenth-century college, the thesis was an agonistic oral performance before the college community, as it had been since the middle ages (and still is, in vestigial form, in the graduate-school tradition of oral thesis defense). In fact, *thesis* was the penultimate exercise in the ancient *progymnasmata*, designed to prepare students for courtroom debate.[21]

But beginning in the late 1860s and 1870s, young American academics who had studied in Germany imported a text-dependent approach to scholarship and, with it, the scholarly thesis or dissertation (the terms were used synonymously, as they are in some contexts today).[22] It was of course not a speech for a forensic occasion but rather a comprehensive display of learning on a narrow topic, replete with extensive textual conventions, such as footnotes and bibliography. German scholarship rapidly set a new standard for academic writing, not only in the sciences but also in the emerging humanities and social sciences, where rigorous "scientific" philology and historical criticism on the German model gained academic respectability as the genteel "life and works" and "great man" traditions of the literary and historical amateur faded.[23] And it is worth recalling that in the new German-inspired university a faculty member no longer taught several subjects, only his specialty, and students took elective courses rather than a common course of study.

The new text-based scholarship, along with the new differentiated academic structure, changed the nature of the academic game. Oral performance for a local academic community demanded only a *display* of learning, but the new text-based standards demanded an *original contribution* to a disciplinary community in written form: a research paper. The American scholarly journals, which developed in the late nineteenth century as a major forum for faculty discourse, contain a great deal more transcription of oral discourse (discussions, speeches, lectures) than do contemporary journals. But disciplines quickly evolved the text-based apparatus of modern scholarship: discipline-specific conventions of argument, style, documentation, and format. The "German footnote" became a mark of distinction among the rising class of research scholars and an object of ridicule to the old academic generalists.

This shift posed a problem: if the primary forums for the faculty's scholarly discourse lay outside the local academic community, where should the forum for students' scholarly discourse lie? The old oral forums, the rhetoricals and the literary societies, were increasingly irrelevant to the production and communication of specialized knowledge, handled primarily in writing. With the passing of the old liberal curriculum, the medium for student academic discourse became, like the faculty's, increasingly *written*, and its sites progressively moved away from the local academic community and into the individual classroom, the domain of specialized disciplinary knowledge in the elective curriculum. The old face-to-face audience of peers and professors from the college community was replaced by an audience of the individual professor representing a disciplinary community. The model of extended student discourse shifted from student-as-public-performer to student-as-disciple or apprentice, conducting individual research under the guidance of a professor and producing critical, "original" interpretations of documents and data using the methods, conventions, and assumptions of a specialized discipline—not the "common knowledge" of a particular social class.[24]

In the late 1860s, a few faculty members began requiring students to write extended "course theses," which increasingly bore the marks of modern, text-based scholarship. Those I have examined range from seventeen to ninety handwritten pages—much longer than the required themes and forensics and too long to be easily read aloud to a group. They often contain such scholarly apparatus as a table of contents at the beginning and a brief bibliography at the end. More importantly, they address questions of interest to a discipline rather than to the general public, though they rarely involve a critical reading of sources or original arguments.[25]

In 1870, when Harvard introduced the elective curriculum, the catalog first announced that "in all departments special investigations may be exacted," indicating that individual faculty could require written work beyond the required themes and forensics.[26] By the late 1870s, original student investigation and written critical analysis of documents had begun to be accepted, though its functions and forms were by no means settled. Henry Adams required written debates from his advanced students, complete with citations; William James required students in Harvard's first psychology course to make a list of inconsistencies and errors in the required readings and comment on them. The Harvard Board of Overseers approved of students examining "for themselves the methods of investigation and the fundamental assumptions which prevail in the 'scientific' school of philosophy" as "immanently liberal and inspiring."[27] Significantly, the overseers used the term *liberal* in a characteristically modern way: broad-minded, free of intellectual prejudices; not in the old sense of the *artes liberales:* free of the need to work for a living. And James' critical analysis and intellectual skepticism was "inspiring" in a modern secular way, not in the old religious way. It was now permissible, even desirable, for student writing to question received truths critically, in the manner of the scientist and philosopher, not merely to communicate received truths persuasively, in the manner of the orator.[28]

Land-grant colleges also began to recognize and encourage student research and extended writing in specific courses and departments. In 1879, Iowa State began requiring seniors to write a "graduating thesis." These theses (and the shorter course "dissertations" which were also required for a time) were painstakingly handwritten on twelve-by-eighteen-inch folio sheets. They are generally short enough to be read in a few minutes, between one thousand and three thousand words, and bear the unmistakable marks of student prose: self-consciously formal style, specious generalities, and impossibly broad topics ("Socialism," "Engineering, Its Relation to Civilization"). The earliest theses and dissertations rarely contain the kind of scholarly apparatus beginning to appear in professional journals, but during the 1880s they increasingly reveal the marks of text-based scholarship. In those from the sciences, occasional parenthetical citations appear, and often there are plates and drawings, carefully labeled. At times it is clear that a student has absorbed important conventions of argument and format from the journal literature of the discipline. An 1881 dissertation, "On a Species of Plant Louse Infecting the Scotch Pine," defines a problem and reviews the literature: "[The species] appears to have received little notice from entomologists, whether from seeming of little importance to them, or from simple oversight, I am unable to state." There is "a table or brief abstract from my notes for two-years" to "plainly show" the original conclusions valid; there are headings for various sections and a conclusion suggesting areas for further research. Sometimes students display clear development from a course thesis to a graduation thesis, as with the student who moved from a flabby summary, "The Uses of Credit," to a more focused survey, "Banking in the U.S."[29]

Throughout the 1890s Iowa State strengthened its thesis regulations, requiring faculty to "criticize and approve" the work "during its progress" and students to "make frequent reports of progress."[30] In 1898 the catalog first requires the thesis to be "the result of the student's personal study or investigation and be throughout original in matter and treatment as far as the nature of the subject will permit" (12). By the turn of the century, graduation theses were replete with footnotes, bibliographies, blueprints, diagrams, plates, and photographs. Without the oral-reading requirement, theses gradually increased in length during the 1890s, and in 1906 they were first bound individually.[31]

Eventually departments dropped the undergraduate theses (engineering was the last to do so, in 1943). And student writing outside of composition courses was entirely at the discretion of the individual professor.

The thesis as a requirement for individual courses came into its own in the late 1880s and 1890s nationwide with the growth of the research ideal in the new universities and the spread of the "seminary" (seminar) or "practice course." The seminar was imported from Germany, where it began in the 1830s as a small, informal group of advanced students gathered around a magnetic senior professor, primarily in history and economics. There it "led a somewhat spasmodic existence," Veysey says, and "did not become a routine part of the curriculum" (154–55). But the young, research-oriented American academics who brought the method back made it a central part of their pedagogical reforms. The professor assigned topics to the seminar students, each of whom presented "a written dissertation" to the class, and "criticized the work of every other."[32] The oral element was clearly subordinate to the written, and the goal was clearly apprenticeship in specific scholarly methods of a narrow discipline, not rhetorical display for a general audience. At Columbia in 1882, for example, one department began an "Academy of the Historic, Jural, and Political Sciences" where each student in the department was expected to read "one original work each year" to the assembled students, faculty, and alumni at weekly meetings, in a kind of moot professional meeting where students were "not simply pupils but coworkers." The author of the best paper won a lectureship in the department.[33]

Faculty prided themselves on sending students to the "original sources" and getting from them "original scholarship," both in the eastern universities and in the new land-grant universities of the Midwest and West.[34] Historian Ephraim Emerton, who began the first *practice course* (a regularly taught seminar) at Harvard in 1882, proclaimed the student "no longer a receiver of other men's thought; he becomes an investigator, a discoverer, a creator." And at Kansas, James H. Canfield in 1878 called the classroom "literally a mutual aid society," where students are "permitted and expected to be a critic of each fellow student," stimulating "careful thought and expression."[35] Emerton regarded the seminar as the pedagogical equivalent of the scientist's laboratory for the "social, moral and linguistic sciences."[36] He pronounced the motto of the seminar—and of the whole research ideal—"The way to that which is general is through that which is special" (133). And by the end of the decade, Harvard and many other universities offered seminars in almost every field, thus effectively stopping the flow of Americans to Germany for advanced study.[37]

The new pedagogy immediately spread to lower-level lecture courses, even to secondary schools, and with it went the ideal of original student writing from original sources. A German-trained historian, Charles Gross, was the first Harvard history professor to require "a stiff thesis" in regular undergraduate courses (and, perhaps not coincidentally, the first member of the department without a Harvard degree).[38] His practice encouraged other faculty to begin using the method of "topics and references" for assigning writing. In larger classes faculty sometimes printed lists of topics, each with references, and appended detailed instructions on the use of sources, notes, tables, and bibliography. Administrative arrangements varied widely. Students in some undergraduate Harvard history courses were excused from a third of the lectures and the midyear examination in exchange for "one considerable thesis, due in April." Other faculty gave over one lecture period per week to "discussion and criticism" of course theses, which were then revised.[39] By the early 1890s the practice of assigning course theses in the social sciences had become so widespread that publishers began to offer collections of primary materials for use by students in research writing.[40]

Topics ranged from William James' intriguingly short assignments ("Make idealism as plausible as you can in two or three pages") to extended treatises of more than two hundred longhand pages. Apparatus and documentation also show wide variation. From the 1860s through the 1880s, citations are often handwritten in the margin, even when the text is typewritten, and styles are irregular.[41] After the turn of the century, formats and styles settled into the familiar footnotes and endnotes. Faculty encouraged students to write "as if for publication" (in a scholarly journal, of course) and some faculty gained reputations for fastidiousness in matters of format.[42]

The rationales for extended student writing were as varied as the writings were themselves. But in the early years of the research paper, at least, faculty often saw writing as a means of improving learning and of introducing students to the activity of the discipline, as well as a means of improving writing. Emerton complained that American students, unlike their European counterparts, have "a deep-seated dread of putting pen to paper." "Writing appears as a kind of extra work; it suggests compositions, with all their train of absurdities." Writing should not be "a thing apart from ordinary studies" but instead "the most useful instrument in pursuing those studies." He even suggested abolishing composition courses and giving the time to "the use of English in the pursuit of other studies."[43] Emerton's colleague Albert Bushnell Hart concluded that "the best writer has also the best general knowledge of the course."[44]

Hart and others sometimes suggested that writing improves learning, but they never developed the notion in any coherent way. The most common rationale for requiring course theses was that they allow the student to "make some small corner of the field his own."[45] Though the Harvard history department's manual of thesis writing mentioned "developing powers of analysis and statement," the primary goal was research: "The purpose of the system [of required course theses] is to train students in finding things out for themselves. It will introduce them to the most valuable authorities; it will make them familiar with the sources of information on American history . . . and interest them in the unsettled questions of our history."[46] Writing a course thesis was thus very different from delivering a rhetorical. The thesis primarily developed specific knowledge and research methods, not general powers of expression; its pedagogical value lay in its relation to the discipline, not to general culture or public discourse. Perhaps because disciplines viewed student writing through the narrow lens of their own research writing, they rarely explored other possibilities for using writing in teaching. Student writing meant the scholar's tools: notebook and extended research paper, in addition to the ubiquitous essay examination.

Although faculty generally agreed that student writing should be scholarly, they by no means agreed on which students should be assigned extended writing. An elitist tendency within the research ideal led faculty to insist that extended writing maintain a "voluntary character" and be reserved for the best students. Writing should be used to promote disciplinary excellence. If a discipline's ultimate goal was to maintain and raise its standards of scholarship, then it was a logical step to conclude that extended writing should be reserved for those few students who had shown particular aptitude for or interest in a specialized field. "To require theses," Hart said, "is to expect more than the average student can give, in time and thought." And there was much sentiment for continuing "drill and recitation" for the great majority of students, without demanding extended writing of them; indeed those methods persisted in the great bulk of secondary schools (and many colleges) well into the twentieth century.[47]

There was also, however, an egalitarian strain within the research ideal that insisted that all students should have some experience in individual research on an important and interesting topic under the tutelage of a master. Elements within the new research-oriented faculty clung to "romantic expectations" (Veysey's term), which held out the hope that mass education could recapture a kind of personal discipleship in learning, despite the gap in knowledge and aims that increasingly separated the research-oriented faculty from the socially or career-oriented student.[48] Vocal advocates of the seminar, such as Herbert B. Adams of Johns Hopkins University, insisted that even secondary students should begin historical study by writing research reports, on town fathers, for example, or on local institutions.[49] Such educators held to the research ideal (and the course thesis) for undergraduates and even secondary students despite the objections from colleagues (and of course students). But the tension between the competing values of excellence and equity left faculty in an ambiguous position with respect to student writing. Should faculty consider it a duty to assign writing to the majority of students or a compromise with disciplinary quality and thus a sheer waste of time? American educators never overcame this tension; they merely developed ways of living with it, ways that marginalized writing instruction.

The idealistic experiments of the modern university's formative decades settled into familiar routine after the turn of the century. Extended writing became standard only at the advanced levels, for the most highly specialized students. Most courses required no extended writing, and those that did made writing an adjunct, offering little instruction. In many cases, extended writing became merely another form of evaluation. Indeed, it was not unusual for faculty to require students to hand in term papers the last week of class and for faculty to return them at the final examination with no marks but a grade.[50]

Just as the last vestiges of universitywide writing requirements died in the 1910s, the research paper began to harden into its familiar form. In the new university, the discourse that finally counted was the discourse that a discipline published. Student term papers became almost as ephemeral as orations had been but with crucial differences. They would be text-bound, individual, discipline-specific, "original" works. Students' verbal performances in the old college had a ritual, celebratory function, as well as an evaluative one. In the new mass-education system, student discourse lost its celebratory, community-confirming role (though it retained the evaluative role).

In theory, student-faculty discourse could now be more focused and purposeful: an individual professor and an individual student interacting within the confines of a specific course in a specific discipline. Yet with knowledge rapidly expanding, the distance between student and faculty discourse separated much student writing from the current activity of the discipline. In the 1880s a student could make a genuine contribution to knowledge by investigating a local problem—the Iowa State student's thesis on the Scotch pine plant louse, for example. But the progress of research and disciplinary differentiation made that increasingly difficult. As academic specialization boomed in the 1890s and beyond, the intellectual gulf between student and professor only widened.[51] Cut off from the old oral, communal tradition and increasingly distant from the new text-bound research of disciplinary communities, the research paper or term paper gradually atrophied as a genre of student writing and gained a reputation as a hollow formal exercise.

Plagiarism was a nagging problem. Of course students in the old colleges cribbed themes and orations, but the oral, face-to-face environment served as a check. In the large, impersonal university, plagiarism thrived. Even the best students yielded to temptation. Samuel Eliot Morison loaned a history term paper (grade of A) to a friend, who "copied it in typewriter and got a B for it in an English Composition course."[52] Infamous "literary gentlemen" began selling papers to students nationwide, much to the chagrin of faculty and administrators. The term-paper industry grew up with higher education, and today there are several companies offering a sophisticated array of "research assistance." One Chicago-based company, for example, boasts a catalog of over sixteen thousand papers, indexed not only by number of pages, footnotes, and references but also by grade level, from high school to graduate school. And this company, like others, will custom-write "research aids" for students.[53] The industry was built on the gap between student and instructor, a gap created in part because faculty ordinarily did not teach or supervise writing, did not require papers be discussed in conference or be revised. But the industry was also built on sheer demand.

One can only guess how widely term papers were (or are) assigned, in what disciplines, in what types of institutions, and at what levels. There has never been a national survey of the term paper in the disciplines, but a few local surveys and records offer fleeting glimpses. A Harvard study of undergraduate courses from 1899 to 1901 found that about one-fifth required a course thesis, but because over half the students never took advanced courses (where theses were most common), many undergraduates may never have written a term paper.[54] Because the Harvard archives contain the undergraduate papers from a few students, it is possible to conclude that conscientious students—those more likely to write (and preserve) papers—did indeed suffer from "constant scribbling," which Grandgent suggested led Harvard to drop collegewide writing requirements. Morison wrote during his undergraduate years (1905–10) at least fourteen papers totaling some four hundred pages, from three-page reports to a fifty-eight-page course thesis.[55]

Elsewhere, a 1930 survey at Kansas State Teachers College—by no means a research institution—found that undergraduates averaged two term papers per semester (out of a four- to five-course course load). Ninety percent of the term papers were due during the last week of class; only 40 percent were returned, and of those returned, 66 percent had no marks other than a grade.[56] By 1931, when the first article with *term paper* in the title appeared, it was already standard practice for high-school students to write a term paper in their junior or senior year.[57] Four decades later, a survey of California higher education (both two- and four-year colleges), found that 15 percent of all undergraduate courses required a documented research paper, and students averaged six to eight papers during a four-year undergraduate program.[58] Even by conservative estimate, tens of millions of papers are written every year in the United States. And the decades-old term-paper-mill industry attests to the genre's persistence, if not to its pedagogical vitality.

As the practice of assigning research papers settled into routine, its pedagogical uses seem to have narrowed, moving from apprenticeship to production. If a discipline was primarily a storehouse of accumulated knowledge (not an active, socially constituted discourse community), then what counted in a research paper was the information it contained, not the methodological processes that led students (or the discipline) to find and value the information. If writing could be treated as a single, generalizable skill, independent of disciplinary context, then so could methods of research. Given these views, it is not surprising that training in methods of research and term-paper writing was soon marginalized. Composition courses assumed responsibility for teaching students research methods along with other aspects of composition, but even within these courses the teaching of research and the research paper was marginalized.

Just after the turn of the century composition textbooks gradually began to treat student research. The influential late-nineteenth-century textbooks of Adams Sherman Hill (1878, 1892) and Barrett Wendell (1891) were largely silent on student research.[59] *Invention* (the process of finding arguments and evidence) was merely assumed; it was observation or inspiration or mere thought, not a discipline-specific method. The few early-twentieth-century composition texts that reflected the classical, oratorical tradition, such as those by John Franklin Genung (1904) and Charles Sears Baldwin (1909), briefly treated note-taking, reference, and citation as part of lengthy discussions of invention, which also included advice on keeping notebooks and commonplace books, writing paraphrases, combining sources, and evaluating authorities (although there was no mention of the question of originality or of plagiarism). Baldwin even suggested using "small, uniform cards," but he was clearly thinking of oral debate, not of a documented essay.[60] In any case, composition textbooks based on the classical tradition of rhetoric quickly faded.

Not until the 1910s did composition textbooks and handbooks, by then ubiquitous, begin to mention research methods, but research methods and term papers were not an integral part of the presentation. Often suggestions on research were contained in an appendix treating the use of the card catalog, note-taking in lectures, and so on.[61] Less frequently research methods were discussed as part of a section on exposition.[62] But there were clear indications that faculty in composition courses assumed students would write research papers and must therefore understand scholarly methods. Chester Noyes Greenough and Frank Wilson Cheney Hersey (1919) stated baldly, "Every long composition upon a subject that has been much written about should contain a bibliography."[63] And the instructions on note-taking in textbooks became more precise and uniform—the sample three-by-five-inch bibliography card made its debut in a textbook.[64] In the 1920s textbooks began treating problems of originality and plagiarism directly, enjoining students to copy quotations exactly, make separate note and bibliography cards, and so on.[65] By the early 1930s the "The Research Paper" had become a chapter to itself, often placed parallel to chapters on letter writing or even description, narration, and exposition.

The term paper had become a genre, with its own terms,

traditions, and functions, but it was still a structurally separate part of composition textbooks and a separate unit or activity in composition courses. Its function was plainly extrinsic. In his chapter-length appendix entitled "The Research Paper," Kendall Bernard Taft (1931) explained, "Since in most courses in the modern university students are required to write term papers or to do other research articles, it has become usual to give students in English some training in the mechanics of research."[66] Such instruction was an add-on service to other departments, not an integral part of teaching writing. In none of the forty-three composition textbooks I examined (1878–1945) was there a mention of differences among the research methods in various disciplines, though a few commented that learned societies had different citation practices. And from the 1940s there was a small but recurring debate among composition teachers over whether the research paper should be taught at all and, if so, how much time should be devoted to it, as if research were an independent technique, unrelated to other writing.[67]

In the wider curriculum, as in composition courses, the genre's function lay mainly outside the central activities of the disciplines. Discussions of the pedagogical value of the research paper centered on "the personal satisfaction that additional information always provides" and "developing good habits of thinking."[68] Students were to "increase knowledge" and "apply knowledge of the course."[69] Few considerations of discipline-specific methods of inquiry or rhetorical conventions entered in. The term paper became fundamentally another means of acquiring and displaying factual knowledge, not a means of entering the rhetorical universe of a discipline, and the formal features of the genre reflected that function: the emphasis on mechanical correctness of form, on the length of the text, and on the number of sources.[70] The traditional place of the term paper in the curriculum reflected its limited pedagogical functions. It was all too often assigned without instruction on methodology, received little class time, and had no revision requirement.

The distance between student writing and disciplinary research was pointed out in George Arms' biting 1943 analysis of the model research papers published in composition textbooks. He found that none of the model papers began with a problem that was not already solved. None had a communicative or rhetorical purpose outside the classroom. The function of the genre, Arms concluded, was classroom specific, a means of adding to and evaluating the student's store of information; it was not an introduction to the intellectual activity of the discipline.[71] The conventions of the research paper suited these narrow classroom-specific functions well, and the tradition of assigning the term paper endured despite occasional criticism that it did not foster "independent thinking," served no real value, and contributed to sloppy, often dishonest writing.[72] A 1982 survey of freshman-composition programs found that 86 percent still required it and for primarily the same reason: students must write them in their other courses.[73] It may be significant that composition courses gradually took on more responsibility for teaching the term paper as rising enrollments (and increasing emphasis on research) reduced the time faculty could devote to teaching, though there is no evidence of a direct connection. In any case, the teaching of the research paper has been so marginalized that only recently, through the WAC movement, have faculty in the disciplines begun to rethink systematically the role of the genre (see chapter 9). But the movement faces a daunting task in resuscitating a genre that was for decades largely cut off from the vital activity of the disciplines that created it.

The Laboratory Report: Writing in the Natural Sciences

From the birth of the new universities and the public secondary-school system in the 1870s, the natural sciences have had, unlike the social sciences and humanities, a unique genre and tradition of discipline-specific school writing: the laboratory notebook and report. In this space I can only indicate the broad outlines of the genre's complex history. But even a brief sketch reveals the same tensions between disciplinary excellence and those of social equity, between the demands of research and those of teaching, that shaped writing instruction throughout the curriculum.

Laboratory-science teaching was a radical innovation in the

---

nineteenth-century liberal curriculum, a dramatic and controversial departure from the textbook- and recitation-bound "natural philosophy" courses out of which it grew. In many respects the laboratory is an ideal site for passing on the rhetorical conventions of a discipline: students are directly engaged in the activities of the discipline, manipulating apparatus, making observations, working with one another under the tutelage of an expert. Indeed, the first college labs were set up privately by faculty in their homes or offices.[74] But as the method spread, the dominant educational theory (mental discipline) and the institutional position of the sciences tended to isolate writing in school and college laboratories from the activity of science. Laboratory notebooks and reports were shaped in the image of other school writing: routine, mechanically correct, primarily evaluative. Several early proponents of the laboratory method, including the influential biologist Louis Agassiz, advocated the "rediscovery" method, in which the students were given a classic problem (though new to them) and then challenged to use laboratory experiments to test their own solutions and write up their procedures, findings, and conclusions.[75] The idea that students should make their own discoveries using the scientific methods of inquiry would have profound appeal for later generations of Deweyan science educators, but in the 1890s this open-ended, student-centered model of instruction contradicted the principles of mental discipline and, in a deeper sense, the positivist research ideal of fixed, steadily accumulating knowledge. Instead of "rediscovery," "verification" became the goal of laboratory work. Students learned facts and principles in lecture and recitation, then verified them in the laboratory. The goals of laboratory work were to "fix principles in the mind," to "acquire skill in making measurements," as the Committee of Ten put it in 1892. Science had to justify its place in the curriculum against the claims of the other disciplines and with the same rationales. It would provide students with mental discipline and thus contribute to a "liberal education."[76]

Before the 1880s, science textbooks assumed no laboratory work (and of course no lab writing). Like textbooks in other fields, they directed students to memorize answers to questions, mainly factual, which were then recited in class or written on examinations; such study questions and problems continued throughout the century (and the next one). The scientific disciplines, in breaking away from the old textbook-dominated natural philosophy, began to insist on laboratory work as a mark of disciplinary rigor and status. Agassiz' motto summed up the approach: "Study Nature, not books."[77] In the 1880s, as the new universities and secondary schools built labs, science textbooks began to include instructions for laboratory experiments. Laboratory manuals proliferated (some thirty in the 1890s), giving students step-by-step instructions for performing and writing up experiments.[78] The laboratory notebook, containing notes on experiments, drawings, data tables, and formal reports, became a standard—and standardized—component of instruction. These notebooks were generally meticulous, elaborate accounts, valued for their neatness and precision rather than for their utility in the lab or beyond.

The same organizational structures and attitudes toward writing I noted earlier guaranteed that laboratory writing would be routine, correctness centered, and largely cut off from the process of scientific inquiry as working scientists used it. Labs were few and classes large; faculty employed lab assistants, who tended to standardize and make routine the instruction. But more importantly, the notebooks came to play a crucial role in evaluation. In the 1880s, entrance examinations at some elite eastern colleges, notably Harvard, began to include a physics or chemistry laboratory component in which college faculty observed and evaluated prospective students' actual performance. As enrollments increased and the geographical distribution of students widened in the 1890s, this direct evaluation became impractical. Instead, secondary-school students had to send in their lab notebooks as an admissions requirement. For the colleges, these notebooks served as a check on the quality of the students' preparation in an era when the quality of secondary science education varied widely. But the requirement also effectively gave research-oriented college faculty control over secondary science education. Eastern colleges produced lists of standard experiments for secondary students to perform and write up as evidence of their competence.[79] Accordingly, secondary laboratory courses focused on these experiments and their written product, gaining in the process a reputation for rigor, standardization—and boredom. Often the laboratory component was largely separate from classroom instruction, a time to fulfill an externally mandated requirement rather than an opportunity to engage in intellectually interesting activities integrated with classroom and textbook study. Because teachers had to certify that the students had themselves performed and written up the experiments, notebooks were often locked up except during laboratory sessions, a practice further separating lab from class, writing from learning. As with the uniform lists of required readings in English and history, the standard experiments served the interests of emerging disciplines by asserting their authority in the secondary curriculum. But in the process, writing came to be used as a means of exclusion, a means of setting and enforcing disciplinary standards, rather than as a means of introducing students to the scientific community through meaningful participation in its activity.

Shortly after the turn of the century, secondary schools began to rebel against this form of college domination in science, as well as in other other fields (see chapter 2). Science, the reformers insisted, should be used not for the purpose of mental discipline but for accomplishing the aims of comprehensive mass education set forth in the *Cardinal Principles of Secondary Education:* health, citizenship, ethical character, "worthy home-membership," and so on. Biology, which had long been tied to botanical classification and drawing (with its opportunities for the mental discipline of memorization and copying), was transformed into a course to teach the virtues of hygiene and temperance to a new class of urban students. As industrial expansion increased the demand for scientists and technicians, "general science" courses were introduced to whet student interest in the "marvels of the age" and to recruit talented students for science careers (particularly after World War I, when the disciplines perceived a shortage of scientists). But laboratory work and writing held a small place in these new courses for the masses, where the goals were social control and appreciation, not disciplinary competence. Physics and chemistry stayed under the grip of the universities and the regime of the laboratory notebook.[80]

Like its counterparts in social studies (1916) and English (1917), the reorganization report in science (1920) was strongly influenced by Deweyan progressives. The report attempted to introduce Deweyan progressive methods into traditional science teaching. Lab writing was a crucial issue in the report, not only because the authors saw it as an oppressive instrument of college control but because it represented an opportunity to break the grip of recitation and "memoriter repetition" in favor of placing students "more nearly in the position of a real scientist . . . getting practice in the use of scientific methods."[81] Dewey's vision of schools, where students were to do meaningful work, lay behind the report's insistence that the laboratory be connected not only to the students' class work but to their lives. For example, instead of recommending the usual method of "covering" the principle of specific gravity in recitation, then entering the lab to verify it, the report suggested asking the students if their milk had been watered, then using the lab to answer the question—in the process teaching them the concept of specific gravity and producing a report for the community on the honesty of its dairymen (53).

If the lab could be used as a "workplace," requiring "simple and direct records," with pupils allowed "much freedom in the precise manner in which the record is made" and "maximum opportunity for self-expression in the immediate problem," then science teaching could break the grip of a moribund tradition (20). Though the report recommended neatness, thoroughness, and accuracy in student writing, it warned that these "should not be exalted above thinking and understanding" (30) and it condemned "printed forms" for lab reports (54). "To require all to use exactly the same plan may make the checking of notebooks more easy and their appearance more satisfactory, but it stifles the pupil's originality and prevents him from discovering and correcting his own faults" (39).

The report's vision of a pedagogical revolution was not to be realized in a mass-education system lacking the resources for labs to teach all students, much less the expert teachers necessary to reform and run them. The report did not succeed in revitalizing laboratory writing, and the overall effect of the report on second-ary-school reformers generally was to discredit laboratory notebooks, while at the same time alienating university-based disciplinary interests tied to the lab-notebook method. Because the report preserved the disciplinary divisions among the sciences—and between science and social studies—it allowed for the continuing stratification of science between biology and general science for the many (with few labs) and chemistry and physics for the elite few (with traditional labs). Physics and chemistry continued to have low enrollments, despite periodic cries of alarm from industrial and military leaders. Secondary-school textbooks in chemistry and physics continued to be written primarily by research scientists, biology and general-science texts by educationists.

Secondary and undergraduate science instruction remained almost exclusively fact bound and textbook centered, with "little space devoted to mastery of principles or generalizations," as a national report concluded in 1932.[82] With his characteristic prescience, John Dewey warned science educators in 1934 that the sciences should be "more concerned about creating a certain mental attitude than they are about purveying a fixed body of information or about preparing a small number of persons for specialized pursuit of some particular science."[83] But the school system and the disciplines did not heed his warning.

The opportunity for reform was short-lived in any case. In the stringent budget cuts of the 1930s, laboratories were often the first casualties. Secondary-school lab work was reduced from two hours per week to one, with similar reductions in undergraduate courses. Political and economic pressures led courses to emphasize practical and technical aspects over the discipline-centered instruction that was traditional in labs—a tendency World War II amplified by its emphasis on "pre-induction" technical-training courses.[84] Empirical studies further discredited lab writing by finding no firm evidence that it enhanced recall of facts—still seen as the goal of lab work.[85] Despite a few progressive experiments to fuse science and other subjects during the 1930s, laboratory writing, where it existed, was generally a routine "cookbook" exercise.

It is not surprising, then, that classroom and laboratory writing in the sciences, like school writing elsewhere, exalted mechanical correctness over intellectual discovery and was used primarily to evaluate students rather than to introduce them to scientific inquiry. From science's first contact with mass education, pressures for disciplinary rigor made writing a tool of exclusion. Early science educators and, later, Deweyan progressives resisted these pressures and promoted writing as an essential activity of learning science for all students; but in the complex struggle between disciplinary excellence and social equity, American education developed no new traditions of extended writing and the old ones were discredited. In time, disciplinary specialization took the activity and the writing of the sciences further from the secondary and undergraduate classrooms and prevented the old tradition from being revitalized through contact with the work and genres of the scientific disciplines (see chapter 8).

At those times in its history when the scientific community perceived a critical shortage of scientists, it attempted curricular reforms to introduce more equity, but it could not resist for long its tendency toward exclusion, nor could it develop its tradition of writing in the sciences to include the great majority of students. As Paul DeHart Hurd, a leading historian of science education, put it, "It has been easier to exclude students from physics and chemistry than to develop courses which make it possible for all students to achieve some understanding of the physical world."[86]

If the sciences did not elaborate their tradition of student writing, they at least had one. The laboratory notebook and report were, in origin and principle (if not in fact), intimately tied both to the research activity of the discipline and to its pedagogy; they were therefore capable of evolving with changes in research and curriculum. It was a tradition flexible enough to include teachers at all levels and in all scientific disciplines yet linked so closely to the disciplines that it could not easily be handed over to outside specialists from the English department. But it was a dispensable tradition. Despite occasional shortages, enough working scientists could be trained to satisfy the demands of the disciplines and the economy without making laboratory writing an essential part of secondary and higher education in science. Such writing competence as was necessary could be passed along tacitly, transparently, through the regular activities of the disciplines at their advanced levels.

The ideal of research shaped student writing so pervasively that it is difficult to imagine classroom writing without its influence. The academic disciplines not only organized curriculum, they also limited the kinds and uses of student writing in the curriculum. Apart from essay examinations, the writing that counted in the mass-education system was that which mirrored the forms used in research. But at the same time, student writing never became a conscious, systemwide means of teaching the activity and rhetoric of a discipline, its methods, assumptions, and written conventions. Because writing remained transparent, disciplinary activity appeared arhetorical to both faculty and students. Thus, the rationales for writing instruction seemed hollow. Helping the English department with its task was not a sufficient motive for faculty to invest much time assigning and teaching writing.

The domination of student writing by the ideal of research was only one of many ambiguities that American academia quietly institutionalized during the first decades of its modern existence, but it had profound consequences for pedagogy. Though generalists regularly attacked the rise of the elective curriculum and the growth of faculty research, they rarely noticed or cared that the extended writing of undergraduate and secondary students was circumscribed by specialized discourse, even in situations where students were not being trained as specialists. The new research-oriented university faculty, caught up in their respective rhetorical universes, rarely questioned the wisdom of making discipline-specific discourse the model for student writing, nor did the university systematically consider ways of more effectively using discipline-specific writing in its pedagogies. Had writing not been largely transparent, the relationship between research and student writing might have become an issue, and academia might have actively developed traditions of conscious, discipline-specific writing instruction and gone beyond the myth of transience. Instead, extended student writing was exiled to an academic limbo: forced to look in only one direction, toward the ideal of research, but effectively cut off from the activities of disciplinary research, which gave academic writing its aims, its methods, and its meaning.

It is worth noting, however, that whatever limitations the research ideal eventually imposed upon student writing (and there were many), the first impulse for assigning and teaching writing in the disciplines arose from a desire to engage students in the discovery of knowledge, to involve them in the intellectual life of the disciplines.

4

WRITING AND THE
IDEAL OF UTILITY

Composition for the Culture
of Professionalism

The founders of the modern mass secondary- and higher-education system often invoked the ideal of utility, as well as the ideal of research. The schools of a democratic nation, they argued, should prepare students for specialized careers. Part of that obligation involved teaching students to write in ways that would serve them beyond academia, or so industrialists and academic administrators frequently assumed. But the mass-education system rarely took conscious and systematic steps to teach students the specialized kinds of writing that were necessary beyond academia, for the ideal of utility had to compete with ideals of specialized research and general culture in the new mass-education system, and the relationship between writing in the academic disciplines and writing in business and industry was rarely explored among faculty or developed in curricula.

As historians of rhetoric have suggested, there were important connections between writing in the new secondary- and higher-education system and writing in the new industrial order, both of which emerged fully during what is broadly called the *Progressive Era* (ca. 1895–1920).[1] But the transparency of rhetoric in both industry and academia made those connections complex and subtle, and thus far historians have only begun to trace the ties between the uses of writing in education and its uses in what Progressive-Era academics came to call "real life."[2] This is a large and vexed question, for the very diversity that characterized the new era makes firm generalizations difficult. But before taking up the history of the most frankly utilitarian writing programs, technical and business writing, I first consider the ways in which writing came to be used in industry as distinct from the ways in which academics viewed it, to understand the limited place of utilitarian writing instruction across the curriculum.

"To Follow Without Wavering Printed Instructions": Writing in the New Industrial Order

In business, as in academia, writing played a role in creating what Burton J. Bledstein has justly called "the culture of professionalism," the "set of learned values and habitual responses" by which middle-class individuals gained power in modern America under the banner of "progress."[3] American industry and government demanded a new class of managers and technicians to run its booming new urban economy; and in this new professional class, writing became increasingly important.

As JoAnne Yates has demonstrated, the shift from oral to written communication played a central role in the development of modern industry, with its far-flung enterprises pursuing highly rationalized activities. Before the 1880s, business management had been a relatively personal matter, with internal communication carried on orally and external communication through handwritten letters. For example, Henry du Pont, owner of one of the nation's largest antebellum manufacturing firms, personally took quill pen in hand to write an average of six thousand business letters per year.[4] But by the turn of the century, industry depended on impersonal bureaucratic organization and the written information that drove it.

Technology made these vast changes possible. The first commercially produced typewriter appeared in the 1870s, as did its "natural partner" carbon paper. The 1870 census found 154 stenographers; in 1900 there were 112,364 stenographers and typists. At the same time, the Linotype and rotary press revolutionized printing, ushering in an age of increasing specialization of publications and readers. Companies began to produce things called memoranda and a host of other internal documents, which they reproduced on the new repeating duplicator (invented in the 1890s) and stored in evermore complex filing systems.[5]

But it was a shift in organizational structure that, Yates argues, made the shift to written communication necessary. In the late nineteenth and early twentieth centuries, American business reorganized human relationships through the new movement toward systematic management, a movement that depended on impersonal written communication to subordinate the individual to a rationalized system. Only with a complex system of upward and downward internal *written* communication could managers safely and efficiently oversee widely distributed enterprises, such as railroads. And more importantly, systematic or "scientific" management effectively broke the power of the skilled craftsmen who had built nineteenth-century industry, for it made their special knowledge accessible to management—written, permanent, capable of being taught by managers to unskilled (and of course lower-paid) workers who could exert less power over the owners. The techniques of time study spread rapidly after Frederick Winslow Taylor and others popularized them in the late 1890s and early 1900s. Professional managers produced detailed *written* analyses of specific jobs, then restructured the workplace "rationally" or "efficiently," as they put it.

The written character of systematic management was a crucial, though largely transparent, factor in its success.[6] The nineteenth-century skilled craftsmen guarded their knowledge in primarily oral traditions, passing it on from master to apprentice. And even where written plans, procedures, and work rules existed, craftsmen preserved a powerful oral shop-floor ethic, which among other things forbade piecework pay, limited the power of managers, and ostracized workers who left the craft to become supervisors (no craftsman was allowed to supervise more than one other worker—his apprentice).[7]

Thus, craftsmen and early trade unions angrily resisted time studies, which they viewed as an attempt to "steal" their knowledge and put it into writing. They ostracized workers who cooperated with management by writing down specifications; they beat up time-study experts who entered the shop floor with notebooks;

and they called strikes at the mere rumor that a factory would be reorganized scientifically. As one machinist said in 1912, workers would make concessions, but they did not care for "a man standing back of you and taking down all the various operations you go though."[8]

Obviously the craftsmen lost their fight. With production rationalized through written knowledge, industry came to value inexperience rather than experience because it cost less, both in wages and in worker unrest. An engineer at Ford Motor Company's Highland Park plant boasted that his workers had "no use for experience."[9] With knowledge centralized in a corporation's engineering department, with skilled labor concentrated in tool and die makers who were removed from actual production, workers became merely machine tenders supervised by management personnel. Workers and their immediate supervisors simply needed the ability "to follow without wavering printed instructions emanating from an unseen source lodged in some far off planning department," as a 1916 federal report on labor described it.[10] Writing was the oil that kept the new industrial machine running smoothly.

Thus, the new industrial order was shaped by the transition from oral to written communication no less than academia. And in industry, as in academia, that transition was so embedded in specialized activities that it was largely transparent. The *quality* of employee writing became something of an issue in business during the Progressive Era, but the *kind* of writing did not. Professionals from "real life" often complained about poor writing and waxed eloquent on the importance of "communication," beginning a tradition that has endured to the present. And they, like academics, placed the responsibility for teaching writing elsewhere: on academics. Business managers frequently attacked schools and colleges for not teaching students to write competently. But they, like academics, rarely noticed that the definitions of competency had changed and multiplied with the increasing differentiation of writing. Only in the last three decades have academics systematically studied writing in nonacademic settings, and only in the last three decades have businesses turned to academics to provide systematic writing instruction for employees (see chapter 8).

Utilitarian Writing and Academia

The characteristic modern uses of writing in business and industry were not shaped by any academic rhetorical theory but by the new communications technology and the new methods of systematic management.[11] Nor did industry model its communication on academic writing. Companies evolved their own genres for written communication—reporting mechanisms, forms, in-house organs, even in some cases their own company-mandated prose styles—all without the aid of academia.

The new universities and secondary schools took up the burden of training and credentialing a new elite of middle-class professionals, which was reorganizing the economy around specialized, written knowledge.[12] But academia, including professional schools, rarely accepted the task of teaching students within their ordinary course work to do the specific kinds of writing that they would encounter after leaving the academy. Academia ordinarily taught the genres of nonacademic professional writing in a systematic way only through composition courses attached to professional curricula, and these tended to become marginalized in the institution and distanced from industrial practice as well. The memo, for example, did not become a regular part of the work in most business- and technical-writing courses for decades after the genre had become an essential part of modern industrial life; even when it was taught, it formed a relatively small part of those courses.[13]

Caught between demands for general culture on the one hand and specialized, research-driven technical training on the other, the mass-education system found no consensus on the specific goals of utilitarian service in the matter of writing instruction that might have forged a viable tradition of writing instruction in technical courses themselves. By the 1890s service had come to mean—even to its greatest proponents—other things besides specific preparation for specific professional roles. To some advocates of the ideal of utility, particularly in the new social sciences, service meant direct political involvement in Progressive-Era social and political reforms. But to the most powerful advocates of utility—administrators responsive to trustees and legislators—service meant something much more individual and much less overtly political: "a new kind of education," as Veysey says, "which would prepare young men directly for a wide variety of employments" (60). Seen in these individual terms, the service that the universities performed meant not merely training students to perform a specific role in a great industrial machine but encouraging those characteristically American values of self-improvement and personal growth.

Secondary and higher education might have embraced the specialization of urban-industrial life in its approach to writing instruction and systematically trained students to negotiate the genres and audiences within each discipline and for each profession. Indeed, educational reformers bent on restructuring education in the image of industry proposed such a plan, as I discuss in the next chapter. But this frankly utilitarian approach never prevailed, except in a very limited way in business- and technical-writing courses. Academic disciplines were organized to further the two other great interests within the academy, culture and research, which held up differing ideals of academic community and different notions of writing instruction.

On the one hand, the genteel amateurs of the old liberal curriculum and their late-nineteenth-century successors in the humanities—what Veysey calls *liberal culture*—fought the idea that secondary and higher education should serve philistine commercial interests through a blatantly vocational curriculum, despite their own increasing professionalization and specialized research.[14] English departments, the bastion of liberal culture in academia, reluctantly agreed to teach general composition as a "service" to other departments but rarely encouraged discipline-specific writing instruction in their own department or elsewhere. Yet "general" composition was clearly oriented toward belles lettres and taught specific kinds of professionally oriented writing only rarely, when local conditions demanded it.

On the other hand, the natural sciences and professional

schools (as well as elements within the social sciences and humanities) upheld the new ideal of research, of knowledge for its own sake, and made another segment of the faculty indifferent or hostile to frankly utilitarian projects, including utilitarian writing instruction. To research-oriented faculty, service often meant the advancement of knowledge, whether immediately useful or not.[15] The ideal of research assumed that service to humanity would inevitably come through service to the discipline.[16] The ethic of disciplinary specialization applied to writing as well. If students needed to learn to write better or in certain ways, they could go to composition teachers. If such problems lay outside the activity of one's specialized research and teaching, the problems at hand, then one had no duty to address them. Teaching meant teaching the specialized material of the course, not the professional genres of writing that applied the fruits of research in nonacademic settings. Those few faculty and administrators who wanted the genres of professional writing incorporated into the professional and scientific courses had to fight an uphill battle against faculty and departments who did not wish to make room in their courses and curricula for writing at the expense of more "content."

Faced with these conflicting ideals of higher education, service-minded administrators tended to fall back on vague pronouncements about the importance of writing for personal success; programs for teaching utilitarian forms of writing in the technical courses themselves rarely materialized or lasted long. Where they did, administrators often had to fight the dogged opposition of English departments and the inertia of research-oriented departments elsewhere.

The Case of MIT: Composition for the Culture of Professionalism

To glimpse the utilitarian ideal of writing instruction in practice, I must turn to one of the new technical universities, MIT, where the educational philosophy emphasized the links between practical and theoretical knowledge. But even here, differing ideals of higher education prevented utilitarian writing instruction from finding a secure place either outside or within composition courses.

Before 1887, MIT's only writing requirement was a one-semester freshman course called Rhetoric and English Composition, followed by three semesters of English literature. Rhetoric was dropped from the title in 1887, and the catalog assured students that the course was "designed to help them in expressing themselves fluently and adequately rather than to develop a theory of rhetoric."

The president of the institute, General Francis Walker, supported the use of writing in the regular courses and taught his own course in economics using "laboratory methods," with "each student doing elaborate exercises in preparing reports, summaries, histories, and graphic statistic charts, from the official records, on given subjects," as the British reformer Sidney Webb admiringly remarked after a visit in 1888.[17]

In 1889, MIT dropped a required literature course and added a required junior course in practical composition, beginning a decades-long negotiation between the competing claims of culture and utility. Moreover, MIT hired a former Harvard instructor, George S. Carpenter, to adapt the Harvard forensic system to the specialized writing in the technical courses, where "the pupil rarely conceives of rhetoric as having much to do with his other work in college."[18] After freshman composition, each student in history, political economy, and, later, technical and scientific courses, such as introductory chemistry, was "by courtesy of the instructor" required to write (and sometimes rewrite) compositions that were read *both* by the course instructor for "content" and by an English instructor for "correction." "What could be better drill in composition," Carpenter asked, "than these reports, theses, and the like, prepared for [the student's] instructors in history, philosophy, or science?" When required to write on "practical information," such as "the effect of algae growths in reservoirs and ponds" or "pin bridges versus riveted bridges, . . . the sound man comes to the front, not the turner of meaningless and quibbling phrases. . . . The man who thought punctuation a useless and finicky operation finds that he must master it if he wants to make perfectly intelligible what he has to say on metallurgical methods in the mines of Bolivia."[19]

This system evolved into a much-admired but rarely imitated program of technical-writing instruction. English faculty critiqued the "memoirs" (technical papers) written in advanced courses in architecture, economics, and several branches of engineering (some 350 papers in 1903, for example). In addition, English faculty critiqued student translations of foreign-language technical documents prepared in advanced courses.[20]

After Carpenter moved to Columbia in 1893, the program continued first under novelist Arlo Bates and then, in 1896, under Bates' assistant, Robert Grosenver Valentine, another former Harvard composition instructor. Valentine's career is worth looking at in some detail, for he developed a composition program explicitly designed to meet the writing needs of engineers entering the scientific and technical professions. After five years he left MIT to serve for a decade in industry and the growing governmental bureaucracy (the Bureau of Indian Affairs, 1904–12), finally turning his attention to the labor-management battles wracking the nation in the wake of gains made by trade unions and socialists. Like other Progressive-Era reformers (Jane Addams comes first to mind), he founded a new profession, industrial relations counselor, to deal "efficiently" with the conflicts. His consulting firm developed and applied "scientific" principles to preventing and negotiating labor disputes. I have chosen to focus on Valentine not because he was a great rhetorical theorist (his great influence lay in industrial management) but rather because he was typical of a whole class of progressives who moved from academia into government and industry to build America's new regulative, bureaucratic order using written knowledge. Precisely because he was so typical (and because he wrote of his experiences both in academia and in industry), Valentine's career offers a convenient window on the ways that utilitarian writing operated in the Progressive Era. Moreover, writing instruction during Valentine's five years at MIT became less tied to the belletristic assumptions of the usual English department (which emphasized the linguistic purity of liberal culture), and thus Valentine's discussions of writing center on the demands of industry rather than on those of literary culture.[21]

Like progressives in many other fields, Valentine carried a passionate belief that science—rationality—could transform society and create in America a truly democratic society through improved communication. But the key to this transformation lay not in a *universal* rise in the ability to communicate but in the *specialized* expertise of career professionals, who discovered and applied universal social laws to specific problems. The ironic prospect that this expertise would create a new elite of its own, as well as serve old elites by legitimizing their uses of specialized discourse in the name of science, seems to have occurred to Valentine and other progressives only fleetingly.

"Hacking Their Way to Power": Writing at the Institute

Valentine reorganized MIT's writing instruction for the new professionals being trained by the institute, technocrats who would climb a competitive career ladder in complex, writing-driven enterprises. Three concepts guided Valentine's writing instruction: "the subject, the reader, and the point of view."[22] Each of these concepts would not only improve students' writing, Valentine argued, but also produce students who are "capable of hacking their way to power."[23] This training should develop in students "precisely those qualities which will be most valuable to him in his work in the world. He becomes wide-eyed in seeing faults, workmanlike in the correction of them, sportsmanlike, hitting hard, and giving and demanding fair play. All this he learns to do with dignity and courtesy."[24] This was "empowerment," not in a modern egalitarian sense, but power for middle-class managers and technicians, carving a place in the new industrial order, fighting the claims of owners and workers. Valentine was educating a professional meritocracy and he knew it—though he also passionately believed that the new elite would discover and disseminate the "scientific" principles upon which a more just society would progressively be built.

Each of these three concepts, subject, audience, and point of view, was crucial in the new industrial order. First, a focus on subject suited professionals who could not draw on a body of culturally shared knowledge but instead had to gather and analyze newly written data. For their subjects, MIT students drew on their own intellectual interests to find topics that "closely concern the student's daily work" (rarely literary), supplemented by readings supplied from their technical courses.[25] Students made meticulous observations and took extensive notes, all designed to increase their "power" in gathering and analyzing information—central to the professional's new role in systematically managed industry.

Second, MIT's emphasis on the reader also suited the professional's new role. Unlike the gentry trained by the old college, whose social place was fixed and secure, the modern professional negotiated his social place in a bureaucratic hierarchy (with owners above and workers below) and in a career hierarchy (with senior colleagues above and junior ones below). Valentine's classroom exercises were particularly sensitive to social registers. Eschewing the romantic emphasis on self-expression common in Harvard's program, Valentine found it "of more benefit to insist on a study of the personality of the reader than of the writer" (443). To master the concept of audience, "of interesting a particular man or class of men," students wrote each paper to "a definite reader." They began with letters to friends, then letters to employers and then to employees, finally progressing to wider audiences, "a railroad board wishing to listen to a plan for a new bridge," for example, or a popular audience: "the whole world waiting for an explanation of a startling discovery." Valentine was adamant about the importance of teaching audience for developing and motivating student writing. "Only in this fashion can a man's audience grow," he said (443). "The fiction of [writing for] 'the average man' paralyzes the interest of the student, and gives to his work inconsequence," while writing for a definite reader "imparts self-possession and clearness" (455). A consciousness of different audiences is crucial, he argued, for academic and professional success, for communicating with "the man who reads his graduation theses or the laborer to whom he sends directions for a day's work" (444). The university classroom, Valentine insisted, was a good place to learn these lessons for a new kind of life.

Third, MIT's emphasis on point of view was broadly conceived of by Valentine as the capacity to understand another person's (or group's) perception of events in order to analyze the situations that written communication negotiates—from the scientist's physical position in relation to an object when describing technical equipment to the politician's ethical stance in relation to an issue of public policy. In one exercise, each student wrote "in ten lines" his stand on a current political issue. After reading them aloud, the class discussed the political, personal, or economic motives for the stances. On the question of annexing the Philippines after the 1898 war, for example, "one [student] wrote what effect he thought annexation would have on his father, who was a manufacturer of cheap furniture; another took the point of view of his brother, who was a soldier in Manila" (448). The realities of writing in the new pluralistic society demanded an awareness of point of view—power relationships (or "interests," to use the term Valentine favored), which professionals negotiated.

Pedagogical practices at MIT, like the concepts underlying the pedagogy, were designed to train vigorous professionals. Valentine insisted that successful pedagogy must unite "the student's work in the class-room and his experiences in daily life," but Valentine had a particular kind of daily life in mind, "the realm of vital affairs" of the upwardly mobile professional.[26] The classroom imitated the bureaucrat's office or technocrat's lab. Instead of formal lectures, instructors used extensive informal discussions to create a collegial atmosphere where students could feel free to express their ideas. As another MIT instructor, Archer T. Robinson, put it, the instructor tried to "remove, as far as may be, the embarrassment of his own critical presence" to allow the students to engage in genuine communication.[27] Students must overcome their tendency to view the instructor as "something between a god and a waste paper basket," wrote Valentine, if they are to develop professional confidence.[28] Instructors made extensive use of student-teacher conferences—"private consultations" as they called them, borrowing the term used to describe professional-client relationships. In these consultations, instructors refrained from criticizing minor errors but maintained a professional manner, with "no chastisement, but a very human and urbane process; it is merely what occurs every day when two people talk on a congenial subject and try to arrive at an understanding."[29] Of course one of the people was a superior, a teacher with the power of a grade, but professional decorum dictated the relationship of a senior colleague to a junior, as in the industrial world.

Relationships between students also mirrored new professional realities. Peer critiques, or "class criticism," as Valentine called them, were important at MIT and elsewhere among progressive composition teachers.[30] The ordinary procedure was for the instructor to distribute the topics that the students had submitted and to ask other students to volunteer to critique a fellow student's paper throughout its composition. The peer critics were responsible for discussing the topic with the author in the preliminary stages, attending the author's private consultation with the instructor, and writing all the comments and corrections on the draft and revisions (the instructor's comments were usually oral). Valentine praised the system for its efficiency (it saved instructors' time) and for its effectiveness (it taught the student "how little he can count on his reader's sympathy or divination"). But the chief benefit, he wrote, was that it built the kind of character necessary for success "in the field of practical dealing between man and man."[31] "A college man soon finds out [through class criticism] that his fellows will not care about him unless he makes himself cared for. . . . If he does not come out of himself, he will be left alone . . . and he will struggle with phantoms. To help him know the real men around him is one of the powers of English composition" (463). Valentine sensed that, in the competitive world of career ladders and ever-increasing responsibilities, the ability to present oneself and one's ideas, to give and take criticism tactfully, to negotiate in an environment where power was exerted subtly—in personal interactions with peers or in writing—was becoming evermore important. His pedagogy therefore aimed at strengthening these young middle-class men for the new realities of life in a new elite, a meritocracy of professionals. And as one follows Valentine from academia into to the spheres of government and industry (the path most of his students took, of course), one can glimpse the importance of the values instilled by MIT through its writing program in the future middle-class professionals "hacking their way to power."

As Valentine found when he left MIT to enter government service and, later, industry, all was not running smoothly. Worker turnover was extremely high owing to the dehumanizing conditions: 416 percent in 1912–13 at the Ford Motor Company's new Highland Park plant, for example. Unskilled workers, even immigrants, showed a surprising ability to organize effectively, bringing a wave of long, often violent strikes.[32]

Drawing on his experience in academia and government, Valentine founded the profession of industrial relations counselor.[33] His goal was to apply "scientific" principles of communication—those he had taught at MIT—to the problems of industry. Like other American progressives who founded professions, Valentine had a faith in science and progress that was almost religious in its fervor. He believed the interests of business and labor could be reconciled through *cooperation* for the general welfare of society. What was necessary, apart from the innate goodwill and good sense of all parties, which he assumed, was the *communications* expertise of professionals who had studied the problems and, of course, written down the answers. Industrial disputes have their origin, he maintained, in "ignorance of the facts."[34] To supply those "facts," Valentine invented the "industrial audit," which *The Independent* admiringly described in 1916: "He takes stock of the human resources of a plant, of its personal frictions and maladjustments, of the effect of its equipment on employees, of the prevailing sentiment of the workers as it expresses itself in their work and attitude, of all the inefficiencies that grow out of the size of modern enterprise and its remoteness of executives from manual workers."[35]

In essence, Valentine in his audit translated human relationships into written form, where his version attained the status of objective fact through the authority vested in him as a professional. These "facts" were then used in labor negotiations. Management almost always hired the audit done, either to defuse

potential strikes by granting inexpensive (though real) concessions in work rules or shop safety, or to make time study appear
more humane. A few moderate (but strong) unions hired Valentine's firm to gain credibility with the press and citizens' groups,
powerful players in an age of civic reform. In either case, the
audit justified claims by giving them the stamp of scientific respectability and rationality.

These audits quickly became institutionalized within personnel
departments, another management innovation Valentine developed.[36] Personnel departments helped management deal with the
staggering turnover rates by rationalizing the hiring process, by
delivering worker benefits that were designed to decrease turnover and unrest, and by providing data useful in managing workers. The human relationships, like the mechanical operations
before them, were thus reduced to "manageable"—written—
form, through the personnel files, questionnaires, and tests which
have now become a permanent part of American industry.

It is important to notice that in the new industrial environment,
the three principles of writing stressed at MIT served professionals well. First, the careful observation and recording of data,
coupled with a distrust of traditional knowledge, was essential
for scientific management's time studies, which required precisely
those skills and attitudes.

Second, a sense of audience was essential for professionals
negotiating the expanding territory between shop floor and
boardroom. Professional managers wrote those "unwavering"
printed instructions based on time studies and composed reports
to superiors on which their jobs, as well as the company's profit-
ability, depended.

Third, an understanding of point of view served them well in
the increasingly complex industrial relations they negotiated. In
addition to owners and workers, managers now also dealt with
labor organizations at local, national, and international levels,
each with different or even competing interests.[37] Managers also
communicated with the press, government, and civic groups,
which became increasingly powerful as labor disputes became
matters of public concern. A manager's success often depended
on his ability to understand and negotiate many interests, each

producing written information. In the New York City garment workers' strike of 1915, for example, Valentine was jointly employed by management and the union to analyze sweatshop conditions—but at the insistence of the mayor and a group of leading citizens, who were aroused to involvement by press exposés of abuses.[38] And the negotiations proceeded in a blizzard of documents: position papers, press releases, laws, regulations, reports.

Finally, the social role that writing instruction helped to instill in students was the very "professional manner" which helped to legitimize the expertise of the new middle class and cement its power. It exalted the accumulation of knowledge and established regularities, separating fact from value. In a telling 1916 comment, Valentine complained that socialism, syndicalism, and capitalism all lacked "a genuine welcome for scientific processes," processes he considered to be independent of political interests when pursued with proper—professional—objectivity.[39] Within these positivist assumptions, the new professional acted as advisor not activist, consulting with other experts to discover regularities in human behavior rather than engaging directly in political action. Instead of revolution, he trusted that organic processes within the existing social hierarchy would reveal the enlightened self-interest of all parties, bringing another kind of "revolution." "The manufacturers, the workers and the state must each therefore share in control," Valentine insisted. But it was the professional who would orchestrate this cooperation, adjusting each "particular job to the complete system of economic and industrial forces in the country." Given the new "scientific" knowledge of industrial relations, "employment can no longer be left to the accidents of bargaining," but must be placed in the hands of experts to avoid "the hopeless anarchy that at present prevails" (588). The progressives' ideal of value-neutral written knowledge removed public discourse from the old face-to-face agonistic encounters of the ancient rhetorical tradition and placed it in a literate world of measured professional distance. The power of persuasive discourse now resided in institutional hierarchies, the property of professionals.

Just before his death in 1916, Valentine confidently predicted: "To some, eager with the haste of uncreative desire, it may often seem that we are lingering in old and abandoned ways. Yet the future is on our side" (588). It was, in one sense. Trained by the new universities, the new class of professionals patiently gathered power under the banner of science and progress. Both the socialism of the workers and the social Darwinism of the owners rapidly gave way to the positivism of modern welfare capitalism, with the interests of state, business, and labor carefully "taken down" and managed. MIT taught the approach to writing that was necessary for the new professional class to perform its duties and, equally important, helped to instill those values which legitimized that class in the new "culture of professionalism." And in a deeper sense, Valentine's career illustrates how writing played a role in reshaping the power structure of modern America. The shift in industrial organization from shop-floor crafts to scientific management was intimately linked to a shift from oral to written knowledge, and the professional manager—through his written knowledge—grew in power as a result.

But in another sense, Valentine and the Progressive-Era reformers failed, for they did not appreciate the ways in which written communication could be used to solidify intellectual and social distinctions in mass society, its capacity to divide as well as to unite. They trusted that social integration always accompanied differentiation, that advances in communication would usher in a new age of community. But in fact, written knowledge furthered the rationalization and specialization of the economic and social life of the nation and strengthened the power of the bureaucratic organization.

MIT's Struggles with Utilitarian Writing

In academia, as well as in industry, writing reinforced the differentiated structure, though in different ways. Like industry, higher education held out the promise of a united community, an academic community; but the institutional structure of higher education, like industry, organized knowledge and activity through specialization in expert elites. Because departments and courses were organized and conducted separately, faculty did not need to negotiate, much less agree on, what kinds of writing should be taught or share responsibility for teaching them.

MIT's cooperative writing program was an adjunct to the technical courses, not an integral, visible part of them. As the *President's Report* for 1894 put it, the program "leaves the heads of the several departments free to lay all their stress upon the technical criticism which they alone are qualified to give" (27). Content and expression were in separate realms, presided over by different departments; the result was, in theory, greater efficiency. Faculty could pursue their specializations without the added responsibility of teaching (or even correcting) writing. Moreover, faculty pursuing specialized research and teaching often did not see the need for devoting time to writing instruction, even when the English faculty were offering their time for critiquing papers. As Carpenter predicted in 1892, "Any large college would encounter many and perhaps great difficulties in adopting such a system and in giving it an organic structure" (445). MIT certainly did. Faculty often withdrew "the courtesy" of cooperating with the English department, and the English department struggled to find courses and faculty willing to give time to student writing.[40]

Despite its difficulties in accommodating the demands of specialized research and teaching, MIT's writing program consciously attempted to train students for the new demands of work in a writing-dominated professional environment, and it attempted to tie writing instruction into the course work in technical areas (faculty in professional programs also critiqued the student papers written in their courses, after all). But when utilitarian writing instruction at MIT came into conflict with the claims of culture, such accommodation was well-nigh impossible. Throughout Bates' twenty-three years as department head, utilitarian writing instruction was the first priority, with literary instruction a secondary though important priority. When Bates retired in 1915, MIT hired a former Rhodes scholar, Frank Aydelotte, as chair of the department. His aim was to "humanize the engineering student's character and his aims of life."[41] The composition courses were restructured to teach general culture. "The widespread demand that our college men, graduates of technical schools and of colleges of liberal arts alike, should be better able to write and speak their mother tongue is really a demand that they have a better literary education," Aydelotte insisted. "A man's writing reflects his habits of thought and it is simply impossible to give him a cultivated style by any other method than by making him a cultivated man" (300).

The cooperative program with other departments was phased out. Training in the specific genres of technical and business writing was relegated to a growing number of specialized advanced-writing courses required of students in specific professional curricula: first Report Writing, then Committee Work, Business English, Human Factor in Business, Engineering Publicity, and The Engineering Field.[42] Again utilitarian writing instruction was marginalized into specialized courses, a pattern that was repeated many times elsewhere. Because the academy included many differing notions of service, many competing versions of academic community, it could not agree on a comprehensive approach to utilitarian writing instruction. Instead, it left systematic writing instruction to the bureaucratic structure, which found a compartment for it within English, a discipline indifferent to, even antagonistic toward, active, direct service to other disciplines through utilitarian writing instruction.[43]

Technical Writing and the Technical Disciplines

MIT's attempts to involve faculty in utilitarian writing instruction were the exception. Engineering schools have valued and consciously taught technical writing as part of students' professional training for almost a century; and since the 1890s secondary schools and colleges have formally taught business writing as well, but almost always in specialized business- or technical-writing courses. The reasons lie in the social structure and mission of these disciplines and their place in the wider institution and society. The ways in which technical schools evolved formal structures for teaching students the written conventions of their disciplines reveal the familiar conflicts between the universities' diverse missions: preservation of traditions (culture), creation of new knowledge (research), and utilitarian service.

In one sense, engineering demands extensive writing by the

very nature of the field, poised as it is between the pure sciences and industry. Engineers "translate" the results of research in the pure sciences into material products. This fundamental need to translate places engineering in a complex social position, engaging communities with different values, goals, and structures. The engineer must not only speak the language of, say, the physicist, but also, in certain instances, the language of the industrial manager, the lawyer, or the foreman on a construction site. And the complexities of playing this intermediate role are vitally apparent in the written products of the engineer, the myriad letters, reports, contracts, specifications, and proposals addressed to audiences with varying interests and technical backgrounds. Unlike the physicist, whose professional writing is almost always addressed to a community or, more often, a subcommunity of other physicists, the engineer in "real life" is much more likely to face complex rhetorical problems in translating information from one community to another. Thus, writing cannot as easily remain transparent.

However, the engineering field, like other disciplines, is also a collection of highly specialized discourse communities, as is evident from the many engineering specialties, which grew up in the late nineteenth century with the explosion of technical knowledge during the early years of modern industrialization. From early in one's training—in the sophomore year, often—each engineering student specializes, eventually becoming a member of a relatively discrete professional community, with its own body of knowledge, methodologies, journals, and associations. He or she is not an engineer, but a chemical or electrical or mechanical engineer. And each subdiscipline in turn specializes as knowledge expands, until the subdiscipline is crowded with bodies of knowledge clambering for a place (or a larger place) in the curriculum.

This conflict between the demands for the professional breadth necessary to translate from one community to another and the ever-increasing demands of disciplinary specialization surfaced early in the development of engineering at MIT and elsewhere. The conflict is evident in the century-long battle over the proper place of writing instruction in the engineering curriculum. Though I cannot here treat the whole history of technical-writing instruction in America, I can point to several themes and crucial moments in its development. Robert J. Connors' article, "The Rise of Technical Writing Instruction in America," provides a thorough and balanced account, upon which my analysis relies heavily.[44]

In the new specialized technology schools, agricultural and mechanical (A & M) colleges, and engineering schools attached to liberal arts colleges, which grew up after the Civil War, the growth of knowledge and specialization forced much of the traditional humanities course work out of the curriculum, though freshman composition remained ubiquitous. While a few engineering schools were just beginning to develop what would later be called *technical-writing courses,* such as Specifications and Contracts, most taught their students to write as part of their regular training, sometimes with specific requirements for papers—"dissertations," "memoirs," or "theses"—in each course, term, or year.[45] With enrollments rising as middle-class students clambered to enter an emerging field with high opportunity and status, these requirements were lowered.[46] Moreover, to handle the enrollment increases (and to keep abreast of developments in industry) professional schools hired faculty from industry who had received little or no liberal arts training. Neither the students nor the faculty were much concerned with niceties of style or liberal learning. Tensions between the two "cultures" increased.

Around the turn of the century, the young engineering schools were assaulted by a chorus of complaints from employers about the poor writing of their graduates.[47] But instead of engineering faculty addressing the problem themselves, using their knowledge, experience, and skill as writers of engineering documents, they invited in specialists, following the model set by the universities thirty years before by giving English teachers responsibility for teaching general-composition courses. The professional associations showed interest in improving student writing—they could hardly afford to ignore it, considering writing's importance to the professional lives of their students. But that interest was professionally detached. Others must solve the problem. Where English departments balked at offering specialized writing courses, engineering schools hired their own English teachers, and in some places even set up their own English or humanities departments.

At the University of Michigan, for example, the College of Engineering hired in 1895 an English professor, Abraham Strauss, to teach composition courses for students in the college. By 1908 these courses had evolved into a separate department of English in the College of Engineering, offering courses in literature and history, as well as in report writing (1914) and other genres. The department also taught students from dentistry, pharmacology, and architecture, who preferred a less belletristic approach than that offered by the English department in the College of Literature, Science, and the Arts. Engineering departments at other comprehensive universities, such as the University of Washington, created similar departments in the period between the world wars to teach writing and humanities courses that fit the program and perspective of their students.[48] But whether the technical-writing teachers were formally attached to English or to engineering, they held low status. English departments considered technical-writing courses a tiresome service to engineering and other professional schools, beneath the teaching of literature. Engineering schools considered writing an important adjunct, but only an adjunct, beneath the teaching of engineering. The growth of specialization, with its consequent increase in knowledge, exerted insistent pressure against writing courses from the beginning, pressure that could only be temporarily overcome.

English teachers in engineering schools responded in the institutionally sanctioned way: they banded together to share knowledge and lobby for their interests. Two English teachers joined the Society for the Promotion of Engineering Education (SPEE) in 1899. Others followed, and by 1914 there was an English Committee, headed by Samuel Earle, a Ph.D. in Anglo-Saxon philology who had agreed to head the Tufts University technical-writing courses for want of work teaching literature. He liked the job and began to realize its possibilities. A professional literature began to develop. Technical-writing textbooks appeared just after the turn of the century, at first highly derivative of general-composition texts, but in time they became more fully responsive to the special needs of engineers. Through SPEE's English Committee, the technical-writing teachers began to develop their own scholarly literature and professional meetings.

The distance between technical-writing courses and technical courses (as well as the professions themselves) is evident in the early approaches to technical writing. With few exceptions, these centered on an atomistic analysis of language ("inserting commas or revamping awkward sentences") and, later, on the form of the final product, rather than on the rhetorical considerations of audience and professional context or the process of composing technical discourse. "A technical-forms approach had become all but absolute by the late thirties," Connors concludes. Because technical-writing teachers ordinarily had little contact with practicing engineers, the language and product approaches were more accessible than the rhetorical or process approaches, which required a familiarity with the activities of the profession.[49]

But despite the organizational separation of writing instruction, technical-writing teachers repeatedly attempted to connect their work with that of the technical courses and enlist the aid of the engineering faculty. There were many coordination experiments between engineers and technical-writing teachers similar to the early MIT program, experiments supported for a time by faculty, administrators, and professional organizations. Samuel Earle had the writing teachers on his staff sit in on engineering courses and participate in discussions of writing in those courses.[50] At several institutions, the English staff commented on reports written for technical courses or even graded the papers for "the writing," as at MIT.[51] At a handful of institutions, engineering professors met with the technical-writing staff to discuss writing assignments.[52]

However, the impetus for coordination came almost exclusively from the writing teachers. They lobbied the professional association for recognition and support, held conferences on writing to which they invited engineering faculty, and asked industry representatives to speak at conventions about the importance of writing to engineers.[53] Coordination programs nevertheless remained only experiments, noted in the literature because they were anomalous. Engineering professors as a group rarely heeded the many calls for coordination between instructors in writing and the technical courses, though the many reports on engineering students' writing problems published over the last century list such coordination as an essential prerequisite to progress. A 1925 survey of English in technical colleges found that only six had some form of coordination, though 70 percent of the responding administrators considered such coordination "fundamental." The 1939 Hammond Report on English in engineering schools noted that only eight institutions had meetings between engineering and technical-writing faculty.[54]

By the 1930s, enthusiasm for such efforts had begun to cool among technical-writing teachers. They complained of a lack of understanding among engineering faculty, for whom writing was thought of too often as "little more than grammar and punctuation."[55] Others resisted coordination because "the department of English almost necessarily becomes subsidiary to the technical departments and consequently suffers loss of prestige which it very much needs."[56] W. O. Sypherd, a leading technical-writing teacher, complained in 1939 that, after thirty years in the profession, the most troubling problem he saw was the "appalling lack of writing in connection with [students'] technical courses" and the lack of time in the curriculum for students to "read and write and think and confer and digest."[57] As Earle had noted in 1912, it was impossible for technical-writing instructors to teach students to write "for all engineering specialties" without the active participation of engineering faculty.[58] Yet the specialization of the curriculum and the consequent pressure for disciplinary excellence (seen in terms of covering more material) tended to squeeze writing into the margins of the various engineering curricula. And even the writing courses themselves had to compete for increasingly scarce space in the crowded curricula. At Iowa State in 1881, for example, there were catalog-mandated writing courses or requirements in all eight semesters; by 1981 the requirements had dwindled to only one semester of freshman composition.

Utilitarian writing instruction was also marginalized by the early and recurring conflict within engineering, which pitted general education—liberal culture—against technical training, both within technical-writing courses and within the whole engineering curriculum. Accrediting bodies periodically recommended more humanities courses for engineers, but generally these discussions considered writing courses not as part of the humanities but rather as "remedial" or "technical." Because most technical-writing instructors were trained in literary studies—another discipline from another and sometimes antagonistic "culture"—tensions were widespread. Within the technical-writing courses, some advocated a literary approach of the kind Aydelotte had introduced at MIT, often structured around readings from the literary canon that treated science. Literary anthologies were even published specifically for technical-writing courses. Others advocated a purely technical approach, intimately tied to the technical content of other courses, instead of "highfalutin nonsense," as one engineering professor described literary courses in engineering.[59] There has been a running debate, from the turn of the century to the present, over whether technical-writing instructors should be drawn from English or from engineering. But the point has been moot. Poor pay, low status, and few opportunities for advancement have deterred engineering students from making a career of technical-writing instruction.[60]

In fact, the problem of a disciplinary home for technical writing solved itself in academia's usual way: technical writing became a discipline itself. After World War II, technical writing evolved into a distinct profession, technical communication, to serve academia, government, and industry (see chapter 8). Ironically, the Progressive-Era faith in democratic communication and cooperation was undercut by its positivistic faith in the power of professional experts. Writing, like other activities, became yet another specialty in academia and in "real life."[61]

Business Writing

Business writing, that most prevalent form of utilitarian communication, was also caught in the net of specialization before the twentieth century was well begun. Throughout the nineteenth century, private business schools and penmanship schools had trained clerks in the mechanical and formal aspects of business writing.[62] Many nineteenth-century rhetorics taught letter writing as well, and there were numerous "letter writers," books of model correspondence to help those Americans who were insecure about their writing. But the rapid growth of business radically accelerated and transformed business education.

In the 1880s, cities created "high schools of commerce" at the behest of industrial interests to train clerical workers. The new service-oriented universities formed business schools and departments to train managers, beginning with the University of Pennsylvania's Wharton School in 1881. The University of Chicago and the University of California followed in 1899 as the Progressive Era gained steam; and by the time the stock market crashed in 1929, there were more than one hundred separately organized business schools and hundreds of degree programs housed within other schools. Business degrees accounted for 3.2 percent of all degrees in 1920, reaching 15.5 percent by 1949 after the influx of GI's.[63]

Many of the first university business schools were founded by economics professors with a practical bent (at Tulane University of Louisiana; University of Chicago) or as training grounds for civil servants (at Wharton School; Harvard University). These schools had a strong liberal arts component. But most business schools, both secondary and university, were founded to meet the demand for functionaries trained in specific vocational skills, such as New York University's (NYU) school of commerce, which began as a course to prepare accountants for the Certified Public Accountant (CPA) examination. Courses with a strong practical component (regular, night, and extension) abounded in all areas of business and public affairs, including typewriting and advertising, even journalism and government.[64] Although academics with cultural and research interests often looked with disdain on the new business schools and commercial courses, trustees, legislators, and administrators supported them, and tolerance won out.

Business-writing courses were in demand in the new schools. High schools of commerce taught letter writing along with typing and shorthand, aided by textbooks that emphasized proper form and formula phrases. The first collegiate business-writing course apparently began at the University of Illinois in 1902, the same year that the business school was founded. Andrew S. Draper, the university's president, had never attended college and insisted that college should prepare students "for all of the skilled employments, all [of] the constructive industries, and all of the commercial activities."[65] By 1909, the first college-level business-writing texts had appeared, generally as formulaic as their high-school counterparts and as dependent on static abstractions as general-composition texts. In 1916, George Burton Hotchkiss of NYU published his highly influential *Business English, Principles and Practice,* in which he introduced the famous "Five C's" (completeness, consideration, clarity, courtesy, correctness), which still endure in business-writing textbooks.[66] By 1930 more than half of all undergraduate business schools required such a course (often the only one required), and many others also required a separate course in report writing.[67]

Both employers and alumni repeatedly insisted that training in writing and in speaking were the most important elements of business education. In James H. S. Bossard's and J. Frederic Dewhurst's massive 1931 study, 92 percent of alumni ranked their training in the "English language" as the most important, 10 percent higher than the next most important element, and other studies before and since have reported similar attitudes. Employers displayed their dissatisfaction with the writing of business-school graduates not only by their frequent complaints but also by their in-house efforts to improve their employees' writing. As early as the 1910s, some companies conducted studies of employee writing to find ways of improving communications and increasing efficiency, though the results of these studies seem to have had little impact on the teaching of writing.[68] The 1920s saw the beginnings of writing components in management-training programs and corporate writing specialists. For example, a major bank hired a "former professor of English to edit and revise all of its letters and reports," claiming it was "cheaper in the long run to handle it this way than to attempt to give a course in English to our executives."[69]

But as in engineering schools, the business schools tended to segregate writing courses from the rest of the curriculum, largely for the same reasons. Business faculty did not feel that they were qualified, or they had no interest in teaching writing. Business schools were highly specialized from the beginning—by industry in the early years (transportation, manufacturing, banking, etc.) and later by function (marketing, accounting, management, etc.). Moreover, large classes in business colleges encouraged the hiring of faculty from recognized specialties, leaving writing courses (not yet a specialty) to be taught by English teachers. Although the major reports on business-school curricula all mention the importance of faculty's teaching or reinforcing student writing, all mention the budgetary constraints on such instruction.[70] Faculty recognized "the primary importance of training in English, albeit there is too often the tacit assumption that this problem, like the weather, is one about which nothing much can be done," as Bossard and Dewhurst lamented (106).

On the other side of the curricular divide, English departments resented the intrusion of commercial courses in their curriculum and either refused to teach them or assigned low-ranking or part-time faculty to the task (often women). Bossard and Dewhurst found that, although there was widespread dissatisfaction with the English departments' instruction among business schools because literature professors were "often not friendly to the atmosphere of business," only a few business schools had their own English department but that "such as do are very pleased with the results" (339). Generally, they found that "where English departments cooperate and consent to the selection or designation of some member of their staff to develop courses adapted to business needs," the business schools were more than willing to let English faculty teach them, but "where English departments have shown no interest in such courses, the adapted courses are given by the school of business, sometimes openly and by mutual consent of all concerned, and sometimes surreptitiously by offering such courses under somewhat flexible titles."[71]

Business-writing teachers, like their fellows in technical writing, responded to the segregation by creating a professional association and literature of their own. Discontented with the position and status of business writing, teachers from secondary schools, universities, and industry joined to form the American Business Communications Association (ABCA) in 1935 and soon published their own journal, books, and position papers. Business writing was on its way to becoming another academic discipline, with its own traditions and interests. As happened to technical-writing instruction, the specialization and marginalization of business-writing courses tended to isolate business-writing instruction from the activity of business. As I noted earlier regarding internal correspondence, business-writing courses took many years, even decades, to reflect changes in business practice. And until recent decades, business-writing courses, like technical-writing courses, emphasized the stylistic and formal aspects of business writing rather than the communicative or rhetorical aspects.[72]

The Case Method: Another Tacit Tradition

Business schools have had since the 1910s an indigenous tradition of instruction that is heavily dependent on extended writing: the case method. But it did not influence business-writing courses until recently. The case method began at the new Harvard University Graduate School of Business Administration, founded in 1908 as a business parallel to professional schools of medicine and law. The law-school-trained dean thought that the study of specific cases would give business education the methodological rigor (and status) of legal training, which had traditionally used written analyses of cases to teach and examine law students. Most of the faculty had practical business experience and saw the case method as a way of tying professional academic training to "real life." Initially, the case method brought students in direct contact with business people and problems. The faculty invited executives into classes to present students with specific problems from their firms. The students then each wrote a "report" recommending a course of action, which the executives, faculty, and students discussed. Writing was initially an important part of the method. Written analysis of cases (known then as WAC, coincidentally) was a frequent activity and, later, a yearlong required course. In addition, students in all courses could be (and often were) required to revise unacceptable case analyses.[73]

Proponents of the case method often praised it as a means of improving students' writing.[74] It offered an intriguing option for incorporating writing into service-oriented courses; united pedagogy, research, and professional practice by rhetorical means in the process of analyzing and producing texts; connected the genres of a profession to students' writing, linking text and context; and acquainted students with the activity of the profession in the process of teaching the rhetorical problems and writing conventions of business. Students had to read, sift, and discuss documents, weigh options, and formulate plans. Research and note-taking were integrated with the discipline's conventions of presentation, and writing could become central to teaching, not ancillary. Moreover, case analysis was collaborative, both through classroom discussion and through study groups, which were organized to expedite analysis and, at times, to write group reports. Indeed, the method has a long and distinguished history in the teaching of rhetoric, dating from Roman education's use of cases for advanced training in public speaking, a tradition that endures in law schools today, though in vestigial form.[75] In addition to business disciplines, other professional fields, such as psychology, sociology, social work, education, and vocational agriculture, experimented with cases in the 1920s and 1930s. And by the 1960s, even some of the traditional humanities disciplines, such as history and literature, were using books of cases published for students.[76]

However, the case method was time-consuming for faculty, as well as for students. At Harvard, the method left little time for research other than the investigation that went into producing the cases. But the pedagogy quickly evolved into a research method itself, as faculty collected cases and published them in handsome volumes on the model of legal cases. Teams of postgraduate assistants helped faculty collect material and write cases, and a large literature evolved. Elaborate conventions of presenting cases quickly developed, so that it became a genre or "literary form," as a pioneer case writer described it, "closest to the detective story."[77]

Despite the possibilities of the method, its potential for writing instruction was barely realized before the 1970s, either by instructors in business or by those in business writing. As the method developed, oral analysis tended to dominate the pedagogy. With ten or more cases per week, writing about each was impossible.[78] Business faculty rarely exploited in a systematic way the method's potential for improving writing. In the early years of the case method, Harvard employed a staff of "women graders" to correct students' case analyses for "grammar and style."[79] Later at Harvard and elsewhere, a few faculty were assigned to teach a separate course in case writing.[80] Efforts to improve writing therefore tended to remain isolated in specific courses, and discussions of the case instruction rarely addressed questions of writing instruction or rhetoric. Writing remained largely transparent in this pedagogy, as it had in others.

Nor did the case method have a continuing influence on business-writing instruction. Beginning in the 1940s, Harvard began a series of efforts to popularize the method. Some 227 faculty from around the nation learned to research, write, and teach cases in a case-method training program sponsored by the Ford Foundation. Not one of the participants was a business-writing teacher. In 1968–69 alone, Harvard's clearinghouse for cases distributed some 1.3 million copies of cases to faculty around the country. But not until the 1970s did writing teachers begin to use extended cases in their teaching in any systematic way. The first attempts to use the massive body of extant case material as a source for teaching writing came in the 1980s.[81] The walls of specialization remained secure, even with a method that was specifically developed to break down the barriers of academic discourse through utility.

If the ideals of research and utility helped to destroy the old curriculum's single, undifferentiated approach to language instruction through unrelenting specialization and professionalization of knowledge and work, the ideals of research and utility nevertheless offered to academia several new options for teaching writing through engagement with the social and material worlds: the new genres of research paper, laboratory report, and case study, as well as the new curricular structures in discipline-specific writing courses. But these new traditions were almost entirely tacit, outside the realm of discussion within or among disciplines. Their advocates accepted the demands of specialization and stayed politely within their respective corners of academia. As a result of the patterned isolation, proponents of these pedagogical traditions rarely became aware that they were options for teaching writing in the disciplines. Cut off from meaningful debate among disciplines, some traditions (such as the case study) have only recently begun to develop their potential for initiating students into discourse communities across the curriculum; other traditions (the research paper, for instance) have become desiccated through lack of contact with the activities of disciplinary research, which might have given them substance and vitality.

Tacit traditions remained tacit because academia had no shared vocabulary, no institutional forums for discussing discipline-specific writing instruction. Because writing within the disciplines appeared transparent, academics found it possible to put aside the problem of discipline-specific writing instruction to pursue the ideals of research and utility without considering the implications of writing instruction for students. And the myth that writing was a transient problem, capable of a single dramatic solution, endured despite continuing complaints about students' "illiteracy."

THE SEARCH FOR
COMMUNITY

Writing and General Education

5

WRITING AND SOCIAL
EFFICIENCY

The Cooperation Movement

As America's schools and colleges entered the twentieth century, they faced a central dilemma. Urbanization and industrialization had specialized knowledge and work to an unprecedented extent. Society demanded that educational institutions create new specialized knowledge and train specialized workers—both professional experts and efficient laborers—on whom urban-industrial America depended for its growth. But the nation also demanded that educational institutions promote the social cohesiveness on which urban-industrial America depended for its stability. As cities grew, the old rural and small-town social structures became inadequate for the complex demands of urban life, and during the Progressive Era, Americans increasingly looked to education to bring about community, cooperation, and democracy in society. Reformers of many stripes sought a "general education" to restore community.[1]

The use and teaching of language reflected this dilemma. On the one hand, language instruction was a means of differentiation. Language served as a tool for sorting students, and writing instruction (or the lack of it) was often a vital part of preparing them for specialized social and economic roles. On the other hand, language instruction was a powerful unifying force, at least potentially—though there were many competing versions of a unified society and of a "common" language. Early-twentieth-century educators' reactions to this dilemma were as varied and contradictory as the Progressive Era itself. But from the Ameri-

135

canization movement in the teeming urban ghettos to the great-books movement in pastoral liberal arts colleges, language instruction in general education became a rallying point for reformers searching for a common denominator to weave together the disparate threads of an increasingly complex polity.

In part two (chapters 5, 6, and 7), I examine three versions of general education—each a response to the widespread desire that education should foster community and social harmony in a society where knowledge and work were becoming increasingly specialized. In this chapter I look at the "social efficiency" version of general education, championed by what Lawrence Cremin has called the "administrative progressives."[2] In those first crucial years of the new century, as the modern curricular and administrative structure of secondary and higher education took shape, a new cadre of professional administrators, preaching the gospel of social efficiency, wholeheartedly embraced curricular specialization and institutional differentiation, stressing the democratic values of variety and choice. Unity would come from diversity, coherence from distribution requirements. Its response to the writing problem was the cooperation movement. The new administrative organization would harness the resources of all schools and disciplines to provide "efficient" or cost-effective language instruction, primarily through remediation. But despite its gestures toward cooperation, the educational philosophy of this "cult of efficiency," as Raymond C. Callahan has dubbed it, was largely antithetical to writing and writing instruction outside of English composition classes; and in the first three decades of the century, this conflict led administrative progressives to abandon a central genre of student writing, the essay examination, in favor of what they considered to be more efficient: "objective" tests.

In chapter 6 I take up the great-books version of general education, which grew out of what Veysey terms "liberal culture" and was most influential in the humanities, particularly in English. Oriented toward the past, it was essentially the newly professionalized humanities' reaction against the unrelenting expansion of scientific specialization in the new elective curriculum, a reassertion of conservative values in the face of rapid change. Its response to the writing problem was to encourage the reading and discussion of literary masterpieces, the "great tradition."

Finally, in chapter 7 I take up a third version of general education, the Deweyan "social perspective," which grew out of the social sciences. Oriented toward contemporary problems and convinced of the schools' role in bringing about rational social change, this version of general education developed the Deweyan progressives' assertion of the social nature of education, affirming the unity of the students' experiences against the alienating effects of modern industrial society. Its response to the writing problem centered on the organic growth of individual writing ability through student-centered activities.

Despite their profound differences, philosophical, psychological, economic, political, and pedagogical, all claimed the names of general education and liberal education for their respective projects, and all promised to knit together an increasingly divided society through "democratic" educational reform. Before the new century was half over, *general education,* like democracy, had become a god-term; everyone proclaimed it a worthy goal, but few agreed on its meaning. To add to the confusion, elements of all three claimed to be "progressive," as did reformers in many areas of national life during the Progressive Era. (In this discussion I follow Cremin by distinguishing "administrative progressives" from "Deweyan progressives," though I am well aware that the two perspectives were often closely intertwined, both in theory and in practice.)

Ultimately, the administrative progressives and their theory of social efficiency won out in the curricular battle over general education. In the institutional structure of mass education, general education became not a coherent philosophy but another set of electives. At certain times and in certain places, both liberal culture and the Deweyan progressives successfully resisted the administrative progressives, but both made crucial compromises with social efficiency because each contained contradictory values that prevented concerted action against it. General-education reformers, pursuing a particular philosophy either of the left or of the right, were often allowed free reign within specific compartments of the curriculum, for the modern educational system, with its additive organizational structure, was big enough and differentiated enough to include them. But mass education ultimately responded to its organizational imperatives rather than to any one philosophy.

All three versions assumed that general education should improve students' writing in one way or another, but there was little consensus on where, when, how, and why it should. Thus, reforms in writing instruction were effectively marginalized into certain courses or programs or specialized institutions instead of becoming truly general. There were even elements within all three versions of general education that sought to abolish general-composition courses—though in different ways for very different reasons. In the end, secondary and higher education retained the fiercely reductive misconceptions of writing and writing instruction, which had grown up in the late nineteenth century, views that coincided with the administrative progressives' reductive view of learning. The myth of transience endured.

Social Efficiency on General Education

The administrative progressives shared the widespread Progressive-Era faith in the power of scientific organization to redeem social ills, including illiteracy (by whatever definition). The dominant curricular theory in secondary schools, social efficiency, was explicitly borrowed from industry, where systematic or "scientific" management had become a dominant force in the 1890s.[3] Scientific management would effect the necessary curricular changes as it rationalized the administration of secondary and higher education by supplanting the old individual, face-to-face structures of control (principal or president to faculty) with an impersonal hierarchical system (a complex educational bureaucracy). Social efficiency sought community through differentiation, on the analogy of an efficient machine and its parts, unlike the Deweyan progressives or advocates of liberal culture who in their different ways sought community through organic functioning, on the analogy of the growing plant. It adapted the methods of industrial organization to build a highly differentiated curriculum, which would prepare students for specific roles in industry after first sorting them by future occupation—"prognosticating," as its central theorist, Edward L. Thorndike, put it—by means of the new "objective" tests first used on a mass scale during World War I.[4]

"Scientific" curriculum specialists carried testing and industrial time study to their logical conclusion. David Snedden, Werrett Wallace Charters, and Franklin Bobbitt analyzed in minute detail adults' daily activities, both on the job and elsewhere, then made copious lists of instructional objectives for schools—some three thousand for English alone in a 1926 NCTE-sponsored study, *The Place and Function of English in American Life*.[5] Administrators tracked students by their probable future vocations (as determined by intelligence tests), selected teaching objectives from the job-study lists and, voilà: an efficient curriculum. Students bound for engineering would study trigonometry; future secretaries would learn Werrett Wallace Charters' 871 "day-to-day activities of secretaries as determined by job analysis," and so on—at great savings to the student in time, to the society in social "maladjustment," to the taxpayer in school funds, and to industry in training costs.[6]

Clearly, social efficiency was probusiness; schools were the direct servants of industry. Though proponents of social efficiency claimed to be apolitical (they merely provided scientific tools to accomplish social progress), their whole methodology reinforced the position of systematic management. Labor conflicts demonstrated the need for schools to teach the scientific principles of "cooperation," which would prevent these conflicts by showing workers and owners that scientific management was in their best interests. In its purest forms, as embodied in Snedden and Thorndike, for example, social efficiency embraced eugenics: the nation would be run by highly intelligent individuals (determined by intelligence quotient tests) with very specialized advanced training; based on IQ tests, "dull normals" would be trained for routine labor, "subnormals" sterilized. Democracy would thus be redefined along more "efficient" and "scientific" lines.[7]

In its more moderate and dominant forms, as expressed by

Bobbitt and Charters, social efficiency allowed schools to preserve the structure of the traditional disciplines but reoriented instruction to accomplish differentiation and improve social control. The majority of social-efficiency experts also held more moderate views on tracking than did Thorndike and Snedden. But all embraced the industrial model, the principle of differentiated schools based on predicted vocational or social role, and the notion that experts would control and manage the curriculum in the interests of social and economic efficiency.[8]

From the social-efficiency perspective, then, general education amounted to teaching each student the skills outlined in the cardinal principles of 1918. Some skills—health, citizenship, "worthy home-membership"—were indeed common to all, though they would be taught differently to students from different social backgrounds. But other skills—"vocation," "worthy use of leisure," and, significantly, "fundamental processes," such as writing—were clearly dependent on one's future role.

Social Efficiency on Writing

In its most doctrinaire form, social efficiency insisted that writing, one of those "fundamental processes," should not be taught as a single, general skill to all students but as specific subskills to groups of students preparing for specific careers. David Snedden, for example, argued that "in the every-day world people do not compose written compositions in the abstract and purposeless manner called for by the schools." Instead, they write in specific genres for specific activities: "friendly letters, and sometimes business letters" for all or almost all; editorials, sermons, newspaper articles, poetry, fiction, scientific articles, for "special classes of men." Accordingly, he called on schools to "abandon general courses designated by such repellent terms as 'written composition' and substitute therefore a variety of courses, each designed to train directly for some one type of functional performance as that is found in the world of real work."[9] With his usual consistency, Snedden suggested that these courses should be taught in the appropriate schools or tracks by specialists in those forms of writing.

140

With his typical iconoclasm, he attacked head-on the conventional wisdom about writing instruction. Despite "traditional dogmas, the inventions of pedants," he said,

the finer expressional qualities of a rhetorical nature can best be produced when the writer has reached the point where he is eager to communicate to a real or imagined audience on the assumption that he has something of importance to say to such an audience. In the absence of such pressure it seems exceedingly doubtful whether valuable stylistic qualities are capable of being produced by systematic training, however prolonged or rigorous [296–97].

And he pointed to mounting evidence of the failure of general-composition courses and the widespread discouragement of composition teachers over their ability to train quickly students in those "finer expressional qualities."

But the schools clung to "traditional dogmas" and continued to teach general-composition courses. The obvious and rigorous tracking called for by hard-line administrative progressives was politically unpalatable—too undemocratic for a system based on increasing educational opportunity. The hard-liners' approach to writing instruction was sometimes incorporated into instruction, though never in any systematic way. Students in various kinds of schools (or tracks within the new comprehensive schools) were taught writing of a vocational nature, and general-composition courses were modified to suit particular clienteles. But overall, moderates held onto the notion of writing as a single generalizable skill, to be taught primarily in English courses as remediation.

As I noted in chapter 1, this view (based largely upon eighteenth-century faculty psychology and, in education, the theory of mental discipline) reduced writing to a discrete mental faculty or set of skills, independent of social or disciplinary factors, which is learned once and for all by mastering specific information, often through mechanical drill. This reductive view of writing fit perfectly with the administrative progressives' need for system and quantification. Progress could be measured in the number of errors reduced per dollar invested, students taught and tracked according to their errors. One of the first actions of the newly formed NCTE was to set up a Committee on Economy of Time in English, headed by Edwin M. Hopkins of Kansas, who a decade earlier had calculated the teacher-hours per forensic and concluded that forensics must end. Studies of "efficiency" in writing instruction abounded.[10]

The psychology of administrative progressives, like that of industrial management, was primarily a mechanistic behaviorism. Students were deficient adults in need of remediation, passive receptors of discrete bits of knowledge and skill. The goal, as Bobbitt put it in 1918, was to make an evermore efficient "man-and-steel machine."[11] This narrow view of writing allowed writing instruction to be reduced to merely another cog in the educational machine, part of a system that reduced all fields to discrete facts and skills. According to the administrative progressives' "deficit theory" of learning, generally educated persons had a certain number of facts and skills at their disposal. Schooling remedied any deficits a person had in as efficient a manner as possible.

A less useful theory in promoting shared responsibility for language instruction would be hard to imagine. It discouraged the study of language in its various disciplinary and social contexts—the very areas where cooperation would have to take root in the differentiated curriculum. Instead, it encouraged classifying and counting errors, atomistic measures of linguistic performance, remedial correctives, and, most importantly, the separation of writing and "content" instruction, a conceptual split between language and learning. Ultimately, it helped further the rationalization and specialization of curriculum and instruction by viewing language as a transparent, objective system, which need not be examined in social terms, instead of as a complex, intersubjective medium, which underlay the specialization of urban-industrial life. And though organicistic, transactional approaches were being developed among composition teachers and, on a wider scale, among educational theorists (see chapter 7), these formulations had comparatively little effect on classroom practice.[12]

Administrative progressives rejected the most radical measures for teaching writing, such as Snedden's, and fell back on a safe, if ambiguous compromise. Responsibility would remain poised somewhere between the English teacher and every teacher. Students would learn to write for everyone in general and no one in particular (except the individual teacher). Writing would remain a way of demonstrating learning, not of acquiring it. And writing would be a low-level, mechanical skill, unworthy of attention at higher levels of education—except through remedial measures. When confronted with complaints about poor student writing, administrative progressives clung to the hope that teachers from all disciplines could be mobilized to reinforce that skill, if only the proper administrative arrangements could be devised. A "generally educated person," they reasoned, must master that skill, that fundamental process, and if one course could not teach the skill, then others would cooperate. As the new century got under way a movement began to organize teachers to deal with the problem, a movement based on a common Progressive-Era ideal: cooperation.

The Cooperation Movement

As with so many other educational and political movements born in the late 1890s and nourished in the climate of prewar optimism, reformers of every stripe, from socialists to genteel reactionaries, embraced the principle of cooperation in writing instruction. But it was administrative progressives who most zealously sought to place writing instruction on a sound scientific foundation by enlisting the aid of all teachers—and even relevant social-service agencies. The cooperation movement reflected the complex and often-contradictory enthusiasm for school reform during the Progressive Era, though it is important to remember that the movement was well launched before "progressive education" congealed into an organized movement after World War I.

Although the Committee of Ten had endorsed facultywide cooperation in writing instruction in 1892, the idea found its first coherent formulation in 1901, when the New England Association of Teachers of English published a leaflet entitled "Successful Combination Against the Inert," which outlined a program of cooperation that would enlist secondary and college faculty from all disciplines to improve students' language, both spoken and written.[13] During the next twenty-odd years, dozens of articles appeared on the subject, both in the professional journals and in the national press. Hundreds of programs began at the school, district, and state levels. In 1924, teachers at the NCTE convention ranked cooperation as the highest priority for improving instruction, and a national survey of freshman-composition courses listed it as one of five significant trends in instruction.[14]

The impetus for cooperation in writing instruction, as with so many other Progressive-Era reform movements, came first from crusading journalists. *Nation, Harper's Monthly Magazine,* and *New Republic* carried on the already-venerable tradition of complaint by pointing out the "illiteracy" of secondary and college students. They called for a cooperative assault on this new educational problem. As a *Nation* editor wrote in 1908, it is a "crying scandal. . . . Merely from the point of view of waste of money it cries for a remedy. . . . What the student gains in one hour he throws out in the next. [With cooperation] the expense of training him in English will be greatly lessened."[15]

Reform-minded administrators responded with such a variety of cooperation programs or "schemes," as they were called, that a single definition of cooperation is impossible. For some, cooperation meant that instructors from outside the English department taught writing within their courses. For others, it meant that the whole faculty set and enforced standards for writing while the English department taught all writing in the curriculum (or corrected student writing from all classes). For still others, cooperation meant that administrators placed controls on writing assignments in the whole curriculum or that there would be community involvement in language instruction organized by administrators. Everyone agreed that each teacher should in some sense be an English teacher, but which English should be taught to which students, by what methods, and for what ends?

Experiments abounded. One fairly common practice was to have English teachers correct papers written in content-area courses, on the assumption that non-English teachers were not qualified to evaluate writing. In a few schools the papers for content-area courses were both written and graded in English classes, and students even used content-area texts in English class—practices that caused some friction.[16]

Reformers often praised the cooperation scheme at Cicero, Illinois, a high school with a high immigrant population. The principal convinced the school board to limit English enrollment to sixty students per teacher. English teachers' release time was spent working with social studies classes to improve students' speaking and writing. English teachers graded every social studies paper according to a formula, and both history and English teachers were required to devote a specific amount of time in each class period to recitation of various types and instruction on specific errors, all closely monitored by the principal, with red pen and stopwatch.[17]

As the systematization of American education marched steadily on, the new bureaucratic apparatus pursued reform measures to address problems of writing instruction on a wider scale. School districts and state education departments made cooperation schemes part of their master plans, prescribing specific kinds and amounts of oral and written work in various components of the curriculum. The new centers of educational research studied cooperation and published their findings. National commissions charged with formulating educational policy addressed the issue. The NCTE in particular devoted a chapter of its landmark reorganization report (1917) to describing and recommending cooperation—in the section of the report devoted to "administrative problems."[18] For the administrative progressives, *efficiency* was the watchword, in the expanding educational system as in the burgeoning industrial sector.

Cooperation and Curricular Specialization

Administrative progressives justified these structures of control by pointing to the most obvious fact of educational life for Progressive-Era schools and colleges: sheer growth in numbers. High-school enrollment jumped from half a million in 1900 to almost three million in 1928, and college enrollment almost tripled (as a percentage of the population) during the same period.[19] To teach writing to so many students, administrators argued, teachers must cooperate. But numbers alone did not create the need for cooperation. There would have been no calls for cooperative schemes if America had simply built more one-room schoolhouses on the rural model or more of the sectarian academies and colleges of the nineteenth century, with their required liberal curriculum, their homogeneous student body and faculty, which generally shared a single body of knowledge and set of values. But instead, America built a highly differentiated curriculum of separate and often-competing disciplines, each forming and asserting its identity through its specialized discourse. In the eyes of the new scientific administrator, differentiation was not a hindrance but a boon to cooperation in language instruction, if only a rational means could be invented to organize efficiently cooperative efforts across disciplines, to take advantage of economies of scale and efficiency of specialized organization.

Yet cooperation schemes never confronted the issue of language and discipline because most administrative progressives (unlike Snedden) saw writing as a generalizable skill, independent of disciplinary content and context: thus, the mandated page requirements, the error counting, the papers graded for "content" in one class and "form" in English class. By viewing writing as a discrete skill, administrative progressives were able to quantify and rationalize its instruction, while ignoring its complex relation to disciplinary learning. This mechanistic view of writing condemned cooperation to superficiality, for instructors in the disciplines (including English, to an important extent) came to see writing instruction as an additional burden over and above the "real" teaching of the discipline, not as an exciting and integral part of the discipline's activity.

Despite the energy that reform administrators devoted to constructing efficient schemes, despite the universally acknowledged need to broaden responsibility for language instruction, cooperation schemes met stiff resistance from teachers defending their disciplines. The very differentiation which administrators had hoped to harness in pursuit of rational language instruction became the chief obstacle. Disciplines fighting for recognition and curricular turf were threatened by many of the reforms imposed from above. English teachers resented having to correct other teachers' papers. The lament of one high-school English chair was echoed in many quarters: "Cooperation begins and ends in the English department."[20] In an angry *English Journal* article, an Ohio State professor, Carson S. Duncan, laid the blame at the door of the educational bureaucracy. Most cooperation programs, he complained, are yet another "new device . . . bequeathed to the teaching of English composition by business"— a means of increasing cost efficiency by relieving other teachers of their responsibility.[21] A few English faculty welcomed such cooperation programs as a way to increase their prestige as specialists in writing and expand the position of English in the curriculum.[22] But as a whole, the new discipline asserted that its primary role was in teaching literature, not in serving other departments (see chapter 6).

While some English teachers resisted cooperation programs, content-area teachers often simply rebelled against programs that made demands on their time and threatened their turf, prompting one principal to remark, "Artificial means of cooperation, especially in large high schools, are hopeless."[23] At the model cooperation program in Cicero, Illinois, for example, the head of the history department resented the administrative requirements for speaking and writing in cooperative classes—"checking-up classes," as he called them.[24] Under the pressures of burgeoning enrollment and curricular ferment, disciplines that had only recently achieved autonomy and professional identity (English, social studies, and laboratory sciences) were loath to give up time and territory to address what was, after all, a very thorny problem. Cooperation efforts were barely a decade old when NCTE founder James Fleming Hosic lamented, "Cooperation is very generally regarded as one-sided. It is supposed [by content-area teachers] to be a device for giving English a larger place in the curriculum or, on the other hand, a means by which teachers of other subjects may unload their manuscripts and escape the grind of correcting them."[25] Ultimately, administrative schemes designed to increase cooperation often simply hardened disciplinary divisions and roles. With cooperation, as with so many other reform efforts inside and outside of education, the promise of scientific management went unfulfilled, and the challenge of creating unity in an increasingly differentiated social and intellectual environment remained.

Most administrative progressives (again, Snedden was the exception) never confronted the central issues of writing and general education: what genres should all students be able to write and who will teach them to write those genres? Answers to these questions demanded more than mere management theory. They required a theory for connecting writing and disciplinary learning; specific, coherent goals for general education; and the political strength and will to overcome those who had different goals. The specialization of knowledge and the departmentalized, additive curricular structure that undergirded it could not be transcended by any cooperative scheme without shaking the foundations of the system.

Cooperation and Institutional Specialization

Of course structural differentiation segregated people as well as knowledge, and in ways designed to serve urban-industrial society. As Lawrence Cremin has forcefully argued, the metropolitan experience overwhelmed earlier models of schooling.[26] The new schools reflected urban-industrial life in their hierarchical structure. Not only were new disciplines formed and old ones transformed but the curriculum became differentiated both through multiple curriculums within single comprehensive schools and universities and through new specialized institutions: the vocational, technical, and professional schools, the settlement house, the reform school, the extension class, and so on. The many new kinds of schools—or new tracks within comprehensive schools—prepared students to play a variety of new social and economic roles in modern America.

Language was a key factor in the specialization of work, as it was in disciplinary specialization. The new roles in the work force demanded varying kinds and levels of linguistic attainment, as did the new branches of knowledge. Through the linguistic forms of various social classes or ethnic groups, language became not only a means of community forming but also a means of sorting and discriminating (on Ellis Island, the inability to speak or write English constituted evidence of a mental defect). Cooperation schemes reflected this differentiation and the administrative progressives' desire to manage it. And the cooperation movement affected schools serving almost every social and occupational level.

Cooperation in Comprehensive Secondary Schools and Universities: The Remedial Model

In comprehensive schools and universities, the most common form of cooperation in language instruction was a system of referrals by teachers in all areas to a remedial English course or courses. The faculty thus did not all teach language, they merely cooperated in finding and isolating those who needed the "hospital squad," a remedial class (which in secondary schools usually met after school) for students deemed deficient in English by their content-area teachers.[27] The concept of remediation was itself an invention of the Progressive Era, an adaptation of the medical—hence scientific—model to education. The inability to use language in some way was traced to mental, even physiological or racial, deficiencies, which could be remedied in some cases by separating the student (the patient) in a "lab" or "hospital" and applying corrective measures.[28] As Gene L. Piché has persuasively argued, the remedial model of writing instruction was at bottom a response to fears that the influx of immigrants would corrupt the purity of American language and culture. Henry James complained in 1905 that the language was in danger of being "handed over . . . to the American Dutchman and Dago . . . without native atmosphere or concern."[29] Agnes F. Perkins, who helped found at Wellesley College what has been called the first remedial college course, voiced a common argument for cooperation in 1907. "Our schoolboys and schoolgirls . . . come from homes wherein [there] is no instinct for culture, no instinct that leads to comeliness of speech or manner." Unlike teachers in the elite English and French schools, she said, we "in this money-getting land . . . deal with another race—a motley, composite, untrained race—and there is vital need that concerted training in our schools act as a substitute for that inheritance and breeding which best of all beget spontaneous and instinctive purity of speech."[30]

Although the goal of "writing hospitals" was to offer all students a common general education, which would assimilate them into a common culture, the actual effect was often the opposite. The remedial model of language instruction segregated students into tracks based on their use of language, which actually reduced "remedial" students' contact with those who used language in the approved way and who could therefore model the approved usage. In both secondary schools and colleges, this "writing police" version of cooperation became an instrument of the growing bureaucratic system of tracking students—often on the basis of national origin, race, or class—rather than a means of sharing responsibility for language instruction across the curriculum. Even elite universities tracked students. At Harvard there was "a foreign squad, an awkward squad, and sections for the rest who showed no great infirmities."[31] At Columbia students were tracked in general-education courses as well as in composition courses, all in the name of more efficient instruction.

The new comprehensive universities, which were admitting an increasingly diverse student population, adopted cooperative remedial programs with particular zest. Barely a decade after most universities dropped collegewide writing requirements, many began a system of faculty referrals to a remedial course to try to deal with the problem of poor student writing—a problem they vainly hoped would be transient.[32]

Harvard's Committee on the Use of English by Students was typical and quite influential.[33] It began in 1914 when yet another committee was formed to carry out the task of "mending English at Harvard" (note the metaphor).[34] It found that writing skills declined after English A. As a result of the study, a standing faculty committee was appointed to improve student writing. The standing committee became, in effect, the writing police, requiring instructors in all courses "to send to the committee any examination book, thesis, or other piece of work which has demonstrated a writer's inability to express his thought." "Delinquent students" were handed over to the English department for "correction," which meant a remedial course called, significantly,

English F, taken without credit until the student "mended" his English. During the twenty-five years for which records are available, the Harvard faculty reported from 4 percent to 22 percent of undergraduates to the committee, and about half of those reported were required to take English F. Other students voluntarily enrolled in the course because it provided the only tutorial and small-group writing instruction on campus.[35]

The committee's struggles, both with faculty and students, highlight the limitations of the remedial model. The committee reported in 1916 that the great majority of the faculty referrals were "based on hastily written class-room tests rather than work done at leisure," and the poor writing resulted from "mere carelessness and lack of revision," not from incompetence. The committee discovered that many supposed writing problems were in fact problems of understanding—either of the material or of the expectations in the course. Students "have been encouraged to believe that recording the facts is all-sufficient," the committee complained in 1934. Many students needed help in organizing the material of the course to write coherently about that material.[36] It also came as a surprise to the committee that the greatest demand for English F came from graduate students in business administration. These students volunteered for the course in large numbers and ordinarily made up one-third of its enrollment. Yet this was quite understandable: pedagogy in the graduate business curriculum centered on written cases and thus included more (and more thoroughly integrated) writing than perhaps any other degree program.

Such experiences might have convinced the Harvard committee and other administrators of remedial programs that successful writing is more than merely an accurate recording of thought, that it depends upon content, genre, social and institutional context. But given the assumptions of the administrative progressives, language instruction was not a question of fostering social or intellectual development but of treating a social or mental illness (as the medical terminology suggests). Remediation found a permanent place within the new comprehensive schools and colleges because, unlike many other cooperation schemes, it reinforced the institutional structure. Institutions gained a means of sorting students into groups that could be taught (or not taught) a certain set of linguistic conventions tied to future occupations and life-styles. The writing police and remedial courses allowed all faculty to share responsibility for language standards without sharing responsibility for language instruction, which remained with English instructors (usually those with low status) and preserved the differentiated curriculum.

Cooperation in Social-Settlement Schools

Cooperative language instruction was also part of the Progressive Era's attack on urban slums through the Americanization and settlement movements. Following exposés of slum conditions by investigative journalists, reformers established private, voluntary institutions to give advice, education, and care to the masses of immigrant and southern poor who were streaming into industrial cities. Following the example of Jane Addams (founder of the first social settlement, Chicago's Hull House), urban-reform groups attempted to transform slum schools into social centers, which would serve the community. A major part of that service was basic English instruction for immigrants and the illiterate poor. Language instruction, and the cooperation schemes that supported it, had two goals: to prepare students, juvenile and adult, to enter the blue-collar jobs available to them, and to encourage social stability by instilling the values of the dominant culture. Reformers harnessed a variety of curricular and community resources to achieve these goals. At a model black ghetto school in a high-crime area of Indianapolis, for example, cooperation in writing instruction served the limited purposes of the curriculum and the social ends of the school. Students were trained to be cooks, cobblers, tailors, carpenters—occupations that required little writing.[37] Indeed, the school had no traditional academic component. Cooperation meant that the English classes wrote notes to the adult night-school students, encouraging them to attend regularly, or invitations to the community to participate in school functions, the cooking class' tea, for example. Thus, the English work focused on surface features: spelling, usage, letter format, and so forth. Such activities helped to accomplish the social-settlement function of such schools and were thought to contribute to a lowered crime rate by increasing civic pride and stability. Cooperation satisfied the urban reformers, without challenging the differentiation of schools or society, and furthered social amelioration among urban blacks, without raising social aspirations.

Among many European immigrants, however, cooperative schemes sparked political conflict. Urban reformers often made English instruction part of a broad program of Americanization, teaching American history and civics, to be sure, but also such values as personal cleanliness, factorylike discipline, and, its critics charged, disdain for ethnic customs and beliefs. In some areas, immigrants resented attempts to use language instruction to expand the role of the schools in ethnic neighborhoods. For example, when school authorities made vocational and social-settlement efforts the emphasis of public schools in some ethnic neighborhoods of New York City, residents attacked what they believed to be a cheapened education for their children. Riots broke out in 1917, forcing local politicians to abandon the proposed "reforms."[38]

On the national level, the wave of immigration (some fifteen million between 1900 and 1915 alone) and the growing racial and labor unrest associated with it, initiated a wave of anti-immigration nativist sentiment. In the wake of the 1911 Dillingham Commission's report, which documented the "inferiority" of immigrants largely on linguistic grounds, wealthy social reformers and business associations redoubled Americanization efforts.[39] They employed a coercive, "melting pot" approach to quell nativist fears and, at the same time, to preserve high immigration levels (and thus cheap labor). Some reformers—including John Dewey—argued for a pluralistic or "orchestra of mankind" approach to Americanization, one that would preserve cultural differences; but the forces seeking to create a "melting pot" won the day. The issue, once again, was not the existence of language instruction. Almost all parties agreed that immigrants should learn English and that the schools must play a central role. The issue was differentiated language instruction, racial and ethnic, as well as economic. What goals would language instruction promote? Ethnic community or national unity? Vocational training or academic education? Long-term, effective cooperation in language instruction, as in anything else, required agreement about goals. And in an increasingly pluralistic society and differentiated economy, such agreement was difficult to achieve.[40]

Cooperation and Vocational Schools

Vocational or manual-training schools were the most visible Progressive-Era educational reform, a clear manifestation of urban-industrial society's power to transform institutions. Though manual training originated in a desire to broaden the education of all children by introducing them to technology, it quickly became a means of sorting and training students for the new (primarily blue-collar) jobs that industrial expansion created. Around the turn of the century, most American cities founded secondary schools of commerce, technology, or industrial arts, directly or indirectly supported by business interests.

Perhaps because these schools had clear goals and relatively homogeneous student bodies, cooperation in language instruction often made more headway than it did in comprehensive schools. At Boston High School of Commerce, for example, English and social studies teachers shared texts, planned and graded assignments together, and even team taught courses. These courses (economics, history of business, civics) were closely tied to the commercial courses, and teachers in all areas used common criteria for marking papers.[41] Such vocational schools justified language instruction on blatantly utilitarian grounds, as a "matter of success in business," in the words of one principal. Margaret Vose, author of a 1925 study of cooperation, called school-wide standards of correctness "an excellent investment," since "in our better stores clerks who desecrate the English language no longer hold their positions."[42]

Cooperation also promised savings to the vocational schools through more efficient instruction and gave English classes a practical connection to the curriculum, which some administrative progressives believed was more appropriate than literary study for students preparing for manual or commercial trades. In the Gary, Indiana, "platoon" schools, considered by many to be the model for vocational instruction, the state curricular requirements were met in part through one hour per day of "English taught by shop and laboratory instructors."[43] Before taking apart a motorcycle in the machine shop, for instance, the students learned to spell the names of its parts, wrote sentences describing its operation, copied and filled in a study outline from the blackboard. Students in many classes wrote up the results of class projects and community-service activities, which were then printed in a student-run shop and distributed, usually as part of school-sponsored public-health or civic-improvement campaigns.[44] Such experiments in cooperation were the exception, however. Differentiation was much easier to create than cooperation, even in schools with a single goal.

Beyond the Progressive Era

In the years following World War I, the heady optimism of the Progressive Era began to fade among cooperation's advocates, as among reformers in many areas of national life. In her 1925 study, Vose surveyed administrators who had reported having successful cooperation programs during the period from 1908 to 1915. She found "the general failure of the practice" and concluded, "Many of the plans are merely nominal or have been frankly abandoned," owing to increased enrollment, teacher turnover, or what one principal called "the complex organization of the school."[45]

That "complex organization" was the central problem. Had the system been willing to restructure the schools to make cross-curricular language instruction a priority, as many Deweyan progressives wished, shortages of time and resources might have been surmountable. But cooperation worked against the system's tendency toward specialization and centralized control, forcing programs to fight continual jurisdictional battles. Moreover, the powerful movement toward efficiency and testing, valued by administrative progressives for the control it afforded them, tended to measure outcomes in discrete, concrete terms—test

155

scores per dollar invested, errors reduced per teacher hired—which made the subtle, less concrete outcomes of language instruction appear irrelevant.

In the deepest sense, then, schools and colleges resisted cooperation because it challenged the stability of a mass-education system founded on the industrial model. A thoroughgoing commitment to cooperation would have made more difficult the already-formidable tasks of integrating masses of students into the burgeoning industrial economy (equity) while preserving disciplinary integrity (excellence). To effect cooperation throughout the educational system would have required consensus among disciplines and differentiated curricula on the goals of writing instruction—and of education itself. Such consensus was neither possible within the system (if that vast aggregate of American educational institutions could be called such) nor within the society that supported it. Thus, the fledgling mass-education system avoided the deeper issues of writing instruction, concentrating instead, almost to the point of obsession, on grammatical correctness.[46] In one way or another, in school or out, Americans gained sufficient communicative competence to perform their roles in the new society. And the unprecedented growth and prosperity during the 1920s reassured the nation that its schools were sound. Talk of cooperation withered among administrative progressives, though the idea of teachers cooperating to improve students' writing stayed very much alive in later versions of general education.

The reformers' disillusionment with administrative cooperation was perhaps inevitable given their assumptions, social, educational, and linguistic. Educators charged with the task of running differentiated schools in the most cost-efficient manner could not be expected to build a single intellectual or linguistic community in those schools, especially since none existed in the society at large. Moreover, Americans labored under commonsense assumptions about language—and particularly about writing—which were inadequate for the new complexities of discourse in modern print culture. At a time when genres were proliferating in mass media and audiences were fragmenting in a deluge of publications, teachers could only fall back on notions of writing as mere recorded thought, or of audience as "the general reader," or of correct writing as an objective quality independent of social and intellectual context. As Dewey had concluded by 1927, when he wrote *The Public and Its Problems,* changes in communication all too often outran the ability to understand them.[47] Efforts to broaden responsibility for language instruction floundered in the same theoretical constraints.

In pragmatic terms, the late specialization that characterized American secondary and most undergraduate education (in contrast to European education) absolved disciplines and administrators from specific responsibility for initiating students into a disciplinary or professional community. Most instruction became "general education" by default. Writing was thus not a pressing issue for any single department, and the curriculum was of course organized by departments. When complaints about poor student writing became loud enough to produce action, administrators simply added more "remedial" writing courses. When the complaints subsided, disciplines reasserted themselves and successfully reclaimed that curricular space. The additive, bureaucratic curricular organization of mass education meant that courses and programs would be the object of interdisciplinary negotiation and institutional concern, not pedagogies—disciplinary "content," not discipline-specific writing.

The Essay Examination as a Genre

Social efficiency's reductive, atomistic view of writing and learning not only condemned cooperation schemes to superficiality but also led administrative progressives to abandon the most visible and important genre of school writing: the essay examination. Significantly, the death of the externally mandated comprehensive essay examination effectively removed a chief motive for cross-curricular writing instruction and practice—as well as the chief vehicle for comprehensively assessing student writing—without offering any other compelling motives or effective monitors for writing across the curriculum. For reasons more political than pedagogical, the curriculum lost yet another important site for writing, another potentially vital genre of student discourse.

157

In the last half century, it has become commonplace to complain that the decline in writing skills is in part due to the prevalence of objective tests. Yet there is no comprehensive historical treatment of the subject, much less any firm body of data to support the notion. Such data may no longer exist given the scarcity of documents on actual classroom writing practices. But the few surviving examination papers and the controversy that has always surrounded written examinations make it possible to sketch their history and trace their decline.

The history of the essay examination illustrates a central shift in the ways that learning was conceived of from the old curriculum to the mass-education system: from communal oral performance in the rhetoricals and oral examinations to an individually written synthesis in an essay examination and finally to an individual performance on an aggregate of discrete "objective" items. Although written examinations were given in England as early as the sixteenth century, they did not challenge the dominance of oral performance until the mid nineteenth century, when a few British universities and, most importantly, the British civil service introduced examination by "papers" (written responses to written questions) to provide admission to coveted social roles based on merit.[48] About the same time in America, educational reformers, such as Horace Mann, introduced written examinations for similar reasons. They, like the British, expected that written examinations would "remove all possibility of favoritism."[49] But more importantly, written examinations helped to standardize and regulate curricula and pedagogies in the growing educational bureaucracy. They took control away from committees of teachers and community leaders (who often examined students orally at the declamation days, exhibitions, or commencements) and placed it in the hands of individual teachers and professional administrators. Written exams became a more politically justifiable means of evaluating, sorting, and rewarding both students and teachers. (In late-nineteenth-century England, for example, secondary schools were funded—and teachers retained or fired—on the basis of how many of their students passed the standard exams.) In an important sense, the introduction of essay examinations in the 1840s made modern mass education possible. Perma-

nent, portable, standard exams facilitated curricular standardization, systemwide teacher evaluations, and a defensible means of
sorting students—all without face-to-face contact among individuals. In education, as in industry, the system could transcend the
individual.

But Mann and the early reformers had pedagogical as well
as organizational reasons for introducing written examinations.
Because time was limited on examination or declamation days,
the oral questions tended "to call forth a factual answer," Mann
lamented. "In the written examination the pupils are able to
develop ideas and show the connections of facts," "quality of
thought," rather than mere recall. Mann called the essay exam
"a transcript, a sort of Daguerreotype likeness, as it were, of the
state and condition of the pupils' minds." Announcing a theme
repeated often in the next hundred years, the superintendent of
the Chicago schools claimed in 1856 that the written exam not
only tests knowledge but is also "one of the best methods of
cultivating freedom and accuracy in the use of language; and it
furnishes a valuable discipline to the pupil's mind, by throwing
him entirely on his own resources."[50]

Despite Mann's hopes, nineteenth-century educators seem to
have thought of the essay exam primarily as a written transcript
of oral recitation answers, as rhetorically transparent, in other
words. There is almost no nineteenth-century literature on essay-
exam design or evaluation or on methods of preparing students
to write exams. This lack of discussion suggests that the exams
were primarily valued as measures of factual knowledge, not as
means of improving students' writing. Surviving college examination papers and a few faculty comments do indicate some movement from written examinations as mere transcriptions of recitation answers (calling for memoriter repetition, summary, and
paraphrase) to examinations that required some "original
thought" (calling for synthesis of collateral readings and lecture,
application of concepts to newly presented data, or analysis of
known information using new categories).[51] As I noted in chapter
3, research-oriented history instructors sometimes prided themselves on examinations that demanded originality. Henry Adams
boasted that his rule in writing examinations was "to ask ques-

tions which I can't answer myself."[52] But the great bulk of the essay examinations I have read from the period (even those from elite institutions like Harvard) called for little higher-order reasoning or synthesis. Most simply required students to repeat the information and interpretations gleaned from lectures and texts, though the mere fact that writing was required forced the students to place information into a meaningful structure, albeit a given one.[53]

With the spread of the elective curriculum and written examinations for each separate course rather than for each class (e.g., sophomores) in the 1870s, higher education began the slow process of moving responsibility for standards and testing away from the whole faculty (and representatives of the wider community) and toward the individual faculty member. Students were to be examined on their performance in each individual course rather than on their comprehensive intellectual attainments.[54] Written exams conducted by individual teachers allowed a specialized curriculum to develop without the whole academic community being collectively responsible for setting institutionwide standards for written performances. The curriculum could be subordinate to the individual teacher as disciplinary specialist; the individual teacher was no longer subordinate to a collectively agreed upon curriculum and standards, as was the case in European schools, where externally graded examinations were (and continue to be) the rule. As the elective system drew increasing fire after the turn of the century, a few universities experimented with departmentwide comprehensive examinations, but these were only partly successful and never spread to the majority of institutions or involved outside examiners, as in Europe.[55] The great diversity of American higher education and its lack of centralized control (unlike higher education in most of Europe and Asia) made outside examinations unworkable, both administratively and politically.

Such was not the case in secondary education. Despite European-style outside examinations having never developed among universities, the founders of the meritocratic modern university, led by Eliot and the Committee of Ten, instituted a series of essay examinations for college admission to assure that those admitted would be worthy. One goal—largely accomplished—was to control and standardize the secondary curriculum, prompting the successful rebellion among secondary-school interests during the 1910s and 1920s that I noted in chapter 2. The college entrance exams (almost all essay) came under increasing fire for being oppressive not only to curricula but to students, who suffered many stress-related physical and psychological problems preparing for and taking the tests, not to mention the financial and social effects of failing them. (The 1913 *Cyclopedia of Education* has a longer discussion of "Examination Hygiene"—dealing with physical and emotional effects of tests—than of examinations themselves.)[56]

But it was a need for control, not compassion, that sealed the fate of the external essay exam. In the first three decades of the twentieth century, administrative progressives dismantled the system of mandated essay examinations in a quest for even more thoroughly rationalized and politically defensible forms of control through "objective" evaluation. Essay examinations suffered two crippling blows during World War I. First, the mental-testing movement gained legitimacy through the widespread use of objective tests by the military. "New-type" or objective tests came to be accepted both by educational authorities and by the public as valid measures of intelligence and performance. Second, the essay exam lost legitimacy in a series of highly publicized experiments to test what today is called *interrater reliability*. English, history, and even mathematics graders achieved rates of less than 40 percent in repeated trials.[57] Stripped of their fundamental rationale, essay exams could not compete with the "scientific" or new-type examination in an age of growing faith in scientific social organization. Several prestigious colleges began accepting a version of the World War I military intelligence test in lieu of the standard college entrance essays, and the College Entrance Examination Board itself slowly began introducing new-type tests in addition to essays in the 1920s and 1930s, in part for simple financial expediency. Rising secondary enrollment, combined with increasing budgetary constraints, had made essay evaluation costly. The New York Board of Regents, for example, hired examiners to read a few more than a thousand sets of essays in

1878, a few more than a million in 1934, at the height of depression-era cuts in funding.[58]

However, essay examinations endured into the 1930s, supported not only by the weight of tradition but also by pedagogical arguments and empirical research. Beginning in the 1920s, studies to improve (and defend) essay exams demonstrated that they *could* be graded reliably (even at more than 90 percent agreement), provided that the exam was well designed; that standards were well defined; and that multiple, well-trained readers were used.[59] More tellingly, research consistently indicated that students studied differently for essay exams than they did for objective tests. They studied longer and used a greater variety of study methods. There was less underlining and more summarizing, outlining, and diagraming; less random note-taking and more studying for broad patterns. Students were more likely to form opinions, "read and review underlying relationships," and "review notes without focusing on details."[60] Alvin C. Eurich and L. B. Kinney, leading advocates of discipline-specific writing instruction, concluded a 1932 summary of research on new- versus old-type exams by stating, "The merit of a test may be intelligently discussed only in connection with the function to be tested . . . from the standpoint of outcomes other than information."[61] But without a long-standing tradition of research into the positive effects of well-constructed and well-integrated essay examinations, such studies could not overcome the administrative progressives' stereotype of the essay examination (largely justified) as a mere catalog of dry information, with little pedagogical value and of questionable value in assessing knowledge.

Advocates of new-type tests argued that information recall was the foundation of all learning and therefore a proper focus of testing, that one had to reason to recall facts, and that their tests could measure the "end product" of a process of reasoning that need not be laid out on paper to be present. Without a cogent theory to explain the relationship between writing and learning, proponents of essay exams could not counter the assumption that writing was transparent, a mere recording of thought. Mental-measurement advocates always protested that they were not attempting to replace essay writing "as a form of training and practice in the clear organization and logical presentation of facts, concepts and ideas," they were merely attempting to *measure* more accurately the outcomes of "content learning." And a few new-type-test advocates even saw a potential danger that "because of the greater reliability and validity of sound objective tests, the educative value of writing essays . . . may be neglected, or, if not neglected, be relegated to classes in English composition alone," as a leading mental-measurement expert, Issac A. Kandel, put it. He conceded that a decline in writing instruction "may be one of the unfortunate but unsupported results of the test movement."[62] But these issues never loomed large to mental-measurement's advocates. The stakes were higher. Ultimately, the issue was not improving pedagogy or learning but rather finding an efficient means of "prediction" and sorting in a modern democratic state.

The final blow to essay examinations came during the depression years when scientific testing became national educational policy, supported by the Carnegie Foundation for the Advancement of Teaching, the Bureau of Education, the College Entrance Examination Board, and other prestigious groups. Their motives were unabashedly political. As greater numbers of students pressed for entrance into secondary and higher education, some rational means had to be found for "vocational guidance," by which administrative progressives meant a politically defensible program for sorting. Particularly troubling to makers of educational policy like Kandel was the social upheaval in Europe, "the unrest due to the overcrowding in the universities and consequently in the professions [which] was without doubt a contributory factor to the Nazi Revolution" and other destabilizing political movements, both on the left and the right, in industrial democracies (4). Mental measurement would address the problem of "social and economic distribution of individuals in society and the danger which may result from educational and vocational maladjustment" (160). Instead of the essay exam's simple pass or fail, new-type exams would make more subtle—and defensible—distinctions, since they tested students on a wider range of "material" and could be designed to demonstrate greater variety in "achievement" over a period of years. The results of these tests, along with other indicators, would be used to track students into a more finely differentiated educational system. No one would fail; everyone would have an appropriate education. The goal was, as Kandel put it, "To enable the right pupils to receive the right education from the right teachers at a cost within the means of the state."[63]

Mental measurement would allow the United States to have common schools without a common curriculum, a differentiated educational system without separate secondary-school systems for different social classes or highly selective postelementary education, as in Europe.[64] But the loss of the essay examination as a central part of the curriculum also meant that educators would no longer need to connect writing and learning in the disciplines. General education, now defined by the administrative progressives as an "objectively" tested body of discrete facts and skills, could proceed without routinely confronting the relationship between students' writing and their future education or employment. Without external essay examinations facing their students, content-area teachers had even less incentive to assign writing or to give their own essay examinations (time-consuming even under the best conditions). Moreover, objective tests offered a powerful disincentive for such activities as writing, which took time away from teaching the "real" content of the discipline (i.e., the information on which students would be tested).

If the loss of comprehensive essay exams decreased schoolwide writing, argued the administrative progressives, then it was a small price to pay for avoiding, in Kandel's phrases, "educational maladjustment" and the "social menace" of overcrowding in the professions (153). Ultimately, the testing movement won so convincingly because there was no powerful constituency to resist reforms being pushed from the top by administrative progressives. To advocates of liberal culture, who complained that the great tradition of liberal learning would be sacrificed, the testing movement replied that it would still be taught but only to students with the capacity and interest to learn it.[65] To Deweyan progressives who complained that schoolwide writing would be diminished, and with it unified, high-order learning tied to experience, the testing movement replied that formal essay exams were to blame for the colleges' stranglehold on the secondary curriculum and that teachers could and should use informal writing more meaningfully in conjunction with individual or group projects. In the climate of social unrest of the 1930s, school reformers from left and right found it difficult to resist administrative measures aimed at restoring order.

The administrative progressives' approach to essay examinations points up the crucial conflict between writing instruction and the industrial model of general education. If the goal is efficient, systematic learning of discrete information and skills, then assigning, teaching, and grading extended writing seems an inefficient use of institutional resources. The success of the industrial model in setting the agenda for American education is tellingly apparent when today's advocates of writing across the curriculum conduct empirical studies attempting to show that students do better on objective tests—learn discrete facts more efficiently—with writing-to-learn pedagogies. But the failure of the industrial model to improve students' writing through remediation is equally apparent. Six decades of research have found that grammar instruction and drill do not improve students' writing. Linguistic and rhetorical theory have thoroughly discredited the atomistic view of language learning. And complaints about poor student writing have not abated. Yet the myth of transience persisted (and persists) among administrative progressives. New forms of remediation continually hold out the promise that, with enough organization and cooperation, drill and reinforcement, students can be trained to write once and for all; that Americans will again possess this elementary skill, this component of general education, and teachers can get on with their "real" work: teaching specific information.

6

WRITING AND THE
GREAT BOOKS

That most limited of all specialists, the well-rounded man.
            —Nick Carraway in *The Great Gatsby*

The industrial model of education won the battle for control of curricula in America and thus set the dominant pattern for general education: a menu of required courses in various fields. But the administrative progressives did not sweep the field. They offered no goal other than efficiency, no vision of community beyond the efficiently run corporation, no philosophy beyond a seemingly apolitical behaviorism. The humanities and the social sciences offered alternative versions of general education, which each held out competing educational goals, ideals of community, and philosophies.[1] But neither the humanities with their great books nor, as I discuss in the next chapter, the social sciences with their Deweyan progressive thought consistently or systematically integrated writing instruction into their general-education programs. In both cases, the increasing professionalization of those responsible for general education thwarted meaningful interdisciplinary dialogue and prevented instructors from appreciating the role of writing in learning. Writing usually remained as transparent in general-education programs as in the disciplines, and the myth of transience continued.

Humanities departments created in the late nineteenth century—English, foreign languages, philosophy—would seem to be the logical place to teach writing. These departments upheld the Renaissance ideal of the well-rounded person, the articulate generalist who could transcend narrow scientific specialization, synthesize wide-ranging knowledge, and communicate with a "general" audience in a clear, forceful style. Moreover, the humanities studied language and texts: *writings,* if not *writing* itself. And of course the English department, the "backbone of the humanities" in the modern university, assumed responsibility for formal writing instruction through the general-composition courses it housed.[2] Yet the new humanities departments rarely supported programs to synthesize students' knowledge in the humanities with knowledge in the social and natural sciences. Nor did the English department make writing instruction a priority or readily cooperate with other departments in teaching composition after the forensic system died around the turn of the century.

Instead of creating interdisciplinary general-education courses and evolving traditions of writing instruction within them, the humanities created its own version of general education, the great-books approach, which asserted its disciplinary values over and against those of the natural and physical sciences, and taught—or rather evoked—writing within its limited discourse conventions. It may seem ironic that humanists, who were committed to the ideal of a well-rounded education, should create a version of general education that was confined to a narrow range of disciplines and give writing instruction a relatively minor place in it. But when the humanities created general education in their own image they were merely conforming to the institutional and professional structure within which they operated. When they abolished or marginalized systematic writing instruction, they were only reflecting the values of the other disciplines for whom specialization and professionalization made rhetoric transparent. Student discourse in the humanities was expected to conform to the standards of the newly professionalized humanistic disciplines, which in turn conformed to the new research mission of higher education: a philosophical or "critical" approach to texts as opposed to the oratorical approach of the old rhetorical tradition. Yet student writing was expected to be "critical" within the constraints of the humanities disciplines, which emphasized formal relations among a discrete canon of texts rather than a critical examination of all texts or of the relationship between literary texts and social, political, and cultural forces beyond the canon. By narrowing the definition of general education to acquaintance with a limited body of texts and their own critical approaches to them, the humanities faculty were able to assume the mantle of the generalist while still pursuing the specialized research and teaching necessary for academic identity and respectability. In this way, the humanities did not need to encounter the discourse of other disciplines, much less teach it, and the effect was to compartmentalize general education and limit the role of writing in it.

Professionalized Generalists

The great-books approach grew out of what Laurence R. Veysey and others have called "liberal culture," a conception of higher learning that grew up in the waning years of the nineteenth century, primarily in the humanities. Liberal culture espoused a "Brahminical romanticism" (Berlin's term), which most visibly defined itself by its opposition to the democratic, vocational, and scientific orientation of the new university and the specialization and commercialism of modern life.[3] Advocates of liberal culture tended to see themselves as embattled humanists in an age of Babbittry and resisted the encroachments of scientific and professional fields as middle-class barbarisms, which thwarted the Arnoldian ideal of the "well-rounded man," a person with "a wide vision of the best things which man has done or aspired after."[4] Liberal culture trusted that philosophical and belletristic literary study among undergraduates would restore a lost community of taste, a "great tradition," which urban-industrial society had betrayed. The books that were accepted into this newly formed tradition were thought to constitute a "great conversation" among the best minds of the past, which students would come to appreciate and perhaps enter.[5]

Like other emerging disciplines, the newly professionalized humanities offered a professional service, which the institution and the wider society valued. They would become arbiters, preservers, and defenders of the great tradition, introducing high culture to the students of middle-class, rural, and immigrant backgrounds who were flocking to the new universities. Liberal culture attempted to justify its position in the curriculum through a missionary pursuit of this tradition, often defined in terms of German idealism (filtered through English romanticism and American transcendentalism), but without the trappings of pettifogging German scholarship. The study of literature, wrote a Cornell University professor in 1894, achieves "the true aim of culture," which is "to induce soul states or conditions, soul attitudes, to attune the inward forces to the idealized forms of nature and of human life produced by art, and not to make the head a cockloft for storing away barren knowledge."[6] In frequent jeremiads, liberal culture lamented the decay of the cultured classes and the loss of the great tradition to scientific specialization and democratic mediocrity, "the worship of the 'Average,' " as Charles G. Osgood of Princeton put it.[7]

Like the old rhetorical tradition, liberal culture was elitist, but it was not the attitude of a secure elite, confident of its social role and the value of the tradition it taught. Liberal culture saw the democratic reforms sweeping the university—particularly the rising enrollment among ethnic minorities and the specialized elective curriculum, which served careerist ends—as a threat to the high standards of the great tradition, which the newly professionalized humanities studied, taught, and in large measure created. In 1909, for example, William T. Foster organized the first explicitly general education curriculum at Reed College to fight "this democratic leniency toward the unfit, favoring self-supporting students at the expense of intellectual standards."[8] The principal role of the humanities in the university and its professional service to the wider society was to uphold standards whose influence would in time elevate the masses through a kind of cultural trickle-down effect.

In its fundamental assumptions, the new humanist project was essentially romantic or Hegelian, not classical. Romantics since at least William Wordsworth had viewed literature in terms of a transcendent liberation. Poetry was the noblest expression of the human spirit, lifting humanity out of the fact-filled scientific age into a higher realm of permanent values and true freedom. The study of literature came to be seen as an antidote to the spiritual ills of the university and, indeed, of society. Thomas R. Lounsbury of Yale insisted that in "the great masterpieces of our literature, lies for the college student his linguistic and literary salvation."[9] The English department in particular had a vital mission. "Democracy," wrote Barrett Wendell, "in old world or new, seems little better than a caricature of government." The great books would be its salvation by instilling "certain external graces and dignity."[10] "The success of the democratic state," his student Oscar James Campbell asserted, lay in "cultivating the sensitivity of the individual," a goal that the study of the great books was uniquely suited to accomplish.[11]

Later critics, such as F. R. Leavis and I. A. Richards, who exerted a powerful influence in American English departments, were successors to the first generation of literary generalists in this regard. For Leavis, the study of imaginative literature was a last-ditch defense of liberal humanism against the chaos and depersonalization of mass society in the scientific age.[12] And Richards baldly asserted that poetry "is capable of saving us; it is a perfectly possible means of overcoming chaos."[13] But it was to be not a collective but an individual liberation, above politics or history. The teaching of appreciation and critical judgment, not communication, was the professional service that the discipline performed. The new profession would willingly teach writing only so far as it served the profession's ends.[14]

The Great Tradition Versus the Rhetorical Tradition

One can perhaps best understand liberal culture's approach to writing instruction by contrasting it to the approach of the old rhetorical tradition. The differences between the two arise in large part from the professionalization of the humanities within the new research-oriented university. Though liberal culture claimed the mantle of tradition and lamented the "decline" of the liberal arts, the humanities actually began their modern existence as a reaction against central aspects of the rhetorical tradition and the old liberal curriculum. The new humanities departments repudiated the old pedagogical tradition in their quest for professional identity within the new compartmentalized university. And the ambiguous position of writing instruction within the humanities in many ways grew out of this tension between a nostalgia for the cultural community of the old college and the necessity of creating a community of professionals to survive in the new university. Liberal culture chose certain general tendencies of the old college to enshrine: reverence for the past, distrust of mercantile values, cultural elitism. It longed for the unity of culture (and class) in the old academic community, where students and teachers shared a set of values and a common fund of knowledge gleaned from books all had read. But in its quest for identity in the new university, liberal culture rejected those central elements of the old college that were incompatible with a new professionalism. In the new secularized institution, the old paternalism, sectarianism, and dogmatic moral philosophy had to go, of course, but so did key aspects of the rhetorical tradition: its focus on classical languages, its communal oral performance, its emphasis on effective expression of received ideas rather than criticism of them.

The most obvious difference was language. The new humanities departments resisted the teaching of classical languages and literature, formerly the backbone of rhetorical study, preferring instead *modern* literature, particularly English and French. To find a respected place in the new curriculum, the new departments had to sever their ties with the old. Without irony, the defenders of general culture founded in 1883 a specialized professional organization for the humanities, the Modern Language Association of America (MLA). And its first task was to overthrow the dominance of Latin and Greek in the curriculum, which it accomplished within a decade.

On a deeper level, though, the modern humanities also rejected the central purpose of rhetorical study in the old liberal arts college: training its students in communal, public discourse on civic issues—the ancient Ciceronian ideal of the "good man skilled in speaking," as Quintilian put it. Isocrates, Gorgias, and Quintilian were absent from the new canon. No text on rhetoric appears on Robert Maynard Hutchins' list of great books, except for Aristotle's *Rhetoric*, which had little influence on the rhetorical tradition until the twentieth century.[15] Even Cicero, the model of the orator-statesman for the old liberal curriculum and its most commonly taught author, was rarely taught, and his works never entered liberal culture's canon of classics (or Hutchins' list).

In a secular institution embedded in an increasingly pluralistic society, the humanities could not retain the Ciceronian ideal of the *vir bonus,* the broadly educated person, versed in all that was good in the culture, and capable of bringing that wide-ranging knowledge to bear on public issues through the use of persuasion. Knowledge was too large, discourse too fragmented, for any person or discipline to teach it all. Recent historians of composition and of general education have lamented the decline of interest in public discourse within the humanities; but given the organization of the institution—and of public discourse outside it—that decline was in many respects inevitable.[16] Public discourse became the province of specialists: academics and other professionals. Professionals in the humanities could not presume to teach students to write about scientific, economic, and political issues—as the difficulties of the forensic system had demonstrated. Even discourse for a "general audience" was increasingly the province of yet another newly professionalized occupation: journalism.

By the 1910s, English faculty seriously questioned whether the teaching of composition was compatible with their professional role in the new universities. In 1915 Edward A. Thurber wrote,

The department of English is straining to become a forum of discussion of all questions that have assailed human intelligence. . . . Those instructors of English [who teach composition] are asked to become actively conversant with science, politics, philosophy. Though still devotees of belles lettres, they are also striving to speak with authority on every other subject. . . . Frankly the assumption is startling. May not a cog have slipped somewhere?[17]

As the cog metaphor suggests, there was no place in the organizational machinery for a course (or a discipline) that took as its province all discourse.

Instead of looking at serious writing in all organized fields of knowledge (*belles lettres* in its original, eighteenth-century sense), the humanities stuck to its limited collection of philosophical and literary texts (belles lettres in its modern sense).[18] A narrow, discipline-specific criticism replaced rhetorical study at the center of this new version of liberal education, as the new canon gave pride of place not to authors in the oratorical tradition but to authors in what Bruce A. Kimball calls the *philosophical tradition,* which since the time of Plato had been suspicious of rhetoric. Rhetoric seeks the probable, as Aristotle put it, the impermanent, conditional agreement of orator and audience, not the permanent, absolute truth of the philosopher arrived at dialectically. As Kimball points out, this critical attitude suited the new university's values: its emphasis on intellect and rationality (versus the emotional and ethical appeals of rhetoric), its individualism and skepticism (versus the acceptance of shared beliefs and communal values upon which the orator depends).[19] Liberal culture's version of liberal education was interested in texts not as public discourse on questions of public policy and morals but as revelations of individual personality and thought, a focus that accorded with the new social role of the university as promoter of individual and personal advancement.

Thus, as the professionalization of the humanities grew, the rationale for humanistic study shifted from expression to appreciation, from formal training in public discourse to informal cultivation of private taste and individual critical acumen. As S. Michael Halloran has pointed out, students in the old rhetorical liberal arts tradition studied texts to internalize models of conduct and uses of language that, as future leaders of society, they could bring to bear on public problems. But the modern student in the humanities classroom—like the modern humanist scholar in the study—would primarily study texts to appreciate their intrinsic beauties, to arrive at an estimate of their aesthetic value, or to offer original critical interpretations.[20] The humanities considered social and historical context outside its purview—mere background to the great books and their great ideas. Other departments could teach the student to address public issues and to use the specialized discourses with which modern technocratic society approached such problems.

Because liberal culture valued "general" knowledge and criticized narrow professional education, it was alienated from the careerist aims of the new university. But because it had itself professionalized, because it did not upset the fundamental structure of the new institution either by imposing its values (and discourse) on the social or natural sciences or by attempting to integrate its values (and discourse) with theirs, liberal culture retained a secure role in the institution as the defender of a narrowly conceived, romanticized version of the old liberal education, aloof from practical consequences, backward looking, timeless. The generalist professor of humanities became a cherished type, immortalized in student memoirs of college life. Like other professionals, the academic humanist played a valuable (and specialized) role in the new order as the arbiter and defender of high culture (though less valued than others, if one judges—as the universities did—by salaries and teaching loads). And like other professionals in the new university, literary generalists did not wish to take responsibility for teaching any writing but their own, though this view often came into conflict with the widespread belief that the English department was responsible for all writing instruction.

Liberal Culture on Writing

The romantic assumptions that informed literary study during the rise of the modern university provided liberal culture with a rationale for abolishing or marginalizing systematic writing instruction in favor of teaching vernacular, imaginative literature. As Richard Young has suggested, romanticism, "with its stress on the natural powers of the mind and the uniqueness of the creative act, leads to a repudiation of the possibility of teaching the composing process, hence the tendency to become a critical study of the products of composing and an act of editing."[21] Liberal culture's attitude toward writing rested on the romantic notion that writing cannot be taught directly. Thomas R. Lounsbury of Yale, one of the most distinguished literary scholars of the age—and a man admittedly bitter about having had to devote "for a quarter of a century . . . a distinctly recognizable share of my time reading and correcting themes"—insisted, "the fundamental fallacy" was that "the art of expression is something which can be made a matter of direct instruction, just as arithmetic can be or history or chemistry or any foreign tongue."[22] Good writing, he argued, is too mysterious, too individual, to benefit even from "the mastery of all the rhetorical rules ever invented" (875). As evidence, he pointed out that the growth of composition courses had not led to a proportional increase in the number of great writers, "the speedy coming of a spotless linguistic millennium" (869).

Liberal culture invoked the romantic model of the composing process to explain why writing is unteachable. Expression is the outpouring in language of preexisting and fully formed ideas and emotions. "Clear thinking precedes clear writing," said Lounsbury, "and does not follow it" (874). "One cannot write any better than he can think," Campbell insisted. "Bad writing is nothing more than the outward and visible sign of bad thinking" (179). Therefore, the only way to improve students' writing is to improve their thinking, and this, they argued, is a very slow process, which cannot be hurried by direct instruction. Lounsbury fell back on the organic metaphors of the romantic tradition: "The ability to write is a growth, and . . . the rapidity and extent of this growth depend upon several agencies which the individual may not and usually does not employ with that particular end in mind" (873). It happens unconsciously, mysteriously, in the great unfolding of life. "All life, if it is worth living, contributes to ability in expression." Even romantic suffering plays a role: "There is nothing like misery to improve the style" (875).

How, then, does education improve writing? Liberal culture answered that a proper education produces deep thoughts, which cannot help but find their proper expression. And the thoughts that most improve one's writing naturally come from studying the great writers, the masters of the art that cannot be taught. "He who of his own accord has sat reverently at the feet of the great masters of English literature," said Lounsbury, "need have no fear that their spirit will not inform, so far as in him lies, the spirit of their discipline" (878). Here, then, is the central paradox of the liberal culture's view: it is the study of literature, not of rhetoric, which ultimately improves students' rhetoric. And the role of English departments in writing instruction is thus to teach liberal culture through belle lettres.

In one sense, liberal culture's advocates had sound theoretical objections to composition courses. Writing, they argued, could only be acquired in the activity of reading and discussing texts. Campbell, a Columbia professor of literature and former teaching assistant at Harvard under Barrett Wendell, claimed that English departments have "pretended time out of mind and to the tune of hundreds of thousands of dollars that we operate a writing shop located in the clouds near the famous thinking shop that Aristophanes built for Aristotle" (180).[23] The traditional freshman English course "is based on a fallacious notion that good writing is a *Ding an sich,* a separate, independent technique. That is, that it can be engendered and grown in a kind of intellectual vacuum." "The pretensions of the teachers of this course in Freshman composition," Campbell complained, "are perhaps the most dangerous symptom of the American belief in educational short cuts, in showy, rather than sound values" (179). But these theoretical objections to general-composition courses led Campbell and others to argue for abolishing composition courses to provide more time in the curriculum for their own discipline, not to investigate ways to embed writing in the reading and writing of all disciplines. Campbell's attack on general composition (like those of other abolitionists) was part of an argument for substituting humanities' general-education courses for composition courses (which he did at Columbia), not for helping other departments (or even his own) to use writing in their disciplines more effectively. Given these views, the process of writing in its rhetorical or communicative context never became an object of disciplinary study for liberal culture. In many ways, writing remained as transparent in the humanities as it was in the other disciplines—and the myth of transience as potent.

Composition and the Professional Humanist

The professionalization of the humanities and the rejection of the rhetorical tradition which accompanied it explains in large part the ambiguous position of composition in English departments.

Though the great-books approach to general education developed primarily out of the new English departments, which had also taken responsibility for teaching general-composition courses, English departments have seen these two responsibilities as deeply contradictory instead of as complementary, so much so that writing instruction has never been a central concern of literature teaching or of the great-books approach to general education; and its advocates have been suspicious of general-composition courses and, indeed, of all systematic writing instruction beyond elementary training. Composition teaching conflicted with the professional humanists' goals and values. Writing instruction was viewed as an unwelcome intrusion on their professional lives and a distraction from a much higher professional calling. Moreover, composition threatened the disciplinary integrity of the humanities insofar as it implied that English should teach the discourse of other disciplines in this "service course."

English departments responded in one of two ways to this conflict: either they attempted to abolish composition courses altogether or, more commonly, they marginalized systematic writing instruction so that it intruded as little as possible on the central professional work of the discipline: the teaching of great books. The abolitionist response was less common, but it influenced the second response in crucial ways; thus I will consider it first.

Just after the turn of the century, some English faculty carried liberal culture's romantic assumptions about writing to their logical conclusion: if, ultimately, writing cannot be taught directly (beyond elementary skills) but only acquired, then writing should not be systematically taught within any course, and composition courses should be abolished as antithetical to literary study and, indeed, to higher education. From the abolitionists' point of view, systematic composition instruction was a dangerous distraction. Its existence in the English department "obscures for everyone concerned the extremely important service that English literature, as one of the still living humanities, must render to college students and through them to this disordered world of ours," as Campbell put it (182).

Given these attitudes, it is not surprising that many advocates of liberal culture resisted the idea that the English department should offer a "service course" in composition for the very scientific and professional fields which threatened the position of the humanities in the new comprehensive university and, in their eyes, also threatened the survival of their Anglo-and Francophile humanism in American culture and thus their professional role in society. In 1910 Lane Cooper, then a young Cornell English instructor, railed against "the popular demand for a kind of education in the vernacular which shall directly liberate the utterance of the masses, rather than raise up leaders in scholarship whose paramount influence might elevate and sustain standards of taste and good usage."[24]

Abolitionists portrayed composition in terms of corruption and enslavement, the very terms that romantics used to describe technology and business. Both students and instructors were thought to be prisoners of compulsory composition. "The average student loathes it . . . he has to have it forced down his throat," said Lounsbury, and qualified instructors "will not persist in carrying on this most distasteful of occupations, unless compelled by necessity" (877). Campbell was even stronger: composition corrupts; it "inevitably stultifies the English department" (179). First there is the hypocrisy of leading students to believe that a composition course or two will teach them to write anything and everything well. Then there is the oppression of "the harried instructor in Freshman English . . . who labors valiantly to accomplish the impossible"—deluded into thinking that his labor will lead to a professorship. He "meekly submits to serving as the vicarious sacrifice for all the sins of all the other departments of the college," which have failed to give students sound knowledge, which is prerequisite to writing. Moreover, self-serving senior professors build graduate programs on the backs of these poor instructors. "The Freshman English machine," Campbell's equivalent of the evil industrial machine, has created an "academic proletariat." "Crowds of young men and women have been lured into the teaching of English by the numbers of positions annually open at the bottom of the heap, and there they stick, contaminating one another with their discouragement and

rebellion" (181). And, Campbell darkly warned, they may overthrow the system if composition is not abolished.

But behind these pleas for compassion and liberation lay a
deeper motive. At bottom, composition instruction represented
the values of equity and inclusion, of vocation and pragmatism,
over and against standards of taste and culture, which professional generalists in the humanities defended. What most dis-
turbed the abolitionists was not the hypocrisy of writing instruction; it was the influx of students who came to the university not
to absorb liberal culture but to prepare for mundane professional
careers. The required composition course represented an intrusion into the English department of people who did not share its
values. Though abolitionists, such as Lounsbury and Campbell,
insisted that writing could not be taught, they favored elective
writing courses in the English department for those who were
willing—and able—to learn. Campbell encouraged courses in
literary writing for "the Freshman who possesses a sincere interest
in some form of artistic writing *and a demonstrated aptitude for
it*" (italics mine) (185). And Lounsbury approved of teaching
composition to the "minority" of students "who would most
profit by it" instead of wasting his time "in vain efforts to overcome the repugnance of the unwilling or to animate the torpid"
(181).

Writing of the kind the abolitionists were willing to teach was
not for the ordinary person, who did not have the talent or the
need to write. The idea that everyone needs to write well, said
Lounsbury, is "a notion born of modern conditions" (by which
he meant the mass-education system). That many did not learn
was actually a blessing. "There is but one way of keeping certain
persons from writing wretchedly, and that is by keeping them
from writing at all" (180–81). With a characteristic late-nineteenth-century social Darwinist fusion of laissez-faire economics
and romantic idealism, he insisted that those men of genius who
have something truly important to say to the world will find a
way to say it, whatever their training.

Liberal culture's contrasting definitions of writing placed responsibility elsewhere. For the gifted, writing was an art; for the

rest it was a useful but mundane skill—mechanical and grammatical correctness. Thus, some abolitionists wanted to require enough of this practical kind of writing instruction "to enable everyone to transact the common business of life," as Lounsbury put it. Unlike the art of writing, correctness could be taught to anyone, chiefly by drill, but it "ought to be learned at a comparatively early age." If students had not learned it by the time they arrived at the university, they were not meant to learn it and should not have been admitted (878). The English department therefore had no unique ability or responsibility to teach writing. If the mundane sort of writing simply consisted of transcribing fully formed thought, then any instructor should be capable of correcting students' errors, which is all writing instruction amounts to in this view. Abolishing composition courses would force other departments to "clean their own doorsteps," as one Harvard English professor put it.[25]

For gifted students, on the other hand, writing was high art, the result of talent and cultivation. English departments began to offer specialized advanced courses in what is today called "creative writing" for students with the talent and interest in the kind of writing that liberal culture most valued. At Columbia, Harvard, and elsewhere, elective creative-writing courses were begun for the talented few, though creative writing did not become entrenched in academia until the new generation of "new critics" arrived in the 1940s.

In the 1910s and 1920s, many articles began to appear advocating the abolition of general-composition courses and the substitution of courses teaching vernacular literary classics of the great tradition. But only Yale and Princeton actually did without composition courses. And only a tiny minority of institutions—almost all small, private colleges with highly selective enrollment—have abolished composition since. But a tradition of complaint about composition has been a recurring theme within the profession, as the many articles on abolition published throughout the century attest.[26]

Although the abolitionist response was most consistent with liberal culture's views on writing, the majority of English departments were not in a position to abolish composition courses.

Academia and the wider public placed responsibility for writing instruction in English departments. Faculty resisted attempts by English departments to abolish composition. And few English departments took that step, in any case, for composition had become an economic necessity for departments at most large institutions. Freshman English provided the higher enrollment that financed graduate (which is to say, professional) programs in the discipline. Composition courses were passed down "like old clothes" to graduate students, paraprofessional temporary instructors, or junior professors, freeing senior faculty for the specialized research and advanced teaching most highly valued by the profession (and by the institution).[27] English came to depend on composition to provide the economic base for its professional work and institutional status, though that work and that status were not achieved through research and teaching in composition. Given these practical constraints, the professional humanists marginalized composition courses in a variety of ways instead of abolishing them.

In 1903 the MLA disbanded its pedagogical section (the only section concerned with writing instruction), and the profession showed diminishing interest in composition teaching in the following decades. English departments had a great many specialized elective writing courses in the 1910s (from theory of rhetoric to agricultural journalism), but these courses consistently dwindled as departments added specialized courses in literature.[28] Like faculty in other disciplines, English faculty viewed the teaching of introductory courses as less interesting than teaching advanced courses in their professional field: literature. Moreover, the general-composition courses were often large, and instructors were expected to assign and correct weekly or even daily themes. As a result, some in the discipline came to view composition teaching with a distaste bordering on outright contempt.[29]

Reductive composition pedagogies also marginalized the courses. The approach to composition that became the norm in English departments limited the content of composition courses to the most specific and concrete features of written discourse (mechanical correctness) and the most abstract and general features of discourse ("unity, coherence, emphasis," and the like).

Composition courses had little to say about the great middle, the communicative aspects of discourse embedded in particular social or disciplinary contexts.[30] Consequently, composition aroused little intellectual interest among English faculty, and there was little research in composition within English departments until composition teachers themselves began to form a professional identity in the 1960s (see chapter 9).

Moreover, the English department taught writing as part of the one context in which it had professional interest and expertise: literary criticism. The single writing course that nearly always remained in the curriculum, freshman composition, was often taught as a course in imaginative literature.[31] And because the contexts for serious intellectual discourse in the university, as elsewhere in the professional world, were almost inevitably tied to a discipline, it is not surprising to find that the most common genres of writing taught in the English department's composition courses—belletristic personal essays and literary criticism—were closely tied to the discipline's professional domain. Composition became an adjunct to the professional work of the discipline. But composition teaching per se finally lay outside its professional interests and, indeed, its expertise, because research in composition was not a recognized speciality.

The Lecture and Writing

The humanities not only rejected the old liberal curriculum's languages and purposes, its concern with rhetoric and public discourse, but also its pedagogical methods of formal verbal interplay and adapted instead the pedagogical methods of the new university, the lecture and the seminar, to accomplish its professional mission. Recitation and the formal study of rhetoric were condemned as being as "dry as bones," and along with them went the oral declamation, oration, and elocution, which had in a sense made the study of rhetoric and belles lettres "a single, undifferentiated process," as Gerald Graff puts it (41). Humanities' teaching took on a much less formal, more impressionistic style, which would let the literary masterpiece "speak for itself" to students in all its immediacy, without locating the work in a historical or social context—a rhetorical context, in other words.[32]

By the early twentieth century, the extempore lecture had become the dominant pedagogy for humanities courses, as well as for most other courses in the new universities. Spellbinding performers in the humanities gained reputations for platform histrionics—and eccentricity. Indeed, the humanities' faculty adopted the lecture with particular zest, and the stereotype of the eccentric professor lecturing to rapt undergraduates is a legacy of late-nineteenth-century academic spellbinders in the humanities, such as Hiram Corson, George Santayana, and William Lyon Phelps.

Phelps, for many years a holdout for the old pedagogy, gave up recitation in 1893, the year after vernacular literature courses were introduced at Yale. He pronounced a kind of credo for popular undergraduate lecturers around the turn of the century.

If a teacher wishes success with pupils, he must inflame their imagination. The lesson should put the classroom under the spell of an illusion, like a great drama. Everything abstract, so far as possible, must be avoided. . . . The interest of the class must be instantly aroused and maintained until the end of the period. This is the first step, the first all-important problem. The teacher must drive out of their minds all other things and substitute an absorbing, jealous interest in the lesson. . . . Minute and exact accuracy must sometimes be sacrificed for emphasis.[33]

Appreciation was the primary goal, not communicative competence, and passive but receptive students, caught up in the "experience" of great literature, would serve the purpose. Barrett Wendell was reported to have sat quietly for a moment in class after reading a poem, then to have cried out in his famous whinnying voice, "Isn't it beautiful!"[34] Research-oriented faculty sometimes complained that these performances cheapened university education by "pander[ing] to the crowd"; the literary generalists answered by charging that specialists ignored the deeper meaning of education and produced in students "a full mind rather than an orderly one."[35] But the literary generalists were allowed to go their way; lecture suited large undergraduate introductory courses, was often popular with students, and left funds and time available for specialized research and teaching.[36]

There was, however, less room for students to develop their powers of expression in the new generalist pedagogy of informal lecture than in the old liberal curriculum, with its frequent performance of student-written texts and the conferences that went along with those performances. The practical difficulties of assigning extended writing to classes of a hundred or even several hundred students are sufficient to explain the lack of student writing. But in a deeper sense, English conformed to the institutional pattern, which valued research and upper-level (professional) education over lower-level (general) education. Although some professors did incorporate a great deal of writing into lecture courses (Phelps assigned brief weekly essays on the readings, for example), the usual practice seems to have been one or two papers and one or two essay examinations per course—essentially the same as in other disciplines. And as early as 1922, some literature professors used objective examinations to test students' reading, though often with essay examinations or papers as well.[37]

Institutional forces tended to marginalize writing in literature classes as they had in other classes. English, like other disciplines, gained recognition and status through specialized research. Eliot specifically hired Wendell to relieve Adams Sherman Hill, the founder of Harvard's composition course, of some of his composition duties. In what was perhaps the first case of faculty raiding, Eliot kept the most prominent literary scholar of the late nineteenth century, Francis James Child, from going over to Johns Hopkins by promising that he would be "relieved at last from the burden of correcting undergraduate compositions."[38] Indeed, some prominent professors assigned *no writing in composition courses.* John Franklin Genung, author of some of the most influential composition textbooks of the era, was reported to have quit assigning writing in his freshman course some twenty years before his retirement.[39] Given the institutional environment, for English faculty to have conscientiously and systematically taught writing as part of a literature course would have been tantamount to losing professional prestige.

But the impressionistic lecture was more than simply a respite from the "academic scullery" of composition. It was an attempt to commune with students, to include them in the great conversation with minds and souls from the past. The teacher was a prophet and mediator, not a mere dispenser of information or analysis. Sympathetic students, who often collected around a charismatic teacher, would enter the conversation; the others were not meant to. The talented few would come to write artfully through reading and discussion, the others would not need to. Thus, students in introductory and general-education courses were relieved of the burden of preparing for formal oral performances and for written performances other than the standard essay examinations and papers.

Columbia and the Great Conversation: General Education as Discussion

Though there had been anthologies of Western literature and introductory courses devoted to its teaching as early as 1900, Columbia's famous General Honors course was the first to receive national publicity, and it set the pattern for general education in the humanities.[40] In 1917 John Erskine, a professor of literature and—significantly—a novelist rather than a scholar, was asked by the United States War Department to develop an adult-education course for U.S. soldiers in Europe, in part to boost morale, in part to teach them the cultural values for which they were fighting. After the armistice, Erskine began the General Honors course at Columbia, with similar content and with similar motives. The course would balance the sterile utility and pettifogging scholarship of the university by inculcating "a humanistic rather than a professional orientation." It would " 'acculturate' a student whose background and upbringing had excluded him from the 'great traditions'."[41] His approach set the tone for many imitators, some thirty between the wars.[42] His students and junior instructors would have wide-ranging influence in American colleges: Lionel Trilling, Mark Van Doren, Clifton Fadiman, and, most prominently, Mortimer J. Adler, who broke with Erskine over philosophical and theological issues but went on to make a long career of promoting his own version of great-books general education.

Erskine's approach was militantly ahistorical and not a little anti-intellectual, from his research-oriented colleagues' point of view, certainly. His idea was to have students read the classics at the rate of one a week, in the vernacular, as "the best sellers of ancient times." The great books, he insisted to his skeptical colleagues, were written for the "average man" in their day and needed no scholarly annotation or historical background to be understood and appreciated by Columbia's undergraduates, at least on the level of the "universal experience" (a key term) which the works evoked.[43] Once a week, fifteen to thirty undergraduates assembled with two professors (later only one) to discuss a classic, whereupon they "formed their opinions at once in free-for-all discussions ... as spontaneously and humanly as they would read best sellers."[44] If the canon of great books constituted a great conversation among the Western world's chief thinkers, students might themselves become a part of that conversation through reading and free discussion.

At first the course aimed at "broadening" students, not so much intellectually as morally and spiritually, in a generalized, secular sense. Through the great books, students would *experience* life in a deeper and more comprehensive way. Erskine warned that students who found a problem in some great book should resist the impulse to go to other books or works of criticism: "It is instead more profitable to go directly to life."[45] "I was concerned with no philosophy and no method for a total education," Erskine wrote, "I only hoped to teach how to read."[46] The great books would "speak for themselves," he insisted repeatedly, without the need of historical and ideological context. This approach would later find a more intellectual rationale as a new generation of professional humanists steered away from the moralistic and "character-building" justifications of literary study that had been associated with the old college and instead justified "criticism" of the great books on the grounds that it developed students' "discernment and rationality of judgement" and made them "sensitive to intellectual sincerity and consistency"—goals more in keeping with the new university's secular and intellectual values.[47] But even after "criticism" became the goal, students were not asked to use the scholarly approaches of the philologist, linguist, or literary historian, much less those of the social or natural scientist. Rationality, discernment, and sincerity were defined in terms of liberal culture, not negotiated with other disciplines, and student writing was expected to remain within disciplinary confines, discussing "artistic processes" in the accepted ways.[48]

The Columbia course profoundly influenced not only the aims but also the pedagogy of general education in the humanities. By the 1910s, liberal culture's romantic distrust of formal pedagogical method made even the extempore lecture seem, somehow, inauthentic. The small group of undergraduates with a sensitive teacher had a "primitive simplicity," as Trilling described it.[49] As with the transition to the lecture a generation earlier, the new discussion pedagogy turned away from the oratorical and rhetorical tradition and toward the philosophical and belletristic traditions. The discussion class was neither the literary society of the old liberal college nor the seminar of the new research university. Erskine disliked both the literary societies and the German seminar for their excessive formality; in General Honors there were to be no formal papers presented and discussed, no propositions debated.[50] Instead, it would be a "free-for-all discussion" in the presence of a man of learning and culture. As with the impressionistic lecture, students would have an inspiring guide, not a mere pedagogue. "The best teachers of literature," wrote Erskine, "try to suggest the experience which such passages [from the great books] are meant to reflect; they remind their hearers of experience mislaid for the moment; they can only remind—they can't impart it."[51] This was the method of Socrates, not of Quintilian; the casual and evocative *causerie* of the salon rather than the intellectual rigor of the seminar. If the great books formed an edifying great conversation, "speaking for themselves" to students, the great-books class would reflect that informal oral model and, in the process, improve the conversation of the young.[52] For advocates of the great books (as for Plato), writing was clearly secondary.

Erskine originally envisioned General Honors as a two-year

sequence for all students, but the college faculty approved only a small colloquium for juniors and seniors, who were admitted by interview. As its title implies, the course was deliberately exclusive. In 1937 the faculty finally approved the English department's proposal for a one-year required freshman humanities sequence based on the great books. Significantly, the English department requested that the college drop its remaining one-semester freshman English requirement, arguing that reading and discussing the classics would improve students' writing through "a more thoroughly vital, and a less provincial, process."[53] The college reluctantly agreed but insisted on a five-thousand-word writing requirement in the general-education courses. However, writing was relegated to a separate "course," English C, taught by graduate students and graded pass-fail. English C was not a formal course but a set of required essays on topics related to the general-education readings, with mandatory conferences for those who did poorly on the assignments. Regular faculty were not required to assign, teach, or grade writing. The writing requirement was thus an adjunct to the "real" work of the general-education courses, which were graded on the basis of discussion participation, weekly objective quizzes to test reading knowledge, and midterm and final exams with some essay and some objective questions. Students naturally did not consider the writing requirements as important as the "regular" course. Plagiarism was a constant problem, and a 1946 report concluded that the time spent on the writing requirement by most students was "quantitatively negligible."[54]

In 1945, with the influx of GI's, the college again forced the issue of student writing. A collegewide committee recommended that the English department return to teaching a one-semester required freshman composition course. The department acquiesced but recommended that a stiff composition examination be the basis for admission. Furthermore, the committee asked faculty who were teaching general-education courses to make extended writing an integral part of those courses by commenting on the assignments "as writing" and by making the assignments part of the course grade.[55] The faculty agreed to do so, but there was no longer any programwide writing requirement; faculty assigned, commented on, and graded writing at their individual discretion. The committee report asked faculty who were teaching general-education courses to give their "moral support" to the effort, but again, the committee placed responsibility for writing instruction in the "Department organized for the purpose" (English). It is worth noting that the course descriptions of Humanities A and B in the committee report did not mention writing at all.[56] And it is clear that the emphasis in Humanities A was clearly on "conversation" not writing, appreciation not expression.

Twenty years later, Daniel Bell's recommendations for general-education reform at Columbia would again call for abolishing composition courses (see chapter 8). The pattern of alternating abolition and restoration had been set by the conflicting notions of general education. The humanities saw their professional role in terms of teaching literary appreciation, not communication. They carried a set of assumptions about general education deeply embedded within the rhetorical universe of the disciplinary "culture," assumptions that were seen by outsiders as vague and elitist. The goal was "to make whole men," or "cultured gentlemen," or "youths of sensibility." But that goal was, as the Columbia General Education Committee put it in 1963, "scorned" by the social and natural sciences as lacking any definable "philosophical or pedagogic ends," a clear "educational thrust." "To what end," the committee asked, was the college "committing our students to this path?"[57] For those steeped in the values of liberal culture, the purpose of reading and appreciating great books was self-evident, the raison d'être of the discipline. Those outside the disciplinary culture expected the humanities to pursue other goals: especially the improvement of written communication and thus the capacity to draw on past cultural formulations to address current problems cogently. But because the goals of general education in the humanities had never been adequately articulated for the whole institution, the shape of writing in great-books courses was never hammered out, its function within the whole curriculum never agreed upon or responsibility defined. To do so would have meant that departments and senior faculty would, in Kimball's words, "discipline themselves by submitting to ... a curriculum with the study of expression and rhetoric elevated from a freshman requirement to a centerpiece."[58] Instead, general education proceeded in neat disciplinary compartments, with little contact between humanities' general-education courses and those in the social and natural sciences.

Chicago and St. John's: The Apotheosis of the Great Books

In the 1930s and for two decades thereafter, Robert Maynard Hutchins kept the great-books version of general education before the public's eye, first as president of the University of Chicago and then, when the Chicago faculty rejected his experiment, through his famous great books adult-education program and his association with a reactionary curricular experiment, St. John's College at Annapolis and Santa Fe. In 1929, the thirty-year-old Hutchins became president of the University of Chicago and set about to restore the intellectual community of the old curriculum by reestablishing a single "theology and metaphysics" to the university, a "common stock of fundamental ideas," which he argued would unify society and make true democracy possible.[59] His program harked back nostalgically to the premodern era when, he insisted, knowledge was orderly and truth permanent. But as Hutchins' critics pointed out—and as he himself admitted—he never proposed "any specific theological or metaphysical system"; he simply had faith that, if enough Americans could be brought to read the great books, a rational consensus would emerge to guide modern society back to intellectual, moral, and political stability.

Hutchins valiantly carried the banner of liberal culture to its logical curricular end (or to its *reductio ad absurdam,* as his opponents said). All great books, scientific as well as literary, formed a single great conversation, which spoke without the aid of historical context or scholarly apparatus to everyone—or everyone "with the capacity to learn from books," as Hutchins qualified the *general* in general education (he estimated that about two-thirds of the population could). He and his "gang" (Mortimer J. Adler, Richard McKeon, Stringfellow Barr, Scott Buchanan) defined the general reader in a somewhat circular way: all "normally intelligent" persons who have acquired the "skill necessary for reading them and make the effort."[60] That skill primarily came from informal discussions, the famous great-books seminars, which he borrowed from Erskine. And like Erskine, Hutchins and his fellows rarely mentioned writing or gave it a central role in their programs.

Hutchins claimed that the trivium—grammar, rhetoric, and logic—was part of general education and of the great tradition, but he distrusted the pedagogical methods associated with it. There would be no formal verbal interplay, no declamation, recitation, or debate. In Hutchins' program, writing was a tool for reading, for understanding and appreciating the great conversation, not for communicating in mundane social and political contexts. "The classics provide models of excellence; grammar, rhetoric, and logic are means of determining how excellence is achieved."[61] Rhetoric, he went on to say, is not self-expression but a tool for dialectical and analytical study of the classics, a means of "learning how to read." Though Hutchins often invoked the ancient rhetorical tradition and attacked modern higher education, his program was, as Kimball has argued, very much in accord with the aims of the modern university; both had as their goal critical and intellectual inquiry rather than the oratorical skill of the old liberal curriculum. In redefining the goal of rhetorical study to de-emphasize its transactional, persuasive uses, Hutchins turned the classical notion of rhetoric on its head: the student writes to find truth, to analyze and evaluate texts, not to persuade others to action by marshaling culturally shared, received truth.

Hutchins thus saw writing in general education as an aid to learning, as a means of cultivating general habits of critical thought useful in future endeavors, including, perhaps, professional training. Though he never used the term "writing to learn," his approach had much in common with some current proponents of WAC who emphasize the relation between reading, writing, and critical thinking. In *How To Read a Book,* for example, Adler suggested writing notes, summaries, and outlines, comparisons between passages, or answers to study questions provided for each text in the great-books series.[62] Occasionally, he said, students might expand those answers into essays.[63] But there was no consideration of genre; that is, of the place of writing in the activities of society or even of the academic disciplines. It was possible, indeed necessary, to ignore genre in the great-books program because the specialized activities that give rise to genres bring students into the vocational, practical realms that Hutchins' program sought to avoid, the world of specific problems and communities and interests negotiated through written discourse.

Moreover, as with other manifestations of liberal culture, Hutchins' model deliberately excluded historical analysis from consideration, despite the chronological arrangement of the readings (a contradiction also present in English and modern language curricula, as Graff has noted) (193). The books will "speak for themselves," said Hutchins, echoing Erskine, "and the reader should decide for himself." Students must read and discuss (and perhaps write about) these books without the aid of commentary or apparatus. "Great books contain their own aids to reading; that is one reason why they are great."[64] If liberal culture made a secular religion of high culture, then the great books were its scriptures—*canon* is the operative term. Interpretation is a hermeneutic activity, confined to a body of texts and a circle of initiates but closed to the uninitiated who cannot or choose not to "learn to read" the texts. For the neophytes, Adler prepared what he called a *synopticon,* a kind of concordance to these secular scriptures, which lists and cross-references 102 "great ideas" as they appear in the 120 great books.[65] Theological and metaphysical "first principles" are the goal of general education, an eternal truth, self-evident to the reader-discussant who truly seeks it, independent of historical exigency or practical applications.

Hutchins was never able to implement fully his "theology of education" at the University of Chicago (though he did transform its adult-education extension). In the first place, the faculty had already approved the basic outline of a general-education program before he arrived, and it was a discipline-centered program arranged around the content of academic fields rather than around great books. But more importantly, the faculty distrusted his attempt to impose a neo-Thomist structure of knowledge on the curriculum.[66] Nevertheless, Chicago took radical steps to create a program of general-education core courses and, with them, a writing program which embodied Hutchins' notion of writing as a tool for reading and learning.

The college relieved lower-division undergraduate faculty of their responsibilities for research and set up a required curriculum of four core courses (humanities, social science, physics, biology) and a separate course in *composition*.[67] Despite Hutchins' objections, each of the cores taught its own discipline: the social sciences read contemporary materials and discussed contemporary problems; the natural sciences went their own disciplinary ways as usual. Only the humanities used something like a great-books approach, and that was modified to teach the content of the humanistic disciplines (by means of textbooks, critical apparatus to the works studied, and the like).

The core courses were taught by lecture and discussion (with labs in the natural sciences); there were no grades, only a final comprehensive examination in each core, made out and scored by an independent examination board. Significantly, all examinations—even the composition examination—came to be primarily new-type or objective tests, for which the examination board was often criticized. There were occasional essay questions, usually paragraph length, of a rather narrow type, which could be graded with high interrater reliability. Interestingly, essay questions were more common on social and natural sciences exams than on humanities exams.[68]

The composition course was at first quite traditional; students read and wrote belletristic essays. But the composition instructors could not convince the board of examiners that the student essays could be graded reliably, and the board (with support from students) insisted the course be completely overhauled to teach the kinds of writing that students would need in the four cores: brief critical and analytical essays in response to academic reading.[69]

In 1933 a committee entirely revised the composition course to support the other cores. The composition course used snippets of readings from the cores as its materials. The first third focused on analytical reading: note-taking, outlining, summarizing, and synthesis ("combining treatments of the same subject"); the middle third took up documentation, use of the library, and stylistic precision; the final third taught students to write the kinds of essays that the comprehensive exams required. In essence, the course taught the genres of the particular educational activities common in the curriculum: notes on lectures and reading, brief critical papers, and short essay examinations. The comprehensive examination in composition was, like the others, primarily multiple choice and short answer. Students were called upon to outline a passage or fill in an outline with details, to summarize a passage in a sentence, to combine sentences using specific grammatical patterns, or to choose the most appropriate word.[70]

The course was popular with students because it taught them specific learning strategies directly relevant to their needs. It served the needs of the curriculum by freeing faculty in the cores from the responsibility for systematically teaching writing and study skills. But as a result, writing was neither fully integrated into the cores nor a full-fledged core itself. Once again, composition instruction was marginalized as a separate "service" course—though not nearly so much as at Columbia (or in the typical English department). Tenure-line faculty taught composition (some from departments other than English), and each composition instructor also usually taught at least one course elsewhere in the college or university.[71] Moreover, the faculty in the cores also assigned writing—as an aid to learning, not as a means of evaluation (there were no grades in courses). The traditional practice of simply marking and returning papers became less common; commenting on papers in conferences and small-group discussions became more common. Faculty noted that, if they assigned writing before a conference or discussion (outlines, syntheses, or analyses of course material, practice essay-exam questions, etc.), students became more involved with the material, as well as with the instructor and the class. By discussing the writing, instructors discovered the students' difficulties in learning. Indeed, students sometimes asked for more writing, because it clearly benefited their preparation for the examinations and gave them a way to monitor their progress. Even so, faculty did not assign more than a few pieces of writing each year.[72] During the first years of the program, faculty were too busy becoming generally educated themselves ("keeping up with the hounds," as Chauncey S. Boucher put it). And although faculty were not required to conduct research, they did so anyway, for that was the road to professional advancement.[73] Hutchins could overturn the college's curriculum, but he could not overturn the system of professions.

Despite its success, the Chicago plan, like most core programs of the 1930s, withered away under the power of departmental interests. The university faculty ultimately rejected Hutchins' "theology of education" as being "at war with the modern temper" and returned to a freer system of electives.[74] The composition requirement remained, but in the late 1930s, as departmental interests reasserted themselves, the third segment of the course emphasized writing papers using the conventions of various disciplines (again anticipating developments in the WAC movement of the 1980s). Faculty were not content with writing merely as an aid to learning; they expected students to attempt the discourse of the disciplines—research papers, reviews, and so on. Specialization resisted a community that was formed on any single philosophy, and composition could only reflect disciplinary divisions, not transcend them. Ultimately, the Chicago plan's approach to composition had little influence; it depended too much on interdisciplinary cooperation and thus slighted the professional interests of departments, particularly English. But it is an important instance of a college systematically exploring the possibilities of using writing as an aid to reading—and therefore learning—academic material.

Hutchins' program finally received a thorough trial at a small, private liberal arts college, St. John's at Annapolis (and, later, at Santa Fe), whose curriculum illustrated the ideal uses of writing from the perspective of liberal culture. On the brink of financial failure in 1937, the college called in two former Rhodes scholars, Stringfellow Barr and Scott Buchanan, whom Hutchins had earlier invited to Chicago to help implement his program. They built the new curriculum around the reading of the 120 great books in discussion groups, supplemented by Oxbridge-style tutorials in mathematics, music, and languages (Greek and French), with laboratory work in the sciences. As in the elite British universities, students wrote essays or translations for all their tutorials (even in mathematics), which the tutors then critiqued but did not grade. Each year students wrote an "annual essay," and seniors wrote a "thesis," which was not defended in the traditional manner but only discussed with faculty members. These essays and theses were in no sense research papers. The college discouraged the use of secondary materials and footnotes; the object was not to trace influences or place ideas and texts in historical context but to struggle with the great ideas (*essay* in its etymological sense: an attempt or trial). The student was expected to produce a piece of writing which "bears traces of this struggle," as the dean of St. John's College at Santa Fe, James Carey, put it. Even if a student's thesis was seriously defective in its writing, the student could pass the oral examination on it with honors. For St. John's College (as for Plato), writing was somehow suspect, capable of concealing truth that face-to-face discussion revealed.[75]

St. John's may have been, as Fredrick Rudolph says, "the first, and only, intellectual community in the history of American higher education."[76] In an almost monastic way, the college created a homogeneous intellectual climate by excluding any specialization, any academic discourse community but its own. All faculty had the rank of tutor and were, in theory, able to conduct a seminar on any of the great books or any tutorial in English, Greek, or French. It was the generalists' dream made flesh. There was no composition course, no curricular question of what or how to write, of who would teach writing.[77] There was one required curriculum, one required conversation. But St. John's achieved this unity, as liberal culture had always done, by narrowing the boundaries and "raising the standards" of discourse to such an extent that other communities were excluded from the conversation.

St. John's curricular unity and its tradition of collegewide writing were of course the exception. Elsewhere in higher education, the literary generalists' romantic assumptions about writing and culture, combined with a need to professionalize in the new system of mass education, led to a divorce between literacy instruction and literary instruction that prevented the old pedagogy from making a successful transition from an oral, face-to-face culture to an industrial society dominated by specialized written discourse. Liberal culture chose to uphold the claims of discipline and excellence over inclusiveness and equity, to define general education in its own specific terms, and to defend that definition by maintaining its curricular turf.

The humanities became professionalized disciplines, as they had to in order to survive in the new university. And when they did so, they evolved discourse communities that made rhetoric largely transparent and writing instruction a marginal activity, as in other disciplines. English departments found themselves increasingly specialized, isolated from the range of activities that had taught students language in the old curriculum and extracurriculum and from the range of texts and ideas that students wrote about across the curriculum. Speech professors broke away from English departments in the 1910s and 1920s to join the social sciences, correctly sensing that their progressive and populist assumptions about the importance of democratic rhetoric (largely rural and midwestern in orientation) had little place in English departments devoted to an urbane and predominantly eastern liberal culture. Debate went with the speech professors to become yet another specialty, curricular or extracurricular, rather than an integral part of the humanities' version of general education. Although English departments often sponsored student theatricals and even theater courses in the early twentieth century, faculty interested in teaching students to perform literature, as well as to read and appreciate it, founded theater departments attached to fine arts schools or found a home in speech departments. Journalism courses were often housed in English departments until journalism professionalized and created its own departments and schools.[78] Even the formal study of language, now called *linguistics,* came to focus on oral rather than written texts and had only loose ties with literary study as practiced in English departments.

Through its great-books version of general education, liberal culture tried to build academic community in its own image but at the same time maintain an insular disciplinary position, though its purposes—maintaining standards of culture and taste—were not the only ones in the new university and not the most important ones, at least from the perspective of other departments. Generating new knowledge and promoting rational social change lay at the heart of the new institution, and another, more forward-looking version of general education soon challenged the great books.

7

WRITING AND
PROGRESSIVE EDUCATION

The search for community took a very different direction in the social sciences than it did either among advocates of liberal culture in the humanities or among the administrative progressives in their drive for "social efficiency." The collection of disciplines that came to be known as the social sciences created a version of general education that was closely associated with Deweyan progressive education.[1] Progressives in the Deweyan mold—unlike the administrative progressives I examined in chapter 5—had the theoretical tools and the philosophical vision to create a form of general education with cross-curricular writing at its center. Yet they did not. The reasons are as complex as progressive education itself, and as full of contradictions.

Progressive education made profound theoretical contributions to writing instruction. John Dewey's early colleague at Michigan, Fred Newton Scott, articulated a social or (to use Berlin's term) *transactional theory* of composition, which offered a sound alternative to the narrow positivism of the administrative progressives or the elitism of liberal culture. Scott trained a generation of reformers in English—Gertrude Buck, Sterling Andrus Leonard, and Ruth Mary Weeks, among others—who developed his notions of composition as a "growth," a complex organic activity incapable of being analyzed on the atomistic industrial model or taught through drill and remediation. In the 1910s and 1920s, Dewey's followers first gave serious consideration to writing as a developing process and first studied writing instruction using empirical methods. Indeed, Deweyan progressives first recognized the broad significance of writing instruction in modern print culture, the "paper civilization" as another progressive, Harold Rugg, termed it.[2]

Nor did they lack vision. Dewey and many of his followers hoped to create a new American community by designing a new integrated curriculum, with communication as its motive center. A reformed general education would produce a generation of articulate citizens who, through improved communication, would heal the divisions in industrial democracy and transcend its dehumanizing specialization and alienation. Like the social sciences out of which it grew, the progressive version of general education focused on the future, not on the idealized past of liberal culture or on the status quo of social efficiency. The goal of progressive general education was to prepare students to transform the social order into a new community, not to recapture the glory of a past one or merely to oil the gears of the current system. Its approach was fundamentally instrumentalist; ideas were plans for action, instruments for adapting to and transforming the environment; they were not fixed repositories of essential truth. The method of education for the progressives and the method of inquiry in the social sciences lay in problem solving; the goal of both education and social scientific inquiry was pragmatic.[3]

But the Deweyan progressives never translated their theoretical insights and their social vision into a coherent plan for teaching written communication in the academic disciplines, much less into practical programs, which might have developed into discipline-specific or systemwide pedagogical traditions. That failure, like the broader failure of progressive education, can be traced to the movement's inability to overcome its profound internal contradictions and to offer an alternative—pedagogical and political—that would appeal to lay leaders, teachers, and professionals in disciplines outside the progressive educators' stronghold in new departments of education.[4] Education departments were largely separate from other departments, including the social sciences, a fact that discouraged dialogue between Deweyan progressives and other faculty on the role that writing might play in discipline-specific learning. Ironically, the hard-won professionalism and disciplinary status that progressive educators found in departments of education kept them from achieving the curricular unity their discipline sought and kept them from exploring the role of writing in learning with the active participation of other disciplines.

Moreover, in cross-curricular writing instruction, as in many other areas, Dewey's followers split between two misreadings of the master: an expressivist, child-centered individualism versus an activist, social reformism. Unable to agree on the structure and purpose of curriculum, much less on the role of writing in it, the progressives never developed their notion of writing instruction in the disciplines beyond a vague allegiance to William Heard Kilpatrick's project method. Lacking a coherent alternative, Deweyan progressives housed in the new education departments were unable to counter the organizational inertia of social efficiency in the school bureaucracy or the entrenched position of liberal culture in the humanities. Later, when their opponents gained strength in the early 1950s, the progressives never successfully countered the charge (often justified) that they ignored writing instruction. But before turning to the divisions in progressive writing pedagogy, I look at the animating vision: Dewey on communication in the curriculum.

Community, Communication, and Curriculum

In the wake of social Darwinism, a generation of American social reformers—Jane Addams, Mary Parker Follett, Charles Horton Cooley, John Dewey—drew on organic metaphors to explain the role of communication in the shift from the small-town to the urban community. If society was an evolving organism, progressing from simple face-to-face agricultural communities to complex urban-industrial centers, then the increasing differentiation of parts must be accompanied by increasing integration for the organism to survive and function. These reformers saw more efficient communication, through expanding education and technology, as the means of achieving social integration in mass society. To those who feared that the complex organization of urban-industrial America would bring alienation, social disintegration, and a breakdown of shared values, organicist theory replied that improved communication—taught in new child-centered schools—would strengthen common values, encourage mutual sympathy, disseminate useful knowledge, and give each citizen a sense of individual importance and potential in the complex social organism. Cooperation would inevitably follow communication. In this view, specialization posed no insurmountable threat to community, for improved communication would mediate social conflicts and create a rational consensus founded on science.[5]

As Dewey argued in his 1916 *Democracy in Education*, technological advances had created a nation "composed of different groups with different traditional customs," and it was the schools' duty to bring community, counteracting "the centrifugal forces set up by juxtaposition of different groups within one and the same political unit."[6] Dewey set out to create schools that would lead to a new and more democratic American community through consensus, not the efficient "man and steel machine" of the administrative progressives, arrived at by coercion. "The parts of a machine work with a maximum of cooperativeness for a common result, but they do not form a community," Dewey wrote. In a true community, all members are "cognizant of the common end and all interested in it so that they regulate their specific activity in view of it. But this would involve communication. . . . Consensus demands communication" (7–8).

From the beginnings of the progressive education movement, Dewey and his followers saw the student as an active participant in the process of learning, not as a passive receptor of discrete information or as a mass of intellectual potential to be developed by mental discipline. Schools, they agreed, shape students; but students also shape schools—as do a host of other forces in a complex set of social transactions which depend on communication. Active, participatory, social, *transactional* instruction would use language to help create community out of American diversity. Dewey's instrumentalist theory saw individual development as a progressive growth in communicative power, which gradually integrated the child into the community and made her a consciously functioning part of a rational, organic whole, a social being forming, as well as formed by, her environment. Thus, improved education in communication would serve both the evolving individual and the evolving society.

But Dewey's goal for progressive education was not only a child-centered pedagogy based on transactional communication but also a new curriculum to replace the old, a curriculum "that would begin with the experience of the learners and end with the organized subjects that represented the cumulative experience of the race."[7] Dewey's instrumentalist method of linking education to society lay in experience, but not in random experience. The new curriculum must select and organize activities drawn from life outside the classroom to show their relation to material from the organized disciplines. Students "learn by doing," as well as by reading, but always under the careful guidance of a teacher steeped in a recognized discipline. In this view, growth in writing ability meant that students would move toward acquiring the conventions of academic disciplines. Curriculum would consciously and carefully balance the interests of the learner with the demands of disciplines.

With uncharacteristic venom, Dewey attacked the sentimentalism of one group of his followers: the child-centered progressives who trusted "planlessness" to develop students' "independent thinking." Intellectual growth, he insisted, must be "systematically wrought out in cooperation with experienced teachers, knowledgeable in their own [disciplinary] traditions."[8] The curriculum must not simply give students new experiences; these new experiences must be "related intellectually to earlier experiences, and this means that there be some advance made in conscious articulation of facts and ideas"—that is, in the use of spoken and written language. A student's experience "can expand into the future only as it is also enlarged to take in the past"— both the student's past experiences and those of the human race as organized through academic disciplines.[9]

In the hands of his followers, notably William Heard Kilpatrick, Dewey's carefully wrought balance tipped away from broader social and disciplinary concerns and toward a narrow focus on the experience of the student. Kilpatrick resisted attempts by the disciplines to structure students' experiences. Such "fixed-in-advance" subject matter, he argued, was the original cause of curricular stagnation and, in the rapidly changing modern world, amounted to a crude guess at the knowledge that students would need as adults. Instead, Kilpatrick hoped to teach students "*how* to think, not *what* to think." Problem solving became a technique to be taught, a method in itself, not an activity embedded in disciplinary matrices. Attempts to teach the process of thinking independent of disciplinary contexts tended to separate writing from the disciplinary organization of knowledge (which of course schools and colleges never gave up). In Kilpatrick's view, writing was as transparent in education as in society. Students would simply write as an ordinary and natural part of their activities, expressing themselves and communicating with others in their various pursuits, not as a deliberately structured process leading systematically to competence in some specific field or fields. For example, students interested in the workings of "a wash-wringer or the ice-cream freezer at home" would describe their functioning "as a basis for such investigation of the working of industries." Or classes might write proposals for "vacant lot gardening, cleaning up alleys, and innumerable other improvements."[10] What they would not do, in Kilpatrick's approach, is learn the written conventions of a discipline, for those, like its knowledge, might become obsolete or, worse yet, hinder the child's independent thinking.

Kilpatrick's great pedagogical innovation, the project method, offered a potentially important site for writing in the curriculum. Writing, in Kilpatrick's view, might be a part of a project to the extent that the project mirrors human activities where writing is necessary and makes education lifelike. The genres of student writing should echo the genres of adult activity: a student report on the quality of milk teaches chemistry, a student newspaper article on slum conditions teaches social studies, a student novel or short story teaches literature. For example, students at Kilpatrick's Lincoln High School at Teachers' College (Columbia) wrote journalism, fiction, and poetry in a regular magazine they published themselves.[11] But in other schools, with less able faculty, the relations between writing as lifelike activity and the disciplinary paradigms, which continued to organize secondary and higher education, were all too often dispensed with, in the name of progressive education. Teachers found it far easier to add isolated projects to the old subject-dominated curriculum than to structure school writing activities in a new curriculum that led coherently from the child's experiences to the intellectual order of the disciplines, from expressive to transactional writing (to borrow James Britton's terms). Because progressive educators had not formulated any intrinsic relationship between expressive student discourse and the transactional discourse of the disciplines, project-centered writing often came to be seen as an "enrichment" activity, an adjunct to the regular curriculum for brighter or more creative students instead of as an integral part of it.[12] Dewey himself found merit in the idea of projects, but as early as 1921 he warned that "too many projects were already so trivial as to be miseducative."[13] Indeed, the project method never developed into a vital tradition in the disciplines, and its potential for writing instruction went unrealized.

That the Deweyan progressives never came to terms with writing in the disciplines is understandable given the disciplinary structure of American education. The study of education along progressive lines quickly became a professional discipline itself, what Arthur Bestor and other critics deridingly called the "interlocking directorate of professional educationists."[14] This disciplinary community formed its own distinct departments and colleges in America (unlike other nations where disciplines retained much more control over curriculum and pedagogy in the schools).[15] This separation from—and, all too often, antagonism with—other disciplines kept progressives from exploring the relationship between secondary education and specific disciplinary inquiry. Progressive educators have never found it necessary, either intellectually or organizationally, to come to terms with the academic disciplines, to investigate along with colleagues in other disciplines what experiences (in the Deweyan sense) lead students to engage disciplinary knowledge in their writing and how those experiences should be arranged and structured to make that written engagement most useful in teaching. Moreover, the few English faculty who took an active interest in composition pedagogy and research (progressive or otherwise) were marginalized within their own departments. As a result, secondary education continued to follow the industrial model: on the one hand, teaching specific, discrete information; on the other hand, teaching generalized, universal "skills"—how to write or learn or think. In the great uncharted middle lay the vital activity of disciplines: the stuff out of which genuinely communicative and educative student writing might come.

But by the same token, the institutional split between pedagogy and "content" gave academic disciplines in colleges and universities yet another reason to devote little of their considerable research energy to the question of how best to initiate students into the discourse of their disciplinary communities. And such discipline-specific pedagogical research as there was had little status among academics and therefore little influence.

Expressivists on Writing in the Disciplines

Fruitful dialogue on writing and learning was impeded not only by divisions between progressive educators and the traditional disciplines but also by a split within progressive education itself. Two stereotypes of progressive education grew up in the 1920s and 1930s and captured, in a sense, the deep tension within the movement's approach to writing, a tension that prevented Deweyan progressives from developing a coherent and persuasive alternative to the writing pedagogies of social efficiency and liberal culture. First, there was the progressive as Bohemian, the self-absorbed individualist teaching children to write avant-garde poetry under a tree while they neglected their spelling. Second, there was the progressive as parlor-pink radical, teaching children to write subversive tracts while they neglected their spelling. To those who had read their Dewey, both were gross caricatures of his philosophy and methods. Yet these stereotypes of progressive writing instruction point to the deep division in progressive thought between those who emphasized writing (and education) as a vehicle for individual self-revelation and improvement and those who emphasized its uses for social reconstruction and improvement. Clearly the two are not incompatible, as Dewey's educational philosophy amply demonstrated, but in the highly charged political atmosphere of the interbellum era, subtleties of Deweyan doctrine were often lost and, in the process, so was the potential for a coherent progressive approach to writing in the disciplines.

The child-centered, individualist strain of progressivism—what Cremin calls its "virulent sentimentalism"—held neoromantic or "expressivist" views of writing instruction (Berlin's term). Expressivist approaches began just after the turn of the century and continued through many versions to the present. All focused on cultivating the student's inner promptings, her originality, imagination, integrity, and authentic voice—romantic qualities which lay beyond rhetorical principles.[16] Expressivists distrusted direct methods of instruction, preferring to evoke writing from students with techniques designed to stimulate the innate potential of the unconscious mind. These techniques were drawn from models of therapy (Freudian in the 1920s and Gestalt in the 1930s) that attempted to free student writers from the inhibitions that blocked their creativity. Writing was thus an essentially subjective, mysterious response to individual experience, and its teaching a set of techniques for evoking that response.

Expressivists dismissed the established genres and styles of academic writing in the disciplines as too confining and encouraged students to find more creative approaches for writing about experience, whether studying English or other subjects. At the famous Lincoln High School at Teachers' College (Columbia), students wrote informal essays in journalistic and literary genres on scientific and historical topics ("In Defense of the Snake"; "Secret History of the Count de Remi"; "The Santo Domingo Corn Dance").[17] These essays were the result of research and observation but clearly engaged the students' interest and creativity.

Hughes Mearns, the guru of expressive writing in the 1920s (and a Lincoln teacher), anticipated a contemporary version of process-based pedagogy by insisting that "the method is writing and revision, many times repeated." He reveled in constant experiment, "the beauty of imperfection," as he called it, and put mechanical correctness as a last, though important, step in writing. Mearns was also the forebear of Ken Macrorie, Peter Elbow, and other contemporary expressivists in his attacks on "the demon of inhibition," which blocks writers' creativity, and in his insistence that teachers should themselves be writers.

But the expressivist approach to writing held little appeal for the traditional disciplines, for its goals lay outside their purview. In the most influential statement of expressivist philosophy, *The Child-Centered School,* Harold Rugg and Anne Shumaker (Mearns' colleagues at Lincoln) insisted that authentic writing must come out of "no formal course of study, no planned list of topics arranged in serial order" (255). The goal was the "enhancement of personality," not the orderly acquisition of knowledge. Knowledge would inevitably come out of the student's unfettered pursuit of her interests—a doctrine that Dewey called "really stupid" but one that appealed to teachers frustrated by the routine and rigidity of the college-dominated curriculum.[18]

At small, selective, progressive schools like Lincoln, where teachers were well versed in their disciplines, the method produced results that impressed even the most vocal critics of progressive education.[19] Teachers could individually guide students to writing experiences that not only enhanced personality but also elucidated the content of the disciplines. In less hospitable environments, with less knowledgeable teachers, the method could not reconcile the interests of the child with the demands of the discipline and became, its critics charged, an excuse for much educational faddishness and tomfoolery. So grew up the stereotype of the student in a progressive classroom writing about his navel instead of his history.

Like the advocates of liberal culture, with whom they shared many neoromantic assumptions, the expressivists attacked the commercialism and superficiality of modern industrial society. The specialization and professionalization of the disciplines was, for them, yet another source of division and inhibition. But unlike the proponents of liberal culture, the expressivists hoped to unleash creativity in *all* students, not preserve disciplinary standards by teaching creative writing only to the gifted. They saw themselves as rebellious artists, battling to free education and, with it, America from the modern evils of bureaucracy, alienation, competition—and some ancient evils as well—religious and sexual repression. A creative revolution in consciousness, begun in the schools, would usher in a new age of community and harmony.[20] The organization of the academic disciplines and the mundane business of teaching discipline-specific writing seemed irrelevant. In time, expressivist methods found a home in specialized creative-writing classes, in one tradition of general-composition instruction, and, most recently, in a segment of the contemporary writing-across-the-curriculum movement (see chapter 9). But until the 1980s, the expressivists never made an impact on writing pedagogy outside English departments.

Social Reformism and Writing: The Correlated Curriculum

The second stereotype of progressive education, the political radical, gained momentum in the 1930s as reformers sought more direct means of creating a new community through secondary education. For cross-curricular writing instruction, the most important of these efforts was the correlated-curriculum movement, an attempt to abolish the formal disciplinary structure and to construct a new and unified curriculum. In a correlated or "fused" curriculum, writing would be integrated into all subjects, and all teachers would be equally responsible for teaching it in conjunction with a whole range of student experiences. Correlation would finesse the problem of writing in the disciplines by transcending the disciplinary organization of curriculum.

The idea of correlation (sometimes called *integration* or *fusion*) had gained currency before World War I in the first wave of progressive reform. In a widely circulated 1913 article, NCTE founder James Fleming Hosic argued that teaching writing in all areas of the curriculum would counteract the "overspecialization" of modern schools, "which can only result in mutual lack of sympathy, and which tends to disintegrate the life of the student instead of unifying and harmonizing it." Writing instruction throughout the curriculum would provide for the student a "consistent unifying of his life" and help schools see "boys and girls as developing beings with whole, undivided lives."[21] "Correlation of subjects" was one of the founding principles of the

Progressive Education Association (PEA) in 1919, encouraging the "direct and indirect contact with the world and its activities and the experience thus gained."[22]

But it was the social dislocations of 1930s that finally brought progressives to attempt a radical restructuring of curriculum. In the fall of 1930, as America was just awakening to the enormity of the Great Depression, the new president of the NCTE, Ruth Mary Weeks, delivered an inaugural address, which she hoped would launch a restructuring not only of English teaching but also of the entire school curriculum and, beyond that, of industrial capitalism itself.[23] This Kansas City high-school English teacher (a former student of Fred Newton Scott) and other influential progressives (such as PEA president George S. Counts) had an explicit political agenda behind their curricular reforms: they would use the schools to reconstruct society along what they considered more democratic and cooperative lines. "American industry," Weeks wrote, "is not yet a democratic institution; but it is destined so to be, and the problem of public education is to make it sanely and efficiently so."[24] Weeks, like Counts and other "social reconstructionists" as they called themselves, believed that industrial democracies would inevitably evolve toward "the socialization of production [public ownership and state control] to a much larger extent than we have become accustomed to expect, and the democratizing of industry as the workers themselves share more and more in the direction of business."[25] For America to achieve such "industrial democracy," schools must teach students from all social classes to understand (and be able to direct) the whole industrial, economic, and political life of the nation—the "correlations" among the social forces which shape (and would be shaped by) the students' lives (46). Weeks was convinced that only through a correlated or fused curriculum could American schools teach "the duty of large scale social thinking" and produce "labor which is prepared for industrial democracy" (48).

Despite their frequent criticisms of industrial capitalism, the social reconstructionists were not Marxists but rather what came to be called New Deal liberals; in fact, they often argued that "industrial democracy," inculcated by public schools, was the nation's best defense against a Marxist revolution. The sweeping social changes enacted by government during President Franklin Roosevelt's first term gave Weeks, Counts, and other theorists of the movement confidence that schools could reconstruct society by reconstructing themselves.[26]

During the turbulent 1930s, this version of progressive education held out the promise of a curriculum that could bring genuine, though moderate, social reform. It offered a liberal alternative to the conservatism of liberal culture and social efficiency. In contrast to the apolitical stance of the others, social reconstructionists explicitly promoted political goals for the schools. "Every teacher," Weeks wrote, "will work from a clearly formulated social and economic philosophy; and the pivotal and central fact in public schooling will at last be a social ideal."[27] The correlated curriculum was at bottom a critique of the administrative progressives' curricular model of social efficiency. An integrated curriculum "most successfully trains not for mere adjustment to life as it is, but for building a new and better world."[28] But Weeks and her allies implicitly attacked the humanists' curricular position as well because it relied on mental discipline instead of having a transactional pedagogy and because it rigidly defended traditional disciplinary boundaries. Schools were not to be merely the keepers of tradition; they were to be a third force in society, gradually transforming "on one hand the capitalist who cannot understand industrial democracy; on the other, labor which is unprepared for industrial democracy."[29]

In 1930, Weeks appointed an NCTE subcommittee, which she herself headed, to study various means of integrating or correlating subjects—the crucial step in restructuring the schools along transactional lines. The subcommittee's report, *A Correlated Curriculum* (1936), appeared six years later. "Meaningful student experiences," Weeks said in the report's introduction, were the bricks of sound schools, but "an integrated curriculum furnishes the straw and clay for these educational bricks."[30] Without a new basis for organizing instruction, student-centered reforms would crumble. In a society with "no general information and no inherited traditions or scale of values by which to pick out a pattern from the educational pieces rattling in the educational puzzle box of the curriculum," only an integrated curriculum in which subjects were fused with one another and with the students' experience can overcome alienation and "prevent students from viewing the world with purposeless despair."[31]

Although *A Correlated Curriculum* was clear and challenging in its theoretical framework, its practical applications of Deweyan transactional theory were timid and predictable—perhaps because the committee was not proposing a model curriculum but surveying current practice to illustrate a wide range of possible models. In its survey of some sixty programs, *A Correlated Curriculum* cautiously moved from "Correlation of English with Other Fields through Incidental References and Isolated Projects," to "An English Course Based on Correlation with Other Subjects but Not Implying the Modification of Courses in Any Other Field," to "Fusion of Subjects and Groups of Subjects," and finally to the ideal: "Integration of All Educational Subjects or Transcending Subject-Matter Divisions." There was something for everyone to call correlation: writing about nature in English compositions, reading historical background in a literature class, or reading a historical novel in a history class. But taken as a whole, the report read less like a "recasting of the whole educational program in the mold of a central purpose"— the committee's avowed intention—and more like "English as a tool for other disciplines" or "the haphazard enrichment of English by materials from related fields," which Weeks deplores in the introduction.[32]

The means of achieving curricular unity and the role of writing within that new unity remained vague: "As English is a study of the tool by which all knowledge is communicated and the repository in which all knowledge is deposited, English naturally becomes the pivot and binding element in any such curricular experiment" (283). If we brush away the grand phrasing, this amounts to saying that students speak, read, and write in the English language. The committee was unsure whether disciplinary divisions should continue to exist, but simply be better "coordinated" (and if so how they should be divided and linked), or, alternatively, whether all instruction should be "fused" around thought centers, social functions, core projects, "culture epoches," or some other rubric, with each teacher supervising all her students' instruction and calling upon specialists in, say, writing or chemistry only when necessary.

Even in the final chapter, "Complete Integration," a coherent curriculum with a clear political agenda never emerged. Liberal and radical programs—the New York City Dalton School's "socio-historical" critique of "cultures in conflict," for example—stood without comment beside very conservative ones, such as the University of Chicago High School's great-books program. In the book's conclusion, Weeks acknowledged the gap between her vision of a correlated curriculum for a new industrial democracy and the reality of educational practice within a heterogeneous urban society. "Our highly specialized culture," she complained, "has this great defect as compared with the encyclopedic culture of our fathers; it creates servants, not masters, of life." And she fell back on religious and romantic metaphors (which recall to the modern reader that old "encyclopedic culture"). "The minute specialization of modern life has been like the dissection and analysis of the parts of a butterfly. . . . How [does one] reanimate the butterfly?" (286). Correlation, she concluded, would require educators to make a leap of faith, "to adopt the Biblical motto, 'Leave all and follow me' " (278). In a sense, the very structure of the report had forced this conclusion. The committee began with the assumption that "the organization of the curriculum as a whole on a correlative basis demands that educators develop a philosophy of education and of life, that they formulate a social program, that they commit themselves to some scale of values" (196). The survey of curricular experiments implicitly showed that there were many philosophies, social programs, and scales of value in America, of which "industrial democracy" was but one. The absence of "the encyclopedic culture of our fathers" made a leap of faith compulsory if curriculum were to be correlated, but not everyone would leap the same way.

Correlation in Practice

Correlation received its major test in the PEA's Eight-Year Study, a nationwide experiment involving thirty schools from 1933 to

1941. The schools were almost all upper or middle class, with a high proportion of private or university laboratory schools, though public schools in a few large cities, such as Denver and Los Angeles, participated. Many cooperating colleges, including most of the prestigious eastern universities, gave the thirty schools' graduates a dispensation from standard admissions examinations, which turned out to be unnecessary: graduates of the programs did well, both on standardized tests and in college. The great challenge turned out to be dealing with almost unlimited curricular freedom. One principal expressed the fears of many, "My teachers and I do not know what to do with this freedom. It challenges and frightens us. I fear that we have come to love our chains."[33]

Almost all of the experimental programs involved some form of English–social studies cooperation, though the complete fusion of subjects was rare, even in private and laboratory schools. Judging from the extensive reports of curricular and classroom practice, writing instruction became part of the project method, which is to say it was submerged in student activities and disappeared as a formal part of the curriculum. Nevertheless, supporters of correlation often suggested that correlation improved students' use of language, including their writing. Reports from teachers in correlation programs emphasized heightened interest and motivation (for their students and for themselves); more discussion, reading, and writing; along with the other social benefits that were the central goal, such as developing a social conscience and an international consciousness. Several small empirical studies at specific schools verified that correlation increased students' scores on nationally normed tests of reading comprehension, language usage, and composition.[34] But there were few data on which to base firm conclusions.

Indeed, the massive evaluation of student performance in the thirty schools did not even attempt to measure writing ability or performance, though it did attempt to measure such intangibles as "social sensitivity," "appreciation of literature and art," and "personal and social adjustment." Moreover, the evaluators moved away from essay examinations in all fields during the course of the study and toward the new-type tests which were coming to dominate all educational evaluation in the 1930s.[35]

In any case, correlation never affected more than a fraction of America's schools. No study ever found more than 8 percent of secondary schools with any form of correlation. The most comprehensive study, that done by the Bureau of Education in 1949, found 3.5 percent of secondary schools with some kind of "core," but 86 percent of these were junior-high civics or "problems of living" courses; and of the 14 percent in senior highs, the majority were for special tracks within comprehensive high schools—usually college preparatory—or in lab schools attached to colleges' education departments.[36] Of the thirty schools that participated in the PEA's Eight-Year Study, none retained an integrated class for more than a year after the study, and most dropped or seriously modified them before the experiment ended. The antiprogressive backlash of the late 1940s and 1950s ended correlation experiments almost entirely.[37] Clearly, public school boards and administrators were not attracted to correlation as a general reform, though they adapted aspects of it for specific (which is to say, specialized) purposes, without adopting either its organizational structure or its theoretical and political assumptions. The vestiges of correlation that endured— the "problems of democracy" course or the junior-high civics course, for example—did so only if they fit easily into the existing disciplinary structure and pursued no controversial agenda.[38]

Teachers and Disciplines React to Correlation

Correlation, both the experiments and the subcommittee's report, aroused strong and generally negative reactions from teachers and disciplines. Weeks had envisioned correlation creating a well-trained teaching corps who planned curriculum democratically. And indeed, teachers in experimental programs generally supported the reforms enthusiastically (and teachers not selected for the programs sometimes expressed resentment at not having been chosen).[39] But as the correlation experiments continued through the 1930s, it became clear that, even where teachers had greater control, they did not represent a united front. In some correlated programs, teachers clashed with administrators and school boards over pedagogical issues. Teachers complained that by giving students greater freedom and individual instruction, correlated or fused programs emphasized student differences and prevented slower students from making the progress that they could with structured, discipline-specific drill and practice.[40] More often, teachers split along disciplinary lines. In several correlated programs, English, art, and music teachers demanded "greater freedom of thought and action" than they had when "dominated by a social sciences theme."[41] Correlation did not erase disciplinary loyalties or interests. Try as they might, reform-minded administrators could not dismantle the old structures without teachers reverting to them when negotiating new ones.

Outside the correlated programs, turf issues also dominated the debate over correlation. English rightly saw itself as the weaker partner in curricular marriages. Articles appeared with such provocative titles as Philip R. Jenkins' "Is English Going Out?"[42] Comments in a 1945 *English Journal* reader survey ran four to one against correlation, with most citing practical problems: increased class sizes or the loss of courses, instructional time, and prestige to social studies in a curriculum with an explicitly social-reformist agenda.[43] But there were theoretical objections as well.

Liberal culture saw correlation as yet another attack on an already-embattled discipline. Such critics as Percy V. Shelly chiefly feared that literary study would die out in American secondary schools unless students took specific courses in it "with a trained lover of literature as a guide."[44] Shelly conceded that studying novels and poems in social studies and biology "is not a bad thing" because it "helps to make tolerable such dismal sciences and adds to the stature and importance of literature" (351). But allowing history and social studies into English class (except as background information) was "to pervert the study of literature." Clearly there was more at stake than curricular jurisdiction. "Our most cherished values," Shelly warned, are threatened by this "extremely dangerous . . . educational hobby horse of the moment" (349).

Although liberal culture rarely cast the debate in political terms, it clearly distrusted the social agenda of correlation. "To-day the attempt is being made," Shelly warned, "to subordinate literature and the study of literature to a new religion—the religion of humanity—and to a new morality—the morality of 'social living' . . . for social reform, for a better 'community life,' for a better understanding of other races and nations, for world peace" (351). Liberal education in the Arnoldian sense, unlike this new "pragmatic liberalism" (Jenkins' term), had higher things to pursue—"to broaden and deepen our perceptions and sympathies and make for ourselves not merely a mind but a soul" and to "remain cognizant of the nature of our subject and of those deeper regions of personality to which it brings life and energy" (344).

Social studies also had much to say about integrating curriculum and, like English, little to say about sharing responsibility for writing instruction. From the social sciences' perspective, correlation, integration, or fusion generally meant some combination of history, political science, geography, civics, or "problems of democracy" centered around "life experiences" or "social living" units.[45] When educators from social studies mentioned writing or English as part of a fusion course, it was always as an adjunct. For example, *Teaching the Social Sciences in Secondary Schools,* a standard methods text from the late 1930s through the 1950s, advocated English–social studies fusion only if "the social studies teacher assumes full charge of the work of the other teachers" because only he has the "wide knowledge" necessary to coordinate the instruction around social themes. Social studies would "provide the basis of the work in composition" and "outside reading" of historical novels would provide the content for literary study.[46] This view of social studies as the core of the curriculum served the interests of the discipline, of course, but it was also a perfectly logical perspective given the social and political orientation of the whole correlation movement. However, social studies' perspective on correlation lent credence to English teachers' dire predictions of the death of literature in the schools, and it fueled disciplinary rivalries, particularly when depression-era funding cuts forced stiff competition for curricular resources.[47]

217

Administrators and Parents React to Correlation

The administrative progressives also resisted correlation, though for different reasons than liberal culture had. In 1937, *English Journal* asked the senior advocate of job study and social efficiency, Franklin Bobbitt, to review *A Correlated Curriculum* after it had appeared in 1936. The English department cannot begin correlating, he predictably argued, until it has "formulated its objectives with sufficient exactness." "To improve the efficiency of its labors," the department must define the specific tasks and set about teaching them. Unless it does so, no program, "whether fused, semifused, or independent, can fully meet the urgent need of our population."[48] Social efficiency rejected the most basic curricular assumption of correlation: that correlation of disciplines would transform education and build a new, more democratic community. "A closer synergism among the parts," Bobbitt wrote, "can occur only when the wholeness or the unity appears first, and the parts are differentiated therefrom."[49] Reading, writing, and speaking consisted of discrete, analyzable skills. The organization of instruction was irrelevant as long as those skills were taught. The traditional disciplines would do just fine as long as each teacher minded her own business and each discipline taught its assigned set of skills.

Administrative progressives also rejected the basic political assumption of correlation: that schools must educate students not for what they would *likely* do after schooling but for what they *wished* to do. Like liberal culture, social efficiency denied the schools a direct role in effecting social change (though for its own reasons). Increasing differentiation would inevitably increase social well-being. The society itself would develop according to its own structural dynamic; schools merely served that end by training students to play their differentiated roles. As one critic of correlation put it in 1936, teaching writing and speaking is "largely a technical job" for which the teacher has "no responsibility to shape the destinies of any individual or group, in any coming social crisis (whether on the scale of a world wide economic construction or on the scale of an afternoon tea)." One merely "performs well his part of the task of preparing the student for a mature life."[50] Administrative progressives considered the social reformists' program a threat, and they dropped their characteristic apolitical stance. Bobbitt charged educational reformers in the social sciences with using "the slogans of democracy as a mere protective smoke screen for a communistic offensive" and charged the "integrators" with presuming "to think and plan for the masses."[51]

In the swirl of ideological and turf battles, pedagogical questions were largely brushed aside, including questions about the role of writing in the disciplines. The drive toward administrative efficiency resisted or coopted reformers' efforts to introduce even limited amounts of extended writing. The widely used textbooks of Charles A. Beard and Harold Rugg, for example, contained numerous projects for student investigation and writing at the end of each chapter, and Beard also published collections of primary sources to accompany his texts to promote the kind of critical inquiry he favored. But soon textbook companies were producing workbooks and objective tests keyed to his texts, with fill-in-the-blank questions designed to drill students on factual knowledge.[52] Moreover, the political assumptions of the social reformers' textbooks aroused virulent opposition from administrators, school boards, and parents.[53] The issue was quickly reduced to *whether* the books and ideas would be used, not *how* they would be used. Beard, Rugg, and other progressive textbook authors never made a large issue of writing in social-science pedagogy, contenting themselves with fighting the more pressing battles over the content and aims of instruction.

Similarly, Deweyan progressives in the social sciences unsuccessfully resisted the administrative progressives' use of objective tests. A controversial 1934 American Historical Association (AHA) report called the tests a "menace to education" because they did not require students to "put forth continuous and constructive effort in *thinking* and *writing*" in the social sciences (italics mine), and the information and values they measured had no "meaning for the lives of pupils in society."[54] But the controversy over objective testing—the one burning educational issue of the 1930s that centered on writing—took on an overtly political character, which eclipsed the issue of writing and learning. Deweyan progressives primarily resisted "objective" tests on the grounds that they were not truly objective. Such tests were, the AHA said, inevitably biased toward one intellectual or political perspective and they were therefore a potentially coercive form of indoctrination.[55] Nevertheless, the objective-testing movement forged ahead, developing tests not only of knowledge but of social attitudes. Such tests, proponents claimed, would allow social studies teachers to measure how well students had absorbed the values and attitudes their courses taught, as well as students' factual knowledge—all without writing.

Parents also generally opposed correlation—so effectively, in fact, that their opposition became the most important reason cited for curtailing or drastically modifying programs.[56] From Oakland to Scarsdale, Minneapolis to Houston, parents organized to protest. Their most common argument was that a correlated curriculum taught their children less than a traditional curriculum, particularly in writing and mathematics. Administrators organized parent-teacher meetings and disseminated information about the new programs in an effort to defuse complaints. The most common defense was test scores. In every controlled trial, students in correlated programs did as well or better than those in traditional classes. But the complaints persisted, for the underlying issue was values, not knowledge; the hidden curriculum, not the published one. Parents resented what they correctly viewed as an attempt to promote values contrary to their own. They insisted it was not the job of a teacher to "take on psychological or family problems" or controversial political issues. In a more general sense, parents often feared the shift in teacher role— "so much talking" and "children wandering around the room at will," as one complained. Correlation was from their perspective a system of "thought control in the classroom," as another parent put it, and indeed the curricula were often specifically designed to change the attitudes of students and thus the political and economic structure of the nation.[57]

Parents, unlike teachers, had the wherewithal to change the system. In upper-middle-class Scarsdale, New York, a city with one of the first and most comprehensive experiments with the Dalton contract plan of individual study, parental pressure forced the board and administration to adopt a series of cutbacks. The Dalton plan accentuated the differences in student ability and maturity, parents complained, and allowed many students to fall behind in subjects for which they had little interest or aptitude. Parents found the results "undemocratic" and the school board finally agreed to reinstate regular classes and grading.[58] In the private high school in St. Louis where the PEA's Eight-Year Study began, parents "in the professional and business classes of the population" insisted that students needed to have "more specific experiences in English."[59] They demanded after-school "skills periods" for students to study grammar; soon these "became so important that the integrated course began to disintegrate," as the principal quipped (379). In many schools, "common learnings" or "core classes" first had their names changed to the less controversial "double period class," then became elective, and finally reverted to two separate classes. In a thorough reversal, correlated "core" courses sometimes evolved into even more specialized elective courses on such topics as "child development" or "psychology of daily living and occupational relations."[60] In the Denver schools, a model of progressivism for twenty years, parents protested the teacher-developed correlated course so vehemently that the school board abolished it. Significantly, English teachers who taught the correlated courses were reassigned to new remedial or skills-oriented courses with such titles as diagnostic English or instructional communication.[61]

From Correlation to Life Adjustment

The 1930s marked the last attempt to do away with the disciplinary structure in public education, and while the urge to create a unified community and shared responsibility for writing remained strong, it manifested itself in ways that acknowledged the permanence and power of the by-then-traditional disciplines, though disciplines had by no means defined their approach to writing in any coherent way.

The failure of correlation was thus significant. It illustrated to all—not least to the social reformists—how thoroughly and rapidly Americans had accepted a new tradition: education based not on a coherent philosophy but on an additive, differentiated structure of discrete disciplines. As Weeks pointed out in the introduction to *A Correlated Curriculum,* "It is, indeed, but a generation or two since English literature was taught in no other way than in relationship to the classics, philosophy, and history; since all training in composition was given in the content-courses."[62] But the "educational home-coming for English" she sought was thwarted at every turn by a tradition of specialization only four or five decades old. Parents, teachers, professional associations, and administrators chose differentiation over correlation and fusion.

It is ironic that in many schools and communities, the democratic process, which the reformers hoped to foster through the schools, was the very process that opponents used to defeat their reforms. Time after time, parents or teachers or both put pressure on school boards or administrators to restore familiar structures, in defiance of the educational experts. Perhaps the greatest irony was that the social reformists' vision of "community" so often conflicted with a community's vision of "community." These reformers harked back to an America of face-to-face communities—the homogeneous small towns where many of them were raised.[63] But the kind of unity they sought required a consensus that no longer existed, a consensus the reformers themselves lacked in their approach to writing, as well as to politics.

By the close of the 1930s, correlated or fused courses had come to be called *core courses* and the buzzword was no longer *correlation* but *life adjustment.* The change was more than in name alone. Gone was the emphasis on unifying the curriculum through fusing or correlating disciplines and with it the emphasis on social reform. Instead, curricular reformers returned to the social efficiency "skills" model, centered around themes "important to adolescents" rather than "important themes." As Weeks had warned, the administrative progressives' goal was to give students the tools necessary to "adjust" to adult life, not a unified philosophy to transform American life.[64] The PEA produced a series of reports organized, significantly, by disciplinary areas: *Science in General Education* (1938), *The Social Studies in General Education* (1940), and *Language in General Education*

(1940).[65] These reports provided the outlines for the "life adjustment" curricular reforms of the postwar era, including the emphasis on "communication skills" (see chapter 8). By the late 1940s, the PEA lost interest in the correlation projects, which had abandoned the most radical elements of the experiment already, and the organization itself died during the McCarthy era. The same methods text that had devoted a whole section to English–social studies correlation experiments in the 1935 edition, *Teaching the Social Sciences in Secondary Schools,* devoted only one sentence to it in the 1952 edition—merely noting that such experiments were no longer common.[66] Educational reformers clung to the dream of an academic community and with it the promise of a society whose members shared a "common learning." But in all the curricular oscillations yet to come, never again would a national movement call for the end of disciplinary boundaries. Ruth Mary Weeks continued to teach English at Paseo High School in Kansas City, Missouri, and turned her attention to reading research and her continuing campaign to end discriminatory work rules for women in education.

As Larry Cuban has pointed out, the Deweyan progressives had their greatest influence on elementary rather than on secondary pedagogy, for elementary education was not organized by disciplines. And the progressives' contributions to writing instruction were also felt most in the elementary school, where an interdisciplinary "language arts" approach became the norm. In the final analysis, progressive education affected writing instruction in secondary and higher education so little because reformers found no meaningful strategy, no vital genres, for introducing and sequencing writing in the disciplines. In their rush to reform curricula and teaching methods, Deweyan progressives never adequately answered the crucial question of what students should write and how they should be taught to write in a differentiated educational system.[67] Its tentative answer, that students should write about their experiences, ignored the demands of the disciplines which structured the curriculum. Thus progressive education never reached the delicate balance John Dewey had envisioned between the student experience and the disciplinary structure; nor did progressives even seek such a balance in any systematic way, divided as they were over matters pedagogical and political. The progressives' faith in the methods of science and the inevitability of progressive change, their professional isolation, their pursuit of sweeping educational reforms blinded them to the demands of other disciplines, other traditions, and thus to the vital contexts, rhetorical and educational, out of which writing and writing pedagogy must inevitably grow.

Nor did progressive education adequately answer the question of who should teach writing. Its tentative answer, that all teachers should help students improve their writing, presupposed an outmoded vision of community inadequate to deal with the fragmenting of discourse communities, disciplinary, social, and political, that carried on the manifold activities of writing and its teaching in modern America. In the compromises that Deweyan progressives made with social efficiency, writing as a transactional, social act was too readily left off of the agenda, and all too often progressive educators were content to let remediation and traditional pedagogy dominate writing instruction while they pursued other agendas.

In the postwar era, the progressives' critics would press for an academic model of instruction and higher "standards" based on the structure and goals of the disciplines. Dewey and progressive education became the villains instead of the heroes. In the backlash against progressive education, schools went "back to the basics" and to the disciplinary structure. Not until the late 1970s and early 1980s did the progressive vision reanimate writing instruction, though in ways so curiously indirect that their early-twentieth-century American heritage was often forgotten.

Writing in the Progressive Colleges

Although Deweyan progressives faced enormous difficulties in public schools, progressive methods profoundly influenced writing in colleges that had been founded or reorganized along Deweyan lines between the world wars. At Antioch University, the model of the progressive college, students combined socially oriented general-education courses, such as Finance 101 (each made a personal budget) and Aesthetics 111 (each reported on the design of a nearby city), with real-world experiences in industry or government arranged by the college. The curriculum specifically used writing assignments to spur the broad synthesis of knowledge and experience toward which it aimed. Each student was required to write a self-reflective paper, first as a freshman, then as a senior, to clarify his educational experience and to chart its direction at those two crucial periods in his education. A faculty advisor then discussed the paper with the student to help him consciously formulate his personal aims, not to evaluate his performance. Comprehensive written examinations over the general-education courses required a student to connect one course with another and the course work with his real-world experience, even when the courses did not systematically do so. And a final senior paper, usually the result of experience or experiment, as well as reading, capped the student's undergraduate years.[68]

At Bennington College and at Sarah Lawrence College, institutions specifically founded on progressive principles (in direct consultation with William Heard Kilpatrick at Bennington), writing was also an important part of learning. Students were required to complete a large interdisciplinary investigative project, almost always written, during their first two years, before they were allowed to begin the last two years. Class time was deliberately kept to a minimum to allow students time for investigation and writing. But even with this emphasis on intensive study of interdisciplinary problems through written projects, Bennington could not avoid a discipline-centered curriculum or evolve as integrated an approach to general education as Kilpatrick had wished. "The [disciplinary] divisions of the college," wrote its second president, Barbara Jones, "became something like separate schools, each offering rival schemes of general education."[69] The social sciences had their small working groups to investigate solutions to social problems; the humanities had their great books; the sciences their laboratory projects; the fine arts their fusion of curricular and extracurricular practice and performance. There would be social community and, as it turned out, a dominantly liberal political community, but not an intellectual one, except in the broadest terms. In the 1940s Bennington revised its curriculum to make a virtue of the necessity of disciplinary specialization. The goal became, as Jones put it, "to make available to all students, in the most effective way, the fundamental language of each of the important fields of human achievement . . . and to bring up for serious common consideration the main lines of philosophical conflict which divide us, as well as those traditional values which unite us, as members of American civilization."[70] Like the research universities, Bennington did not escape differentiation, but it did at least confront it by acknowledging that students could visit—if not inhabit—several of the disciplinary universes through their written projects.

Bennington's "sister in progressivism," Sarah Lawrence, also engaged students in social issues and activities through writing. Without grades or formal class meetings, the project method subsumed all other instructional methods. Students investigated problems that interested them, and New York City, only thirty minutes away, became a huge educational laboratory. For example, in one of the general-education "exploratory" courses in psychology, called Observation of Personality and Behavior, students walked through Harlem, then along Fifth Avenue, making notes on "ten people in different settings" and taking pictures. They then wrote characterizations of four of them to illustrate "significant types of personality produced by modern civilization."[71] One student in a sociology course claimed that stories of depression-era poverty were exaggerated, so her advisor arranged for her to do volunteer work in a relief bureau. Over a period of months, she wrote case histories and in the process changed her previous view. In literature courses students wrote analyses of texts in terms of contemporary social (rather than purely aesthetic) issues: "women and the conventions of society," "culture of social minority groups," and modern novels on economic problems. In conferences and small-group discussions, students were required to explain their research and defend their stands. This education was "liberal" in a new way, a political way, as upper-middle-class parents discovered when their children came home for vacation sounding like "parlor pinks," as one Bennington freshman's father noted.[72]

At Alexander Meiklejohn's Experimental College, attached to

the University of Wisconsin, writing also played a central role in what its founder called "this never-accomplished but never-to-be-abandoned enterprise of the human spirit—the search for unified understanding."[73] Meiklejohn began the college with a typical great-books curriculum, Greek literature in translation discussed in small groups, supplemented with Oxbridge-style tutorials. But the Experimental College quickly moved toward a progressive concern with contemporary problems and student interests. In the "Athens-America curriculum," as it came to be called, students read classical Greek literature and nineteenth-century American texts not as masterpieces to be admired but as examples of cultures solving problems. The goal of analyzing the past in its historical context was to enrich understanding of present problems and, Meiklejohn hoped, to build social values and active social involvement, which would lead the next generation to forge a new, uniquely American culture.

The writing assignments at the heart of the program—the only method of evaluation apart from discussions with students—often asked students to confront issues in a way that liberal culture avoided as irrelevant. After reading Thucydides, for example, freshmen were asked, "Describe the conflict about wealth with which Solon had to deal. What did Solon do about this conflict? . . . Do you find any similar conflict today? If so, what is your opinion and your attitude toward it?" (77). In proper progressive fashion, sophomores went to their home "region" and studied its cultural heritage, analyzed its values in relation to some institution "of greatest interest and closest acquaintance to" themselves, and made maps, charts, and illustrations. They were to turn in not only the final report but "any record of your attitude toward it as it developed during the progress of your work" (83). In other assignments, students imagined themselves ancient Greeks, American presidents, and so on. The genres were deliberately varied and provoking, mixing notes, journals, and tentative opinion statements with more conventional finished forms.

Faculty evaluations of students were also written, one version for the eyes of the student's next advisor-tutor (a new one each semester) and a different report for the student and his parents.

Reading these evaluations, one sees the faculty grappling with the problems of student writing on a deep level. Faculty commented on the medical and psychological, the cultural, economic, and ethnic factors that conditioned their students' writing. Some excerpts from the confidential reports about three students will illustrate.

[Jensen] missed most of his conferences, for which he always had excuses which he did not profess to regard too adequate. He couldn't get at what Henry Adams was saying, so he wrote nothing. Knowing he had an interest in horses, I proposed he write a paper on the evolution of the horse for his science period. He did. He made a sort of outline sketch from a technical book on the subject, cataloging periods and species with labels which I fear he understood no better than I. He is a likable boy and can be got to respond readily and volubly in most any argument on his own terms. On the whole, I think he is wasting his time.

In part [Joe's] trouble is imagination and organization; he saw little continuity between the chapters of his regional study until I pointed it out to him. In part his difficulty is an inability to exclude irrelevant details. In part it is paucity of background brought from a small-town high school, and here I think the college has helped him and may continue to help him a great deal.

He writes better than most others, with only an occasional slip in idiom which he is pleased to have you point out. A good earnest, hard-working, thinking student [179].

From a prosperous family . . . [Peter's] military school attitude tells the story of his life here. He rolls up his sleeves, reads his "assignment," slams the book closed, and writes his paper. The papers are usually short, clearly thought out, but superficial. He wrote one very long paper which reflected a fine job of fact-finding and organization, but little critical thought. He swore he would never do a paper that thoroughly again—but he will if he is challenged—he will do anything on a "dare."

Lately his blithe acceptance of the social order has been undergoing changes; he begins to doubt the divinity of our political system, though the industrial system is beyond reproach [181].

The faculty clearly saw writing as a central means of achieving the intellectual and personal integration at which the program aimed. The opportunity to guide the writing of a small group of students over a semester allowed faculty to see the students' social and intellectual development as a whole. This writing-rich education depended not only on low student-faculty ratios (about six to one) and low research expectations on faculty but also on the homogeneity and independence of the faculty. But most importantly, no remedial stigma was attached to writing or its improvement because the activity of writing was an integral part of doing and learning, not merely a means of showing learning.

Writing in General-Education Programs at Public Universities

General-education programs built on progressive assumptions (and the variety of student writing they evoked) did not find as secure a place at research universities as they did at private colleges, for the compartmentalized, research-driven universities could not find interdisciplinary genres and forums for student writing. The most influential and long-lasting (if not the first) general-education program at a research university was Columbia's Contemporary Civilization course, whose humanities counterparts, General Honors and, later, Humanities A and B, were built on very different assumptions (as I noted in the last chapter). CC, as it was called, is worth looking at in some detail, for it illustrates the social sciences' response to the problem of writing for general education in public schools and universities.

CC was born of political controversy. Just after America entered the European conflict in 1917, the War Department asked Columbia to develop a war-issues course to indoctrinate officer candidates on the cultural and political reasons for America's involvement and to prepare them for service in Europe. Several Columbia faculty and administrators had been vocal opponents of American entry into the war, and the trustees had ordered an investigation of the faculty's political views (which led to the resignation of several faculty, including Charles A. Beard). After the war, several faculty asked that a peace-issues course be developed to prepare students for peacetime. The result was CC, first taught in 1919 by a group of faculty from history, philosophy, government, and economics.[74]

Despite its origins (or perhaps because of them), the course did not seek confrontation but "objective," rational cooperation—on the disciplinary model of the politically progressive and liberal social sciences. Although the course was not an introduction to any specific discipline, its philosophy and aims accorded with those of the new social sciences, which privileged recent social history over ancient history, studies of the common man and economic conditions over chronicles of great men and events. (Beard's economic interpretation of the U. S. Constitution is perhaps the best example.) A critical, objective "historical-mindedness" was necessary, the "new historians" argued, for promoting intellectual liberty on which social progress depended in a democracy.[75] Columbia faculty member James Harvey Robinson (the doyen of the new historians and a close associate of another Columbia professor, John Dewey) did not plan the course, but its planners consistently credited him with its inspiration. The bulletin described the goal: "To give the student early in his college course objective materials on which to base his own further studies and his own judgement will, it is believed, aid him greatly in enabling him to understand the civilization of his own day and participate effectively in it."[76] Here is the progressives' vision of the active democratic citizen, rationally transforming the future through understanding the past, a call to develop civic judgment, not the aesthetic judgment of liberal culture. But neither is this the classical, rhetorical education of the citizen orator, committed to teaching the overtly persuasive expression of received ideas and communally shared values. It was to be an education growing out of the social scientist's new quest for objectivity. The speeches and actions of great men would no longer guide the student, as they had in the rhetorical tradition of *imitatio* so central to classical education. Instead an objective reading of the past would create a distanced, rational understanding.

These aims complicated two crucial questions of pedagogy: what to write and why. Students would not be asked to use the formal conventions of the social science disciplines because the course was to be *general* education, not discipline specific. But neither was it academically respectable, or politic, to have students writing in popular genres: partisan political journalism of the kind faculty were avoiding as unbecoming a social scientist in academia. In fact, the organization of the curriculum finessed this problem, as it did the problem of writing in the humanities' general-education courses. The freshmen (and, beginning in 1929, the sophomores also) were divided into groups of twenty-five to thirty, each meeting with a single professor for a year. They read and discussed the same materials, which were collected (and sometimes written) by the instructors. However, instructors did not use the same writing assignments. Though diversity was lauded as a virtue, it removed a forum for raising conflicts over pedagogical and disciplinary methodology. It avoided discussions of the real sticking points—what should be *taught* and how—by limiting the issue to what should be *read* and when (but even here there was enough disagreement to prompt six major revisions in twenty years). Once again differentiated structure brought an organizational solution to an ideological problem.[77]

To find room in the curriculum for CC, the college dropped one year of composition, hoping that the CC discussions would make students more "articulate" and obviate the need for formal writing instruction.[78] (The remaining year of composition was gradually reduced until the introduction of Humanities A and B erased it entirely.) Had writing improvement been a concrete objective for the course, the faculty might have developed assignments (and thus genres) that were part of the activity of the course. But the course aimed to refine understanding and judgment, not to teach content or disciplinary method, and these less concrete goals, the instructors found, could be accomplished with oral instruction. Instructors were not required to assign papers. In fact, students were tracked into sections based on their scores on objective tests. Only the sections for high-scoring students typically required essays; students in the middle- and low-scoring sections usually kept notebooks on their readings instead of having to write essays. Once again writing became a way of discriminating among students instead of a way of making education general.[79]

Moreover, the students' attainment of these goals was measured without resorting to writing. Edward L. Thorndike, the champion of mental measurement, was also in residence at Columbia with Dewey and James Harvey Robinson, and his philosophy shaped the course as well, through administrative channels. The only universal requirement for CC classes was that instructors report students' progress quarterly (and of course assign grades each semester). At first instructors gave midterm "papers"—hour-long essay examinations—to meet the requirement. The year after the course began (and two years after Columbia began accepting intelligence-test scores for admission), the dean encouraged the CC faculty to experiment with new-type tests as a means of providing a more comprehensive and reliable measure of students' adjustment to the demands of college study than the individual responses of two dozen CC instructors could give. Though the faculty were skeptical at first, trials of essay-exam reliability undercut their arguments. In a two-year experiment (the first large-scale trial of new-type exams in a course—as distinct from entrance or exit exams for an institution), the new exams proved to be as reliable as essays—and, predictably, far less time-consuming to administer.[80]

According to Issac L. Kandel, a faculty member from Teachers' College who advised CC instructors on new-type tests, "Instructors soon became convinced of their utility; in some cases perhaps they became too convinced, since the value of the essay examination was in danger of being depreciated, and more particularly by those who had been in the habit of employing it regularly than by the advocates of the new type test."[81] Although some faculty continued to use essays to supplement the standard tests, citing the need to test the student's "power of accurate and cogent expression, and his ability to organize his material," others came to rely exclusively on new-type tests. The administration supported the change not only to save faculty time but also to provide more defensible data for advising freshmen.[82] The bureaucratic demands of the system left no real reason to assign and teach writing conscientiously.

The CC staff were mainly junior faculty who needed time for research, and the new-type exams not only freed them from much paper grading (secretaries scored the new-type tests) but also simplified their interactions with students. After the new tests were instituted, faculty had fewer complaints about unfair grading or inconsistent instruction. As one instructor wrote in his evaluation of the experiment, "The New Examination relieves the teacher of the necessity for defending his position; an endless source of unpleasant bickering."[83] The lack of mandated extended writing and externally graded essay exams also relieved the faculty (and students) of any need to negotiate a collective meaning of general education (other than the reading of certain books to obtain a certain score on a standardized examination).

The absence of written forums within general-education programs where students (and faculty) could confront issues was yet another manifestation of the relentless professionalization of academia along bureaucratic lines, the classroom correlate of the social scientist's carefully circumscribed discourse. As Burton J. Bledstein has said, "Universities quietly took divisive issues such as race, capitalism, labor, and deviant behavior out of the public domain and isolated these problems within the sphere of professionals—men who learned to know better than to air publicly their differences."[84] A general-education course, involving faculty from different disciplines with divergent interests, also encouraged limitations on discourse—what Veysey calls "patterned isolation," a "need to fail to communicate," which minimized conflict but created a general education "without recourse to shared values."[85]

Historians of general-education programs at Columbia and other universities have pointed to the conflict between departmental specialization and general education as a cause of tension.[86] Certainly, general-education programs struggled to find faculty who would place the general-education program (including writing instruction) on par with their commitment to research and thus their career prospects, which were intertwined with specialized research. The temptation to devote time to one's own writing at the expense of students' writing has been present since the research ideal restructured institutional values in the 1880s. But the failure to develop a tradition of writing instruction in general-education courses also grew out of the university's tendency to narrow the kinds of writing that it accepted as legitimate. Faculty were caught between the demands of specialization—with the responsibility to communicate in ways appropriate to their disciplines—and the demands of teaching a broad, general-education course. They were limited by their *views* of writing, as well as by the time available for it.

To liberal culture, writing was an unteachable response to inner promptings, a mode of appreciation or an indication of genius. Writing did not aid learning; it showed the state of mind. For progressive education, writing was a means of therapy or a vehicle for political consciousness-raising. To the social sciences in general, writing was a distanced, objective response to a problem defined by the discipline, not by political or personal exigencies, with a solution circumscribed by the discipline, not negotiated with those outside it. Students wrote primarily to demonstrate knowledge, not to discover or communicate it. Consequently, none of these academic cultures evolved a tradition of writing instruction in general education, and the roles that writing could play were primarily evaluative rather than pedagogical.

Finally, there was little contact between the humanistic and the social science versions of general education. Without a shared sense of values and purposes, an academic community, there could be no meaningful discourse community. Even in the 1940s, when CC's faculty borrowed from Humanities A the practice of using original historical documents in their entirety, they used them for different ends than did the humanities' faculty. "In CC [primary texts] are read as sources, as data; in Humanities they are read as self-sufficient creations, as ends in themselves."[87] Caught in their own rhetorical universes, the two versions ultimately compromised with the regulative, bureaucratic demands of social efficiency, a curricular structure that kept the peace through a policy of containment. Daniel Bell and, twenty years later, Gerald Graff have argued that the most meaningful general education might come from an encounter between liberal culture and the social sciences, CC and Humanities A, to force the two cultures to confront their differences.[88] The final test of such a curriculum, I suspect, would be whether faculty from competing disciplinary cultures could design a common writing assignment to achieve a common goal, formulate criteria for evaluating it, and reliably apply those criteria. That test may not be possible given the deep divisions in modern academia. But without such concrete agreement on the role of writing in general education, a unified academic discourse community will continue to be an unexamined—and unrealized—ideal, and the myth of transience will continue to hold out the false promise that some comprehensive means of dramatically improving student writing lies waiting in yet another reform of general education.

III

THE POSTWAR ERA

8

THE DISCIPLINES ENTER
THE INFORMATION AGE

The years following World War II were crucial for writing instruction, not so much because American secondary and higher education took a new direction but because the pace of change accelerated so dramatically. The growth of higher education in the postwar era, not only in the size and number of institutions but in the variety of programs they offered, increased differentiation exponentially. Moreover, the explosion in knowledge during and after the war—aided for the first time by massive federal and corporate research funding—only multiplied and reinforced disciplinary boundaries and thus the distance between faculty and student, university and secondary school. Higher education fully became, in Burton Clark's phrase, a vast aggregate of "small worlds, different worlds."[1]

Academia reflected the increasing differentiation and rationalization of the whole society as America entered the information age. In 1956, the year William H. Whyte published *The Organization Man,* white-collar workers outnumbered blue-collar workers for the first time in American history. For the first time in any nation, secondary education was expected of all, and the word *dropout* carried a social stigma. For greater numbers of Americans, a college education came to be thought of as a necessity, perhaps a right. And even graduate education became common, to the amazement of Europeans. The claims of equity and inclusion had clearly won a decisive victory, but the claims of excellence and exclusion were also heard.

Frequent exposés of Americans' "illiteracy" made it clear that the demands for writing were increasing, both in schools and on the job. Americans learned that poor writing was a serious problem, from the high-school dropout to the Ph.D. candidate. And there were new villains: television and progressive education. But the real culprit was the very success of the economic and educational systems in raising expectations, combined with the old assumption that writing was a single skill, independent of specific contexts. Increasing specialization in education and in work demanded that students be taught to write for a host of new situations. But the system, still tied to a reductive conception of writing, did not provide the means to teach writing in new contexts. The myth of transience grew in power as one panacea succeeded another: life adjustment, "new criticism," communications courses, computers.

In this chapter I first trace developments in several earlier traditions of writing instruction as they entered the information age: essay examinations, theses, lab reports, and business- and technical-writing courses. On the whole, these developments accelerated differentiation and made writing and writing instruction even more transparent to faculty and less important in the classroom. I then take up the most important of the postwar general-education reforms, the Harvard "Redbook" and the communications movement, to examine the ways in which they coped with the effects of increasing specialization.

Essay Examinations

In the postwar era, American education carried out the testing movement's policies with a vengeance. Objective tests almost entirely replaced essays on external examinations: national, state, and local. Machine-scored testing became the primary means of sorting students into the proliferating and increasingly differentiated institutions and programs. As both opponents and proponents had feared, objective tests made extended writing instruction even more difficult. Postwar technological advances, such as the IBM computer, made machine-scored tests so economical that even individual schools and classrooms could use them, ushering in the age of Scan-Tron. With machine-scored tests providing the most important measures of performance, essay writing became increasingly distant from the activities of education that mattered most to the system. The 1940s and 1950s saw very few studies of essay examinations in the United States. The testing movement evolved into its own disciplinary community, which resisted "subjective" measures.[2] The rest of the industrialized world retained essays as the primary means of evaluation and for precisely the reasons the U.S. critics of new-type tests had marshaled in the 1930s. Research and development of essay-testing procedures continued abroad; standards remained high, and the social pressures for educational equity also continued, focused as always on examinations.

However, beginning in the mid 1960s and growing throughout the next two decades, pressure mounted in the United States for a return to some essay component on external examinations. The College Entrance Examination Board exams, the medical college exams, the General Equivalency Degree (GED) exam, the national teacher exam, and other nationally normed tests introduced or reintroduced essays—though usually to test composition skills not to test content-area learning, which only reinforced the split between writing and content learning. The research literature on writing evaluation has begun to grow accordingly. But the genre of the essay examination is no longer an integral part of American educational activity, and its future is still greatly in doubt.[3]

Writing in Graduate Education

The postwar era saw a boom in graduate education to match the boom in undergraduate education that had occurred five decades earlier, and with it came the first widespread discussion of writing in the graduate curriculum. Graduate schools preserve the last institutional vestiges of traditional rhetorical education in America, the final thesis with a formal oral defense (though some elite liberal arts colleges preserved or revived the senior thesis and there is some interest in undergraduate "portfolio" evaluation or a "capstone" writing experience today).[4] Discipline-specific writing competence is therefore essential. Graduate faculty are expected to be mentors, guiding the apprentices as they learn the written conventions of the discipline. In graduate schools papers are expected frequently; there are seminars in which faculty and students discuss their writing. The thesis or dissertation provides the final written evidence of membership in the community.

However, expanding graduate schools suffered the same pressures on writing instruction as did the undergraduate and secondary schools which produced their students and faculty; often those pressures generated similar responses, as complaints about poor graduate-student writing—and writing instruction—over the last four decades make clear.[5] In the postwar era (and much earlier in some professional fields, such as in education), graduate-school-enrollment increases put a premium on faculty time. Research pressures, already highest among graduate faculty, further reduced the time available for mentoring. And the graduate school was and is the most highly specialized and therefore the most loosely organized level of education, with faculty operating independently, almost as private entrepreneurs, in competition for research funds and graduate students. These institutional pressures, combined with the same reductive assumptions about writing acquisition that I have noted throughout, led to a separation between graduate course work and the all-important writing requirements, echoing the split between content courses and writing at the secondary and undergraduate levels. The two parts of graduate training, course work and thesis or dissertation, have traditionally been functionally independent (though, of course, theses have often grown out of course projects). Responsibility for developing graduate students' writing has thus been as diffuse as in undergraduate and secondary education.

Graduate students have often had little formal supervision of the writing requirement. As a 1957 Association of Graduate Schools report put it, they are "cast adrift" to write the thesis.[6] In his 1964 book *The Writing Requirements for Graduate Degrees,* Paul E. Koefod noted that undergraduate and graduate courses do not often train students in the research methodology and the writing conventions necessary for thesis work. Too often such training "falls wholly on the thesis or dissertation. . . . It imposes the necessity of self-training on the candidate at the wrong point in time"—after the student has invested years in course work and is cut off from structured contact with fellow students and faculty.[7] Along with alienation comes confusion, for "their capstone degree requirement is neither familiar to them or made readily understandable" (3). Koefod mainly attributes this confusion to the rapid differentiation of graduate education. In the rush to create new knowledge and new degree programs, the genres of academic writing proliferated. Faculty accepted as theses novels, plays, films, reports of specific experiments, and performances. With little agreement among faculty about what a thesis or dissertation should be, students could often be confused. The writing requirement was clearly both an intellectual hurdle and a rite of passage, but its educational purpose, its role in a student's professional development, its connection with the course work was never well defined across the system; and where the writing requirement was well defined locally, it was often, like many rites, communicated to the neophytes indirectly, tacitly, in the day-to-day affairs of departments and committees, rather than directly, as a consciously held tradition of rhetorical practices shared by the discipline.

As a result of the alienation and confusion associated with the writing requirement, many graduate students have felt intense anxiety. The phenomenon is long-standing and widespread. As early as 1903 there were complaints about the "Ph.D. octopus," which entangled students in confusing and irrelevant writing requirements.[8] The lore of graduate school is of course replete with horror stories. Indeed, the graduate student defeated by the writing requirement is so common that in the postwar period America has coined a title for her: the ABD. Spurred by high attrition rates in graduate schools, higher-education research has produced a significant literature on the problems of graduate study.[9]

However, American researchers have almost entirely ignored that these problems are partially the result of the system's inability to teach writing as part of its regular work.[10] Research in composition is only now beginning to address the problem. Patricia Sullivan's longitudinal study of the classroom writing of English graduate students concluded that "writing is valued for evaluative properties or an academic exercise, as the basis of a grade." Although graduate students in English wrote a great deal in their courses, they were almost never given specific assignments, direct instruction in writing, or the opportunity to discuss their writing with faculty or other students. Faculty had an "arhetorical" or "black box" view of writing: reading goes in and writing comes out. "Students are seeking to learn discipline-specific languages that will allow them to participate in discipline-specific conversations, but the discipline itself seems to assume that those languages have already been mastered."[11] At the graduate level, as at lower levels, institutional attitudes and structures all too often inhibit rather than promote writing competence.[12]

Once again, the transparency of writing and the agonistic institutional and disciplinary structure promote these attitudes. Because faculty are often blind to the rhetorical structures that lie behind the writing requirements, they attribute students' difficulties to lack of intelligence or initiative in penetrating the intellectual difficulties offered by the discipline, instead of to the complexity and inaccessibility of those rhetorical structures. Moreover, in the institution and in the discipline, the values of excellence come before those of equity. The institution tends to interpret high attrition rates as evidence that standards are high, not that the system neglects students' writing development. The agonistic structure of the academic discipline—scholars competing for position and recognition—is reflected in the agonistic structure of graduate education. Faculty are merely reinforcing the competitive values of the discipline when they refuse to "spoon feed" graduate students by devoting time and conscious effort to tutoring their writing. Only the "best" students will master the rhetorical forms without being consciously taught them.

The measures that students and graduate schools take to deal with the problems mirror those that are taken at lower levels. Commercially produced self-help books on thesis writing have been published since the 1920s. Next came discipline-specific guides as fields gained enough graduate students to make such guides commercially feasible. The first were in education, but after the war graduate study in other disciplines created a thriving market. These how-to's always included advice on form and mechanics, but sometimes they introduced the research methodology of the discipline, which students were presumably not taught in their courses or textbooks. In other words, these books tried to make explicit the rhetorical universe, the disciplinary paradigm, which is so often transparent to the faculty who live in that universe but frustratingly opaque to the students. Indeed, the guides' authors occasionally present themselves as revealing professional secrets. A guide to economics writing began with an anthropological metaphor: "The mysteries of writing research papers, theses, and dissertations have virtually been handed down from supervising professor to supervising professor as part of the tribal rites for generations of those seeking initiation to higher education."[13] These guides have become so specialized that there are books to teach graduate students in engineering and business how to write *academic* papers as distinct from the *professional* genres taught in business- and technical-writing courses and textbooks.[14]

It was only a short step from such self-help guides to full-fledged graduate writing courses. During the 1960s, the greatest boom years in graduate education, many universities instituted general graduate-level writing courses to help students prepare papers and theses, and many departments set up discipline-specific graduate writing courses. In such courses, graduate students found direct help with crucial writing tasks that the regular faculty could not or did not give. Faculty appreciated the "cleaner" writing submitted, and administrators pointed with pride to this concrete action in response to complaints by faculty and editors about the poor writing of graduate students and graduates.[15] The largest survey of such courses found that 50 of the 144 graduate schools responding had regular graduate writing courses, offered for full graduate credit.[16] Though most discipline-specific writing courses were offered within the individual departments rather than through English—and thus might logically have been staffed by regular faculty in the field—departments turned to lower-paid and lower-status teachers trained in English departments to staff the courses, as business and engineering had done a half century before. Some departments even referred to their graduate writing courses as "remedial." The same logic, the same institutional structures and attitudes, which had led to the founding of composition courses almost a century earlier in secondary and undergraduate education, now brought graduate schools to adopt the same marginalized structures for writing instruction. Again, regular faculty were never forced to look closely at the rhetoric of their discipline and the ways in which they introduced (or failed to introduce) it to neophytes. The myth of transience had spread to graduate education: others had failed to teach students to write; others must solve the problem.

Developments in the Natural Sciences

World War II and Sputnik dramatized the need for more effective science education and produced another attempt to "make science education scientific."[17] In the late 1950s, as in the 1880s, curriculum revision was largely left to research scientists, who set out to raise standards and increase disciplinary rigor, this time with hefty federal funding. Teams of scientists at elite research and liberal arts schools received grants to develop new college and secondary courses, which were then disseminated nationwide.[18]

The movement toward disciplinary rigor produced an influential new theoretical formulation of the role of language in learning in the work of Harvard psychologist Jerome S. Bruner, who took into account—as most child-centered progressives had not—the structure of disciplinary inquiry in the process of education. At the influential 1960 Woods Hole conference of educators (mainly from the sciences), Bruner introduced the notion of the *spiral curriculum*—a concept he may well have borrowed from Dewey's most impassioned attack on the excesses of child-centered education, his 1936 essay "Progressive Organization of Subject Matter."[19] Like the child-centered progressives, Bruner favored a "discovery" method of learning, which connected learning to the student's experience, but, unlike them, he assumed (as did Dewey) that the experience of the child was by itself inadequate for education and had to be systematically connected to the knowledge and activity of organized disciplines through conscious articulation. The central concepts of a discipline could be taught, Bruner insisted, "in some intellectually honest form to any child at any stage of development."[20] Curriculum thus becomes a progressive elaboration of those central concepts at more and more sophisticated and abstract levels. But development can only take place if students are confronted with progressively more sophisticated uses of language, especially written language, which when set against concrete experience give the student "multiple means for representing his world, multiple means that often conflict and create the dilemmas that stimulate growth."[21]

For the first time an American educational theorist looked closely and systematically at the role that language plays in *acquiring* knowledge, not merely in communicating or demonstrating it. And perhaps more importantly, Bruner's theorizing showed the possibility of consciously, systematically using writing as a tool for learning in a specific disciplinary context, rather than as a generalized skill. In the deepest sense, his work can be seen as a call to build the careful curricular balance Dewey had urged between the interests of the learner and the structure of the disciplines (though he criticized Dewey on many points).[22]

The "discovery" or "inquiry" method revived interest in laboratory work, though without the child-centered progressives' emphasis on connecting science with the life of the student, which was seen as a concession to watered-down "applications" courses. Laboratory writing was part of this effort, though a small part. One method was simply to allow more white space in lab manuals for students to write. The student was encouraged to "learn like a scientist," "to write the results and interpretations of the experiment as he sees it." Teachers were encouraged to use lab writing as a "measure of the capacity to reason, not to follow directions," to have students write outside the lab, as a means of prompting further questions, in the way practicing scientists used writing as a vital part of their activity.[23]

However, science itself had changed dramatically since lab instruction was introduced almost a century before. The most obvious difference was the sheer amount of scientific knowledge available to the instructor, which made attempts to cover the subject even more absurd than they had appeared in 1920, when the reorganization committee had recommended teaching a few principles, through fully relevant laboratory experiments, rather than teaching a broad factual overview supplemented by rote, "cookbook" laboratory exercises. Not only had the amount of knowledge grown but the very nature of scientific activity had changed. In the mid and late nineteenth century, American science was still something of an amateur affair, and much scientific writing remained within the reach of high-school students and undergraduates. Student labs (and writing) could engage even beginning students in scientific activities very close to those of practicing scientists. But in succeeding decades, the activity of science and, with it, the genre of the experimental report had become much more theoretically based, quantitative, and specialized in its vocabulary. In many scientific fields (physics is the best example), descriptions and drawings of apparatus, so vital to late-nineteenth-century amateurs and their student apprentices, virtually disappeared, replaced by abstract diagrams or specialized, highly conventional descriptions accessible only to specialists already familiar with the equipment. Discussions became highly theoretical and quantitative, filled with technical terms understandable only to small subcommunities of specialists playing a narrow professional role.[24] Intellectually, socially, and rhetorically, the activities of scientists were far removed from the majority of students.

It was therefore much more difficult to connect student laboratory work and writing to the activity of the scientific disciplines, to close the distance between scientist and student as Dewey had urged. Moreover, in a dwindling pool of science teachers, fewer and fewer secondary and even undergraduate instructors had themselves been socialized into a community of research scientists. When research scientists at elite institutions attempted to lead the profession away from textbook-oriented, fact-centered instruction toward more abstract, theoretical, and quantitative science teaching based on discovery and inquiry, teachers were often ill equipped to follow.

Because lab notebooks had been discredited and reports reduced to fill-in-the-blank exercises during the 1920s and 1930s (see chapter 3), the sciences had no vital tradition of student writing to develop by the late 1950s, and the profession made feeble attempts at understanding and redeeming the remaining one. Quantitative and graphic competence, so central and conscious a part of contemporary science, took attention from writing, which generally remained transparent. A 1985 national study of secondary-school lab use reported that 83 percent of science teachers used the lab less than forty-five minutes per week. And a 1979 study found that even the most commonly used post-Sputnik lab manuals, based on inquiry and discovery methods, emphasized such rote activities as manipulating apparatus, recording data, and repeating preformulated conclusions, with "few opportunities to discuss sources of experimental error, to hypothesize and propose tests." "In spite of the curriculum reform of the last twenty years, students still commonly work as technicians, following explicit instructions and concentrating on the development of low-level skills."[25]

In recent years there has been a small but growing body of research on laboratory practice, focusing on such issues as cooperative versus competitive activities and structured versus unstructured approaches.[26] But there has been virtually no research on the role of writing in science learning. The little research on writing that has been undertaken in science education grew out of the 1970s WAC movement, not out of the tacit writing traditions of the discipline, and that research primarily treats the effectiveness of notebooks in lecture classes or experimental plans for English-science cooperation, not of lab writing.[27]

Developments in Technical and Business Writing

Technical writing reached something of a crisis just before World War II. Many faculty were discouraged by the lack of status, pay, and promotions, as well as by the lack of cooperation from engineering faculty. Some counseled abolition of technical-writing courses.[28] But the war set in motion forces that finally solidified technical writing as a specialized field, both in and out of the academy. The massive influx of students in technical courses created a need for writing teachers, certainly; but more importantly, the technological advances during and after the war created a need for technical writers. Corporations and governmental bodies began to hire technical-writing specialists to produce manuals, instructions, reports, proposals, and myriad other documents that accompanied America's postwar economic boom. By the late 1950s, technical writing had become a profession, with a secure institutional role. The 1950s saw the first comprehensive professional organization, including both teachers and practitioners, the first technical-writing journals, and the first graduate program.[29]

Real gains in status also came after World War II, when industry began to compete with academia for skilled technical writers. Technical writers sometimes commanded salaries above those of academics in the humanities, and writing instructors in engineering schools sometimes had salaries above those of their English department colleagues teaching literature. Today there are almost two dozen graduate programs, with more planned. And technical writing has a valued role in business, industry, and government.

Of course engineers still must write a great deal, despite the presence of technical-writing specialists. And there are still complaints about their poor writing. The information age produced the need for more and more writing, and even with writing specialists who can translate information from one community to another, engineers must still communicate in writing with those in other communities. Specialization of responsibility did not solve the problems of written communication, either in academia or in industry; it merely allowed a profession or discipline to manage those problems while maintaining its boundaries. Technical-writing courses meant that engineering professors did not have to bear the brunt of writing instruction and could thus focus on what they were primarily paid to do: specialized teaching and research. The presence of technical writers in an organization meant that engineers in the laboratory or field did not have to tackle the big writing tasks alone and could thus focus on work within their disciplinary community. The system guaranteed that few people would have to enter thoroughly another discourse community.

Business writing went through similar though even more complex changes as it moved toward a separate identity as a disciplinary community after World War II. In the late 1940s, a few management faculty began studying the process of communication within business. This new research area had little interest in practical writing issues, and even when organizational communication, as it came to be called, mushroomed into a fully developed area of specialization in the 1960s, with its own required courses and majors, it did not involve itself with writing instruction.[30] Meanwhile, traditional business-writing courses came under increasing fire, as business schools sought the theoretical rigor and liberal arts orientation that would earn them a prestigious place within an expanding university system. Two influential reports in 1959 condemned business-writing courses as trivial and essentially remedial, with "no place in university curricula." "If English composition is degraded by teaching such topics as 'business correspondence' and 'report writing,' for example, it becomes a trade course which regiments thought, cramps originality, and ceases to be a subject of college level at all." General composition would do as well, since "businessmen speak and write the same language as the rest of us."[31] The reports recommended more literary study instead, to "humanize" business curricula. In regard to the "writing problem," the reports found it "surprising and disconcerting that English departments have not taken the lead in attempting reform," and they reluctantly recommended that business schools "assume main responsibility" for bringing writing into their regular courses—principally by hiring "specially qualified readers to grade student reports for organization, style, grammar and spelling," as Frank C. Pierson put it.[32]

Many schools, particularly the most selective ones, dropped or reduced business-writing courses, though few hired special graders or reduced faculty loads to allow for more writing in other courses. Business-writing teachers were forced into rethinking their discipline. They introduced more theoretical rigor, began doing research, and sometimes called themselves teachers of *organizational communication* (another very different disciplinary community used the same title).[33] In the late 1970s and 1980s business writing regained its position and found new status, both in the curriculum and through real-world writing and consulting.

Business- and technical-writing teachers began to offer short courses or institutes for professionals in business, industry, and government. Research traditions began to develop which tied instruction to real-life practice. And in the 1970s, business and technical writing came of age as an academic discipline.[34]

General Education Redux: The Harvard "Redbook"

The second world war, like the first one, produced a wave of general-education reform, and for similar reasons. The challenge to democratic institutions sent educators searching for some ideological common ground on which to build postwar society.[35] Harvard president James Bryant Conant spearheaded the highly influential report, *General Education for a Free Society* (known as the Redbook) to counteract "the impact of the European radical doctrines of the nineteenth-century based on the notion of class struggle" and revive "our native American traditions . . . the type of political, social, and economic system . . . on trial in the grim world of the mid-twentieth century."[36] The report might have been titled "General Education for the Cold War," for like the Columbia experiments of the previous generation, the new experiments were fundamentally conservative in character, stressing the great books and the great ideas of Western civilization as an antidote to the ideological dangers at home and abroad. The Redbook, like its predecessors, was disarmingly vague about what that tradition and that ideological common ground consisted of, or how they might be taught. Again humanities, social science, and natural science cores were recommended—and again there was no effort to find common ground among the three perspectives.

The Redbook was silent on the kinds of writing that students might do in the natural and social sciences. In the area of the humanities, the report was influenced by I. A. Richards' insistence on a "new critical" method of close reading and explication devoid of historical or ideological criticism (Richards helped draft the report). A "great text of literature" must "speak for itself," said the Redbook, echoing Hutchins and Erskine (205). Students would absorb the literary tradition without studying its relation to the historical and social contexts out of which the great texts grew.

The Redbook devoted only two pages to the specific question of writing instruction (199–200) and mainly repeated the broad generalizations common in such reports. Writing, "a never-ending discipline which can only be begun in schools and must be continued in college," is nevertheless "remedial." Though the Redbook affirmed the English department's responsibility for teaching composition, the report insisted that composition should "not be associated with the English department only," but "functional to the curriculum, a significant part of the student's college experience . . . associated with general education." The Redbook not only expressed the usual generalized concern that "segregating training in writing from the fields of learning" is a "weakness" it also made a specific suggestion for reform. The second semester of freshman composition should take the form of individual tutoring "in connection with the courses in general education then being taken by the student," a system Columbia had tried for almost a decade and then had given up. The phrasing of the proposal was cautious and avoided giving regular faculty any firm responsibility for assigning and teaching writing. "During the first experimental years the writing would probably be directed and coordinated by the instructors in composition, but it is hoped that later all instructors in these courses might share in the task. Instructors in composition thus would come to have an intimate relation to the courses in general education. So far as proves feasible they should become members of [the individual core course] staffs" (200). The report never considered what kinds of writing students would do or how that writing would be taught and evaluated. How the faculty should be brought to "share the task" and how it might be "feasible" for composition instructors to "be members of their staffs" was equally obscure.

Despite these obstacles, the Redbook's proposals for composition reforms were in part carried out at Harvard—unlike most of its other recommendations. Beginning in 1950, Harvard phased in a general-education (GE) requirement for freshmen and sophomores: one course each in the humanities, social sciences, and natural sciences, chosen from a menu of courses. The catalog specified "four or five" longer essays in each GE course.[37] Syllabi and assignments from these courses indicate that faculty often found alternatives to the standard research paper due during the last week (typical of other courses). In a 1954 natural science GE course, for example, students wrote a rather standard essay outlining the Copernican system, but they also traced the effects of the industrial revolution on some "domain," such as on an industry or institution. On some papers, both the social and natural science cores gave students a choice of topics, each with several references—the system that had begun at Harvard in the 1880s.[38] To judge from the assignments, the writing requirement seems to have encouraged faculty to look more closely at the possibilities of writing for learning. Moreover, a general-education course in composition (GE A) replaced English A. Richards' influence is clear in the course's emphasis on "the study of the semantic and logical functions of language." But significantly, GE A instructors also offered students "practical" help with their essays in the other general-education courses, particularly during conferences. And the course was administered by a GE committee rather than by the English department.

It is important to note, however, that Harvard did not begin a program of core courses as the Redbook recommended; instead, the faculty offered several optional courses in each area. "Not a 'great ideas' or 'great books' course, the Harvard program, in effect, became a 'great man' course," as Bell says, with prominent faculty teaching lecture courses.[39] The faculty concluded that it would be enough simply to expose students to a "great mind at work"; questions of what, when, and how students wrote were left to the individual instructors, and the writing instruction and grading were left to graduate assistants. The GE A course was taught by TA's and the writing in GE courses graded by TA's. Composition instruction was still marginalized. And in the 1960s, the Harvard catalog dropped any mention of writing requirements in its GE courses—apart from the composition course, which was then called Expository Writing and eventually came to be administered as a separate unit within the college.[40] Nevertheless, the 1950s' reforms represented Harvard's first collegewide writing requirement outside freshman composition since the death of the forensic system in 1900.

Though the Redbook helped bring back some cross-curricular writing requirements for the lower-division students, it subverted Harvard's only structure for cross-curricular writing instruction among upper-division students. The Redbook recommended doing away with the then-current system of required faculty tutorials for upper-division students, a Harvard tradition that had given all students individual, supervised writing practice in their major fields. The committee agreed that tutorial instruction was "of immense value, *particularly when combined with the writing and critical analysis of essays,*" (italics mine) and "can make very great contributions to general education, inasmuch as the results of successful tutorials are to be found in increased skill in analysis and expression, in the capacity to deal with general ideas, and to make and defend value judgements, in those intangibles which are surely of the very essence of a successful general education" (232). However, the high cost of tutorials and the difficulty in recruiting senior faculty to teach them led the committee to recommend that only honors students, those "best qualified for, and most deserving of, tutorial instruction," should be eligible for it, and only in their fields of concentration. Again, Harvard made writing instruction part of a meritocratic system of sorting. Ironically, the pedagogy best able to develop democratic generalists was to be reserved for an elite group of students confined to their narrow disciplines.

In the next two decades, the tendency toward exclusionary restrictions on writing instruction appeared in many institutions. In the 1960s, Daniel Bell's *Reforming of General Education* again gave higher education (and Columbia in particular) an opportunity to rethink the clichés and compartments into which general education had settled. Commissioned by Columbia, the book called for restoring historical and ideological context to the study of the humanities, but again writing was outside the discussion. Bell reflected the views of many faculty when he proposed dropping composition altogether and simply raising entrance requirements. He repeated the by-then ritual assurances: "Student are, of course, required to write papers in different courses and more of this is necessary."[41] He offered no thoughts, however, on how to encourage more writing; instead, he looked to others to solve the problem: "It is entirely the responsibility of [secondary] schools to assure the proficiency of their students in English composition" (234). Bell was following a half-century-old Columbia tradition when he suggested that another humanities course replace composition. Only in the early 1980s would general-education reformers return to the issue of writing.

The Communications Movement

The most visible effort to improve writing during the postwar years was the communications movement. While the correlation movement of the 1930s had aimed for nothing short of restructuring and reuniting the differentiated curricula, the communications movement merely asked for a new emphasis on "practical" communications and increased cooperation among instructors and departments teaching general composition and speech to freshmen—especially to the massive influx of GI's.

The communications movement sprang from two sources, one theoretical and one practical: the new interest in semantics and scientific study of communication, and the mobilization of American education for the war effort and postwar adjustment. Though existing intellectual currents would likely have pushed writing instruction in the direction of communications theory in the years after 1940, the war created a surge of interest and produced a generation of teachers and administrators who talked of communications. But the movement seldom engaged the question of writing in the disciplines, at either a theoretical or a practical level. Thus, it is not surprising that the movement did not shake the disciplinary structure or permanently alter the usual arrangements for writing instruction that helped that structure work so efficiently. And for the most part, the movement did not change the way teachers in the disciplines approached writing in their courses and programs. By encouraging a widespread rethinking of the problems of language instruction, the communications movement did lay the groundwork for a revival of interest in rhetoric in the 1960s, which in turn led to the WAC movement in the 1970s.

Communications in Theory: The Four Skills

The communications movement drew its theoretical framework largely from I. A. Richards, who in *The Philosophy of Rhetoric* (1936) called for a transformed discipline of rhetoric, which would study all types of discourse as *functions* of linguistic behavior. The revived discipline would discover, as he put it, "how much and in how many ways good communication may differ from bad"—questions that Hitler's propaganda machine had dramatically brought to the nation's attention.[42] With his extraordinary combination of modern linguistics, behavioral psychology, and traditional rhetoric—coupled with a strong interest in pedagogy, evident from his earlier *Practical Criticism* experiments—Richards became a powerful advocate of reforms in language instruction. In 1939 the PEA put together a blue-ribbon committee on language instruction in the public schools, as they had earlier done with science and social studies. With Richards as chief advisor, the committee looked beyond English education to the role of language in the whole curriculum—and in the school environment as a whole. The final report, *Language in General Education*, advocated "the interdependence of English and other subjects" and the improvement of "language skills" across the curriculum.[43] Like earlier reports in this genre, the PEA report lacked either analyses of specialization's effects on language instruction or substantive recommendations for writing across the curriculum. The few specifics were generally disclaimers: communications study should not replace content courses, including literature courses; it should not force teachers to give up disciplinary autonomy (86). The failures of correlation had perhaps taught the committee caution.

But in addition to the usual calls for more attention to language in all courses, the report for the first time connected the development of language skill with learning in all disciplines—and in terms that have since become commonplace. Facility in language, the committee wrote, lies behind "critical thinking" (60). It makes possible "classifying, sorting, ordering, clarifying" of experience in the whole curriculum. Despite the broadening of terminology and focus, Richards and the committee still saw writing as a single attainment, independent of disciplinary context. Instead of one skill, there were now four: listening, speaking, reading, and writing—and a host of subskills. But the PEA committee never asked how the "four skills" (as they were called) shaped and were shaped by the different activities of the disciplines. This was a significant limitation, for it led to the same marginalizing of composition instruction outside the disciplinary structure, the same preoccupation with remediation and efficiency that was characteristic of the industrial model.[44] Still, the theoretical emphasis on communication did move the discussion out of the conceptual fetters of the writing-as-mechanical-transcription approach and place it in a rhetorical context—language as communication rather than language as manners—which would become crucially important in the revival of rhetoric in English departments during the coming decades.

As America drew closer to World War II, the treatment of critical thinking in content learning took a backseat to the more pressing issue of its importance in understanding threats to democracy, such as propaganda (a subject closer to Richards' theoretical interests anyway). In the late 1930s, such theorists as C. K. Ogden, Alfred Korzybski, and S. I. Hayakawa popularized the study of semantics as a means of understanding propaganda. An Institute for Propaganda Analysis was set up, and textbooks in English, speech, and social studies began to incorporate units on the subject.[45] With America's entry into the war, the schools mobilized to teach *communications,* a term that now encompassed not only effective use of the four skills but also the ability to tell true communication from false, propaganda from democratic values. The communications movement had none of the leveling cast which the correlation movement had taken on in the 1930s.[46] As the NCTE Basic Aims Committee wrote in the "Basic Aims for English Instruction in American Schools," on the eve of the war, language "is a basic instrument in the maintenance of the democratic way of life"—with the emphasis on *maintenance.*[47]

Communications in Practice:
Government-Issue Writing

The communications approach to language instruction received its first thorough interdisciplinary test in officer candidate schools. Faced with the task of producing competent officers in ninety days, the navy decided to drop composition and speech courses from the curriculum and instead incorporate writing and speaking into the technical program through a writing lab. The army's Specialized Training Personnel Program also taught a communications course, which combined speech and writing instruction (this time on college campuses), for students who needed to work with technical course material.[48] Not surprisingly, the rationales were frankly utilitarian. With the combined course, fewer teachers and class hours were necessary, and the writing instruction was to reinforce the content of other courses. Both programs found the experiment successful and recommended it to colleges after the war.

The massive postwar influx of GI's into higher education made colleges and universities receptive to the idea of a communications course, for it combined scientific and patriotic rationales with managerial efficiency. Enrollment tripled between 1945 and 1949, sparking a host of experiments with communications courses. But unlike the military programs, which integrated writing instruction into technical courses, these were essentially core courses, which combined speech and composition, sometimes adding elements of the new field of semantics, particularly the analysis of propaganda and advertising. To deal with the enrollment crisis, NCTE and the Speech Association of America jointly sponsored a conference on freshman courses in 1947, calling for a new emphasis on language instruction across the curriculum but primarily spending its efforts on revising freshman-composition courses. The two associations went their separate ways within three years as the crisis waned; however, each formed an organization to study communication pedagogy.[49] The NCTE's contribution, the Conference on College Composition and Communication (CCCC), outlived the curricular trend which gave birth to it and became the leading professional organization for writing teachers and a major force not only in the revival of rhetoric in English departments but also in the creation of the WAC movement in the 1970s.

Less than a year after the joint conference, there were some two hundred communications courses at the college level.[50] These courses evolved out of many institutional settings and naturally took many forms. Programs housed within a department (or informal arrangements among departments to share faculty) quickly faded as disciplines reasserted their interests after the postwar enrollment crisis passed. The longest-lived programs developed as separate units outside departmental authority, administered by deans or faculty committees. Some were for students in two-year programs, such as the one at the University of Minnesota's General College (which actually began before the war). Others, like Michigan State University's American Civilization freshman course, were part of a "general" or "university" college, which offered courses to freshmen. Michigan State's program began in the late 1940s as a standard speech-English communications course but in 1950 became an interdisciplinary humanities-writing course, combining an American studies program with writing instruction. The University of Iowa's rhetoric program is perhaps the best known (and longest lived) of the postwar communications programs. Though it originally drew mainly on tenure-track faculty (as did Michigan State's program), it eventually came to rely on graduate assistants, primarily from English and speech, to teach freshman rhetoric courses that combined instruction in writing and speaking.[51]

Although freshman communications courses were common in the late 1940s and early 1950s, comprehensive cross-curricular writing programs were sporadic at best. Most programs never went beyond speech-English core courses, and other departments were rarely involved.[52] Because communications programs had no recognized disciplinary status or research role, they all sooner or later became marginalized, with few tenure-track faculty and heavy reliance on temporary instructors or graduate assistants. As Berlin puts it: "Their fatal shortcoming in the end was the threat they posed to departmental autonomy and academic specialization. It is significant, for example, that the alternative to them commonly proffered by the English department was writing about literature" (104). But it is also important to remember that the programs offered no reason for departments to take an active role in their work, for they treated writing as a generalizable skill, unrelated to the specialized activities of the disciplines. Thus, the communications courses all too often reinforced the myth of transience, holding out to departments the false hope that writing could be taught quickly and efficiently without deep institutional changes.

A few institutions did make a conscious effort to develop writing across the entire curriculum, actively involving many departments and faculty. I focus on two such programs that anticipated, in many ways, current WAC programs: the Functional Writing Program at Colgate University (1949–61) and the Prose Improvement Committee at the University of California at Berkeley (1947–64). Both programs conceived of writing as a complex developmental process and recognized its capacity to improve learning; both developed collegial relationships among faculty, which could discover links between disciplines. The experiments at Colgate and Berkeley are thus atypical, but they provide a useful contrast—one from a small, private liberal arts college, the other from a large public university—and illustrate the possibilities that the curricular ferment of the communications movement offered to higher education.

The Functional Writing Program

Like many small colleges, Colgate had in the 1930s adopted core courses, one of which was speech-English. Colgate also had a "preceptor" program, which provided tutoring in writing for students in core courses. Borrowing the functionalist, behaviorist vocabulary that Richards had brought to the communications movement, Colgate's English department chair, Strang Lawson, transformed the preceptor program into the Functional Writing Program (FWP) in 1949, with strong administrative backing.

Lawson replaced the preceptors with a writing lab and gave a young English faculty member, Jonathan Kistler, the task of helping core-course instructors design a series of writing assignments based on the idea that "writing is a process involving several stages."[53] Each assignment, outlined on a single sheet, emphasized the process by giving specific suggestions for invention, arrangement, audience, revision, and editing. (To encourage revision, students whose papers received a grade of C or below rewrote them with help from the FWP's writing lab.) The core instructors themselves taught and graded the assignments, basing the mark on a paper's "total effectiveness as communication."

"Instead of floating in the unmotivated limbo of detached 'exercises,' " Lawson wrote, the assignments were "rooted in the materials and educational purposes of the courses" and served to improve not only the students' writing but also their learning, their "grasp of those materials and purposes." Writing became "a function of the day-by-day learning process."[54] Moreover, the assignments consciously drew on the students' experiences to encourage connections between learning and life, which reformers in the progressive tradition had long advocated. A writing assignment in physics, for example, asked students to define several terms with one example from the reading and another from "your recent personal experience, perhaps unrelated to science."[55]

As its emphasis on communication in the learning process suggests, the FWP was consciously developmental, not remedial. Its goal was, Lawson wrote, "a progressive *maturing* of the young people in an important and complex aspect of their behavior" (251). It treated writing as "a tool to be whetted with everyday use" (289). The assignments were sequenced over the four years to move from simple tasks (enumeration, definition, summary) to more complex assignments (comparison, evaluation, research, and analysis). The director kept a four-year calendar of each task assigned in the program, both to keep track of the sequence and to ensure that the writing load was moderate. As the students progressed, the assignments began to incorporate the conventions of each discipline, the appropriate evidence, format, and documentation, until students were handling sophisticated writing tasks.

The FWP was also consciously collegial: an attempt to draw

the faculty and students together. The FWP approached writing as a form of social behavior, a response to a community "whose opinion we respect, cherish, or fear," as Lawson described it (288). In the university, that community is "the educated Faculty" who model the behavior for the student (290). The program's organizational structure was collegial, too, in the sense that the faculty developed and made the assignments, taught and graded the writing, while the program director merely encouraged and educated his colleagues. Kistler recalls "sitting down with a physics or history or philosophy professor and planning a paper, clarifying its aim, limiting its scope, and making sure the student who is to write the paper knows exactly what's expected, and then suggesting ways to go about the job. In the process of meeting and thinking together, I made a lot of friends."[56] Faculty who participated in the program were also enthusiastic about its effects, both on the students and on the faculty. Philosophy professor Huntington Terrell found "appreciable improvements" in the style of student prose when writing was linked to the reading that students did in their courses and stressed the value of the program in making the campus aware that "writing is everybody's business."[57] The program was not able to sustain the enthusiasm long enough to make cross-curricular writing a permanent part of the institutional structure, but Colgate nevertheless used the foundation of the communications movement to build a developmental, collegial writing program of the type that, two decades later, gave rise to the current WAC movement at other small, private liberal arts colleges.

Writing in the "Multiversity"

At the same time that Colgate was beginning the FWP, the Prose Improvement Committee began at the University of California at Berkeley. Organized in 1947 at the urging of English professor Benjamin H. Lehman, the committee began a developmental (rather than remedial) program, which confronted the complex issues of cross-curricular writing at a large public institution, with its entrenched departmental structure and its large research mission. In 1950–53 a committee survey of student writing, like so many other surveys elsewhere, found that student writing did not improve during the undergraduate years, but the committee rejected the usual remedial measures as misguided and ineffective. Nor was it possible, they reasoned, for the English department in the large "multiversity," which its president, Clark Kerr, was building, to work closely enough with other departments to achieve the cooperation possible in small liberal arts colleges.[58] Instead, the committee concentrated on providing writing instruction not through the professors but through the teaching assistants and graders in each cooperating department, on the theory that they were "the ones most directly responsible for correlating writing and learning" in a large university (6). The committee set up a course (in the English department) to train them in techniques of writing instruction—apparently the first such course in the nation. The TA's then regularly taught writing in large lecture classes and in the smaller discussion sections they led, while graders helped students rewrite papers in conferences.

Though the program did not ask professors to teach writing, it was very much interdisciplinary and collegial. TA's and graders were not selected for their writing ability or training in English but for their command of the subject they taught. While the training course was supervised by English faculty, it was sometimes taught by faculty in other disciplines: Benbow Richie, for example, a psychologist whose perspective on cognitive development informed the program. In addition, the committee attempted to interest the general faculty by holding regular open meetings to discuss not only pedagogical questions, such as essay-test construction and evaluation, but also broader theoretical issues, such as the role of audience in academic discourse and the uses of discipline-specific conventions (e.g., continuous present tense and impersonal pronouns in scientific discourse and the rhetorical effects of graphics and format).

From its inception under Benjamin H. Lehman, and continuing with its new chair, Josephine Miles, the committee based its work on many of the tenets that were later adopted by the WAC movement. Its first assumption was that writing is closely related to learning. The program undertook what Lehman called "the controlled correlation of writing and learning; that is, the guiding of the learning process as it is evidenced in writing" (5). The goal was "a deeper integration of writing and learning throughout the university," as Miles put it, not only for the improvement of student prose but for the improvement of the whole intellectual life of the university community.[59] Miles explained the effects of poor writing with a metaphor borrowed from Richards: "Writing defective in logic or grammar or rhetoric short-circuits ideas and prevents their successful functioning. Thus bad writing short-circuits the potentialities of departments, instructors, readers and students who believe that good writing is a function of good thinking and a continuing force in the process of learning" (12). To teach effectively, therefore, is to teach writing. "Learning a subject," she wrote in the committee's 1958 report, "involves learning how to write about it. Teaching a subject involves teaching how to write about it."[60]

Like their predecessors in the progressive tradition and their successors in WAC programs today, the Prose Improvement Committee saw writing instruction as developmental. "It is not an ability simply acquired once and for all," Miles argued, "but a complex and maturing ability growing along with knowledge."[61] The problem with traditional writing instruction, the committee repeatedly insisted, is that it does not teach writing as a function of maturing thought but rather as a set of discrete mechanical skills. On the other hand, by placing "explanatory adequacy" over "mechanical accuracy," as its last chairman, Ralph W. Rader, put it, the committee developed a pedagogy that was "constructive, not corrective," focusing on guiding revision in individual conferences.[62]

But the committee, particularly Miles, struggled with questions that went beyond pedagogy to explore the role played by discourse in the university itself. In the committee documents and in essays published in *College Composition and Communication* and elsewhere, Miles placed the committee's work in a much larger context than prose improvement. Rational discourse, she argued, is essential to the university. The tradition of rational discourse embodied in writing formed the university and constitutes, in large measure, its intellectual life. Composition, "composing our thoughts," as she put it in *Working Out Ideas,* is thus the ultimate purpose of the institution, drawing students and faculty away from the poles of "raw material" and "self-expression" and moving them "toward the center, where they can meet in thoughtful argument." In the university it is possible to "build a community between personal and impersonal" through rational discourse.[63] This then was the goal of the Berkeley program: "If a prose committee, which is made up of faculty members from so many fields, can succeed in its efforts to persuade students that their knowledge in every field has meaning only in their embodiment of it in language, that sheer fact is inert and generalization dogmatic unless related to perceptive questions and answers, it will have achieved something not only in the realm of prose composition, but in the realm of reason as well" (21).

The committee learned through its experience that writing is not some generalized ability, a single skill transferable to any discipline. It is intimately bound up with the language of each discipline. "When student writing is deficient, then," Rader concluded in his final report, "it is deficient . . . in ways having directly to do with the student's real control of the subject matter of his discipline and not in ways having to do with the special disciplines of English or Speech departments."[64] The Prose Improvement Committee was quite consciously struggling against the myth of transience, aware that many other institutions had expended massive energies and resources on general-composition courses with little effect. "We can take heart in the knowledge," Miles wrote in a 1958 memo, "that we can do no worse, and may learn how to do better."[65]

Academic Erosion

Despite their high aims and long successes, both programs died out in the early 1960s. They were victims of the compartmentalized structure of academia and the entrenched attitudes in the university both toward writing and toward interdepartmental programs. At Colgate the death process apparently began in 1954 when the core requirements were relaxed, forcing the program director to recruit faculty from outside the core courses.[66] Although Kistler had what he described as "full support—more than mere backing—"from the dean and from the president, a great deal of his time went into promoting and developing the program: enthusiastic memos, meetings with interested (and less than interested) faculty. Thus the program succeeded, Kistler said, only with "as many departments as we could persuade that we had a hot thing going."[67] When Kistler became department chair, the directorship passed to another faculty member, who was in turn assigned to other administrative duties. A new English department chair decided to return to a tutorial system, and the FWP ended. Because the FWP was not part of the regular departmental and administrative structure, it could not resist institutional inertia which militated against interdepartmental efforts—especially such time-consuming ones—despite the best intentions of all concerned and the nearly ideal atmosphere of a small, private liberal arts college with selective enrollment and relatively low student-teacher ratios.

At Berkeley, the Prose Improvement Committee suffered much the same fate. As early as 1953, after the initial three-year survey of student writing was complete, chair Benjamin H. Lehman argued that centralized committee administration of the program would not work in the long run owing to the time and expense of recruiting faculty and TA's, as well as to the lack of individual departmental responsibility when a committee ran the program. He proposed that the university fund vice chairs in writing for interested departments, making writing instruction part of the institutional structure. The vice chairs would be given release time to recruit and train faculty and TA's in writing instruction, with consultation from an English department specialist. The proposal was never adopted, however; and for the next decade, the committee was forced to enlist support from year to year. Although the faculty involved in the program "almost unanimously reported themselves pleased with the gain in student expression and comprehension," as Rader stated in the committee's final report, the results of the program were "local and temporary."[68] In the eighteen years of its existence, the program never attracted more than a dozen departments, and by 1964 so few departments sent TA's for training that the program's budget had an embarrassing surplus. The committee dissolved itself, though not without sharp words for apathetic colleagues.

> To raise the level of student writing . . . would be in effect to raise the student's level of intellectual attainment in the subject matter itself. To say this is to indicate . . . the reason for the lack of response to the committee program: faculty are by and large satisfied with the intellectual attainment of their students. The Committee is suggesting, then . . . that the faculty should not be so easily satisfied [5].

Institutional Inertia

The FWP and Prose Improvement Committee were atypical in that they lasted more than a decade. Most interdisciplinary efforts—even those limited to speech-English cooperation—were much shorter-lived.[69] These programs failed not because they lacked substance but because they could not overcome institutional inertia, which the differentiated structure of mass education creates. Cross-curricular writing instruction goes against the grain of the modern university, with its research orientation, specialized elective curriculum, and insular departmental structure—all of which make it extremely difficult to change faculty attitudes toward writing instruction. Despite strong administrative support and an enthusiastic core of faculty members, the Colgate and Berkeley programs were unable to integrate writing into the organizational structure of the university to the extent that cross-curricular instruction could become self-sustaining, independent of the dynamic personalities who began the programs.

From the early 1950s through the early 1960s, critics attacked communications courses as interlopers in academia. Speech departments complained that the courses were too literary or not scientific enough in their approach. English departments complained that the courses did not teach enough literature and that semantics was a quasi-scientific distraction from the real mission of the humanities. In the structure of patterned isolation, communications courses had no permanent place. The professional communities and faculty who make up academia and, beyond it, America's "culture of professionalism" felt no need to introduce concerted training in the specialized discourses. They were already selecting and educating enough competent professionals within their communities without reaching beyond to other disciplinary communities or to students who needed conscious instruction to learn the discourse of the discipline.

Indeed, American education demobilized rapidly, mothballing the majority of communications courses. The nation's schools and colleges returned to an "academic model" (Applebee's term), a model that explicitly hardened the boundaries between different specialties and different educational levels. In secondary schools, critics of progressive education dealt that movement its death blow by installing a new curriculum with heightened concern for the talented student (with the inevitable testing and tracking), a return to "basic issues" (required-reading lists in English), and more emphasis on "discipline" in both senses of the word. For example, Rudolph Flesch's enormously popular *Why Johnny Can't Read* called for a return to rigorous drill and made literacy instruction a political issue by its "subtle linking of progressivism and communism," as Arthur N. Applebee has put it (188). A new emphasis on English as an academic discipline, an accepted body of information to be mastered, led directly away from the interdisciplinary efforts of the communications movement. America's reaction to Sputnik only accelerated the tendency toward differentiation and exclusion by putting into place discipline-specific funding of curriculum development and by encouraging ability grouping and tracking. Disciplines focused on educating the "best and the brightest" secondary students, particularly in the sciences.

In colleges and universities there was a similar circling of the wagons. After the tide of GI's ebbed, admissions standards rose again and continued rising into the 1960s. Disciplinary boundaries also tightened in higher education. English departments championed the new-critical method of close textual analysis, which divorced reading—and writing—from communicative contexts outside the academic specialty. General-composition courses focused more on imaginative literature and less on writing about social and political issues. Richards and others expected that literary criticism would be, in Graff's words, "therapy for ideologically based miscommunication and misunderstanding" and produce a generation of students immune to the blandishments of propoganda (133). By and large the debates over writing competence lost even what little interdisciplinary focus they had earlier. With a more homogeneous student population and a stable institutional climate, the pressures came chiefly from advocates of higher standards and the status quo. Institutional inertia led academia back to the structural and curricular differentiation that is the normal state of America's mass-education system.

9

THE WRITING-ACROSS-
THE-CURRICULUM
MOVEMENT

1970–1990

Cross-curricular writing programs were almost always a response to a perceived need for greater access, greater equity. They
set out to assimilate, integrate, or (in the current phrasing) initiate
previously excluded students by means of language instruction.
So, it is not surprising that the greatest efforts came as the pressure
for access increased. The cooperation movement and the first
general-education initiatives began just after the turn of the century, when middle-class, rural, and immigrant students were
clambering for admission; the core-curriculum experiments at
Chicago and elsewhere, as well as the correlated curriculum
movement, flourished in the 1930s when economic pressures
forced students out of the job market and back into school—and
when social agitation for egalitarian reforms was at its height in
modern America; the communications movement and the postwar reforms in general education were explicit responses to the
massive influx of GI's into higher education; and the current
WAC movement was born in the early 1970s, when open admissions in universities and racial integration in secondary schools
forced educators to rethink language instruction.

When pressures for greater access abated in the late 1950s and
early 1960s, writing in the disciplines received little attention
within English, as pressures for disciplinary excellence increased.
At the secondary level, English, like the sciences, was immediately
influenced by Jerome S. Bruner's emphasis on the structure of the

271

disciplines. In the early 1960s, federally funded Project English centers pursued a disciplinary model, strongly influenced by the new-critical approach to literature, and had distant relations with other disciplines.[1] However, the emphasis on disciplinary rigor, higher standards, and education of the "gifted" students ignored Bruner's deeper theorizing on the process (rather than on the product) of education and on the role of language in all learning.[2] Once again, writing remained largely transparent. Only later, in the 1970s, would composition teachers begin to explore his work on the unique role that writing plays in learning.[3] And only in the 1980s did writing teachers and researchers begin to investigate the ways in which students can gradually and systematically acquire "the underlying principles that give structure to a subject" through writing in the disciplines.[4]

Higher education also had more pressing matters to attend to than writing instruction. It accomplished a vast building program while bearing much of the brunt of America's social and political upheaval. The "baby boomers" entering college allowed old institutions to keep both enrollment and admission standards high. And the system built a host of new institutions or expanded old ones into "regional universities" to meet the demands for higher education of excluded students. Indeed, the 1960s saw massive cutbacks in general-composition courses; and despite a few isolated experiments, writing instruction stayed in its usual places. Almost one-third of all four-year colleges and universities dropped or reduced their composition requirements, with many of them abolishing freshman composition altogether.[5]

Yet the 1960s set into motion the forces that produced the current writing-across-the-curriculum (WAC) movement, or rather amplified those waves of reform that, moving in several different directions, had successively rocked American language instruction for a century. In the 1970s those waves met in a dramatic burst of interest in writing instruction and produced what is certainly the most widespread and sustained reform movement in cross-curricular writing instruction.

One legacy of the 1960s for writing instruction was ideological. The political and cultural upheaval of the decade revived the communitarian vision in American social and educational thought that had spurred previous generations of curricular reformers, but it had its own antiauthoritarian, utopian, and romantic cast. Such theorists as Peter Elbow, Ken Macrorie, Donald Graves, and James Moffett profoundly influenced the generation of teachers and curricular reformers who were nurtured in the 1960s and gave to the WAC movement its focus on the classroom as community; its student-centered pedagogy, often with a subversive tinge; and its neoromantic, expressivist assumptions, reprising themes familiar among child-centered progressives of the 1930s.[6]

There were also crucial foreign influences. At the 1966 Dartmouth Seminar, a meeting of NCTE leaders with their counterparts in Britain's National Association of Teachers of English (NATE), Americans pursuing rigid disciplinary or industrial models were fundamentally challenged by the British emphasis on the linguistic, social, and personal development of the student, "a personal growth model, based on principles of language in operation and creative expression."[7] Loosely structured classroom "talk," dramatic improvisation, and personal response to literature took precedence over disciplinary knowledge embodied in literary classics and rhetorical or grammatical principles. Students' own creations were valued as literature and treated as texts worthy of serious analysis. The British were also reprising themes from the American progressive tradition—Dewey, in a broad way, but mainly expressivists in the "sentimental" progressive tradition, such as Hughes Mearns and Harold Rugg. However, the British, like Bruner, also had Continental influences, notably Jean Piaget and Lev Vygotski, who had studied the relationship between language and cognitive development in children. One British educator at the Dartmouth Seminar, James Britton, would shortly provide an influential theoretical framework to link the development of writing in the disciplines with personal writing, a connection the American progressives had not yet systematically explored.

But the communitarian and expressivist vision, though broadly influential, could only have shaped WAC through another legacy of the 1960s: the newly professionalized writing instructor. During the 1960s, the interest in writing instruction that had been evident in the communications movement coalesced into a "revival of rhetoric," which not only gave composition teachers a professional identity apart from literature (the MLA had shown diminishing interest in composition teaching since disbanding its pedagogical section in 1903) but also provided institutions with recognized experts who could design and implement curricular reforms in writing instruction.[8] The CCCC outgrew the communications movement to become a large professional organization for writing teachers, with its own traditions of research that increasingly went beyond freshman-composition courses to investigate wider issues of writing and learning.

The decade of the 1960s left its greatest legacy, however, in less obvious, though far more important changes in the structure and social role of mass education. The first was racial integration. As America's secondary schools and colleges haltingly moved during the 1960s to implement *Brown v. Board of Education of Topeka, Kansas,* the social differentiation of schooling became glaringly apparent, especially so in language policy. In the wake of the civil rights movement and the race riots of the late 1960s, as the nation began to take affirmative action to rectify educational inequality, schools and colleges faced—many for the first time—the task of teaching the dominant language to excluded populations.

The second was the massive boom in higher education, which created far more—and more differentiated—institutions of higher learning, preparing students from increasingly diverse backgrounds (primarily first-generation college students) for increasingly diverse roles. By 1980 there were 3,125 institutions, up from 2,006 in 1960. Significantly, many were open admission. Like integration, the rapid growth in numbers forced colleges to face the task of initiating students whose language background was radically different. For example, one of those new institutions, City University of New York (CUNY), began project SEEK in 1965 to prepare students whose grades excluded them from admission. Social and political upheavals in the late 1960s forced CUNY to begin open admissions in 1970, five years earlier than planned. Out of that experience, Mina Shaughnessy, a former copy editor and part-time writing instructor at CUNY, founded the study of *basic writing,* a new, more politically and pedagogically sensitive approach to "remedial" writing instruction, which would become important in the growth of the WAC movement.[9]

Moreover, the new institutions, and increasingly the old ones as well, came to be managed by a new class of academic executive. These managers—like their secondary-school counterparts half a century earlier—adopted the techniques and attitudes of industrial management in an attempt to make the institutions more effective in instruction and more accountable to the society that supported them and employed their "products." In the late 1970s the new academic executive would discover in WAC a tool for curricular reform and faculty development.[10]

Finally, in the wake of the social upheaval of the 1960s—much of it focused in schools (through integration) and colleges (through student political movements)—government and industry became directly involved in those social aspects of education that bore on language and culture. Though the post-Sputnik National Defense Education Act had been belatedly extended to the humanities and social sciences in the early 1960s, federal and private granting agencies had paid little attention to writing instruction until the educational crises of the late 1960s and 1970s. But as pressures for widening access increased, new public and private funds fueled the WAC reform efforts of the coming decades and encouraged their spread.[11]

In the early 1970s, these social and institutional factors produced the widest social and institutional demand for writing instruction since the mass-education system had founded composition a century earlier to solve the problem of integrating new students into academia. An outcry against "illiteracy" in the 1970s, like those of the 1870s, 1910s, and 1950s, coincided with the attempt to broaden access to schools and colleges for students who had formerly been excluded from them; though the 1970s crisis, like its predecessors, almost ignored the complex political issue of rising social expectations and focused instead on the popular issue of declining standards. Like the earlier literacy campaigns, the new one became a cause célèbre of the reformist press. The national press greeted with shock and indignation the release of the 1974 National Assessment of Education Progress

(NAEP) results on writing ability, a study of actual student writing (not another multiple-choice test) conducted every five years by the Education Commission of the States. The 1974 NAEP showed an apparent decline in some areas of secondary students' performance since the test was first administered in 1969. *Newsweek*'s 9 December 1975 cover story, "Why Johnny Can't Write," brought to a head the national discussion—some said crisis—over literacy, particularly writing instruction, with its inflammatory conclusion: "Willy-nilly, the U.S. educational system is spawning a generation of semi-literates." Even NEH Chairman Ronald Berman fanned the flames with his warning that the results presaged "a massive regression toward the intellectually invertebrate." The next NAEP administration (1979) revealed an all-time high in many of the very areas that had shown the greatest decline five years earlier, leading the Education Commission to conclude that "changes in overall writing quality are basically undramatic for any particular age group" and to recommend "caution in making global statements about writing."[12] But the nation was already aroused, and the educational establishment had already mobilized to meet the crisis. As in previous decades, with the coming of heretofore excluded groups to academia, there were also fresh attempts to broaden responsibility for language instruction. This time, though, the resources were greater, the organization more flexible, and the theoretical basis firmer.

Theoretical Bases: James Britton and the British

In 1975, as the newest American literacy crisis reached a fever pitch, two new British books were published that gave researchers and reformers in composition a name and a theory to catalyze disparate experiments into a full-fledged educational movement. *A Language for Life* (The Bullock Report) and James Britton's *Development of Writing Abilities (11–18)* both came out of the British tradition of educational reform, which had its first impact on America at the 1966 Dartmouth Seminar.[13]

In 1972 Margaret Thatcher, who was then secretary of state for education and science, asked Sir Alan Bullock, vice-chancellor of Oxford, to head yet another of the blue-ribbon educational commissions that Britain periodically forms to look into some current crisis in education. Britain had weathered its own literacy crisis only a few years before America's—also precipitated by pressure for widening access to comprehensive secondary schools and new universities. The commission was thus charged with reporting on "all aspects of teaching the use of English" in British education. In 1975 its six-hundred-page report reached a more informed conclusion than had most American educators about the extent and cause of the "crisis." While it is "extremely difficult to say whether standards of written and spoken English have fallen," the report said, changing patterns of employment and higher education are today "making more widespread demands on reading and writing skill and therefore exposing deficiencies that have escaped attention in the past."[14]

Its recommendations generally followed progressive lines instead of remedial lines, emphasizing informal classroom talk, especially in small groups; expressive writing; and teacher-student collaboration. The commission particularly listened to a theory of natural language acquisition and development propounded by James Britton, one of its members, whose 1970 book *Language and Learning* had argued that language is central to learning because through language we "organize our representation of the world."[15] Britton's study of children's language acquisition convinced him that, for students to learn language effectively, the classroom, like the home, must have a climate of trust and shared contexts for purposeful communication. Britton was a chief contributor to The Bullock Report's chapter entitled "Language Across the Curriculum," which emphasized the roles played by language in discipline-specific learning. "While many teachers recognize that their aim is to initiate students into a mode of analysis," the report concluded, "they rarely recognize the linguistic implications of doing so. They do not recognize, in short, that the mental processes they seek to foster are outcomes of a development that originates in speech."[16]

Britton also led the British writing-across-the-curriculum research project, which produced the other influential 1975 book, *The Development of Writing Abilities (11–18)*. Britton and his colleagues conducted a survey of student writing for the Schools

Council, a prestigious advisory group composed of leaders from business, government, and education. That survey was based on Britton's theory that children develop writing ability by moving from personal forms of writing (what he calls *expressive* and *poetic*) to more public, workaday forms, which communicate information (what he calls *transactional*). Britton and his associates found that the overwhelming majority of writing in British schools was transactional, that students were given very few opportunities to do expressive or poetic writing, and thus, he argued, they had little chance of developing in a natural way their writing abilities. The Schools Council's writing-across-the-curriculum project recommended a thorough revamping of pedagogy to rectify the imbalance.[17]

On reaching America, Britton's theory and the British pedagogical reforms found a warm reception among reformers in composition who were doing research along similar lines. The British reformers gave the Americans a new theory, a new set of tactics, political and pedagogical, and, most important, a new title for their response to the most recent literacy crisis: writing across the curriculum. In the spring of 1977, America's leading researcher in writing development, Janet Emig, published a seminal essay, "Writing as a Mode of Learning," which wove together the British research, the Continental theories of Vygotski and Piaget, and American theorists' ideas, from Dewey, Bruner, and George Kelly, to support the central contention of the nascent WAC movement: that writing has "unique value for learning."[18] Robert P. Parker and others organized an NEH seminar for college teachers at Rutgers in the summer of 1977 to introduce the new theories and pedagogical techniques to fifty American composition teachers in higher education. Future leaders of the WAC movement, such as Toby Fulwiler, were exposed to the works of Britton, Moffett, and others in a writing-rich workshop environment of the kind that would become the hallmark of the WAC movement. In the next few years, the CCCC and NCTE held convention sessions on WAC, and the journals in composition and English education published many articles on writing and language development, writing and learning. The movement had found its intellectual moorings.

The choice of Britton and the British is surprising in some respects. The British educational system, unlike America's, is based on external written examinations—essays that are graded outside the classroom, the school, even the country. Teachers across the curriculum must and do teach students to write for those exams, and they have a long tradition of doing so. British reform, then, did not aim to introduce or extend writing across the curriculum, as in America, only to modify the kinds of writing and its pedagogical uses.[19] America's rapid adoption of Britton's theory is surprising as well. The idea that language is central to learning forms a recurring theme in Deweyan progressives' thought, beginning with Dewey himself. And Britton was profoundly influenced by his American contemporary Bruner. Britton's discourse classification system is in many ways similar to the theories of Americans James Moffett and James L. Kinneavy. But Britton entered the American scene at a climactic moment. His student-centered pedagogy struck a deep chord within American reformers fresh from the 1960s' climate of experiment with radically student-centered education; but despite its domestic roots, Britton's work carried few of the "educationist" overtones of the discredited American progressive tradition. His theory was simple in its outlines and readily adapted to a student-centered pedagogy, without the complexities of rhetorical or communications theories, which had been the staple of the rhetoric revival in the 1950s and 1960s.

Perhaps most importantly, Britton and the British popularized a methodology that fit well with student-centered pedagogy: an adaptation of anthropological descriptive inquiry variously called *classroom ethnography, naturalistic inquiry,* or *qualitative research.* He and his associates entered classrooms to listen and observe, to learn from teachers and students, not to prescribe "teacher-proof" methods and test them in controlled statistical trials. Broadly empirical, yet humanistic, these methods seemed to bridge the gulf in American academia between social science and the humanities, a gulf that English departments were encountering as composition research, with its social science (education department) model, encountered the departments' liberal culture.

279

WAC *in Secondary Schools*

In the 1970s, the ferment in public schools brought about by racial integration gave new life to the old industrial model, now transformed by a "systems approach" into the back-to-the-basics movement. Conceived as a corrective to the laissez-faire educational approaches of the late 1960s, the back-to-the-basics movement introduced competency-based education in the three R's— little more than the familiar remedial labs and workbooks, though supported now by computers and federal monies.[20] Administrators spoke of "accountability" and "behavioral objectives," and textbooks stressed mechanical drill and practice, reinforcing the remedial, atomistic "skills" conception of writing— as well as the myth of transience. The few writing-across-the-curriculum programs that this movement produced were, like their forebears in the 1910s, little more than "grammar and spelling across the curriculum."

But one program sympathetic to Britton's approach achieved national prominence and influenced cross-curricular writing instruction in secondary and higher education: the Bay Area Writing Project (BAWP). In 1971, administrators at the University of California at Berkeley, recalling the demise of the Prose Improvement Committee almost a decade earlier, began a program to improve the writing of college freshmen by improving their secondary-school writing instruction. In 1974, BAWP held its first summer institutes for area high-school teachers—primarily composition teachers, though disciplines from history to home economics were represented. The idea was not to supply them with "teacher-proof" materials or prescribe expert-developed methods but to provide a forum for successful teachers to share their insights and methods for using writing in the classroom. Participants presented their own methods, shared experiences, and, most importantly, wrote a great deal themselves. In this collegial environment, the BAWP staff, while disclaiming any single theory or methodology, could disseminate the results of composition theory and research that they considered most important: the work of Britton, Francis Christiansen, Moffett, Macrorie, and others.

Two years later, in 1976, the California Department of Education adopted BAWP as a model for staff development statewide and, as with some later WAC programs, funded it with federal monies (earmarked for compensatory education under Title IV C of the National Defense Education Act). In 1977 the NEH provided money for a National Writing Project (NWP) at sites in several states. By 1979 there were sixteen California sites and sixty-eight others nationwide, each offering summer institutes, a newsletter, and in-service follow-up visits in the schools by NWP staff members.[21]

In 1979, Arthur N. Applebee conducted a national survey of writing in the schools. He and his collaborators found that there was little extended writing, though a great deal of copying, filling in of blanks, and other "writing without composing," as he called it. Such extended writing as there was fit the pattern the British had found: transactional writing for an audience of the teacher in the role of examiner.[22] Further studies have confirmed these findings and sought to understand the resistance to secondary-school pedagogical reform in the structure of mass education. The American secondary-school system faces unique difficulties in implementing WAC programs. The system is organized on an industrial model, which uses writing primarily to assess students' performance, not to improve it. Teachers operating within this system lack the time and training necessary to integrate meaningfully process-oriented writing into their instruction. Even education departments have sometimes attempted to "reign in" such efforts as BAWP, for it challenges their research paradigm and their professional turf.[23] Furthermore, research into writing and learning in the disciplines has not yet formulated an analysis of the ways in which writing can be meaningfully integrated into discipline-specific learning activities to produce increasingly more sophisticated levels of understanding and writing performance—the kinds of pedagogical "scaffolding" that Bruner suggested in the 1960s.[24]

However, in the 1980s, with the spread of Britton's theories and the WAC movement in higher education, many secondary schools and school districts began successful WAC programs despite the obstacles. With support from administrators, curriculum coordinators in some districts began in-service training programs for teachers in the disciplines, produced extensive materials to aid teachers in their efforts to incorporate meaningful writing activities into their content teaching, and provided ongoing support for these activities. In several states, school districts began cooperative programs with universities to reform writing instruction.[25] And some states passed regulations to encourage or even mandate writing instruction, though these efforts have been more prevalent in elementary schools and secondary-school English courses than in the disciplines. Several of the content areas (particularly social studies) have also begun to investigate uses of writing in secondary-school teaching, and a small but growing literature on secondary-school writing in the disciplines now exists.[26] These efforts suggest that, during its first decade in the secondary schools, WAC has had an increasing influence and in some districts has become part of the institutional structure. Although secondary education resists deep pedagogical and curricular change, WAC programs have survived and grown, building on BAWP's collegial approach to reform.

The Birth of WAC in Higher Education

Though WAC projects in the United Kingdom were almost exclusively concerned with elementary and secondary education and James Britton's first American followers were secondary-school reformers, his most visible influence was on higher education. The first WAC programs in higher education appeared in small, private liberal arts colleges with selective admissions, where general education and other interdisciplinary programs had always found a more congenial atmosphere. In the 1970s, enrollment and affirmative action pressures sparked a renewed interest in literacy issues and produced experiments in cross-curricular writing instruction. Carleton College in Northfield, Minnesota, faced problems of rising enrollment (a near doubling in five years) and "the diversity in ability that accompanies the increase in numbers of students," as one faculty member tactfully put it.[27] The college first responded by reducing the composition requirement and exempting more students, as other "abolitionist" colleges had done in the 1960s, and like many colleges in the early 1970s, it established special sections to allow for that "diversity in ability." But the college also instituted what it called "the college writing proficiency requirement" to give "formal recognition of the fact that teachers in departments other than English may assume the responsibility of judging a student's ability to read and write well" (8). Volunteering faculty attended a two-week conference on improving and evaluating student writing in all courses, beginning in the summer of 1974. The faculty then developed criteria that allowed students to satisfy the proficiency requirement through writing in courses from several departments. Moreover, a Carleton administrator, Harriet W. Sheridan, set up a program of "writing fellows" to tutor fellow undergraduates on writing assignments for their courses in the disciplines, an idea that would be developed elsewhere in the coming decade.

Further south, Central College, a liberal arts institution of twelve hundred students in Pella, Iowa, began a similar program, which embodied most of the central features of what came to be called the writing-across-the-curriculum movement: faculty development workshops, a facultywide supervisory committee, a writing lab with a writing specialist as coordinator, student tutors, departmental responsibility for students' writing proficiency, a system of student writing portfolios, and external funding (federal and corporate) to defray start-up costs.

Faced with rising numbers of students whose reading and writing skills the faculty considered inadequate, a group of Central College faculty, led by Barbara Fassler, began in 1971 a week-long seminar, held once each semester, to discuss student writing. In 1975, as part of curriculum restructuring, the college opened a writing lab and trained upper-division students to tutor writing. With a grant from HEW for "Special Services for Economically Disadvantaged Students," the college hired a full-time "skills coordinator" to supervise the program, recruited a "skills council" from the faculty to oversee the program, and in 1976 voted to give each department responsibility for teaching and certifying the reading, writing, and oral communications skills of its students. Central College then obtained further funding from the Exxon Corporation to expand its peer-tutoring program.[28] The skills coordinator organized workshops to train faculty from other disciplines to foster (and evaluate) student writing in their classes.

The most influential of the early private, liberal arts college WAC programs—inspired in large part by the Carleton College experiment—was at Beaver College in Glenside, Pennsylvania (with some eight hundred students). In December 1975, the *Newsweek* exposé led the dean to call in the new composition director, Elaine P. Maimon, and charge her with the task of improving student writing in conjunction with the Educational Policy Committee (EPC). Rather than adopting a remedial approach, as some advocated, she and several colleagues from psychology, anthropology, and biology interested in student writing began sharing ideas and collaborating on research and pedagogy to "galvanize scholarly and research interests" in composition.[29] By 1976, the ground of argument had moved away from remediation, and the EPC endorsed wider-scale faculty involvement in writing instruction. Maimon obtained outside funding to organize workshops for faculty, beginning in 1977, which treated writing as a serious intellectual and scholarly activity (Harriet W. Sheridan from Carleton led the first one, using as the first text Aristotle's *Rhetoric*). A $207,000 NEH grant in 1977 funded a program to create "a liberal arts college committed to teaching writing in all parts of the curriculum." The earlier informal collaboration among colleagues led to a collegewide "course cluster" experiment. In each cluster, three instructors (one from the English department) met to plan ways to make writing, in Maimon's words, "a natural part of each class meeting." In these clusters, loosely organized around a few themes or a text—such as Charles Darwin's *On the Origin of Species* for a history-biology–British literature cluster—students wrote projects acceptable in two courses.[30]

The Beaver College program emphasized the connections between writing instruction and faculty research. Writing and its teaching were treated as serious intellectual activities intimately related to disciplinary inquiry, activities that go beyond mere skill building or correction of surface features. As Maimon put it, "The teaching of writing is scholarly not scullery."[31] At one level, of course, the emphasis on research and scholarship simply reflected the growing seriousness of the new writing professionals who came out of the revival of rhetoric in the 1960s. Maimon was deeply influenced by Shaughnessy, Britton, Emig, and others, who valorized composition as a field of study. But there were also political advantages. The attempt to recreate the role of writing instruction in higher education by giving it the mantle of academic respectability (research) was an essential element of WAC's success in institutional settings where research was valued over teaching.

At the deepest level, reconceiving writing as a serious intellectual activity, worthy of study and consideration by academia, was a means of breaking down the century-old academic notion of writing as an elementary mechanical skill or a romantic inspiration and replacing it with transactional theories and student-centered pedagogies in the Deweyan progressive tradition. (Maimon called Dewey the "presiding ghost" in her early efforts.) The workshops gave many faculty their first opportunity to discuss writing and teaching in an environment of communal scholarship, without the "educationist" stigma or the belletristic assumptions of the English department determining the ground. In a collegial, interdisciplinary atmosphere, a faculty member could explore the relationships between the structure of the discipline, as revealed in its discourse, and the ways in which students learned that structure and discourse.

Such dialogue was not without its conflicts, of course. There were interdisciplinary battles over the nature of "jargon" and of "proper" academic writing. The ambiguous role of the English department, where many faculty had taught writing but few had studied or taught it in contexts outside their own field, produced other jurisdictional battles—an experience repeated often elsewhere.[32] But in this new forum, writing could not remain transparent. And the specialization of academic discourse, the dependence of writing on discipline-specific contexts and genres, could no longer hide behind unexamined notions of a universal "plain English" or a "general reader." Discussions of the various contexts of academic writing and the genres that those contexts produced was deeply stimulating, by all accounts. Out of the collaboration of Maimon and her colleagues grew an influential composition textbook, *Writing in the Arts and Sciences*, one of the first texts to portray students wrestling with the intellectual complexities of assignments from many disciplines, and federally funded seminars at Beaver drew faculty from across the country who founded WAC programs at many kinds of institutions.

WAC at Public Colleges and Universities

The mid 1970s' literacy crisis also prompted several public colleges and universities to institute programs that spread the WAC movement to this, the largest segment of American higher education—and the segment most affected by pressure for widening access. Some programs grew out of the abolition of freshman composition. For example, at Eastern Oregon State College, a four-year college of seventeen hundred students, the faculty reduced the composition requirement in 1965. In 1975, during the national debate over students' writing proficiency, the faculty abolished the course requirement in favor of a proficiency exam. Although most students continued to take optional composition courses to prepare for the exam, some faculty in other disciplines added or increased writing assignments and instruction in their courses. Three years later the college began a voluntary summer training workshop for faculty, though it was discontinued in 1983 as the program struggled to maintain the commitment of faculty.[33]

The most famous of the WAC programs at public institutions is at Michigan Technological University (with some six thousand students). The program began after the usual complaints from faculty about student writing, complaints bolstered by the *Newsweek* article and other national publicity. There were demands for higher standards, specifically a junior-level objective examination over grammar and mechanics, with English department remediation for those who failed. Instead of adopting the usual belletristic and remedial approaches, the head of the humanities department, Art Young, and the new composition director, Toby Fulwiler, set about designing a program more appropriate to a technical university, one that would involve many faculty in improving student writing. At the 1977 CCCC convention, the two learned of programs at Central College, Oregon State, and elsewhere; and at the Rutgers NEH summer seminar, Fulwiler was exposed to the new British and American composition research and, more importantly, to the writing-rich workshop environment of the NWP used by such seminar leaders as Lee Odell (a NWP meeting was also going on in a nearby room). There Fulwiler conceived two central elements of the Michigan Tech approach: writing workshops to change faculty attitudes toward the role of language in the classroom and journal writing across the curriculum. Young and Fulwiler then convinced the Michigan Tech faculty to provide opportunities for student writing, supported by a writing lab in the humanities division. In October 1977 Fulwiler and Young led the first of their influential faculty writing retreats (at a mountain lodge in northern Michigan). They borrowed Britton's fundamental notions of the importance of language—particularly expressive language—for active, student-centered learning and his focus on teachers as the agents of curricular change. They borrowed their methods primarily from the expressivist pedagogical tradition of the 1960s: free writing, personal journal writing, and dialogue, from Peter Elbow (*Writing Without Teachers*), Donald Murray, James Moffett, and others. But they also stressed what had come to be known as "the writing process": an emphasis on heuristic invention or "prewriting" and conceptual revision rather than mere proofreading for mechanical correctness.[34]

Art Young described the response of the fifteen volunteer faculty as "heart warming if not epidemical."[35] The most enthusiastic faculty described it in terms of a conversion experience: it restored a sense of their mission as teachers and their identity as part of a collegial academic environment. During the following year, the retreatants revised their courses to incorporate more writing, with the help of several two-hour follow-up sessions and a WAC newsletter. More faculty retreats, this time funded by the General Motors Corporation, spread the word across campus, and the English department's commitment to hiring writing specialists and their ongoing research and evaluation of WAC further drove the program.

Elsewhere, large research universities were forced to approach

WAC with more complex organization and less dependence on the faculty consciousness-raising model, as Richard Lanham has described Michigan Tech's approach.[36] The most common model at large research universities was and is a campuswide writing requirement administered by a committee of faculty from several disciplines, which students satisfy by taking a certain number of "writing intensive" (WI) courses offered in several—sometimes all—departments. Faculty in each discipline agree to assign a specified amount of writing, sometimes with a revision requirement, and to guide the students in writing the assignments. These WI courses usually have fewer students than typical sections so that faculty will have time to grade assignments. Often the university also requires one or more general-composition courses of most freshmen and makes a writing lab available to students in the WI courses. For example, at the University of Michigan at Ann Arbor, the first large research university to adopt the model, the interdisciplinary English Composition Board oversees a large number of WI courses, approving syllabi, providing training for faculty and teaching assistants, and administering a writing lab, which supports the WI's.[37]

Realizing that faculty in large research universities often give undergraduate teaching lower priority, other institutions have revived (without realizing it) the plan of the 1950s Prose Improvement Committee and focused their efforts on training graduate assistants or adjunct faculty to teach writing in support of regular courses—often large-enrollment lecture classes. In 1975 the University of Washington began a program of linking writing courses to large lecture classes—usually lower-division general-education or honors classes. It was expanded in 1978 with a Fund for the Improvement of Postsecondary Education (FIPSE) grant and grew to its present level of twelve Writing Link sections, as they are called. Students enrolled in specified lecture courses have the option of also taking its Writing Link course: prepared, taught, and graded separately by a TA or an adjunct instructor who attends the lecture course and structures the Writing Link assignments around the lecture course's material and schedule. About 10 percent to 15 percent of the students in the participating lecture courses also enroll in the Writing Link. Contact between the two instructors may be minimal or extensive, depending on their relationship. But any such contact between writing instructors and other faculty promotes discussion of writing and learning issues, which would likely not exist otherwise. Similar programs at UC San Diego, UCLA, and elsewhere use the linked-course concept in upper-division classes, often with support from a peer-tutoring program, a writing lab, or some combination of other models.[38]

A less common model for WAC in some public midsize and large institutions is peer tutoring, another means of getting around the problem of recruiting faculty whose time and interests may not allow them to restructure their courses to include more writing. In 1972 programs began at Brooklyn College and at California State College, Dominguez Hills.[39] Peer tutors were recruited from undergraduates through a competitive program, trained in writing instruction, then assigned to a particular course (as at Cal State) or to a writing lab (as at Brooklyn College). Based on research in group process conducted in the 1960s, the peer-tutoring model addresses what Burton Clark and Martin Trow concluded in 1966 was a central problem of mass higher education: to overcome students' "indifference to ideas, and the irrelevance of their education to their associations and relationships with other students." The research of Kenneth A. Bruffee of Brooklyn College on group process in writing and learning was particularly influential in the development of this aspect of WAC.[40] Paired courses and peer tutoring are what Tori Haring-Smith calls "bottom-up" approaches, attempts to influence faculty to use and value writing in their teaching by creating an atmosphere among the students where writing is used, valued, and expected.[41]

Evolving Models

In the 1980s, the movement spread to many more institutions. Theories, methods, and organizational models of the pioneering programs gained currency among administrators and faculty in a multitude of ways: through sessions devoted to WAC at professional conferences such as NCTE and CCCC; through summer workshops at Beaver College, the University of Chicago, and elsewhere; through hundreds of retreats and workshops nationwide, led by Fulwiler, Young, Maimon, Fassler, and others; and through articles in the pedagogical journals of several disciplines. In time, some administrators, as well as composition specialists, came to see these programs not only as ways of improving student writing but also as faculty development efforts, a means of initiating discussions of pedagogy among faculty and increasing contact between faculty and students.

Just as WAC gained momentum, however, the political climate of educational reform changed profoundly. Enrollment at traditional four-year colleges and universities decreased as the baby boom generation left college, though enrollment increased in community colleges (as did WAC programs).[42] Pressure for affirmative action and integration subsided; minority enrollment began to decline in higher education. The literacy crisis of the 1970s, with its impetus for school writing reforms, became in the 1980s a return to general-education core courses. In a spate of highly publicized reports on secondary and higher education, several national commissions recommended a return to "common learnings" or "core curricula," and while each of the commissions recommended strengthening programs to improve students' writing skills (and in some cases specifically praised WAC efforts), they had little to say about discipline-specific writing instruction and, indeed, criticized the increasing specialization of education. In the absence of social pressures for widening access, the focus of language policy shifted to the agenda of liberal culture, now under the rubric of *cultural literacy*. In the curricular ferment that accompanied the publication of the reports, WAC became only one of many reform movements, though it served as a model for several: speech communications, critical thinking, ethics, computer literacy—all "across the curriculum." WAC also became part of a general rethinking of pedagogy and assessment, as institutions sought to increase student "involvement in learning," as one of the reports put it, through faculty-student mentoring programs, offices of faculty development and teaching, "freshman experience" programs to retain students in an era of dwindling enrollment, and a host of other programs.[43]

The change in climate had an immediate effect on the fledgling WAC movement: federal and corporate funding became more scarce, forcing programs to find ways to move beyond the initial enthusiasm of retreats or workshops or pilot programs that had begun with outside funding to permanent curricular structures in the institutions. WAC programs entered their "second stage," adapting (and sometimes succumbing) to the increasing pressures.[44] Some institutions took over full funding of WAC or found permanent endowments when outside funding ended. Other institutions reduced their programs, attaching them to a writing center or to English department writing courses. Still others merged WAC efforts with one or more of the other curricular reforms of the 1980s. Capitalizing on the renewed popularity of general-education core programs, some WAC programs focused their efforts on writing in core courses. George Mason's Plan for Alternative General Education (PAGE) program, for example, grew out of a WAC program. Other WAC programs became "critical thinking" programs or evolved into consulting services under the auspices of faculty development offices.

Despite these changes, the WAC movement far surpasses any previous movement to improve writing across the curriculum, both in the number of programs and in the breadth of their influence. Susan H. McLeod's 1987 survey of 2,735 institutions of higher education found that, of the 1,113 that replied, 427 (38 percent) had some WAC program, and 235 of these had had a program in existence for three years or more. The persistence of so many programs and their ability to secure ongoing internal funding (rather than external grant funding) suggests that WAC programs have found a secure place in many institutions.

The range of activities that WAC programs embrace suggests that WAC is having a diverse impact on higher education. McLeod's respondents reported efforts to encourage individual departments to make writing a part of their teaching, through departmental faculty workshops and through the recruiting and training of faculty writing consultants within individual departments. Some institutions have begun interdisciplinary discussions of rhetoric, through workshops on discipline-specific uses of language and through cooperative research projects to describe and classify discipline-specific conventions of written discourse. Other institutions have organized workshops or made consultants available to help faculty with their own writing. Still others have sponsored faculty debates on writing issues, organized national teleconferences on WAC, and published faculty handbooks, videos, newsletters, anthologies of student writing in the disciplines, and many other materials. Some WAC programs have even reached beyond faculty involvement to sponsor writing-to-learn workshops for administrators.[45]

Reform and Resistance

The WAC movement has clearly had a broad and growing influence on American higher education over the last fifteen years. By conservative estimate, tens of thousands of faculty, students, and administrators at hundreds of institutions have been exposed to the movement, and many have made it an important part of their work. Yet the same attitudes and organizational structures that ended or marginalized earlier reforms continue to place large, often insurmountable obstacles in the way of current efforts to make writing a central part of American education. And without minimizing the unprecedented success of the WAC movement in the 1980s, it is important to understand the historical roots of the resistance that the movement faces as it enters the 1990s.

WAC challenges deeply held institutional attitudes toward writing, learning, and teaching: attitudes that are reinforced by the differentiated structure of knowledge and education. Faculty who grew up with the century-old notion that writing is a generalizable mechanical skill, learned once and for all at an early age, have difficulty experimenting with alternatives, even when teaching loads might permit time to be spent on their students' writing. Ideas of "correctness" inherited from the nineteenth century make some instructors reluctant to accept writing (even in drafts, notebooks, or journals) that is not edited by the teacher. The instructor's role as examiner is difficult to step out of because it is assigned to faculty by the institutional hierarchy. Assumptions about the nature of writing in their disciplines may also make faculty reluctant to assign personal or expressive writing (again, even in drafts, notebooks, or journals). Faculty who are accustomed to complete autonomy and authority in the classroom often feel threatened by reforms in pedagogy that necessitate personal and intellectual involvements with students and colleagues.

WAC is therefore sometimes perceived as an attempt to take time away from content and thus lower standards. Specialized instruction is, by its very nature, elitist, in that it is carried on by specialized communities with certain powers, sanctioned by the wider society, to regulate areas of public knowledge and life. When WAC programs threaten those elites—by asking them to change the pedagogical practices that form new members, or by altering the examination processes by which those entering a discipline or profession are selected and credentialed—then resistance comes. An instructor (or discipline or institution) may consider it a violation of her professional role to cover less material in a course to make room for more writing (particularly since the almost-ubiquitous standardized tests primarily measure such coverage).[46] Fulwiler and Young note that high-school administrators have even reprimanded teachers "for asking students to write before they completed workbook exercises—the required preparation for an upcoming [objective] test" (292).

Moreover, the instructor's role has been traditionally (and logically) defined in terms of "discipline": showing students the "right" way within the constraints of that discipline. Thus, he may find his identity as a teacher of a discipline challenged by student responses that propose answers or use evidence or methods of inquiry not accepted by the discipline. Even simply allowing students to revise drafts is sometimes seen as lowering standards. Faculty are naturally hesitant to risk a reexamination of their roles as teachers and as representatives of a discipline. Thus, relatively few faculty commit themselves to WAC.

Not surprisingly, some of the most entrenched opposition to WAC has come from English departments, who see programs challenging liberal culture's view of writing as an unteachable gift or infringing on the department's century-old institutional prerogatives. Most WAC programs began with (and are still led by) composition teachers in English who reach out to like-minded colleagues in other disciplines, and many English departments actively support WAC programs. But the claims of discipline are as strong in English as they are in any other department (as I discussed in chapter 6), and if writing is perceived as a threat to the department's literary mission, then it can be marginalized or ended. Fulwiler and Young again report that a number of programs have been "dismantled by a change in departmental administration or by the curricular or personnel decisions of unsympathetic English faculty" (289).

Perhaps more surprising is the controversy among composition specialists over whether students should be taught the conventions of specific disciplines, though this controversy is understandable given the historical divisions within the progressive tradition of writing instruction. An expressivist element in composition studies today, like its forebears in the "sentimental" progressive tradition of the 1920s, sees the teaching of disciplinary conventions as a denial of students' "authentic voice" and a rejection of the possibility of true academic community in a reformed institution, where knowledge and discourse will not be controlled by disciplinary elites. Expressivists, such as Kurt Spellmeyer, argue that students should be encouraged to do personal writing (the personal essay of the belletristic tradition, mainly) *instead of* learning to write in the public genres of the disciplines, a practice that in his view "encourages both conformity and submission" through a naive and formulaic "cookie cutter" approach to composition.[47] Proponents of writing in the disciplines argue that, as did Dewey, this line of reasoning rests on "a badly formulated opposition—a wrongly forced choice," in Joan Graham's words.[48] They insist that the student's experience, individual and personal, must interact in complex ways with disciplinary discourse, communal and public, in order for meaningful learning—and writing—to take place in academia. Britton, Maimon, Fulwiler, and Charles Bazerman, as well as other WAC proponents espouse varying theories and pedagogical approaches, but all favor students doing both personal and public writing at various stages of their writing and learning. They agree that learning to write is part of a dialectic between self and society, which can transform both, but only if students learn how disciplines are constituted through their discourse.[49]

Thus, given these reductive notions of writing among academics in all quarters, a central theme of many versions of WAC today is the transformation of faculty attitudes toward writing and an emphasis on the intrinsic motivation of more successful, satisfying teaching. The WAC movement, unlike most of its predecessors, attempts to reform pedagogy more than curriculum. In most of its theory and much of its practice, writing to learn overshadows learning to write. This is one reason WAC has eclipsed all of its predecessors. It asks for a fundamental commitment to a radically different way of teaching, a way that requires personal sacrifices, given the structure of American education, and offers personal rather than institutional rewards (perhaps this explains the religious metaphors common in the movement).[50] A group of faculty who are personally committed to WAC can ride out any administrative changes (and perhaps increase their number), for the reforms are personal not institutional, and their success depends on conversion not curriculum. But on an *institutional* basis, WAC exists in a structure that fundamentally resists it.

Faculty tend to retain narrow attitudes toward the role of writing in pedagogy not only because of disciplinary constraints but because those attitudes reflect the priorities of academia and are reinforced by its structure of rewards.[51] Even faculty who recognize the importance of writing for improving learning may not have the time to restructure their courses and pedagogies to incorporate writing more effectively, for faculty must work within institutional and disciplinary contexts that embody competing values. The century-old complaint of faculty that they do not have time to assign and respond to student writing is frequently a just one, but it begs deeper questions of institutional values. At research institutions, for example, undergraduate instruction typically holds a lower priority than graduate teaching or research. And responses to WAC reflect those priorities, despite jeremiads on the crisis in undergraduate education. Faculty at such institutions have little extrinsic motivation for introducing or continuing to incorporate writing in a course if it takes time away from research or graduate teaching; and there are many extrinsic motivations for dropping it. To initiate WAC programs, institutions have therefore had to offer release time, smaller classes, or other forms of compensation as carrots, but these are, of course, very expensive and easily cut when priorities or personnel change. What is less common is a deeper change in the way teaching is assessed and rewarded in the institution. If WAC is to become more than a marginal activity, criteria for promotion, tenure, or merit pay must measure and value the kinds of teaching and learning that WAC promotes, though this, like measuring and valuing writing itself, is far more difficult than looking only at more easily quantifiable "outcomes."

Without a strong base of support from faculty who see writing and learning in less reductive terms—and are committed to using writing in their teaching—WAC efforts easily fall victim to the institutional inertia of academia's differentiated, hierarchical structure. The myth of transience reasserts itself, and WAC programs, like composition courses, tend to become marginalized. This reassertion of the status quo takes many forms.

Some WAC programs never progress beyond (or may revert to) remedial labs, outside the curricular structure. Today many universities carry on the tradition of writing police and remedial labs; faculty prescribe treatment (often using computers), administered by a staff member or tutor—but rarely by a tenure-line faculty member. Responsibility remains outside the disciplinary communities, dropout rates are high, and the status quo is preserved. Many labs are attempting to shake the remedial image (and some are succeeding) by encouraging students of all backgrounds in all courses to use their services. Writing tutors have become "writing fellows"; labs have become "centers"; and at some institutions faculty members are encouraged to consult the center for help with their own writing. Yet the exclusionary attitudes remain. Some campuses have even attempted to overcome the stigma by separating a writing center from a remedial lab—further marginalizing the students who most need intellectual contact with students and faculty who use language in the approved ways.

WAC programs are also marginalized when writing "in the

disciplines" is confined to general-composition courses. One of the most common models of WAC amounts to a revised general-composition course, usually taught by English department graduate students or by junior faculty trained in literary analysis. This model simply shifts the emphasis of composition courses toward reading (and writing about) nontechnical, often belletristic essays collected in "WAC readers," on topics from the sciences and social sciences, as well as from the humanities: Stephen Jay Gould, Loren Eiseley, and so on.[52] Such a program need not require (or even ask for) the active involvement of faculty from across the curriculum or even those in the English department outside the composition staff.

Writing intensive courses, sometimes supported by a lab, are another common curricular model for WAC, but these WI's may also tend to marginalize writing in the disciplines.[53] WI courses again concentrate in a few professors or TA's the responsibility for initiating students into the discourse community, while freeing most faculty resources for other activities which the community views as more important. As Tori Haring-Smith points out, when a few courses are labeled *writing intensive,* students sometimes object when other courses require writing. Writing is viewed as an adjunct to a course, even a punishment, not as an accomplishment valued by the community. And WI's do not necessarily provide students with more writing (as a recent survey of such courses at Cornell indicated) because faculty are not always held accountable for writing instruction in these courses.[54] Moreover, WI courses often substitute for one or more semesters of composition, further decreasing the little formal writing instruction that students typically receive.

Even when WAC programs attempt to make writing part of every class, every discipline, the writing can be marginalized if it is perceived as an additional burden rather than as an intrinsic part of learning. At some institutions, administrators have attempted to impose WAC by fiat, sometimes without providing training and support for faculty or securing their consent. Naturally, faculty resent and resist the imposition, considering it "doing the English teacher's job" or "adding writing" of the traditional evaluative kind, often a research paper divorced from the "real" content and activity of the course.[55] For the new generation of upwardly mobile career administrators, advancement often depends on their ability to initiate and support visible, innovative programs. WAC easily becomes part of administrators' curricular and pedagogical reform initiatives. As one administrator recently remarked to me, "WAC is the cheapest faculty development program you can buy." But the danger is that these "top-down" programs may simply reinforce the myth of transience. As Fulwiler points out, "Many administrators believe or want to believe that writing across the curriculum is a quick fix. They seek the immediate gratification of a visibly successful program, one that quiets legislators and enhances administrative careers."[56] Christopher Thaiss, coordinator of the National Network of WAC Programs, sees these administratively mandated programs as one of the most troubling trends in WAC in the 1980s, for it destroys the grass-roots efforts of faculty and breeds resentment.[57]

Without deep changes in the ways that disciplines and institutions approach writing, the WAC movement will, in all likelihood, remain on the margins of the curriculum at many, perhaps most, institutions. What Rudolph said of interdisciplinary programs in the past is no less true of WAC today: "Unless handsomely funded and courageously defended, efforts to launch courses and programs outside the departmental structure [have] generally failed."[58] There is no specific constituency for interdepartmental programs within the structure of the American university, much less for interdepartmental programs that incorporate writing, because the academic community is fragmented, and there is thus no permanent defense against the slow erosion of programs under the pressure of well-defined departmental interests. Until individual disciplines accept the responsibility of studying and teaching the writing of their community to students, WAC programs will continue to be marginalized, subject to the vagaries of existence in an institutional no-man's-land. Writing will continue to be transparent and the myth of transience powerful among those who do not understand or acknowledge the relationship between writing and the creation and acquisition of knowledge.

Rhetoric, Research, and Reform

Like its many predecessors, the current WAC movement encountered an institution whose very structure eroded meaningful reforms. But unlike its predecessors, the current WAC movement has elements within it that do not ignore or attempt to supplant institutional divisions; rather they work through the disciplines to transform not only student writing but also the ways the disciplines conceive of writing and its teaching. The WAC movement (and, with it, elements within the academic disciplines themselves) are attempting to develop new traditions of inquiry into writing and its pedagogy that examine the structure of academia's divisions and the ways that students and faculty may learn to travel among them, not transcend them.

In the late 1970s and 1980s, research into rhetoric and writing has taken a new direction. Instead of examining writing as a single set of generalizable skills and its teaching a set of generalizable principles and techniques, new lines of investigation have examined writing as a constituent of communities, differentiated by the structure of knowledge and the activities of each community. Drawing upon such diverse fields as the history of science, anthropology, sociology, and social psychology, these investigations attempt, as Steven Weiland recently put it, to "assemble the rudiments of rhetorical interpretation and instruction in composition on a field-by-field basis."[59] After a century of working under reductive nineteenth-century assumptions, this research may at last give academia an intellectual foundation on which to construct pedagogies, one that acknowledges the differentiation of written knowledge in modern academia and, indeed, the modern world.

Appropriately, this new direction in rhetorical research began within composition studies as an attempt to resuscitate the research paper, the oldest tradition of extended student writing in the modern university. In the mid 1970s, CUNY professor Charles Bazerman revised his freshman course to strengthen its research-paper component and found that there was almost no research on the rhetorical conventions of various disciplines or on the relationship between college-level reading and writing. His 1979 article on the "conversation model" of academic discourse and his 1981 textbook, *The Informed Writer*, approached writing as a means of drawing students into "wider public, professional, and academic communities." He and others began research into disciplinary rhetorics, the differing ways communities use written discourse in their activities.[60] He found that other disciplines, such as the sociology of science, were also investigating the social and rhetorical dimensions of knowledge. By the mid 1980s, research in disciplinary rhetorics was going on in many fields, both among composition scholars and among scholars in philosophy, anthropology, literary theory, economics, biology, business, history, law, and other fields, as I noted in chapter 1. Even physics, that most theoretical of the modern disciplines, is engaged in a lively debate over whether it should change the conventions of its written discourse to acknowledge the social dimensions of research.[61] It is by no means clear if those who view knowledge in social and rhetorical terms will prevail in their disciplines, but at least the role that writing plays in shaping knowledge is now an issue. Writing cannot so easily remain transparent.

This is a crucial step. For unless disciplines first understand the rhetorical nature of their own work and make conscious and visible what was transparent, the teaching of writing in the disciplines will continue to reinforce the myth of transience and the current WAC movement may share the fate of its predecessors. Writing in content courses will be seen merely as a further opportunity for evaluation or remediation, a means of introducing pedagogical variety, or as a favor to the English department and not as a central part of disciplinary research or teaching.

What is most promising about this line of investigation for those interested in improving student writing and learning is that faculty now have an intellectually respectable avenue for investigating and discussing writing, an avenue that acknowledges the institution's curricular and structural differentiation, instead of lamenting academia's fall from the homogeneous community of the nineteenth-century college and longing for some linguistic homecoming. However, understanding the rhetorical nature of a discipline is no guarantee that the discipline will find and embrace pedagogies for teaching its rhetoric more effectively (or to more students). We must not only understand how a discipline constitutes its discourse but also understand how students learn the discourse of a discipline, how writing plays a role at various stages in their initiation into that community.

A second line of research has begun to investigate these pedagogical implications of disciplinary rhetorics. Faculty from English departments and their colleagues across the curriculum have in the last decade begun to study in specific, concrete ways how students learn the discourse of various disciplines. This research has grown directly out of the WAC programs as participating faculty from many departments have become interested in tracing the development of writing ability in its relation to learning in specific disciplinary and classroom contexts. Such research uses qualitative *and* quantitative methods; it traces the relationships between a discipline's texts, its pedagogy, and its students' texts; it reassesses the old notions of writing as a generalizable skill; it even addresses those central issues of evaluation that have been neglected under the reign of machine-scored tests. For example, some departments and institutions are experimenting with portfolios of student writing, gathered over several months, even years, to measure and promote students' intellectual and communicative development through time.[62]

Through this research, disciplines may eventually be able to design the pedagogical "scaffoldings" that Bruner theorized, curricular structures built of meaningful experiences with language, which will lead students toward progressively more sophisticated engagement with the activities of each discipline through its discourse. And the dream of Dewey—a curricular balance between the interests of the learner and the demands of the disciplines— may be realized as disciplines at last come to grips with the concrete ties between language and the process of learning. After more than a century of complaints and recriminations, the mass-education system may bridge the old rift that has divided student-centered from discipline-centered education and marginalized writing in both.

But discipline-specific rhetorical and pedagogical research is still in its infancy, and it faces major obstacles in translating its results into pedagogical reform. To influence scholarly activity and pedagogy deeply, such research must be valued and supported by the disciplines themselves—not merely by individual scholars inspired by a WAC program, as has largely been the case thus far. By its very nature, WAC research challenges the convenient notion that disciplines are static repositories of knowledge and replaces it with a model of disciplines as communities that are continually being reformed through their discursive practices, including those of students. It opens for criticism the structures of disciplinary formation and initiation, and those critiques can threaten the central assumptions that the members of a discipline have come to take for granted (as faculty participants in WAC research have discovered).

Yet these are the very obstacles WAC must overcome if it is to achieve its ultimate goal: reforming American pedagogy. Reform efforts will continue to depend largely on the goodwill of individual faculty and administrators until disciplines assume responsibility for making writing a central part of their pedagogy. As the fundamental unit of academic organization, disciplines have many means for assuming this responsibility: through their professional associations, their training of graduate students, their accreditation procedures, their support of pedagogical research, their relations with secondary teachers. Some few disciplines have taken small but important steps in this direction. The accrediting body for engineering schools, for example, has made comprehensive writing instruction one of its criteria.

Ultimately, these efforts in the disciplines will themselves depend on broader changes in the structure of secondary and higher education to overcome institutional inertia, which has eroded previous reforms. If writing is to become a central focus of pedagogy, then it must be structurally linked to the values, goals, and activities of disciplines; faculty must see a connection between encouraging better writing among their students and advancing the value and status of their disciplines—and of their own individual careers. Disciplines must find or create places where student writing matters to the disciplinary community. The oral communal performance of the old college is of course unworkable and irrelevant in a writing-based academic culture, but written forums for opening student discourse and its teaching to the communal discussion and criticism of disciplines are possible. For example, if student writing is critiqued by a faculty member's disciplinary peers outside the individual classroom, outside the institution even, then standards for student writing and its teaching will inevitably develop, as will pedagogical traditions for preparing students to meet those standards. European systems provide models of external evaluation of student writing by faculty in a discipline, though the traditional autonomy of American academics in the classroom and the diversity and independence of American institutions in setting curriculum will make such peer review difficult. "Lifting the veils that normally shroud the teaching behavior of individual professors and departments," says Clark, is "perhaps the best way to improve teaching competence in large systems," but it is immensely threatening.[63] Even so, a few institutions have begun programs in which faculty in a WAC program or a discipline review student portfolios. One institution, Swarthmore College, has even begun external reviews of senior honors theses.[64] Such attempts, along with the renewed efforts to improve the evaluation of writing, may again allow written performance to become a viable complement (or in some contexts, even an alternative) to machine-scored tests.

Administrative structures can play an important role in encouraging disciplines to value writing—not by mandating writing or its teaching but by setting up structurally integrated forums that open writing to discussion and critique within and across disciplines. Faculty workshops, WAC committees, writing centers, and consultants provide forums, of course; but these are structurally independent of the fundamental disciplinary organization of institutions and therefore easily dispensed with. If writing is to become a valued part of teaching and learning, then the evaluation of student writing and its role in curricula must become integrated into the disciplinary structure of the academic system: through departmental reviews, teaching evaluations conducted by peers, promotion and tenure procedures, and so on. Peer review of faculty-written texts forms the very basis of disciplinary structure, organizing each disciplinary community's energies toward greater efforts and higher standards. Applying some analogous process to student-written texts may allow the American system to evaluate (and thus value) students' writing performances across a discipline or even across institutions.

Finding ways to harness the efforts of the disciplines—where the faculty's primary loyalty and interest lie—will perhaps achieve more in the long run than structurally separate programs, no matter how well intentioned and well financed. Here again there are political costs and trade-offs. The energies that departments and disciplines expend on student writing might be spent elsewhere, and the critique of learning and teaching that writing opens will challenge both students and faculty. WAC will become part of the ongoing negotiation among the many interests that comprise the system (as Robert Morris College recently discovered when WAC became an issue in contract talks with the faculty union). But without structural changes to integrate writing into the disciplinary fiber of institutions, without a commitment to permanent change in the way academia values writing in pedagogy, WAC programs will always work against the grain.

Despite these formidable obstacles, there are reasons to believe that academia will support research and reform in writing—perhaps even evolve traditions of writing instruction in the disciplines that are fully integrated into the structure of academic work. Industrial society, which gave birth to composition courses a century ago—with its compartmentalization of roles and knowledge, its alienating bureaucratic management, its separation of mental and manual labor—is evolving, some say, into postindustrial society, where new knowledge is created through disciplinary and interdisciplinary collaboration, where competitive advantages are derived from more effective communication (often written) among workers at all levels, and where new management structures replace the rigid hierarchies of the past. Writing instruction may be part of this shift, as it was part of the shift in the American economy a century ago. For example, the recent interest in collaborative-writing and student-writing groups within academia may reflect and support, more or less consciously, collaborative management and worker productivity circles within the business community. WAC may also reflect and support a postindustrial economy in subtle, but crucial ways. Writing instruction is potentially a way of making connections between individual scholars and disciplines, either directly, through the contact many WAC programs encourage among faculty, or indirectly, through research into the discourse of various disciplines, which opens their central assumptions, methodologies, and rhetoric to examination and invites useful comparisons and interactions with others. Unlike many previous cross-curricular writing programs, most versions of WAC today do not posit a unified structure of knowledge, a "theology of education," as did Hutchins' neo-Thomism. But WAC may nevertheless forge links between scholars and disciplines, without attempting to create and impose a single overarching discourse community on academia.[65]

WAC also may have profound implications for preparing students to enter a postindustrial economy (as granting agencies acknowledge, more or less explicitly, through their funding of it). Those who study employment trends generally agree that in fifteen years most jobs will involve information processing, in one form or another, almost always with computers. But in the electronic office of the information age, "computer literacy" may mean much more than mechanical or clerical skill. The productive capacity of America—and perhaps its social cohesion as well—may increasingly depend on rhetorical skill, the ability of an ever-growing portion of the work force to communicate in writing, both in and out of an organizational unit, not only from one person to another but also from one community to another.[66] The rising demand for writing skill, which The Bullock Report noted fifteen years ago, will not likely be reversed, and the growth of information technology may continue to increase it. WAC is one way to prepare students for the complex new roles many of them will play in professional communities. Ideally, cross-curricular writing instruction would initiate students into the discourse of one professional community and give them extensive experience in negotiating the discourse of several other communities, other disciplines. While students cannot be fully initiated into the discourse of all the communities to which they are exposed in their schooling, making writing central to the whole curriculum may give students, in Maimon's phrase, "a sense of intellectual tact," a kind of liberal education that would encourage students to take an intellectual interest in several communities and to respect the logic and diversity of written conventions they find there.[67]

There is indeed much that is new and promising in the current WAC movement, but it would only be reinforcing the myth of transience to assume that these differences, as important as they are, will guarantee WAC's survival. When cross-curricular programs seek to modify the attitudes and compartmental structure of academia, when programs seek to broaden access to professional discourse communities, they become forms of resistance, threats to the institution (or to the century-old conceptions of it). Thus, as with all movements to extend literacy, WAC has political, economic, and social consequences. The empowerment that literacy affords demands power sharing. In composition studies, the identity of the field—perhaps its existence as a discrete discipline—is negotiated in WAC. Will writing specialists be tenure-track faculty, members of a department, or will they primarily be administrative staff consultants, temporary instructors, support personnel? In the postmodern education system, how will various kinds of knowledge and instruction be organized and funded? It is worth contemplating the fate of Great Britain's "new universities," which were founded in the 1960s as innovative centers of interdisciplinary teaching and research but are now suffering from a bureaucratic malaise caused in large part by budgetary and administrative strictures of the present government, a government that discourages the intellectual risk taking that interdisciplinary innovation requires.[68] And finally, WAC has implications for the wider society. If the educational system teaches greater numbers of students to enter academic discourse communities and, through them, coveted professional roles, there may be increased competition, economic dislocation, and political conflict. If, however, the system frankly acknowledges that it is excluding students from professional communities on the basis of their language rather than committing its resources to teaching the linguistic forms of those communities to those students, the results might also be painful. The recent rioting in France over access to higher education (determined there primarily by written examinations) should give one pause. In any case, there are powerful reasons for preserving the myth of transience and equally powerful reasons for reformers to construct alternatives, consciously, deliberately, with some attention to their historical precedents, and great regard for their long-term consequences.

For in historical perspective, WAC is not a single trend or movement; it is, like its predecessors, a collection of often-conflicting approaches to the problem of linguistic differentiation in the modern world. It offers no panacea, but it need not support the myth of transience either. Seen in its full dimensions, WAC can become a convenient tool for focusing our attention in a very practical way on the contradictions of American secondary and higher education, a means of examining rather than skirting the deepest problems. With WAC, the old battles between access and exclusion, excellence and equity, scientific and humanist worldviews, liberal and professional education, all come down to very specific questions of responsibility for curriculum and teaching. WAC ultimately asks: in what ways will graduates of our institutions use language, and how shall we teach them to use it in those ways? And behind this two-part question lies a deeper one: what discourse communities—and ultimately, what social class—will students be equipped to enter? That is an extremely complex question in our heterogeneous society. It is a question that Americans have consistently begged because it forces us to face painful issues of opportunity, of equality, of democracy in education. But underneath the buzzwords and the bustle of programs, it is the question we will inevitably answer by pursuing WAC.

THE WRITING-ACROSS-THE-CURRICULUM MOVEMENT

1990–2000

In the ten years since the first edition of this book appeared, the myth of transience has remained very much alive, and writing is still transparent to the great majority of teachers and students. But signs of change are even more evident than a decade ago, in individual faculty, in disciplines and institutions, and in the U.S. education system in general.

It should come as no surprise that the change has been incremental rather than radical. Writing across the curriculum is still not so much about curriculum per se (what gets taught and learned) but about fundamental reform of teaching and learning (the process of teaching and learning what gets taught and learned). And the same institutional structures fundamentally resist it: the decentralized nature of education; its separation of research and teaching within higher education; its divisions into institutions, disciplines, and discrete courses; and particularly the very loose structures of collaboration—and accountability—that go with decentralization. Similarly, the WAC movement has been very much decentralized, so change is not neatly linear but immensely varied and dispersed.

Yet education in the U.S., like education worldwide, moved in the 1990s to a recognition of these fundamental structural barriers to change. WAC has both supported and benefited from the increasing attention to educational reform. Indeed, the story of WAC in the 1990s is part of the story of an emerging culture of innovation in education, higher education in particular. There is greater attention to teaching, to programmatic improvements in teaching, to student academic life, and particularly to accountability and assessment. One dramatic sign is that many research institutions have begun to tenure and promote some (though few) faculty primarily on the basis of teaching.

In broad structural terms, education has continued to expand in the 1990s, particularly in higher education. The percentage of high school graduates in the U.S. population increased from 77 percent in 1990 to 83 percent in 1999. And, the percentage of college graduates increased from about 21 percent in 1989 to almost 25 percent in 2000.[1] The percentage of the population that has pursued higher education increased even more dramatically. Yet expanding higher education did not bring more open admission, as in the 1970s, but greater sorting, with elite institutions raising requirements and others expanding enrollments, as budgets tightened in the 1990s. This move toward sorting ushered in what has been called an age of accountability in higher education and had important consequences for WAC.

The most important consequence is that WAC had to position itself in relation to other education reforms. In the late 1980s, WAC moved toward what McLeod and Soven called the "second stage" of WAC programs (2). Funding from granting agencies, relatively plentiful in the 1980s, largely dried up in the 1990s, as granting agencies moved on to other priorities in education reform, such as assessment. Internal funding and, much less often, private donations became the mainstay of WAC programs' funding, forcing WAC programs to compete and cooperate with other initiatives to a greater extend than they had ever done before.

Because the WAC movement is so diverse and intertwined with other reform efforts, it is difficult to know how widespread the WAC movement is. The most recent national survey was in 1987 (McLeod and Soven). It indicated that somewhere between 20 and 50 percent of higher education institutions had a WAC program (a 40 percent response rate accounts for the uncertainty.) Surveys of WAC websites and of attendance at the yearly National Network of WAC Programs meetings do not suggest higher figures. But there is clearly a need for research on the extent and composition of efforts nationally (made more difficult by the loose structure of the WAC movement, which I noted above).

Nevertheless, it is possible to trace the development of WAC in the 1990s in terms of changes visible in programs and in the growing WAC literature. In this chapter, I'll look first at some of the major program types as they evolved in the last decade, at various levels, beginning with higher education. I'll then look at four of the most crucial national developments: discipline-based WAC, assessment, research, and dissemination (national and international). Finally, I'll look at some of the ways WAC has aligned itself with other education reform initiatives, such as oral communication and computer-aided learning. But first a word on the two terms that came to define—and split—the movement in the 1990s: writing across the curriculum and writing in the disciplines.

WAC and WID

An unfortunate but understandable controversy pitting writing across the curriculum against writing in the disciplines (WID) developed in the 1990s, which tended to divide rather than unite efforts to improve students writing and learning. In the 1970s and 1980s, WID was usually seen as an integral to WAC, not something separable. But in the 1990s, many composition scholars and programs began to draw distinctions between learning to write *in* the ways disciplines do (which they called WID), and writing *about* the subjects disciplines study (which they called WAC).

As I mentioned in chapter 9, many first-year composition programs taught general composition courses called WAC courses in which students read popular essays and wrote essays (or themes) about subjects that other fields took up. They did so without looking at the writing of those other fields or their activity, their questions, their methods of research, or their epistemologies. Indeed, there were a great number of textbooks published to support such WAC-emphasis composition courses, with thematic units arranged loosely around disciplinary interests.[2] Such courses don't require (or, usually, ask for) the active involvement of faculty from across the curriculum.

Another way of separating WID from WAC was to consider WAC as fundamentally "writing to learn," developing cognitive performance in a field, while WID was considered fundamentally "learning to write" professional discourse, the rhetorical marshalling of arguments in a field. Thus, a WAC approach to a general education course (for example, history) would use "writing-to-learn" techniques, such as journals, or "public discourse," such as letters to the editor. As with the WAC-emphasis composition courses, there is no need to write (or even consider) the discourse of the discipline.[3]

Rationales for splitting WAC from WID often argued that WAC is interdisciplinary (a freeing thing) while WID is merely disciplinary (a confining thing). Still others saw WAC as being about public discourse and WID as being about highly specialized academic discourse.[4]

This WAC/WID distinction grows out of the contradiction in higher education that produced a need for the WAC movement in the first place—the separation between general and professional education, which led to institutional arrangements that try to separate a hypothetical general writing from writing in the disciplines. The dream of an overarching discourse community or super-discourse is still very much alive in English departments and composition programs alike. Indeed, some dismissed what they termed WID programs as mere "grammar across the curriculum" or claimed WID programs lacked ideological edge and "institutional critique."[5]

In a profound sense, the WAC/WID split is the legacy of the "professionalized generalists" discussed in chapter 6. English departments have seen themselves as training generalists, often without seeing that their work (and discourse) is also highly specialized. And there has been a tendency to be suspicious of professional education and specialized discourse (of others).

However, other voices in the WAC movement attacked as a false dichotomy these attempts to split WAC and WID. They argued that WAC and WID are two sides of the same pedagogical coin; or rather, that WID is always a part of WAC, even when faculty imagine that they are teaching students general cognitive skills. Jones and Comprone, for example, argued that research into specialized writing is a hallmark of the WAC movement. Without attention to interaction of WAC with specific disciplines, "WAC may well be absorbed into a potentially amorphous review of general education" (61). In 2000, McLeod and Maimon, reviewing the debates of the 1990s, rightly pointed out that the WAC movement has from its beginnings been more than "grammar across the curriculum," that it has always been concerned with ways knowledge is made in the disciplines.

The institutional contradiction between general and professional education has reinforced the epistemological contradiction that writing is an elementary (and largely transparent) set of skills rather than a central tool for learning and doing myriad human activities. Writing is viewed as a general skill to be taught in composition—or general education—courses, and the myth of transience is reinforced.

General education in higher education (a product of late specialization in the U.S. system) means that most students in an introductory course in some discipline (or even an advanced course) will not pursue a career in that discipline. Thus, most will never need to write the kinds (genres) of discourse that people in the field write. This raises the profoundly difficult question for faculty: What genres do I assign and teach students to write?

To answer this question and get past these contradictions, we will have to have a much better sense of how students of different kinds gradually learn to write the genres of particular disciplines—and how they learn those specialist genres called "public discourse" (usually written by professional journalists). That is, we will have to learn ways to articulate writing development from secondary to higher education, across all four years of higher education, and into further education and work.

The early WAC movement finessed its way through the problem by having students in disciplinary courses do personal writing (for example, journals) or public writing (for example, editorials) or "the essay" (really school themes)—the genres assigned typically in composition classes. The audience for such writing is other students, when it is not the teacher as examiner.

The problem is that, without specific instruction in the specialized discourse of the discipline, students rarely have a chance to develop in a systematic way over their undergraduate years the kinds of writing they will need when they leave higher education, where they will have to write to audiences other than instructor or students. Nor do they see the textual ways a discipline carries on its work and (re)produces its ideology. It is difficult, in practice, to separate writing-to-learn from writing like those in the field, without sacrificing a deep understanding of the field. What counts as good writing in a course or a field is profoundly shaped its questions, goals, methods, and epistemology. But unless higher education confronts these "writing" problems, the divisions remain untouched, and the curricular isolation is reinforced rather than broken down by WAC.

The WAC/WID split was most evident in the articulation between composition courses and WAC initiatives, to which I now turn.

First Year Composition, WAC, and the Abolitionists

The relations between the writing-across-the-curriculum movement and first-year composition (FYC) programs got much more complicated in the 1990s. In some programs, the articulation between WAC and composition was strengthened by extending writing instruction over all four years. One way was to create courses and requirements throughout the undergraduate program, perhaps by moving or expanding composition courses to the sophomore year, by adding or revising writing courses for the junior year, by providing writing-intensive courses or discipline-specific writing courses that consciously build on first year courses, or by a combination of these methods. At Ohio State University, for example, writing requirements were instituted in all four years, some general, others discipline-specific. Other universities transformed FYC into discipline-specific first-year seminars, taught by faculty and graduate students in the disciplines, as we will see.

But at many other higher education institutions—perhaps the great majority—WAC and composition programs retained separate identities, and the articulation was not particularly close. The additive structure of American higher education made it easier to add a program than to rethink the relationship between writing instruction among units, to create a sequence of articulated experiences with writing.

Indeed, some composition teachers and programs have seen WAC as a threat to their existence. If faculty other than composition can and do improve students' writing, then, they argued, there is no need for a general composition course. There were calls from some in composition to abolish general composition courses and substitute instead writing requirements in the disciplines (or nothing at all). Though, as we noted in chapter 6, similar abolitionist proposals had been made over the last century (and a few elite institutions had actually abolished composition), the success of the WAC movement lent a certain credence to recent abolitionist calls.[6]

There have apparently been no institutions that abolished general composition courses in the 1990s (though a handful of institutions have made them optional). The vast majority of WAC programs, theorists, and researchers have seen composition courses, in one form or another, as an important component of writing development in higher education. But the tensions remained, fueled by the suspicions about faculty in the disciplines we noted above. We now consider how the most common curricular models of WAC developed during the 1990s.

Curricular Models of Writing Across the Curriculum

Writing-Intensive Courses

During the 1990s, writing-intensive (WI) courses became the most common curricular model for WAC. Often called "writing enhanced courses" (so they would not sound so intense to faculty and students) or "writing-in-the-major courses," they are regular courses in the disciplines with special writing requirements. Often, students must take two or more to graduate. Pioneered at the University of Michigan and Indiana University in the 1970s and spread through the influence of outstanding programs, such as the University of Missouri at Columbia's, they are an appealing institutional choice because they provide a relatively inexpensive institutionwide structure without requiring fundamental changes to departments or to all but a relatively few individual courses and faculty.

There are many anecdotal reports that WI programs have raised the level of awareness of writing and even changed the institutional culture. And several studies have found that students perceive WI courses as enhancing their education. But the courses can also marginalize writing as students complain of being assigned writing in non-WI courses. WI courses can become little more than formal requirements if standards are lax or unenforced and junior faculty are assigned to teach them. Finally, as Martha Townsend says, "It is hard to make WI programs work" administratively (239). Studies have also found that such courses can provoke faculty resistance.[7]

Freshman Seminars

Freshman seminars are another WID model that made widespread gains in the 1990s. Pioneered at Cornell in the late 1970s, freshman seminars have faculty or graduate students in the disciplines teach a seminar-style course to freshmen (usually a smaller number than in the typical FYC course) about a topic of interest to the instructor. These are not introductory courses, per se, but seminars on special topics, from which the students choose. At Cornell and elsewhere, these seminars have evolved into a comprehensive WID program, including, for example, sophomore seminars, writing-in-the-majors courses and programs, and discipline-specific tutoring.

Since 1997, Cornell (with funding from the Knight Foundation) has formed a consortium of institutions to evolve WID models, specifically. Representatives of participating institutions—public and private, U.S. and European, large and small—meet each summer to share ideas for discipline-based programs, then consult over time with each other and with outside experts. Some thirty institutions have participated thus far.[8]

Writing Centers

In the 1990s, writing centers became full partners with WAC programs. This helped writing centers move beyond their marginalized position as providers of remedial skills to play a more central role in teaching and curriculum. They provided tutoring not only for students in composition courses but also, increasingly, for students in the disciplines. In this way, writing center staff became involved with faculty in the disciplines, in some cases working closely with them.

Partnerships between WAC and writing centers took many forms. Sometimes WAC programs were housed in writing centers, or writing centers were housed in WAC programs. At institutions without formal WAC programs, writing centers often became de facto WAC programs, providing faculty development or consulting with faculty in the disciplines and paving the way, sometimes, for more formal campuswide efforts. At many other institutions, writing centers cooperated closely with WAC programs. For example, some kept files of assignments in various disciplinary courses or offered specialized tutoring for students in WI courses, as some tutors were trained by writing center personnel or faculty in the disciplines to help students in certain courses or programs. This cooperation sometimes evolved into discipline-specific "satellite" writing centers in departments, where tutors from the discipline are trained by writing center personnel. At their most ambitious, partnerships between WAC and writing centers attempt to create a campuswide "writing environment" to facilitate what Barnett and Blumner call "ongoing dialogue about writing and its relationship to thinking and learning among faculty as well as students" (1).

Partnerships between WAC and writing centers were not without their tensions. Established writing centers are sometimes threatened by WAC initiatives, and WAC programs can marginalize writing center work. But some of the most ambitious WAC efforts of the 1990s flowed from these partnerships.[9]

Community Colleges

Two-year (community) colleges grew dramatically in the 1990s, as demand for higher education expanded while funding (and open admissions at four-year state universities) diminished. Community colleges have become leaders in WAC innovations. First-year composition courses are sometimes more thoroughly articulated with other disciplines than in four-year institutions. Undergraduate "writing fellows" trained to tutor writing in the disciplines are a common and successful model, in the absence of graduate students. And two-year colleges have been leaders in introducing electronic and oral communication into pedagogy across the curriculum.

Funding cuts and new initiatives have forced two-year colleges, like four-year colleges, to merge with other new initiatives, such as critical thinking and assessment. Stanley, editor of one of the two collections on two-year college WAC (both published in the early 1990s) found that the programs of contributors had been merged with or absorbed into other initiatives. But even here, innovation is widespread. For example, Longview Community College won a national award for its assessment-based WAC program (see under Assessment below). Moreover, some of the best research has come out of two-year colleges as well.[10]

Much remains to be done, particularly in terms of four-year institutions articulating WAC efforts with those of community colleges. And rising teaching loads make curricular and pedagogical innovations all the more difficult. But WAC is clearly a viable option for community colleges and will be more so as innovations are disseminated through publication in such journals as *Teaching English in the Two-Year College*.

Secondary and Elementary Schools

In the last decade, some two hundred articles and books, representing almost every subject area, were published on WAC in secondary schools, representing almost one third of the total. But the literature on secondary school WAC reflects only part of the growth. From individual teachers' collaborative efforts and pioneering districtwide reforms in the 1980s, such as Volusha County schools in Florida, secondary school WAC evolved into larger district, state, and national efforts.

The most widespread and coordinated efforts have come out of assessment initiatives, which drove change in every aspect of WAC in the 1990s. At the state level, Vermont's portfolio requirement, begun in the 1980s, was developed by other states, Kentucky most visibly. In Kentucky, beginning in 1992, students in grades 4, 8, and 12 were required to submit a portfolio of their work, to include some pieces of writing from subjects other than language arts. This high stakes exam, assessed collaboratively by teachers, led many schools to involve subject area teachers in writing development in-service and portfolio assessment, efforts supported and encouraged by the state through a team of itinerant writing consultants.

The National Writing Project (always the leader in secondary school WAC) collaborated with assessment efforts in many states— and with national alternative assessment efforts, notably the New Standards Project. Many attempted to develop "tests worth teaching to" by including writing in all subjects. Though cross-curricular writing assessment (like all assessment) has been very controversial, it has certainly raised awareness of the role of writing in learning. And the future of WAC in secondary education depends on whether and how well writing appears in assessment and how teachers in subject areas support (and are supported in) developing students writing and their learning through writing.[11]

Elementary schools might be said to have always used WAC because students typically write as part of studying all subjects, and elementary teachers teach all subjects. But the 1990s saw increased attention to writing in those areas beyond language arts—in science, social studies, and even math. The whole language movement emphasized an integrated approach to teaching writing, in which students read and write about a range of subjects in a range of forms or genres. Studies of children's writing found that students in classrooms where teachers frequently used children's literature, integrated reading and writing, and taught skills in context developed reading and writing skills at higher levels than students in classrooms where teachers used other practices.[12]

The resurgence of standardized testing in the 1990s often worked to constrain WAC in elementary schools, as in secondary schools. But materials that emphasize writing in areas beyond language arts have proliferated in spite of the constraints. And alternative methods of assessment that meaningfully incorporate student writing are now viable options for making integrating writing more effectively, as recent research on the effects of the most visible of these, the Primary Learning Record, has shown.[13]

Relations to Other Movements and Organizations

In 1996, Walvoord warned that WAC must "dive in or die" (70). That is, WAC programs must find a ways to work with other education reform initiatives in order to prosper—and avoid being swept way in the massive wave of educational reform, where faculty are often "initiatived to death." We now look at how WAC has "dived in" by forming alliances with disciplines; with assessment efforts; with learning communities; and with oral, visual, and electronic communication.

Disciplinary Developments

Disciplines and professions still hold the greatest unrealized potential for developing students' writing across the curriculum. Faculty in both higher and secondary education see themselves primarily as members of a discipline. And the fundamental unit of institutional organization is the department. If faculty within a department or, more broadly, a discipline can find intellectually respectable avenues for investigating and discussing writing in relation to pedagogy, then WAC can flourish in ways that are impossible when change comes only through the efforts of individual faculty, however well supported by a central WAC program.

Unfortunately, there has been relatively little development in the past decade of departmental approaches to WAC. This is due perhaps to several factors. WAC programs have made little attempt to involve departments and disciplines, per se, as historically the WAC movement has focused on individual faculty in interdisciplinary workshops or WI courses centrally administered. Moreover, the WAC movement grew out of composition, primarily, where disciplinarity has not been a central concern, and out of general education programs, which attempt to transcend disciplines. As we noted above, there is much suspicion in composition of disciplinary writing as jargon-laden and, more recently, oppressive to students' attempts to find an individual voice.

Yet there have been a number of WAC programs that take as their unit of change the individual department. At some institutions, department-specific efforts grow out of goal-setting and assessment efforts universitywide. Each department develops (often in consultation with the WAC program) discipline-specific goals (outcomes) for their students and a departmental plan for meeting those—which differ widely among departments. At these universities, departments are now revising courses and teaching methods to sequence communication experiences throughout departmental curricula. These sorts of programs produce a cycle of development and responsibility for continuous improvement that can outlast any singe faculty member or administrator.[14]

Even where departments are not the primary focus, many WAC programs work with departments on an ad hoc basis to sequence communication experiences into departmental curricula. Department-specific colloquiums, workshops, and planning grants are common. Statewide demands for accountability, as in Virginia, have led in some cases to training departmental faculty to assess student writing—and, ideally, teach more with it. In other programs, departments or colleges select undergraduate or graduate students to be trained by the WAC program for tutoring students in courses, providing "backdoor" faculty development. There are also a number of college-specific WAC programs, such as Iowa State's AgComm and programs in business and engineering at Clemson.[15]

Though a programmatic focus on disciplines has been rare, the publishing industry has produced discipline-specific guides to writing for faculty who wish to improve their students' communication and learning through writing—especially faculty teaching WI courses. For example, HarperCollins publishes "short guides" to writing in seven disciplines, several of which have gone into multiple editions, and other publishers cover these and other disciplines with their own guides.[16]

Perhaps the most encouraging developments in the disciplines and professions are discipline-specific movements to incorporate writing in teaching. Though it may seem surprising at first glance, mathematics has been a leader in this regard. Science teaching has also produced a range of innovative pedagogical strategies and materials that incorporate writing—beyond the traditional cookbook laboratory report. Indeed, the National Science Foundation has funded dozens of studies of writing to learn science, math, and economics. These efforts, like similar efforts in social sciences such as history, have not yet been analyzed in terms of either the collective import of their findings or in terms of their dissemination with in the disciplines. Whether or not the professions are moving—or will move—in the direction of writing in the discipline is an important but unanswered question.[17]

Professional education has also moved in some cases toward systematically incorporating writing into its teaching. Law schools have for many years employed staff to improve students' writing. But the most dramatic changes have come through accreditation and certification processes requiring writing. In the late 1990s, engineering revamped its accreditation process (ABET) to make communication a requirement across the curriculum. No longer is a separate technical communication course adequate. Students must demonstrate communication skills in engineering courses. ABET has spurred many engineering departments and colleges to rethink how they are improving students' communication—and their learning through communication. In many cases, fruitful collaborations with WAC programs and technical writing programs began. Similarly, in the 1990s, the accounting profession added significant written components to the CPA examination, which may bring accounting departments to make explicit efforts to teach the writing necessary on the exam—and perhaps in the field itself.[18]

These are very positive developments, but it remains to be seen how individual disciplines and professions will accept the responsibility of investigating and teaching the writing of their community to students or whether writing will continue to be largely transparent.

Assessment

Assessing WAC programs and the students writing in them emerged as a central concern in the 1990s. Assessment is in many ways the "growing edge" of WAC as it enters the twenty-first century. During the 1980s, assessment was primarily concerned with programs, making a case for funding, usually. WAC programs looked at the number of faculty who attended workshops, taught WI courses, or revised syllabi to include more (and more effective) writing. But these outcomes were perceived as too narrowly defined when higher education moved into what Walvoord has characterized as "a new era—the era not of access but of accountability" (69). Faculty involvement and development proved to be much more complex than workshop attendance or syllabus revision, as Walvoord showed in her longitudinal study of participating WAC faculty in three institutions.[19] And the big question remained: Are students writing and learning better?

Thus, administrators, funding agencies, and other stakeholders began demanding assessment of *student performance* to measure the effectiveness of WAC programs. This posed thorny problems as it is devilishly difficult to measure either writing or learning and even more difficult to measure whether the changes are due to the WAC efforts. Early studies showed that learning did not significantly improve as measured by the usual multiple choice tests, and writing did not significantly improve as measured by timed assessments of general writing skills. But these were not valid measures of the higher-order learning or writing that WAC aimed to improve. Later, an increasing number of studies showed that higher-order thinking did improve, as well as discipline-specific writing. And new measures were developed that got at the discipline-specific features of writing.[20]

With these demands for and improvements in assessment, an increasing number of programs used assessment to drive WAC. For example, in Longview Community College's national award-winning program, students submit a paper from a course in the disciplines to be assessed by faculty across the curriculum, involving faculty and other stakeholders in the process. North Carolina State made departmental goal-setting and assessment in oral and written communication the engine for WAC.[21]

Elsewhere, portfolios of student writing across the curriculum were widely promoted and experimented with as a way to involve a range of stakeholders, promote faculty involvement, and make writing relevant to assessment (and vice versa). At Washington State University, for example, entering students take a placement writing exam for FYC, and then as juniors they submit a portfolio of writing from several courses, to qualify for writing-in the-majors courses. Some institutions have even moved toward an electronic writing portfolio.[22]

On a wider scale, portfolios can be used to assess writing and learning beyond the individual school. In Kentucky, as we noted,

K–12 portfolios are assessed by teams of teachers within the school, then by teachers judging samples taken from several schools or districts, to ensure consistency. This process, called "moderation," was developed in England by James Britton, who provided much of the theoretical basis for WAC, though his work in assessment is much less known in the U.S. In England, national comparisons of writing portfolios across schools (and of student writing across universities) within each discipline are routine. The moderation system was imported to the U.S. through the Primary Learning Record and was used to assess students' learning in elementary and secondary schools in some districts. Studies have shown that such cross-institution assessment not only makes reliable comparisons but also involves teachers and other stakeholders more than traditional timed writing tests or multiple choice tests. A number of studies have also shown that teachers' Primary Learning Record assessments of students are at least equal in rigor to standardized tests.[23]

Efforts to meaningfully assess student performance in writing (and learning) across the curriculum are still not widespread, however. They often encounter resistance, both from teachers who (often justly) distrust them as a dangerous intrusion and from administrators and other stakeholders who advocate traditional assessments as less expensive and more objective (as they understand that term). Yet collaborative assessment of writing done in courses can provide more authentic measures and at the same time bring stakeholders together to develop and apply standards. This can lead to a different—and often more useful—kind of objectivity, where mutual understanding and consensus building is the key. In my view, the future of WAC depends on these sorts of innovations, as only assessment (combined with disciplines' rising awareness of the importance of communication in learning and teaching) can organize the resources necessary make WAC central to education nationally, rather than leaving it as only an exciting option for individual teachers and institutions.

Learning Communities

In the early 1990s, many universities began programs to place first-year students in what are variously called freshman interest groups (FIGs), learning teams, or learning communities, to give students a sense of belonging and to increase retention. From the mid-1970s, some WAC programs had "linked courses," in which a course in the disciplines was tied to an accompanying WI section or sections where students wrote about the content of the disciplinary course. These linked-course programs quickly developed relationships with learning community programs. For example, the University of Washington had an outstanding linked-course program since the 1970s and joined with a FIG program in 1990 so that students in almost all of its some twenty-five linked courses were also in FIGs. Research showed that students in FIGs with writing links responded most favorably to the FIG program. Kerr and Picciotto found significant gains in student performance within the disciplines at Oglethorpe University in a program of linked FYC courses combined with WI courses in later years. At George Mason University, a linked-course program evolved into an "integrated studies program," where students complete virtually all their general education requirements in one year, through four interdisciplinary team-taught learning community courses that integrate writing assignments across disciplines.[24]

Some programs have found it is difficult to retain the integrity of the composition course in a link, particularly where the writing teacher is a graduate student who may have little expertise in the linked discipline and little clout or long-term investment in the collaboration. But in the most successful versions of learning communities, FYC, WAC, and student services (such as residence life) collaborate to provide students with a rich and integrated experience. Writing teachers—or even undergraduate tutors—collaborate with faculty in many fields to become resources for each other on writing and learning in the disciplines, sharing their expertise.

From WAC to CAC

WAC moved in the 1990s toward *communication* across the curriculum (CAC) in many places, incorporating oral and even, at times, visual communication. At North Carolina State University, Clemson University, Tidewater Community College, and elsewhere, faculty were given encouragement and training to incorporate oral elements to courses, such as group discussions, speeches, and oral presentations. At Iowa State University, visual communication was added, with training for faculty on incorporating visuals into documents and oral presentations.

The discipline of speech communication also made national efforts to build programs across the curriculum, though there are similar tensions between CAC and first-year courses. Sometimes these efforts were in conjunction with WAC efforts, sometimes in separate programs. And a literature is emerging in the discipline on CAC.[25]

As new technology facilitates multimedia communications, oral and visual elements will become increasingly conjoined and important. Many WAC programs are now calling themselves "CAC" (an equally unfortunate acronym). Indeed, some are already wondering whether the term WAC is obsolete.

Computers and WAC

Another profound change in education in the 1990s was, of course, electronic technology. In the early 1990s, Michigan Technical University (home to one of the most important early WAC programs) began offering each summer a "computer camp" for faculty in the disciplines nationally, which developed and disseminated strategies for improving student writing using computers, especially e-mail discussions.[26]

In the mid-1990s, WAC took to the web like a duck to water. After all, the web is primarily made of written documents. Programs were able to communicate efficiently with faculty and students through the web. A survey of colleges and universities showed that some 128 U.S. institutions had a WAC website. Almost one third of the 88 Research I schools had one, the highest percentage. Only 0.6% of the 1,471 two-year institutions have one. WAC programs also used the web in conjunction with writing centers, in "online writing labs" (OWLs), such as the pioneering site at Purdue. At other institutions, undergraduate writing fellows were trained to assist faculty in assignment design and writing instruction electronically, using the web.[27]

One of the most promising developments in WAC in the 1990s is computer-aided writing instruction for specific disciplines.

Teachers in many disciplines experimented with electronic journals, discussions, chats, web-based student research, publication, and self-evaluation. E-mail and MOO connections with students in other courses (and even other disciplines) at the same institution or at others around the nation or the world provided innovative pedagogy. Though the web made it easier for students
to purchase term papers, it also provided ways to catch plagia-
rists—and may force more faculty to consider WAC alternatives to the old pastiche of quotations that too-often passed for
a "term paper."

Web-based instructional software was developed in a number
of fields, first with virtual cases in specific disciplines that could
be shared by faculty in that field, later with more sophisticated
software and web-based materials to integrate writing into learning and teaching that would otherwise have little or none.[28] For
example, National Science Foundation grants have provided support for numerous web-based efforts to teach science writing online
in support of courses. Lab-Write, developed at North Carolina
State University, provides students with sophisticated heuristics and
other direct instruction for writing laboratory reports, transforming what is often a "cook-book" classroom genre that requires
little thinking beyond following instructions into a way of teaching the structure of scientific thinking and argument.[29]

Some institutions made electronic multimedia training for faculty the center of their WAC faculty development efforts. At
Spellman College, for example, a multimedia facility taught faculty how to develop materials and activities that integrated writing and speaking as the faculty learned to use computers.[30]

Distance education—growing by leaps and bounds—provided
enormous opportunities to integrate writing and learning in new
ways. Most communication in distance education is of course
written, in many ways forcing new attention to writing. For example, the InterQuest philosophy course assignments are carefully sequenced to "scaffold" learning as students write progressively more sophisticated responses to the material. Finally,
experiments with electronic portfolios and online learning records
in the late 1990s offer the possibility that students can display
their work for formative and summative assessment, allowing

others in the course, the institution, or the discipline to see and comment on the work.[31]

Computer-aided instruction promises to make discipline-specific writing experiences available to students and faculty who would otherwise not have the expertise to develop and use them. The World Wide Web has made writing ever more pervasive in our lives. And WAC is both making use of it and helping us make sense of it.

Research and Dissemination Efforts

Research

Research on writing and learning exploded in the 1990s. One of the most significant developments in writing research over the last decade has been the large number of naturalistic studies of college-level writing in the disciplines, over two hundred. Qualitative studies have predominated in recent years because the early attempts to perform quantitative experimental studies yielded confusing results. As we noted, when these studies attempted to test a central claim of WAC, that writing improves learning or thinking (Emig), they found that writing does not automatically improve either. Indeed, when writing was used to improve students' performance on the usual kinds of school tests, it sometimes had no effect or a negative effect. However, when students were given tasks differing significantly from the standard knowledge-transmission purposes of the schools, writing helped students learn.[32]

Qualitative research on how students write and learn to write has been profoundly influenced by cultural-historical ethnographic and discourse-analysis studies of literacy. Individual case studies of students in secondary and undergraduate education have begun to map the many and often messy paths students take to gain agency, authority, and identity through writing in the specialized ways that mediate specialized activity in a field. Studies have also shown the "mismatch" between what students and their teachers expect. There have also been many remarkable recent studies of internships, which describe student/professionals in transition, struggling to make sense of a professional network's writing using the tools they picked up in their schooling. Similarly, studies of the transition from undergraduate to graduate education have broadened our understanding of the complex play of power and identity with writing processes in complex hierarchical professional systems of activity. And all these studies are informed by studies of writing in the professions, in communities, and in personal life histories, which also blossomed in the 1990s.[33]

Despite the remarkable output of research, two great challenges remain. Research has found no neat path of development in writing. It is immensely variable and messy. We still do not have an analysis of how students (from various backgrounds) come to write in the ways the various disciplines expect (or how students change those expectations). So it is difficult to structure activities that balance the demands of the discipline with the interests of the learner and move students toward increasingly productive engagement with the discipline or with civil society in their writing—"scaffolding" as Bruner termed it.

The other challenge is dissemination. Though some review essays and some faculty development books that are research based appeared in the 1990s, the insights of research are not readily available to faculty and program directors. As research expands and becomes more sophisticated, new ways will have to be found to make it useful in classrooms across the curriculum.[34]

National Dissemination: Conferences, Journals, and Awards

As Walvoord pointed out, WAC has never had a strong national organization but has remained a loose, grassroots structure, which she characterized as "independent congregations linked by itinerant preachers rather than a strongly organized central church with a central orthodoxy" (61). The only permanent national structure is the National Network of WAC Programs, which publishes an annual list of member institutions and has held, since 1981, an evening meeting at the annual Conference of College Composition and Communication convention.

But in 1993, a group of South Carolina WAC programs organized a National WAC Conference, which has been held every two years since. This conference attracted faculty from a very wide range of disciplines and, of course, WAC program directors. The WAC conferences, attracting as many as five hundred participants, have been instrumental in raising the awareness of WAC nationally. Moreover, there have been several disciplinary conferences emphasizing communication, such as the regional conference on CAC in Agriculture at Iowa State University in 1999, sponsored by the U.S. Department of Agriculture.

The 1990s also saw new journals devoted to WAC. In 1996, a journal was launched specifically devoted to research on WAC/CAC programs, *Language and Learning in the Disciplines*. And a comprehensive electronic journal, *Academic.writing*, was launched in 1999, providing not only research articles but a comprehensive clearing house for teaching materials, program descriptions, and even online reprints of important books on WAC.[35]

WAC programs continued to get national recognition, and that increased dramatically as national organizations honored WAC programs. Indeed, in 2001, Clemson University, Cornell University, and Longview Community College were awarded the *Time/Princeton Review* "College of the Year" awards in their respective categories. In each case, the award was given specifically for their work with WAC.

For a decade, there has been a steady stream of textbooks, teaching materials, and faculty development guides in print and electronic format—some very innovative. For example, Robert Morris College, in collaboration with PBS Adult Satellite Service, produced five interactive videoconferences. Each videoconference was received live, via satellite, by between 150 and 300 locations across North America, for a total of 10,000 to 25,000 viewers each, and the programs received several prestigious national awards.[36]

Despite this widespread effort, WAC is still not a major influence in national organizations devoted to education reform, such as the American Association of Higher Education or the Carnegie Foundation for the Advancement of Teaching. Writing is still marginalized. The national presence of WAC became more visible in the 1990s despite a lack of an organized voice. But a more organized effort will almost certainly be necessary if WAC is to maintain an identity and become a major voice in national reforms. Whether or not such an identity and voice are worth giving up the freedom of the grass roots is a question often debated within the WAC movement.

International

By the end of the decade, WAC had become an international movement. The same contradiction between greater access to higher education and increasing work specialization that had fueled the WAC movement in the U.S. led many nations to take a new interest in academic writing development. On one end, far more students and far more *diverse* students are streaming into higher education worldwide—bringing in a far greater diversity of linguistic resources: returning students, first-generation university students, international students, students from previously excluded groups. On the other end, students are leaving higher education to enter far more diverse workplaces—not only in terms of the backgrounds of entering workers (age, national origin, class origin, and so on) but also in terms of the sheer specialization of knowledge and work.

General composition courses in higher education are almost unheard of in other nations, so efforts tend to focus in the disciplines. And their assessment systems are much more dependent on mass written assessment, raising the stakes for writing. In Europe, traditional language programs for international students (part of student support units) began to respond to new demands from nontraditional native students for writing help by encouraging faculty to use writing in new ways.

In England, where the WAC movement began at the secondary level, widespread changes in higher education led in the mid-1990s to programs, research efforts, and a yearly conference, called Writing Development in Higher Education. Similar efforts in a number of European countries led to the formation of the European Association of Teachers of Academic Writing (EATAW), in conjunction with the European Writing Centers Association. And the International Association for the Improvement of Mother Tongue Education (IAIMTE) focused on writing development as never before. At the beginning of the new century, there are two journals being formed, and a book series on academic writing has ten volumes published. Developing nations also feel the pressures of writing in higher education, as well as at all other levels. And there are major program and research initiatives in Africa and the Pacific Rim.[37]

International efforts have been influenced by U.S. efforts, but they are creating innovative responses to their particular national and local needs, many of which can offer the WAC movement in the U.S. fresh approaches by "making the familiar strange."

Conclusion

The WAC movement is now over thirty years old—a very long run indeed for an educational reform movement. Clearly, it meets a need—better learning and writing for students, better teaching for faculty. By learning to write in new ways, students are expanding their involvement with the different worlds that make up our world. Writing organizes our lives, our worlds, even more now than a decade ago, as the Internet and intranets reach into every domain of modern life. And for faculty, WAC is ultimately about finding textual pathways to help students enter and eventually transform powerful organizations of people. Our lives are linked by the written word in ways so pervasive and mundane that we forget sometimes how powerful writing is to our futures and to the futures of students. WAC reminds us, students and faculty, that writing is powerful, even when it seems transparent—and that the problems of learning to write in new ways are not transient but a permanent condition of (post)modern life.

In this sense, writing and WAC focus our attention on the deep contradictions of education and of our civic life. The need for specialization versus the call for a unified, democratic civic life drives the debates over general versus professional education and thus the WAC/WID split. The need to initiate students into the powerful ways with words of disciplines and professions, which I emphasized in chapter 9, are now more than ever held in tension with the need for a wider and often more critical sense of civic responsibility and a need for civic action. The seemingly simple questions, "What will my students write?" and "How will I assess it?" lead to questions of the futures we envision, questions of equity and access for traditionally excluded groups, questions of who our students, and we, are and will be as members of society. WAC is a way of still answering those deepest questions.

As I think back over the whole history of writing in the academic disciplines, the most inspiring and troubling questions are those raised by Dewey, still the "presiding ghost" of WAC, as Maimon put it.[38] Dewey dreamed of a curricular balance between the interests of the learner and the demands of the disciplines, between our lives as individuals and our lives in democratic communities mediated by technologies of communication. We have still not yet formulated an analysis of discipline-specific learning activities to produce increasingly more sophisticated levels of critical understanding and writing performance—instructional scaffolding that can bridge the rift between student-centered and discipline-centered education that have marginalized writing for so long. But the WAC movement has made important strides toward that through research and program development over the past decade. And I think such a balance is now possible.

It is possible because WAC has become an institutional presence, much more so than a decade ago. It is likely that every institution of higher education (if not K–12 education) now has faculty who have worked with WAC at some institution, even if their current one does not have a program. And administrators more and more see campuswide WAC as a viable option. But WAC is not yet an expectation (as, for example, assessment is). The U.S. education system will have to find new ways of organizing teaching and assessing learning through writing in order to make WAC an expectation rather than an exception.

Students learn by expanding their involvements, academic and civic. So too must the WAC movement learn by expanding, as it has for three decades now. And the 1990s showed how crucial are the intersections of writing and learning with assessment, communication in other media, electronic links among us, and the disciplines and professions that organize our worlds. The future of WAC, like its past, is about forging alliances, expanding with new connections, even as we wrestle with the inevitable contradictions of education and civic life.

NOTES
WORKS CITED
INDEX

NOTES

Abbreviations

On the left are the code letters used to cite each manuscript collection in the notes.

CC   Columbiana Collection. Columbia University. Faculty papers and memorabilia.

CCA   Central College Archives, Pella, Iowa. Papers of the Communication Skills Program.

CUA   Columbia University Archives. Committee records, faculty papers, and correspondence.

FWP   Colgate University Archives. Papers of the Functional Writing Program.

HUA   Harvard University Archives. The Curriculum Collection is perhaps the largest and most complete collection of course materials and student papers in the United States. A fifty-year limit makes materials unavailable from the Redbook reforms of the 1940s to the present.

ISU   Iowa State University Archives. Student dissertations, commencement orations, and senior theses. Faculty papers and curriculum materials.

KU   Kansas University Archives. Papers of Oread and Orophilian societies; faculty papers and minutes; student papers of alumni.

MIT   Massachusetts Institute of Technology Archives. Curriculum materials. Papers and correspondence of faculty.

MU   University of Missouri Archives. Papers of Athenaeum and Union literary societies; faculty papers and minutes; student papers of alumni.

OSU   Ohio State University Archives. Papers and correspondence of faculty. Departmental records.

PIC   University of California at Berkeley, English Department Records. Papers of the Prose Improvement Committee (courtesy of Ralph W. Rader).

UCA   University of Chicago Archives. Papers and curriculum materials from the University College. Papers and correspondence of faculty.

UMA University of Michigan Archives. Papers and personal correspondence of faculty. Curriculum records.

YA Yale University Archives. Papers and correspondence of faculty. Papers of alumni.

1.
Introduction: The Myth of Transience

1. For the following analysis, I am deeply indebted to Susan Miller, *Rescuing the Subject: A Critical Introduction to Rhetoric and the Writer* (Carbondale: Southern Illinois U P, 1989) chap. 2.

2. On the expanding role of writing in industrial management, see JoAnne Yates, *Control through Communication: The Rise of System in American Management* (Baltimore: Johns Hopkins U P, 1989).

3. From the mid nineteenth century to the late twentieth, definitions of adult literacy rose from the ability to write one's signature or recognize letters to the ability to read and write at a twelfth-grade level. On increasing standards of literacy in response to industrialization, see Jeanne S. Chall, "Developing Literacy . . . in Children and Adults," in *The Future of Literacy in a Changing World,* ed. Daniel A. Wagner (Oxford: Pergamon, 1987) 65–80.

4. Harvey Daniels, *Famous Last Words: The American Language Crisis Reconsidered* (Carbondale: Southern Illinois U P, 1983); see also Leonard A. Greenbaum, "A Tradition of Complaint," *College English* 31 (1969): 174–78.

5. "Report of the Committee on Composition and Rhetoric," no. 28 in *Reports of the Visiting Committees of the Board of Overseers of Harvard College,* 1902, 155 (HUA).

6. Mike Rose, "The Language of Exclusion: Writing Instruction at the University," *College English* 47 (1985): 355.

7. For studies of the appropriation of progressive ideas, see David B. Tyack, *The One Best System: A History of American Urban Education* (Cambridge, MA: Harvard U P, 1974); Michael B. Katz, *Class, Bureaucracy, and Schools* (New York: Praeger, 1971); and Roderic C. Botts, "Influences in the Teaching of English, 1917–1935: An Illusion of Progress," diss., Northwestern U, 1970.

8. See, for example, Christopher Thaiss, "The Future of Writing Across the Curriculum," in *Strengthening Programs for Writing Across the Curriculum,* ed. Susan H. McLeod (San Francisco: Jossey, 1988) 94; Tori Haring-Smith, "What's Wrong with Writing across the Curriculum?" CCCC Convention, Atlanta, Mar. 1987.

9. C. W. Knoblauch and Lil Brannon, "Writing as Learning through the Curriculum," *College English* 45 (1983): 465–74.

10. James A. Berlin, "Contemporary Composition: The Major Pedagogical Theories," *College English* 44 (1982): 770; see also Jasper P. Neel, *Plato, Derrida, and Writing* (Carbondale: Southern Illinois U P, 1988) chap. 4.

11. On the process of commodifying expert knowledge, see Andrew Abbott, *The System of Professions: An Essay on the Division of Expert Labor* (Chicago: U of Chicago P, 1988) chaps. 6 and 7.

12. This line of investigation, on which my historical analysis is based, draws on the theoretical resources of several disciplines: social history, sociology, history and philosophy of science, anthropology, sociolinguistics, and poststructuralist literary theory. The framework—really a bricolage—I outline here is deeply indebted to the synthesis of recent theories on the social nature of writing by Charles Bazerman, *Shaping Written Knowledge: The Genre and Activity of the Experimental Article in Science* (Madison: U of Wisconsin P, 1988). I have also borrowed heavily from historians and sociologists of education to connect the production of written knowledge with the differentiated structure of modern mass education and professional culture, particularly Burton R. Clark, *The Academic Life: Small Worlds, Different Worlds* (Princeton: Carnegie Foundation for the Advancement of Teaching, 1987); and Burton J. Bledstein, *The Culture of Professionalism: The Middle Class and the Development of Higher Education in America* (New York: Norton, 1976).

13. Terezinha Carraher, "Illiteracy in a Literate Society: Understanding Reading Failure in Brazil," in Wagner 101.

14. Carolyn R. Miller, "Genre as Social Action," *Quarterly Journal of Speech* 70 (1984): 159; qtd. in Bazerman, *Shaping* 7n.

15. Arthur N. Applebee, *Writing in the Secondary School: English and the Content Areas*. NCTE Research Report no. 21. (Urbana: NCTE, 1981) 4.

16. Bazerman, *Shaping* 302–4.

17. Donald N. McCloskey, *The Rhetoric of Economics* (Madison: U of Wisconsin P, 1986); Greg Myers, "The Social Construction of Two Biologists' Proposals," *Written Communication* 2 (1985): 219–45; Glenn Broadhead and Richard C. Freed, *The Variables of Composition: Process and Product in a Business Setting* (Carbondale: Southern Illinois U P, 1985); James Boyd White, *Heracles' Bow: Essays on the Rhetoric and Poetics of the Law* (Madison: U of Wisconsin P, 1986); Hayden White, *The Content of the Form: Narrative Discourse and Historical Presentation* (Baltimore: Johns Hopkins U P, 1987); Yates, *Control;* Ludwig Fleck, *Genesis and Development of a Scientific Fact* (Chicago, U of Chicago P, 1979); Bruno Latour, *Science in Action* (Cambridge, MA: Harvard U P, 1987); Harriet Zuckerman, *Scientific Elite* (New York: Free P, 1977).

18. See S. Michael Halloran, "Rhetoric in the American College Curriculum: The Decline of Public Discourse," *Pre/Text* 3 (1982): 246–49.

19. See James A. Berlin, *Writing Instruction in Nineteenth-Century American Colleges* (Carbondale: Southern Illinois U P, 1984) chap. 7; and James A. Berlin, *Rhetoric and Reality: Writing Instruction in American Colleges 1900–1985* (Carbondale: Southern Illinois U P, 1987) esp. 15–19 and 155–79.

20. Jerome S. Bruner introduces the concept in *The Process of Education* (Westminster, MD: Random, 1963) 52–54. The quotation is from Bazerman, *Shaping* 306.

21. Lev Vygotski, *Thought and Language* (Cambridge: MIT P, 1962).

22. Clifford Geertz, *Local Knowledge: Further Essays in Interpretive Anthropology* (New York: Basic Books, 1983) 84.

23. Applebee, *Writing* 4.

24. For an overview of the issue of discourse community in institutional contexts see Richard C. Freed and Glenn Broadhead, "Discourse Communities, Sacred Texts, and Institutional Norms," *College Composition and Communication* 38 (1987): 154–65. For an overview of second-language research in discourse "domains," see Larry Selinker and Dan Douglas, "LSP and Interlanguage: Some Empirical Studies," *English for Specific Purposes* 6 (1987): 75–85.

25. For attempts at cross-national comparisons of writing performance see *An International Perspective on the Evaluation of Written Composition*, ed. Alan C. Purves and Saule Takala (New York: Pergamon, 1982); and *The IEA Study of Written Composition*, ed. T. P. Gorman, Alan C. Purves, and R. E. Desenhart (New York: Pergamon, 1988).

26. See Halloran, "Rhetoric" 249–56.

27. Daniel P. Resnick and Lauren B. Resnick, "The Nature of Literacy: An Historical Exploration," *Harvard Educational Review* 47 (1977): 385, qtd. in Rose 355. On the increasing and proliferating standards of literacy, see also Dell H. Hymes, "Foreword," in Wagner xi–xvii.

28. Gerald Graff, *Professing Literature* (Chicago: U of Chicago P, 1987) 6–15. See also theoretical discussions in *Interdisciplinary Relationships in the Social Sciences*, ed. Muzafer Sherif and Carolyn W. Sherif (Chicago: Aldine, 1969); and Stanley Fish, "Being Interdisciplinary Is So Very Hard To Do," *Profession* (1989): 15–22.

29. See Clark, *Academic Life* esp. chap. 5.

30. Laurence R. Veysey, *The Emergence of the American University* (Chicago: U of Chicago P, 1965) 338.

31. See Ernest L. Boyer and Arthur Levine, *A Quest for Common Learning: The Aims of General Education* (Washington, DC: Carnegie Foundation for the Advancement of Teaching, 1982) chap. 1.

32. Burton Clark, *The Higher Education System: Academic Organization in Cross-National Perspective* (Berkeley: U of California P, 1983) chap. 7, esp. 251–53.

33. See Albert R. Kitzhaber, *Themes, Theories, and Therapy* (New York: McGraw, 1963) 14–15.

34. Worth Anderson, Cynthia Best, Alycia Black, John Hurst, Brandt Miller, and Susan Miller, "Cross-Curricular Underlife: A Collaborative Report on Ways with Academic Words," *College Composition and Communication* 41 (1990): 11–36; Rosemary L. Hake and Joseph M. Williams, "Style and Its Consequences: Do as I Do, Not as I Say," *College English* 43 (1981): 433–51.

35. Three of the most important recent studies are Berlin, *Rhetoric*; Richard Ohmann, *English in America: A Radical View of the Profession* (New York, Oxford U P, 1976); and Greg Myers, "Reality, Consensus, and Reform in the Rhetoric of Composition Teaching," *College English* 48 (1986): 154–73.

2.

Nineteenth-Century Backgrounds: From the Liberal Curriculum to Mass Education

1. For a theoretical discussion of the transition from oral to print culture in America, see Miller, *Rescuing the Subject* chap. 5, esp. 151–59. On the decline of orality in the mid-nineteenth-century college, see Graff 46–51; and Walter J. Ong, *Orality and Literacy* (London: Methuen, 1982) 112–16.

2. Edmund Wilson, *The Triple Thinkers: Twelve Essays on Literary Subjects* (New York: McGraw, 1948) 162, qtd. in Graff 21. Standard treatments of the old college include Fredrick Rudolph, *Curriculum: A History of the American Undergraduate Course of Study Since 1636* (San Francisco: Jossey, 1978) chaps. 2–3; Fredrick Rudolph, *American College and University: A History* (New York: Knopf, 1962); Veysey chap. 1; and Douglas Sloan, *The Scottish Enlightenment and the American College Ideal* (New York: Teachers College P, 1971).

3. On the teaching of rhetoric in the old college, see Donald C. Stewart, "The Nineteenth Century," in *The Present State of Scholarship in Historical and Contemporary Rhetoric,* ed. Winifred Bryan Horner (Columbia: U of Missouri P, 1983); Halloran, "Rhetoric"; Porter G. Perrin, "The Teaching of Rhetoric in American Colleges Before 1750," diss., U of Chicago, 1936; Carolyn R. Miller and David A. Jolliffe, "Discourse Classifications in Nineteenth-Century Rhetorical Pedagogy," *Southern Speech Communication Journal* 51 (1986): 371–84.

4. Ronald F. Reid, "The Boylston Professorship of Rhetoric and Oratory, 1806–1904: A Case Study in Changing Concepts of Rhetoric and Pedagogy," *Quarterly Journal of Speech* 45 (1959): 239–57; and Veysey 38.

5. For an overview of the oratorical tradition in education, see Bruce A. Kimball, *Orators & Philosophers: A History of the Idea of Liberal Education* (New York: Teachers College P, 1986).

6. See Perrin 137.

7. See, for example, *Charles Francis Adams, 1835–1915: An Autobiography* (Boston: Massachusetts Historical Society, 1916) 33–37.

8. Lyman H. Bagg, *Four Years at Yale, by a Graduate of '68* (New Haven: Charles C. Chatfield, 1871).

9. See, for example, Henry Adams' pleas to be allowed to teach instead of hearing recitations, recounted by Ephraim Emerton, "History, 1838–1929," in *The Development of Harvard University: Since the Inauguration of President Eliot, 1869–1929,* ed. Samuel Eliot Morison (Cambridge, MA: Harvard U P, 1930) 154–57; see also George Ticknor, *Remarks on Changes Lately Proposed or Adopted in Harvard College* (Boston: Harvard College, 1825); William Lyon Phelps to R. H. Catterall, 1 Sept. 1891 and 5 Oct. 1893 (YA); and George Santayana, *Persons and Places* (New York: Scribner's, 1945) 77–78.

10. Notebooks of George Dudley Wiles, 1868 (HUA).

11. For detailed descriptions of Yale's twice-weekly rhetoricals, the "Junior Exhibition," and the commencement orations in 1869–70, see Bagg 554–65,

661–64, 665–80. Note that he always refers to "reading" speeches composed in writing beforehand.

12. The practice of printing college catalogs began in the 1820s.

13. Kansas University catalog, 1878–79 (KU).

14. On the structure of the *progymnasmata,* see Miller and Jolliffe 380–83; and Donald Lemen Clark, *Rhetoric in Greco-Roman Education* (New York: Columbia U P, 1957) chap. 6. On the absence of rhetoric from freshman requirements, see John Michael Wozniack, *English Composition in Eastern Colleges, 1850–1940* (Washington, DC: U P of America, 1978) 33–38.

15. Wozniack's survey of 36 eastern colleges (50–51, 245) showed that 18 of 30 colleges in the 1850s and 1860s combined rhetoric with another department (other than oratory, elocution, belles lettres, or literature). The most common marriages were with history, logic, or philosophy; my research for midwestern colleges shows a similar pattern.

16. S. Michael Halloran, "John Witherspoon and the Formation of Orators," CCCC Convention, Atlanta, Mar. 1977. For examples of student rhetoricals from the mid nineteenth century, see Frederick H. Viaux, Themes, 1868 (HUA).

17. University of Missouri catalog, 1870, 46 (MU).

18. Direct evidence of revision can be seen in the many pencil or ink drafts on inexpensive, lined, white composition paper attached to a revised, "fair copy" in ink on more expensive blue paper (HUA, KU, MU).

19. University of Missouri catalog 1870, 46 (MU). Cyrus Northrop: Letter to the President, 1869, in Oscar W. Firkins, *Cyrus Northrop: A Memoir* (Minneapolis: U of Minnesota P, 1925): 216–17.

20. Rudolph, *Curriculum* 146–47. See also Mary L. Smallwood, *An Historical Study of the Examinations and Grading Systems in Early American Universities; A Critical Study of the Original Records of Harvard, William and Mary, Yale, Mount Holyoke, and Michigan from Their Founding to 1900* (Cambridge, MA: Harvard U P, 1935) 15–18, 41–86.

21. Robert J. Connors, "Personal Writing Assignments," *College Composition and Communication* 38 (1987): 168.

22. The title is from a sophomore theme by W. R. Thayer, 1878 (HUA).

23. These topics are from Connors, "Personal" 170; Albert R. Kitzhaber, "Rhetoric in American Colleges, 1850–1900," diss., U of Washington, 1953, 170; and Harvard student themes of the 1860s (HUA).

24. Connors argues that the "idea of a specific research paper would have been without meaning in 1880, of course, because prior to the reign of personal writing, teachers naturally assumed that the students had no choice but to write something transmitted and synthesized from their reading" ("Personal" 178–79). Though research papers per se were not assigned in rhetoric courses in the 1870s, written forensics did allow specialized, researched writing. And curricular documents indicate that, in other disciplines (history courses at Harvard, for example), research papers or course "theses" were often an important part of the work, as I discuss in the next chapter.

25. Connors suggests that the emphasis on "narrowness and novelty" in the

new-style composition assignments of the late 1880s and 1890s was a function of a revival of romanticism, the decline of invention teaching, and the loss of "a considerable store of cultural knowledge" among students ("Personal" 171). But it can also be seen as a function of growing specialization and the rise of the ideal of original research in the whole university.

26. The standard treatment is David Potter, *Debating in the Colonial Chartered Colleges: An Historical Survey, 1642–1900* (New York: Teacher's College P, 1944); see also Graff 51; and Rudolph, *Curriculum* 94–98. For the literary societies' relation to composition instruction, see Wozniack 45–47; and Anne Ruggles Gere, *Writing Groups: History, Theory, and Implications* (Carbondale: Southern Illinois U P, 1987) chap. 1.

27. Clifford S. Griffin, *The University of Kansas: A History* (Lawrence: U P of Kansas, 1974) 92–93; Veysey 27.

28. Potter 70.

29. For meeting procedures, see records of the Athenaeum Society (the first society west of the Mississippi) 1847–1958 (MU) and the Oread and Orophilian societies, 1867–90 (KU). See also Gere chap. 1.

30. University of Missouri catalog, 1866 (MU).

31. Colleges occasionally found it necessary to exert prior censorship on student writing and oratory because of its political content. See Jonas Viles, *The University of Missouri: A Centennial History* (Columbia: U of Missouri P, 1939) 184; and Griffin, *University of Kansas* 91–93.

32. On the old college and its transition to the new university, see Rudolph, *Curriculum* chaps. 4–5; Rudolph, *American* chaps. 1–10; Veysey chaps. 1–2.

33. Adams Sherman Hill, LeBaron R. Briggs, and B. S. Hurlbut, *Twenty Years of School and College English* (Cambridge, MA: Harvard U P, 1896) 17.

34. Adams Sherman Hill, "An Answer to the Cry for More English," *Good Company* 4 (1879): 234–35. See also George R. Carpenter, "English Composition in Colleges," *Educational Review* 4 (1892): 338–46.

35. See Kitzhaber, "Rhetoric" 56–57; and Hill, "Answer" 237. Marie Hochmuth and Richard Murphy also stress the shift from oral to written language as a motive for composition courses' emphasis on correctness but in the context of the rise of speech courses. See Marie Hochmuth and Richard Murphy, "Rhetorical and Elocutionary Training in Nineteenth-Century Colleges," in *A History of Speech Education in America,* ed. Karl R. Wallace (New York: Appleton, 1954).

36. Hill, "Answer" 237; see also Connors, "Personal" 172–76.

37. Hill, "Answer" 234; see also Paul E. Cohen, "Barrett Wendell, A Study in Harvard Culture," diss., Northwestern U, 1974, 48.

38. Harvard University catalogs, 1894–1900 (HUA). Berlin (*Writing* 59), following Rudolph (*American* 294), says that Harvard reduced required courses to freshman composition in 1894, but, in fact, the sophomore themes and junior forensics "half-courses"—really a collegewide writing requirement—endured until 1900, and they did so in the Lawrence Scientific School until 1907.

39. For an overview of the literature, see Stewart in Horner, *Present State.*

40. The first and most often cited analysis is Kitzhaber's ("Rhetoric"); he de-emphasizes the impact of writing requirements not attached to specific composition courses (55) and emphasizes the impact of the creation of freshman composition in 1885 (101). Potter discusses the forensic system as a last vestige of curricular oral debate (33–63); but apart from two mentions (59n, 62), he does not treat its written character and its relation to writing in the curriculum. Neither do Berlin (*Writing* 59) or Wozniack discuss Harvard's collegewide writing requirements, English B and C.

41. Kitzhaber ("Rhetoric" 55–56) and David A. Jolliffe ("The Moral Subject in College Composition: A Conceptual Framework and the Case of Harvard, 1865–1900," *College English* 51 [1989]: 168) mention other writing, and Wozniack briefly notes the importance of these requirements in eastern colleges (36, 76, 122).

42. The first use of the term *forensics* occurs in the 1867 catalog, where it replaces declamations in the list of requirements. Whether this indicates a shift to exclusively written work I cannot tell from the curricular documents and student papers preserved.

43. Harvard catalog, 1872–73 (HUA).

44. Student papers of Frederick H. Viaux, 1868–70 (HUA).

45. Hill, "Answer" 237.

46. Hill, "Answer" 238; Harvard catalog, 1879–80 (HUA); Charles H. Grandgent, "The Modern Languages, 1869–1929," in Morison 75. On the Oral Discussion course, see Albert Bushnell Hart, *English 6: Oral Debate,* 1892 (a pamphlet outlining course procedure and topics) and briefs for the course by a student, Ralph C. Larrabee, 1892 (HUA).

47. Harvard *Crimson* 28 June 1882: 111, and 9 Dec. 1882: 82 (HUA).

48. Grandgent in Morison 75. Before coming to Harvard, Royce had taught composition at the University of California at Berkeley and written *A Primer of Logical Analysis: For the Use of Composition Students* (San Francisco: A. L. Bancroft, 1881).

49. *Annual Reports of the President and Treasurer,* 1883–84, 84 (HUA).

50. See for example E. W. Forbes, English B Themes, 1894 (HUA); and George Converse Fisk, Forensics, 1893 (HUA).

51. George Pierce Baker, *Specimen Briefs,* 1891 (HUA).

52. Forensic I of Ralph Clinton Larrabee, "The Algo-Fungal Theory of Lichens," 1891–92, graded by JBF (Jefferson B. Fletcher) (HUA).

53. Harvard catalog, 1897–98 (HUA).

54. The Lawrence Scientific School preserved English B until 1907 under the title "Written Exercises and Conferences"; see papers of Frank B. Duvineck for an example, "The Chemistry of Negative Marking for the Amateur Photographer," 1907 (HUA).

55. Wozniack, tables I, III, VI, X, and XIV. My examination of twelve midwestern college and university catalogs shows a similar pattern, though I have not replicated Wozniack's statistical analysis.

56. Bucknell University catalog, 1910–11, 64–65; Wesleyan University catalog, 1911–12, qtd. in Wozniack 161–62.

57. On the persistence of rhetoricals at small, private colleges, particularly Catholic ones, see Wozniack 133–34 and 194–95.

58. *Annual Reports of the President of Columbia College,* 1866, 6–13; 1868, 11–13; 1869, 2–14 (CUA); and Wozniack 43–44.

59. Ohio State College catalog, 1891–92, 1892–93, 1895–96 (OSU); See also *One Hundredth Centennial of the Ohio State University,* Departments of Speech and English, 1970 (OSU).

60. Joseph Villiers Denney, "College Rhetoric," *PMLA* 20 (1894–95): 51.

61. Joseph Villiers Denney, *Two Problems in Composition Teaching* (Ann Arbor: Inland P, 1897) 6.

62. Enrollment statistics of the university (OSU). See also Don Faules, "Joseph Villiers Denney: English Scholar and Contributor to the Emergence of Speech Theory," *Speech Teacher* 20 (1964): 105–9; and David R. Russell, "Rhetoric Entering the Twentieth Century: Joseph Villiers Denney at Ohio State, 1891–1933," unpublished essay, 1987.

63. Iowa State College bulletins, 1869–78 (ISU).

64. Iowa State College bulletin, 1879 (ISU).

65. Iowa State College bulletin, 1879 (ISU).

66. Iowa State College bulletin, 1879 (ISU); in Britain, undergraduate research projects are still called *dissertations.*

67. Iowa State College bulletin, 1887 (ISU).

68. Iowa State College bulletin, 1888 (ISU). See course descriptions for English, history, philosophy, and engineering, Iowa State College bulletins, 1888–93 (ISU).

69. Kansas University Faculty Minutes 1887, 185; 1892, 243 (KU). This apparently meant a visit to the dean and a return to freshman composition if necessary.

70. Kansas University Faculty Minutes, 1888, 185; 1890, 122; 1903, 120; 1905, 138–39 (KU); "English Department Bulletin," 1899, 1 (KU). Similar staffing problems existed elsewhere, in part as a result of a 62 percent increase in male students in colleges between 1890 and 1900 (and a 153 percent increase in female students in coeducational institutions); see Kitzhaber, "Rhetoric" 72–73.

71. See Susan Miller, "An Archeology of English," CCCC Convention, Chicago, Mar. 1990.

72. Grandgent in Morison 69.

73. *Digest of Educational Statistics* (Washington, DC: GPO, 1989) 166.

74. Hill, "Answer" 240; Carpenter, "English Composition" 446.

75. The most thorough treatments are in Berlin, *Writing;* Kitzhaber, "Rhetoric"; Donald C. Stewart, "Two Model Composition Teachers and the Harvardization of English Departments," in *The Rhetorical Tradition and Modern Writing,* ed. James J. Murphy (New York: MLA, 1982) 118–29; and Donald C. Stewart,

"The Status of Composition and Rhetoric in American Colleges, 1880–1902: An MLA Perspective," *College English* 47 (1975): 734–46. For a brief treatment of the genesis of English departments and the role of composition courses and teachers in them, see William Riley Parker, "Where Do English Departments Come From?" *College English* 28 (1967): 339–51.

76. Hill, "Answer" 234.

77. See Burton R. Clark, "The School and the University: What Went Wrong in America?" Comparative Higher Education Research Group Working Paper no. 8. Urbana: ERIC, 1985 (ED 265 797): 17–22.

78. Samuel Thurber, "English in the Secondary Schools: Some Considerations as to Its Aims and Needs," *School Review* 2 (1894): 476.

79. *Report of the Committee on Secondary Schools* (Committee of Ten) (1893; New York: Arno, 1969) 90–91.

80. Homer E. Woodbridge, "Freshman English Course," *Educational Review* 66 (1923): 8.

81. On the controversy see, for example, "Our Infant Critics," editorial, *Nation* 27 Feb. 1908: 188–89; and J. H. Gardiner, "Our Infant Critics," *Nation* 19 Mar. 1908: 257–58.

82. National Education Association. *Cardinal Principles of Secondary Education: A Report of the Commission on the Reorganization of Secondary Education* (Washington, DC: GPO, 1918).

83. Arthur William Dunn, comp., *Social Studies in Secondary Education: Report of the Committee on Social Studies of the Commission on the Reorganization of Secondary Education of the National Education Association.* (Washington, DC: GPO, 1916); James Fleming Hosic, comp., *Reorganization of English in the Secondary Schools,* Bureau of Education bull. no. 2 (Washington, DC: GPO, 1917); Arthur N. Applebee, *Tradition and Reform in the Teaching of English: A History* (Urbana: NCTE, 1974) 64–67.

84. On the history of secondary teaching methods, see Larry Cuban, *How Teachers Taught: Constancy and Change in American Classrooms, 1890–1980* (New York: Longman, 1984) esp. 132–33.

85. Although competition from social organizations (intercollegiate athletics, the YMCA-YWCA movement, the Greek system) has often been cited as the primary cause of the literary societies' decline in the last two decades of the century (see Potter 91–93), there is much evidence to suggest that the proliferation of specialized academic extracurricular organizations accounts for much of the decline. At the University of Missouri in 1900, for example, the venerable literary societies, Union and Athenaeum, competed with fifteen new clubs that had been organized by specific departments, from agriculture and engineering to philosophy and Latin. Sometimes literary societies themselves became an arm of the English department (producing a literary magazine, as at Kansas University) or, later, an arm of the speech department (sponsoring intercollegiate forensic tournaments). See University of Missouri catalog, 1900 (MU); records of the Union and Athenaeum societies, 1900–58 (MU) and *Oread Magazine* (KU).

3.

Writing and the Ideal of Research: Some Tacit Traditions

1. The ratio went up significantly after 1960 if one excludes graduate assistants (*Digest of Educational Statistics* 166).

2. See, for example, Edwin M. Hopkins, "Can Good Composition Teaching Be Done Under Present Conditions?" *English Journal* 1 (1912): 1–8.

3. S. F. Wolverton, "Professional Scullery," *Educational Review* 60 (1920): 407.

4. Lawrence A. Cremin, *American Education: The National Experience* (New York: Harper, 1980) 405.

5. John Merle Coulter, *The Elements of Power* (Chicago: 1894) 3, 7, qtd. in Veysey 144; for Eliot's views on recitation versus lecture, see "President Eliot's Inaugural Address," in Morison lxiv.

6. Ephraim Emerton, "The Practical Method in Higher Historical Instruction," in *Methods of Teaching History,* ed. G. Stanley Hall, 2d ed. (Boston: Heath, 1883) 31.

7. Hall x.

8. See Albert Bushnell Hart, "Methods of Teaching American History," in Hall 28; and Emerton in Hall 57.

9. Hart in Hall 21.

10. Emerton in Hall 33, see also 51–52.

11. Emerton in Morison 151–52; on the increasing availability of libraries and books to students, see Rudolph, *American* 145–46; and Veysey 175.

12. Hart in Hall 5.

13. See, for example, "Methods of Instruction in History," Kansas University catalog, 1878, 58 (KU); and Hart in Hall 4–5, 30. On note-taking suggestions, see Hart in Hall 28. Hart initially printed his syllabi on one side of the page and left the other half blank for the students' notes. On Hart's teaching methods, see Carol F. Baird, "Albert Bushnell Hart: The Rise of the Professional Historian," in *Social Sciences at Harvard, 1860–1920: From Inculcation to the Open Mind,* ed. Paul Buck (Cambridge, MA: Harvard U P, 1965) 147–74. On "microthemes" and the WAC movement, see John C. Bean, Dean Drenk, and F. D. Lee, "Microtheme Strategies for Developing Cognitive Skills," in *Teaching Writing in All Disciplines,* ed. C. Williams Griffin (San Francisco: Jossey, 1982).

14. Hart in Hall 5, 30. For representative examples of syllabi and questions, see Henry Adams, "Syllabus for History II," 1874 (HUA); and Edward W. Wheeler, "Study Guide for Economics I," 1892 (HUA).

15. For examples of notebooks as a course requirement, see "Metaphysics," University of Missouri catalog, 1885, 41 (MU); and Herbert B. Adams, "Special Methods of Historical Study," in Hall 121.

16. Hart in Hall 4. On Henry Adams' teaching, see Stewart Mitchell, "Henry Adams and Some of His Students," *Proceedings of the Massachusetts Historical Society* 66 (1936–41): 294–321.

17. Compare, for example, notebooks of Frederick H. Viaux, 1869, and those of Francis Minot Rackemann, 1909 (HUA).

18. Henry Adams, "Syllabus: History II," 1874 (HUA); and "An Attempt To Answer the Syllabus in History II," 1875, 12 (HUA). These unauthorized professional tutors' outlines are one of the most common items in the HUA curriculum holdings from the 1880s and 1890s, but after the curriculum reform of 1903 they almost disappear.

19. Morison xlvi. An unauthorized professional tutor's outline of Lowell's own course, Government I (1902), may help explain the vehemence with which he pursued reforms. It contained résumés of all lectures and readings, all quiz answers, and all final-exam questions, 1897–1900 (HUA).

20. James E. Ford, Sharla Rees, and David L. Ward, "Research Paper Instruction: Comprehensive Bibliography of Periodical Sources, 1923–1980," *Bulletin of Bibliography* 39 (1982): 84–98.

21. See Clark, *Rhetoric* chap. 4.

22. On the debate over terminology, see Paul E. Koefod, *The Writing Requirements for Graduate Degrees* (Englewood Cliffs, NJ: Prentice Hall, 1964) chap. 2.

23. For the debate over the general influence of German scholarship, see Richard J. Storr, *The Beginnings of Graduate Education in America* (Chicago: U of Chicago P, 1953) chaps. 3–5; and Carl Diehl, *Americans and German Scholarship, 1770–1870* (New Haven: Yale U P, 1978). On the German influence on scholarship in the humanities, see Graff chap. 4; in the social sciences, Hazel W. Hertzberg, *Social Studies Reform, 1880–1980* (Boulder, CO: Social Science Education Consortium, 1981): 5–6.

24. For a theoretical discussion of the shift from oral to written scholarship and its effects on students, see Miller, *Rescuing* chap. 5. For the influence of the new pedagogical model see Rudolph, *Curriculum* 144–45; and Veysey 156–57.

25. See, for example, Frederick H. Viaux, "Crete: A Historical Essay," 1868; "The Great Pyramid: Its Age, Builders, and Purpose," 1869; and "Milton's Public Life and Political Writings," 1870 (HUA).

26. Harvard College catalog, 1870–71 (HUA).

27. On Adams, see Baird in Buck 148; for James' pedagogy and the Board of Overseers, see Sheldon M. Stern, "William James and the New Psychology," in Buck 189.

28. On the distinction between the *artes liberales* ideal of the old classical curriculum and the modern identification of liberal learning with intellectual freedom, see Kimball chap. 5.

29. Dissertations, 1879–82 (ISU). Senior theses at Kansas have a similar pattern after they were required in 1881.

30. Iowa State College bulletin, 1895, 30; and 1898, 43 (ISU).

31. See the volumes of bound "Theses," 1880–1904 (ISU).

32. Emerton in Hall 38.

33. John W. Burgess, "On Methods of Historical Study and Research in Columbia University," in Hall 219–20.

34. See discussions of teaching methods in history at Cornell (Andrew D. White, "Historical Instruction in the Course of History and Political Science at Cornell University," in Hall 75); at Johns Hopkins and at Smith College (Adams in Hall 114–18); at Columbia (Burgess in Hall 219); and even at Roxbury Latin School (W. C. Collar, "Advice to an Inexperienced Teacher of History," in Hall 82).

35. Emerton in Hall 34; Kansas University catalog, 1878–79 (KU).

36. See Emerton in Hall 33, 51–52; Veysey 153–55.

37. See Emerton in Morison 154–55, 163; Veysey 180.

38. Emerton in Morison 161.

39. Henry Scott, "The Courses of Study in History, Roman Law, and Political Economy at Harvard University," in Hall 188–90.

40. See, for example, Harvard's "Work for Students [in] History," 1889 (HUA); Charles Franklin Dunbar, "Topics and References in Political Economy," 1889 (HUA); W. F. Allen, "History Topics [at] Wisconsin University," in Hall 324–26; *American History Leaflets: Colonial and Constitutional,* nos. 1–36, ed. Albert Bushnell Hart and Edward Channing (New York: Lovell, 1892–1913); Baird in Buck 169–70.

41. For examples of student writing, see "University Studies," 1884 (KU); *Dissertations,* 1879–89 (ISU); George Lyman Kitteridge, Theses in Classical Philology, 1882 (HUA); Charles Lewis Slatterly, Theses in Philosophy IV and XII, 1890 (HUA); Ralph Clinton Larrabee, Papers in Philosophy I and II, 1891–92 (HUA); Charles Merlin Barnes, History of Education Course Reports, 1898 (MU). On most extant papers from the period no grade or comments appear. Perhaps comments and grades were given orally or appended and then lost; but student comments suggest that many faculty collected papers at the end of the term and simply assigned a course grade, returning the paper unmarked.

42. Baird in Buck 159–60.

43. Emerton in Buck 59. See also Canfield's remarks in the Kansas University catalog, 1879, 46 (KU).

44. Hart in Hall 28.

45. Emerton in Morison 163.

46. "Work of Students in History," 1888–89, 25 (HUA).

47. See Burgess in Hall 216; Emerton in Hall 54. On secondary-school pedagogy, see Cuban chap. 2.

48. On this "romantic" strain in the research ideal, see Veysey 156–58.

49. Adams in Hall 126.

50. See Edwin J. Brown and Maxele Baldwin, "The Term Paper in College," *Education Administration and Supervision* 17 (1931): 306–16. See also Morison's notes on his undergraduate papers at Harvard (HUA).

51. On the effect of specialization on student-faculty relationships during the period, see Veysey 294–302; see also LeBaron R. Briggs, *Routine and Ideals* (Boston: Houghton, 1904) 42, 165–66.

52. Note in Morison's hand on the title page of his paper, "The Expedition Against Cadiz, 1596," 1905 (HUA).

53. For late-nineteenth-century attitudes toward "literary gentlemen" who sold

mail-order papers to Harvard students, see Briggs 166–69. On the contemporary term-paper industry, see Thomas Mallon, *Stolen Words: Forays into the Origins and Ravages of Plagiarism* (New York: Ticknor, 1989) 90–94.

54. "Report of the Committee on Improving Instruction in Harvard College," A. Lawrence Lowell, chair, 1902 (HUA).

55. Morison undergraduate papers, 1905–10 (HUA); see also "Selected Theses for Classical Philology," 1910 (HUA); papers of James Ford, 1903–5 (HUA); Albert Waite papers in Economics 9, 1903 (HUA); and Warren J. Samuels, "The Teaching of Business Cycles in 1905–6: Insight into the Development of Macroeconomic Theory," *History of Political Economy* 4 (1972): 146.

56. Brown and Baldwin 315–16.

57. Frances N. Ahl, "The Technique of the Term Paper," *High School Journal* (1931): 17–19, 53.

58. Veronica Tischer Wills, "An Investigation of the Use of the Documented Research Paper in College Courses," diss., United States International U, 1970.

59. Adams Sherman Hill, *Foundations of Rhetoric* (New York: Harper, 1892); and Adams Sherman Hill, *Principles of Rhetoric and Their Application* (New York: American Book, 1878); Barrett Wendell, *English Composition* (New York: Scribner's, 1891).

60. Charles Sears Baldwin, *Composition: Oral and Written* (1909; New York: Greenwood, 1969) 163–71; John Franklin Genung, *The Working Principles of Rhetoric* (Boston: Ginn, 1904) 417–19.

61. See, for example, Mervin James Curl, *Expository Writing* (New York: Houghton, 1919).

62. As in Bernard Levi Jefferson, Harvey Houston Peckham, and Hiram Roy Wilson, *Freshman Rhetoric and Practice Book* (Garden City, NJ: Doubleday, 1928).

63. Chester Noyes Greenough and Frank Wilson Cheney Hersey, *English Composition* (New York: Macmillan, 1919) 367.

64. George Benjamin Woods, *A College Handbook of Writing: A Guide for Use in College Classes in Composition* (Garden City, NJ: Doubleday, 1922).

65. See for example Jefferson et al. 182–88.

66. Kendall Bernard Taft, John Francis McDermott, and Dana O. Jensen, *The Technique of Composition* (New York: Smith, 1931) 338.

67. In Ford et al., see the entries on pages 85–87; and see Richard L. Larson, "The 'Research Paper' in the Writing Course: A Non-Form of Writing," *College English* 44 (1982): 811–16.

68. Mathilda Bailey and Bunnar Horn, *English Handbook* (New York: American Book, 1949) 349.

69. Brown and Baldwin 306–16; see also Roy C. Woods, "The Term Paper: Its Values and Dangers," *Peabody Journal of Education* 11 (1933): 87–89.

70. See Brown and Baldwin 307.

71. George Arms, "The Research Paper," *College English* 5 (1943): 19–26.

72. For criticisms of the practice of assigning term papers, see John W. Stevenson, "The Illusion of Research," *English Journal* 61 (1972): 1029–32; A. L.

Bader, "Independent Thinking and the Long Paper," *English Journal* 25 (1936): 667–72; Thomas E. Taylor, "Let's Get Rid of Research Papers," *English Journal* 54 (1965): 126–27; and Larson.

73. See James E. Ford and Dennis R. Perry, "Research Paper Instruction in the Undergraduate Writing Program," *College English* 44 (1982): 825–31.

74. See Stanley M. Guralnick, *Science and the Antebellum American College* (Philadelphia: American Philosophical Society, 1975).

75. George W. Hunter, *Science Teaching at Junior and Senior High School Levels* (New York: American Book, 1934) 27–28; see also Lane Cooper, *Louis Agassiz as a Teacher* (Ithica, NY: Comstock, 1917).

76. See Josiah P. Cooke, "The Value and Limitations of Laboratory Practice in a Scheme of Liberal Education: Report of the Director of the Chemical Laboratory to the Visiting Committee of the Overseers," 1892 (HUA).

77. Hunter 27.

78. Carlton H. Steadman, "An Examination of Science Texts from Early America to the 1900s for Evidence of Inquiry Oriented Presentations," Urbana: ERIC, 1986 (ED 271 291).

79. Cooke 15–16 (HUA); Hunter 41–49; Edwin H. Hall, "Physics, 1869–1928," in Morison 285–86.

80. See Paul DeHart Hurd, *Biological Education in American Secondary Schools 1890–1960* (Washington, DC: American Institute of Biological Sciences, 1961) chaps. 1–3; and Paul DeHart Hurd, *New Directions in Teaching Secondary School Science* (Chicago: Rand McNally, 1969) 44–47, 110–11.

81. *Reorganization of Science in Secondary Schools: A Report of the Commission on the Reorganization of Secondary Schools*. Bureau of Education bull. no. 26 (Washington, DC: GPO, 1920) 53.

82. Ralph S. Powers, chair, "A Proposal for Teaching Science," in *Thirty-First Yearbook of the National Society for the Study of Education*, pt. 1 (Chicago: U of Chicago P, 1932): 1. For a summary of research in the 1920s and early 1930s, see Morris Meister, "Recent Educational Research in Science Teaching," *School Science and Mathematics* 2 (1932): 875–89.

83. John Dewey, "The Supreme Intellectual Obligation," *Science Education* 18 (1934): 3.

84. Hurd, *New Directions* 114.

85. Victor H. Noll, *The Teaching of Science in Elementary and Secondary Schools* (New York: Longmans, 1939).

86. Hurd, *New Directions* 6.

4.
Writing and the Ideal of Utility: Composition for the Culture of Professionalism

1. Berlin, *Rhetoric;* and Wallace W. Douglas, "Rhetoric for the Meritocracy: The Creation of Composition at Harvard," in Ohmann 97–132.

2. On late-nineteenth-century academics' views of "real life," see Veysey 61–68.

3. Bledstein x.

4. George H. Douglas, "Business Writing in America in the Nineteenth Century," in *Studies in the History of Business Writing,* ed. George H. Douglas and Herbert W. Hildebrandt (Urbana: Association for Business Communication, 1985) 127.

5. See Douglas in Douglas and Hildebrandt 131; Bledstein 37.

6. Yates' 1989 study was the first book-length treatment of the role of written communication in systematic management.

7. See David Montgomery, *The Fall of the House of Labor: The Workplace, the State, and American Labor Activism, 1865–1985* (Cambridge: Cambridge U P, 1987) chap. 5.

8. Qtd. in Montgomery 218.

9. Horace L. Arnold and Fay L. Faurote, *Ford Methods and Ford Shops* (New York: Engineering Magazine, 1919) 41–42, qtd. in Montgomery 234.

10. Qtd. in Montgomery 116.

11. See JoAnne Yates, "The Birth of the Memo: A Study in the Evolution of a Genre," Association for Business Communication Annual Meeting, Indianapolis, Oct. 1988: 26; and Yates, *Control* chap. 1.

12. Bledstein 33.

13. Yates, "Birth of the Memo" 24–26.

14. See Veysey 114.

15. On the "uneasy marriage" between ideals of utility and research, see Veysey 104, 119, 174, 257.

16. See Veysey 140–45.

17. Sidney Webb: To Graham Wallace, 13 Oct. 1888, in *The Letters of Sidney and Beatrice Webb,* ed. Norman MacKenzie, 3 vols. (Cambridge: Cambridge U P, 1978) 2: 116.

18. Carpenter, "English Composition" 439.

19. Carpenter, "English Composition" 443. See also MIT *President's Report,* 1890–91, 23–24 (MIT); and MIT catalog, 1890–91 (MIT).

20. *President's Report,* 1903–4, 74 (MIT); and MIT catalog, 1896–97 (MIT). See also Henry Latimer Seaver, "English at the Institute of Technology," *Nation* 26 Dec. 1907: 586–87.

21. Gertrude Buck praised MIT's program in 1901 as exemplifying the "doctrines" of socialized rhetoric "in active operation in the classroom" ("Recent Tendencies in the Teaching of English Composition," *Educational Review* 22 [1901]: 374n). However, despite Valentine's insistence on the differences between composition at Harvard and MIT ("Instruction in English at the Institute," *Technology Review* 1 [1899]: 587), there were many similarities between the pedagogies of Valentine and Wendell, as Wallace W. Douglas pointed out to me.

22. Valentine, "English" 442.

23. Robert Grosenver Valentine, "On Criticism of Themes by Students," *Technology Review* 4 (1903): 358.

24. Valentine, "Criticism" 460.

25. Valentine, "English" 445.

26. Valentine, "Criticism" 460.

27. Archer Tyler Robinson, "The Teaching of English in a Scientific School," *Science* 30 (1909): 659.

28. Valentine, "Criticism" 463.

29. Robinson 661.

30. On the use of writing groups at MIT and elsewhere in the period, see Gere chap. 2.

31. Valentine, "Criticism" 660.

32. On worker turnover and unrest in the 1910s, see Montgomery 234–44.

33. On Valentine's influence on scientific management and labor relations, see Milton J. Nadworny, *Scientific Management and the Unions, 1900–1932: A Historical Analysis* (Cambridge, MA: Harvard U P, 1955) esp. 74–77.

34. "Sketch: Robert G. Valentine," *Outlook* 114 (1916): 629.

35. Ordway Tead, "Industrial Counselor: A New Profession," *The Independent* 88 (1916): 394.

36. See "Sketch" 629; and Nadworny 81. On the functioning of personnel departments in the period, see Montgomery 236–44.

37. On the new demands that systematic management made on managers, see Yates, *Control* esp. 6–19; and Montgomery chap. 5.

38. Melvyn Dubofski, *When Workers Organize: New York City in the Progressive Era* (Amherst: U of Massachusetts P, 1968) 93–101.

39. Robert Grosenver Valentine, "Cooperating in Industrial Research," *Survey* 36 (1916): 586.

40. Chemistry, architecture, foreign languages, economics, and four engineering departments participated at various times during the three decades the program was in place; but most participated for three years or less, none for the whole time.

41. Frank Aydelotte, "Training in Thought as the Aim of Elementary English Course as Taught at MIT," *Engineering Record* 24 Feb. 1917: 300.

42. MIT catalogs, 1915–22 (MIT); MIT *President's Report,* 1918, 65 (MIT).

43. MIT's struggles with the issue of specialized training versus general culture are outlined in Robert G. Caldwell, "The Humanities at Technology," *Technology Review* 42 (1941): 210–28; and "Course XXI—A History," anonymous, unpublished manuscript, n.d. (MIT).

44. Robert J. Connors, "The Rise of Technical Writing Instruction in America," *Journal of Technical Writing and Communication* 12 (1982): 329–52.

45. See *Dissertations* and *Theses* 1879–82 (ISU).

46. See T. J. Johnson, "Engineering English," *Society for the Promotion of Engineering Education (SPEE) Proceedings* 11 (1903): 361–71. The *SPEE Proceedings* published "English Reports" beginning in 1903. These volumes contain not only the papers read at the annual convention session on English but also stenographic transcriptions of discussions after the formal presentations, which occasionally provide glimpses of faculty speaking informally.

47. See, for example, Johnson, "Engineering English" 361–62; and J. Martin Tellen, "The Course in English in Our Technical Schools," *SPEE Proceedings* 16 (1908): 61.

48. *A Century of Engineering Education* (Ann Arbor: U of Michigan P, 1954) 1252–53. James Souther, personal interview, 10 Apr. 1990; see also Ray Palmer Baker, "Problems of Administering English Work in Engineering Colleges," *SPEE Bulletin* 23 (1932): 282–91.

49. See James Souther, "Teaching Technical Writing: A Retrospective Appraisal," in *Technical Writing: Theory and Practice*, ed. Bertie E. Fearing and W. Keats Sparrow (New York: MLA, 1989) 3–5; Connors, "Technical Writing" 338. On the isolation of technical-writing instruction from professional practice, see Souther in Fearing and Sparrow 3.

50. Samuel Earle, "English at Tufts College," *SPEE Bulletin* 2 (1911): 29–43.

51. Arthur Starbuck, "Technical English: A Diagnosis and a Prescription," *SPEE Bulletin* 9 (1919): 470–80.

52. *Instruction in English in Technical Colleges* (The Hammond Report), published as an appendix to *SPEE Bulletin* 31 (1940): 24.

53. See, for example, a letter from J. Raleigh Nelson to the SPEE Board of Investigation and Coordination, *SPEE Bulletin* 13 (1922): 251–52; and "Report of the English Committee," *SPEE Bulletin* 12 (1921): 573–74.

54. Otto Birk, "Interdepartmental Cooperation To Promote the Habitual Use of Correct English," *SPEE Bulletin* 16 (1925): 231–32; *Instruction in English* 24.

55. Baker, "Problems" 286.

56. "English Report," *SPEE Bulletin* 28 (1937): 181. See also Johnson, "Engineering English" 364; and John J. Clark, "Clearness and Accuracy in Composition," *SPEE Proceedings* 18 (1910): 349.

57. W. O. Sypherd, "Thirty Years of Teaching English to Engineers," *SPEE Proceedings* 47 (1939): 164.

58. Samuel Earle, "English in Engineering Schools," *SPEE Bulletin* 2 (1912): 387–88.

59. Tellen 90.

60. See Sypherd 162–64.

61. For the history of technical-writing textbooks and the growth of technical writing as a discipline, see Connors, "Technical Writing"; and Souther in Fearing and Sparrow.

62. Edwin K. Knepper, *History of Business Education in the United States* (Bowling Green, OH: Edwards, 1941) esp. 42–53.

63. Robert Aaron Gordon and James Edwin Howell, *Higher Education for Business* (New York: Columbia U P, 1959) 21.

64. Frank C. Pierson, *The Education of American Businessmen: A Study of University-College Programs in Business Administration* (New York: McGraw, 1959) 35–50.

65. Qtd. in Veysey 71.

66. Francis W. Weeks, "The Teaching of Business Writing at the Collegiate Level, 1900–1920," in Douglas and Hildebrandt 202.

67. James H. S. Bossard and J. Frederic Dewhurst, *University Education for Business: A Study of Existing Needs and Practices* (Philadelphia: U of Pennsylvania P, 1931) 338–39.

68. Yates, "Birth of the Memo" 13–25.

69. Bossard and Dewhurst 106.

70. Bossard and Dewhurst 48; Pierson 180–82; Gordon and Howell 154–56.

71. Bossard and Dewhurst 340; see also Pierson 177.

72. As I discuss in chapter 8, the study of organizational communication actually evolved in three rather distinct disciplinary communities, one from speech departments and one from traditional management research, in addition to the ABCA business-writing instructors with their ties to English departments.

73. Pierson 180.

74. See Michael Masoner, *An Audit of the Case Study Method* (New York: Praeger, 1988).

75. Michael Mendelson, "The Historical Case: Its Roman Precedent and the Current Debate," unpublished manuscript, 1988.

76. See, for example, D. Henryetta Sperle, *The Case Method Technique in Professional Training: A Survey of the Use of Case Studies as a Method of Instruction in Selected Fields* (New York: Teachers College P, 1933); Aretas W. Nolan, *The Case Method of Teaching Applied to Vocational Agriculture* (Bloomington, IL: Public School Publishing, 1927). Casebook series in the social sciences include the Inter-University Case Program in public policy, which began in 1948 in imitation of the Harvard University Graduate School of Business Administration's use of cases, and in literature, the Crowell Literary Casebooks series.

77. Andrew R. Towl, *To Study Administration by Cases* (Boston: Harvard U Graduate School of Business Administration, 1969) 66.

78. James A. Erskine, Michiel R. Leenders, and Louise A. Mauffette-Leenders, *Teaching With Cases* (London, Can.: School of Business Administration, U of Western Ontario, 1981) 216.

79. Pierson 180.

80. Erskine et al. 217.

81. See Towl 305–12, 230; Ben J. Barton and Marthalee Barton, "The Case Method: Bridging the Gap between Engineering Student and Professional," in *Courses, Components and Exercises in Technical Communication,* ed. Dwight W. Stevenson (Urbana: NCTE, 1981) 22–33; John R. Brockman, ed. *The Case Method in Technical Communication* (Lubbock, TX: Association of Teachers of Technical Writing, 1984); and Mendelson.

5.

Writing and Social Efficiency: The Cooperation Movement

1. On the broad social changes in the Progressive Era, see Robert H. Weibe, *The Search for Order, 1877–1920* (New York: Hill, 1967).

2. Lawrence A. Cremin, *The Transformation of the School: Progressivism in American Education* (New York: Vantage, 1961) 179–200; see also Raymond C. Callahan, *Education and the Cult of Efficiency* (Chicago: U of Chicago P, 1962).

3. As JoAnne Yates has pointed out (*Control* 9–15), the Taylorite school of scientific management was only one manifestation of the broader movement known as *systematic management*.

4. For the influence of systematic management on curriculum theory, see Barry M. Franklin, *Building the American Community: The School Curriculum and the Search for Social Control* (London: Falmer P, 1986); on Thorndike and sorting, see Franklin 52–56.

5. John M. Clapp, *The Place and Function of English in American Life: Report of an Investigation by a Committee of the National Council of Teachers of English* (Chicago: NCTE, 1926).

6. Werrett Wallace Charters and Isadore B. Whitley, *Analysis of Secretarial Duties and Traits* (Baltimore: Williams, 1924). See also Herbert M. Kliebard, *The Struggle for the American Curriculum, 1893–1958* (Boston: Routledge, 1986) 108–22; and Franklin chap. 4.

7. See Edward L. Thorndike, *Human Nature and the Social Order* (New York: Macmillan, 1940) esp. 456.

8. See Kliebard chap. 5; Franklin chap. 4.

9. David Snedden, *What's Wrong with American Education?* (Philadelphia: Lippincott, 1927) 295.

10. Edwin M. Hopkins, "The Cost and Labor of English Teaching," *Journal of Proceedings and Addresses, National Education Association* 53 (1915): 114–19. See also "Standards of Efficiency in the Teaching of English," editorial, *School Review* 23 (1915): 719–20; John J. Maloney, "Economy of Time in English," *School and Society* 2 (1915): 96–98; and Alfred M. Hitchcock, "Economy in Teaching Composition," *Education* 24 (1904): 348–55.

11. See Franklin Bobbitt, *The Curriculum* (Boston: Houghton, 1918) chap. 7.

12. Berlin, *Writing* chap. 7.

13. G. H. Browne, "Successful Combination Against the Inert," leaflet no. 3. (Cambridge, MA: New England Association of Teachers of English, 1901).

14. J. W. Searson, "Determining a Language Program," *English Journal* 13 (1924): 274–79; Warner G. Taylor, *A National Survey of Conditions in Freshman English*, bull. no. 11 (Madison: U of Wisconsin P, 1929).

15. "English and Other Teaching," editorial, *Nation* 19 Mar. 1908: 258.

16. See R. T. Congdon, "Some Forms of Cooperation in English Composition Teaching," bull. 16 (New York: New York City Association of Teachers of English, 1915); H. F. Fore, "Harvard English Plan," *Nation* 29 July 1915: 146–47; William Rollo Lyman, *Summary of Investigations Relating to Grammar, Language, and Composition*, Supplementary Educational Monographs no. 36 (Chicago: U of Chicago P, 1925) 235–43; Ruth M. Vose, "Co-operative Teaching of English in the Secondary Schools," MA thesis, U of Illinois, 1925, 14–22.

17. Vose 44, 77.

18. Hosic, *Reorganization* chap. 14.

19. Figures are from the Bureau of the Census, *Historical Atlas of the U.S.* (Washington, DC: GPO, 1975); see also Applebee, *Tradition* 280.

20. Qtd. in Vose 56.

21. Carson S. Duncan, "Rebellious Word on English Composition," *English Journal* 3 (1915): 155.

22. See, for example, Fore 147.

23. Qtd. in Vose 19.

24. Qtd. in Vose 64.

25. James Fleming Hosic, "Effective Ways of Securing Cooperation of All Departments in the Teaching of English Composition," *Journal of Proceedings and Addresses, National Education Association* (NEA) 51 (1913): 480.

26. Lawrence A. Cremin, *American Education: The Metropolitan Experience* (New York: Harper, 1988).

27. See, for example, Werrett Wallace Charters, "A Spelling Hospital in the High School," *School Review* 18 (1910): 192–94.

28. On the history of remediation, see Rose 344–50; and Andrea A. Lunsford, "A Historical, Descriptive, and Evaluative Study of Remedial English in American Colleges and Universities," diss., Ohio State U, 1977.

29. Henry James, *The Question of Our Speech* (Boston: Houghton Mifflin, 1905) 12; Gene L. Piché, "Class and Culture in the Development of High School English Curriculum, 1800–1900," *Research in the Teaching of English* 11 (1977): 17–25.

30. Agnes F. Perkins, "Cooperation in English," *Nation* 24 Oct. 1907: 373; See also Gardiner 257–58.

31. "Harvard Plan," editorial, *Nation* 22 Apr. 1915: 431. On Columbia see chapter 7.

32. In 1912 Kansas University began the first such program I have been able to locate (Faculty Minutes VI, 1912, 26; VI, 1914, 93–94 [KU]). For a survey of college-level programs in the early 1920s, see Vose 4–8.

33. For descriptions of the Harvard program, see "Harvard Plan" and Vose 4–8. For letters from other institutions inquiring about Harvard's program, as well as about details of its everyday workings, see "Chairman's Scrapbook," in Records of the Committee on the Use of English by Students, 1914–40 (HUA).

34. Nineteenth Annual Report of the Committee, 1934 (HUA): 2.

35. Nineteenth Annual Report of the Committee, 1934 (HUA): 3.

36. Second and Nineteenth Annual Reports of the Committee, 1916, 1934 (HUA). The committee eventually published a pamphlet to guide instructors in making referrals. It contained samples of poor student writing that were due to causes beyond the committee's purview; see *A Brief on the Use of English in Exams by Students in Harvard College,* 1939 (HUA).

37. John and Evelyn Dewey, *Schools of To-morrow* (1915), in *John Dewey: The Middle Works, 1899–1924,* vol. 8 (Carbondale: Southern Illinois U P, 1979) chap. 8.

38. Cremin, *Metropolitan* 236–37.

39. United States Immigration Commission, *Reports of the Immigration Commission: Abstracts,* 61st Congress, 1st Session (Washington, DC: GPO, 1911).

40. See Cremin, *Metropolitan* 237–39.

41. See O. C. Gallagher, "Cooperation in English," leaflet no. 67 (Cambridge: New England Association of Teachers of English, 1909).

42. Jesse L. Newlon, "Stronger Foundation for, and a Better Command of, Spoken or Written English," *Journal of Proceedings and Addresses, National Education Association (*NEA) 55 (1917): 698; and Vose 3.

43. Randolph S. Bourne, *The Gary Schools* (New York: Houghton, 1916) 74; on machine shop English, see Bourne 126.

44. Dewey, *Schools* 327, in John Dewey, *The Middle Works.*

45. Qtd. in Vose 55.

46. See Gene L. Piché, "Revision and Reform in the Secondary School English Curriculum, 1870–1900," diss., U of Minnesota, 1967; and Piché, "Class."

47. John Dewey, *The Public and Its Problems* (New York: Holt, 1927) 125–26.

48. The standard treatment of British examination practices in the nineteenth century is John Roach, *Public Examinations in England, 1850–1900* (Cambridge: Cambridge U P, 1971); see also Walter Roy, *The New Examination System* (London: Croom, 1986); and *Cyclopedia of Education,* vol. 2, ed. Paul Monroe (New York: Macmillan, 1911) 534–38.

49. See Issac A. Kandel, *Examinations and their Substitutes in the United States* (New York: Carnegie Foundation for the Advancement of Teaching, 1936) 24–27.

50. Horace Mann, "Boston Grammar and Writing Schools," *The Common School Journal* 1 Oct. 1845: 1–3; W. H. Wells, "Public High School in Chicago," *American Journal of Education* 3 (1857): 532.

51. Compare, for example, the Harvard examination papers of George Dudley Wiles, 1868–72, and Frederick H. Viaux, 1869–70, with those of Edward Roes, 1884–85, and Ralph Clinton Larrabee, 1891–92 (HUA).

52. Qtd. in William Dusinberre, *Henry Adams: The Myth of Failure* (Charlottesville: U P of Virginia, 1980) 87.

53. Only a more systematic study of surviving examination papers than I have been able to perform could adequately assess their character. For late-nineteenth-century debates on the structure and goals of essay examinations, see Smallwood esp. 104–6; Baird in Buck 161–62; and Hart in Hall 30.

54. See, for example, Michigan Faculty Records, 27 June 1864 (UMA); Reports to the Overseers, vol. 13, 1871, 11 (HUA).

55. See, for example, Harvard's experience with comprehensive examinations (Morison xlviii–l; Emerton in Morison 174–75; and Frederick C. Shattuck and J. Lewis Bremer, "The Medical School, 1869–1929," in Morison 584–85).

56. Monroe, *Cyclopedia* 534; on early criticisms of essay exams, see Kandel 27–34.

57. See Daniel Starch and Eliot C. Elliott, "Reliability of Grading High School Work in English," *School Review* 20 (1912): 442–57; "in History," 21 (1913): 676–81; "in Mathematics," 21 (1913): 254–59.

58. Kandel 40.

59. See Carol Dwyer, "Achievement Testing," *Encyclopedia of Educational Research* (1982) 15.

60. George Meyer, "An Experimental Study of the Old and New Types of Examination and Methods of Study," *Journal of Educational Psychology* 26 (1935): 38; and George Meyer, "An Experimental Study of the Old and New Types of Examination," *Journal of Educational Psychology* 25 (1934): 656–57.

61. L. B. Kinney and Alvin C. Eurich, "A Summary of Investigations Comparing Different Types of Tests," *School and Society* 36 (1932): 544.

62. Kandel 68, 85–86, 161; see also Ben D. Wood, *Measurement in Higher Education* (Yonkers, NY: World Book, 1923): 118.

63. Kandel 162. The College Entrance Examination Board (CEEB), which administered the largest program of essay examinations in the disciplines, instituted an objective examination for college entrance in 1926, the Scholastic Aptitude Test (SAT), but retained essay examinations in the disciplines, the College Board Examinations. In 1937, CEEB added an objective College Board Examination administered in April as a supplement to the regular essay examinations administered in June. By 1940, only a handful of eastern colleges with highly selective admission standards were using the June examination scores. In 1941, CEEB dropped the June essay examinations in the disciplines, citing the pressures of the war effort, though it retained a forty-minute essay component in the English composition examination. In 1956, CEEB instituted Advanced Placement Examinations, which again used essays in the disciplines, and retained the essays into the 1970s despite difficulties with scoring reliability. See College Entrance Examination Board, *Forty-Second Annual Report of the Executive Secretary* (New York: CEEB, 1942) 1–8; and College Entrance Examination Board, *Fifty-Sixth Annual Report of the Executive Secretary* (Princeton: CEEB, 1956) 5, 40.

64. The British considered but rejected objective testing for most purposes; see Philip Hartog, chair, *The Marking of English Essays* (London: Macmillan, 1941).

65. See Kandel 57–61, 152–53.

6.
Writing and the Great Books

1. These two broad versions of general education are discussed in different terms by Gary E. Miller, *The Meaning of General Education: The Emergence of a Curriculum Paradigm* (New York: Columbia U P, 1988) and by Kimball. The following discussion is deeply indebted to their analyses, to Graff, and to S. Michael Halloran,"On the End of Rhetoric, Classical and Modern," *College English* 36 (1975): 621–31.

2. Rudolph's term (*Curriculum* 140).

3. Berlin, *Rhetoric* 44.

4. Charles F. Thwig, *The College of the Future* (Cleveland: Western Reserve U, 1897) 12–13, qtd. in Veysey 186.

5. John Erskine apparently coined the term *great conversation* in the late 1910s, and Hutchins popularized the notion in the 1930s and beyond.

6. Hiram Corson, *The Aims of Literary Study* (New York: Macmillan, 1895) 81–82, qtd. in Veysey 185.

7. Charles G. Osgood, "Humanism and the Teaching of English," *English Journal* 11 (1922): 159.

8. Qtd. in Veysey 211.

9. Thomas R. Lounsbury, "Compulsory Composition in Colleges," *Harper's Monthly Magazine* (Nov. 1911): 878.

10. M. A. DeWolfe Howe, *Barrett Wendell and His Letters* (Boston: Atlantic Monthly P, 1924) 112–13.

11. Oscar James Campbell, "The Failure of Freshman English," *English Journal,* coll. ed. 28 (1939): 182.

12. See Terry Eagleton, *Literary Theory* (Minneapolis: U of Minnesota P, 1983) 30–53.

13. I. A. Richards, *Science and Poetry* (London: Haskell, 1926) 82–83.

14. On the relationship between liberal culture's political stance and the teaching of the great books, see Graff 86–89; and Veysey 189–91.

15. See George Kennedy, *Classical Rhetoric and Its Christian and Secular Tradition from Ancient to Modern Times* (Chapel Hill: U of North Carolina P, 1980) 189–90.

16. See, for example, Kimball 240; and Halloran, "Rhetoric."

17. Edward A. Thurber, "College Composition," *Nation* 9 Sept. 1915: 328.

18. On the origin of the term *belles lettres* and its shifts in meaning, see Wilbur Samuel Howell, *Eighteenth-Century British Logic and Rhetoric* (Princeton: Princeton U P, 1971) 519–36.

19. Kimball 119–22.

20. Halloran ("Rhetoric" 258–62) discusses this point in relation to belles lettres and the elective curriculum.

21. Richard Young, "Concepts of Art and the Teaching of Writing," in Murphy 31. The implications of this conflict for composition theory and pedagogy have also been explored by others, notably Berlin, *Rhetoric;* and Lester Faigley, "Competing Theories of Process: A Critique and a Proposal," *College English* 48 (1986): 527–42.

22. Lounsbury 870.

23. Campbell 180.

24. Lane Cooper, "On the Teaching of Written Composition," *Education* 30 (1910): 421.

25. J. M. H. "English in College," *Nation* 1 July 1915: 16.

26. For an account of the tradition of abolition, see David R. Russell, "Romantics on Writing: Liberal Culture and the Abolition of Composition Courses," *Rhetoric Review* 6 (1988): 132–48.

27. Harold C. Binkeley, "If the Salt Have Lost Its Savor," *Journal of Higher Education* 11 (1940): 182.

28. See Miller, "Archeology of English."

29. On the low status of composition teaching (and on the pains of theme grading) see, for example, Woodbridge 7–13; Wolverton 407–8; and Lounsbury 180.

30. For an overview of approaches common in English departments in the early twentieth century, see Berlin, *Rhetoric* chap. 3.

31. See Osgood.

32. Berlin, *Rhetoric* 43–46.

33. William Lyon Phelps, *Teaching in School and College* (New York: Macmillan, 1912): 51, 96–97, qtd. in Veysey 225.

34. Qtd. in Veysey 232–33.

35. Graff 95. On faculty complaints, see Graff 49.

36. Veysey 222.

37. See Phelps 141; and Wood 266–71.

38. Henry James, *Charles W. Eliot* (Boston: Houghton Mifflin, 1930) 14–15.

39. John Erskine, *My Life as a Teacher* (Philadelphia: Lippincott, 1948) 16. For a portrait of Genung's teaching methods earlier in his career, see Wozniack 93–100.

40. Graff 134.

41. On the origins of Columbia's great-books courses, see Daniel Bell, *The Reforming of General Education: The Columbia Experience in Its National Setting* (New York: Columbia U P, 1966) 13–14.

42. Rudolph, *Curriculum* 256.

43. John Erskine, *The Delight of Great Books* (Indianapolis: Bobbs, 1928) 14.

44. John Erskine, *The Memory of Certain Persons* (Philadelphia: Lippincott, 1947) 343.

45. Erskine, *Delight* 28.

46. Erskine, *Memory* 343.

47. Robert MacDougall, "University Training and the Doctoral Degree," *Education* 24 (1904): 261–76.

48. On liberal culture's shift in intellectual tone, see Veysey 197–212. On student writing and new criticism, see Graff 171–73, 230–32.

49. Qtd. in Graff 135.

50. Erskine, *Memory* 344.

51. Erskine, *Delight* 28–29.

52. On the importance of conversation, both as a method and as a goal of teaching the great books, see Harvard Committee on General Education, *General Education in a Free Society* (Cambridge, MA: Harvard U P, 1945) 68–69.

53. Justus Buchler, "Reconstruction in the Liberal Arts," in *History of Columbia College on Morningside* (New York: Columbia U P, 1954) 76.

54. See Columbia College Bulletin, 1937–1938 (CUA); Alan Brown to Harrison Ross Steeves, 7 Jan. 1937 (CUA); Buchler in *History* 117–24; and *A College Program in Action: A Review of Working Principles at Columbia College by the Committee on Plans* (New York: Columbia U P, 1946) 150.

55. *College Program* 151–52; Charles W. Everett, " 'Most Glad To Teach,' " in *History* 145.

56. Committee on the College Plan, Minutes, 7 Feb. 1922 (CUA); English department response to the committee, 29 Nov. 1945 (CUA); Letter of H. R. Steeves to English Department, 5 Feb. 1946 (CUA); *College Plan* 35–40, 146–54.

57. Stern Committee report, qtd. in Bell 225.

58. Kimball 240.

59. On the origins of the Chicago experiment, see Rudolph, *Curriculum* 278–80; Chauncey S. Boucher, *The Chicago College Plan* (Chicago: U of Chicago P, 1940); and *The Idea and Practice of General Education: An Account of the College of the University of Chicago,* by Present and Former Members of the Faculty (Chicago: U of Chicago P, 1950).

60. Mortimer J. Adler, *How To Read a Book: The Art of Getting a Liberal Education* (New York: Simon and Schuster, 1940) 16.

61. Robert Maynard Hutchins, *The Higher Learning in America* (New Haven: Yale U P, 1936) 83.

62. See, for example, the apparatus in Mortimer J. Adler and Seymour Cain, *Religion and Theology* (Chicago: Encyclopedia Britannica, 1961).

63. Adler, *How To Read* chap. 9.

64. *The Great Conversation: The Substance of a Liberal Education,* ed. Robert M. Hutchins (Chicago: Encyclopedia Britannica, 1952) xxv.

65. Mortimer J. Adler, ed. *The Great Ideas: A Synopticon of Great Books of the Western World* (Chicago: Encyclopedia Britannica, 1952).

66. Rudolph, *Curriculum* 279.

67. See Boucher, esp. 64–73.

68. See *Manual of Examinations,* 1932–40 (UCA). See also Bell 38; Boucher 66–68.

69. For a description of the Chicago course, see C. W. Kerby-Miller and Wilma Anderson Kerby-Miller, "A New Type of Composition Course," *English Journal,* coll. ed. 26 (1937): 715–25; and see their continuation, "What Is Wrong with Freshman Composition?" *English Journal,* coll. ed. 26 (1937): 625–37.

70. See *English 102: Syllabus and Readings,* 1934; and *Manual of Examinations,* 1934 (UCA).

71. *Idea of General Education* 210.

72. For instructor comments on writing, see Boucher 288–90, 296, 299.

73. Boucher 63.

74. See Rudolph, *Curriculum* 279.

75. James Carey, personal interview, 11 Sept. 1990. On St. John's curriculum, see J. Winfree Smith, *A Search for the Liberal College: The Beginning of the St. John's Program* (Annapolis, MD: St. John's College P, 1983) 27–38.

76. Rudolph, *Curriculum* 280.

77. In 1985, St. John's at Santa Fe funded two "student writing assistants" to help students with the "mechanics of writing," as Carey put it. Carey also said the college is reluctantly considering instituting writing classes to address the students' lack of secondary-school preparation in writing.

78. See Viles 411–22.

7.
Writing and Progressive Education

1. In this chapter I use the terms *Deweyan progressive* or simply *progressive* for Deweyan educational reforms, reserving Cremin's term *administrative progressives* for the advocates of industrial efficiency in education. My goal is to set complex problems of terminology aside to focus on the roles that writing played in curricula. I realize that contradictory terminology and positions sometimes came together in uneasy alliances, even in the works of Dewey himself.

2. Harold Rugg and Anne Shumaker, *The Child-Centered School: An Appraisal of the New Education* (New York: World Book, 1928) 244. On Scott and the progressives, see Berlin, *Writing* chap. 7; Berlin, *Rhetoric* 58–91; and Donald Stewart, "Rediscovering Fred Newton Scott," *College English* 40 (1979): 539–47.

3. On the social sciences' version of general education, see Miller, *Meaning* chap. 4.

4. I am applying Cremin's central thesis to the specific issue of interdisciplinary writing instruction in progressive education; see Cremin, *Transformation*, esp. 183–84.

5. For Progressive-Era theories of communication, see Jean B. Quandt, *From the Small Town to the Great Community: The Social Thought of Progressive Intellectuals* (New Brunswick, NJ: Rutgers U P, 1970) chap. 2.

6. John Dewey, *Democracy in Education* (1916) in *John Dewey: The Middle Works* 9: 25–26.

7. Cremin, *Transformation* 220.

8. Cremin, *Transformation* 234.

9. *Experience and Education* (1938), in *John Dewey: The Later Works, 1925–1953*, vol. 13 (Carbondale: Southern Illinois U P, 1980) 51.

10. Sterling Andrus Leonard describes and classifies these and many other composition projects in *Composition as a Social Problem* (Boston: Houghton, 1917) 24, 27.

11. *Lincoln Verse, Story, and Essay*, selected in Hughes Mearns, *Creative Power* (Garden City, NJ: Doubleday, 1929) 279–91.

12. See, for example, the written projects in The Association of Teachers of Social Studies of the City of New York, *Handbook for Social Studies Teaching* (New York: Holt, 1941): 194–95.

13. Cremin, *Transformation* 220.

14. Arthur Bestor, *Educational Wastelands: The Retreat from Learning in Our Public Schools* (Urbana: U of Illinois P, 1953) chap. 7.

15. On the historical alienation of education departments, see Geraldine Joncich Clifford and James W. Guthrie, *Ed School: A Brief for Professional Education* (Chicago: U of Chicago P, 1988) esp. chap. 4; and Clark, "The School and the University" 17–22.

16. On the expressivists in composition instruction, see Berlin, *Rhetoric* 73–

81; and Kenneth J. Kantor, "Creative Expression in the English Classroom: An Historical Perspective," *Research in the Teaching of English* 9 (1974): 5–29.

17. For these and other such essays, see Mearns, *Creative Power.*

18. See John Dewey, Albert C. Barnes, Laurence Buermeyer, Mary Mullen, and Violette de Mazia, *Art and Education*, 2d ed. (Merion, PA: Barnes Foundation, 1947) 23–40.

19. Arthur Bestor, one of the severest critics of progressive education in the 1950s, was himself a graduate of Lincoln High School in the 1920s and complimented the education he received there; see *Educational Wastelands* 45–47.

20. Cremin, *Transformation* 183.

21. Hosic, "Effective" 485.

22. Cremin, *Transformation* 243.

23. Ruth Mary Weeks, "Teaching the Whole Child," *English Journal* 20 (1931): 9–17.

24. Ruth Mary Weeks, *Making American Industry Safe for Democracy*, bull. no. 5 (Chicago: Vocational Education Association of the Midwest, 1918) 3.

25. Ruth Mary Weeks, *Socializing the Three R's* (New York: Macmillan, 1920) 22–23.

26. On the social reconstructionists' politics, see Hertzberg 47; and Walter Feinberg, *Reason and Rhetoric* (New York: John Wiley, 1975) esp. chaps. 3 and 5.

27. Weeks, *Socializing* 5.

28. Ruth Mary Weeks, comp., *A Correlated Curriculum*, NCTE Educational Monograph no. 5 (New York: Appleton, 1936) 4.

29. Weeks, *Socializing* 48.

30. Weeks, *Correlated* 4.

31. Weeks, *Correlated* 3–4.

32. Weeks, *Correlated* 10.

33. Qtd. in Wilford M. Aikin, *The Story of the Eight Year Study* (New York: Harper, 1942) 16.

34. See Weeks, *Correlated* 234–38; and Loaz W. Johnson, "The Effect of Integration on Achievement," *English Journal* 25 (1936): 737–44.

35. See Eugene R. Smith, Ralph Tyler, and the Evaluative Staff, *Appraising and Recording Student Progress* (New York: Harper, 1942) esp. 84–86.

36. Figures are from Grace S. Wright, *Core Curriculum in Public High Schools: An Inquiry Into Practices, 1949.* U.S. Office of Education bull. 1950, no. 5. (Washington, DC: GPO, 1950).

37. Applebee, *Tradition* 142; Cuban 67–83.

38. The preponderance of correlated programs in junior-high schools is worth noting in this light. When junior-high schools were founded in the 1910s to offer a place for educational innovation outside the tradition-bound secondary-school curriculum, most of their graduates never went on to high school. Correlated courses offered a convenient way to give most students a first and last taste of academic subjects—history and literature, mainly—while still preserving time in the curriculum for vocational courses, such as wood or metal shop. In the 1930s

and beyond, as a greater proportion of students continued on to high school, junior highs retained correlated courses as a means of giving all students a try at various subjects before they were tracked into college preparatory or vocational training. But increasingly, the correlated courses centered on "problems of living," such as managing money, etiquette, hygiene, and other skills thought necessary for a safe and productive adulthood in American society—socialization in its most direct sense.

39. See, for example, *Thirty Schools Tell Their Story* (New York: Harper, 1942) 228.

40. Carol A. O'Connor, "Setting a Standard for Suburbia: Innovation in the Scarsdale Schools, 1920–1930," *History of Education Quarterly* 26 (1980): 306.

41. Mark Neville, "Sharing Experiences with Farmville," *English Journal* 34 (1945): 371.

42. Philip R. Jenkins, "Is English Going Out?" *English Journal* 31 (1942): 439–44.

43. "Our Readers Think: About Integration," *English Journal* 34 (1945): 496–502; continued as "Our Readers Think: More About Integration," 555–59.

44. Percy V. Shelly, "English as an Independent Subject in the Curriculum," *English Journal*, coll. ed. 28 (1939): 356.

45. Hertzberg 56–58.

46. Arthur C. Bining and David H. Bining, *Teaching the Social Sciences in Secondary Schools* (New York: McGraw, 1935) 212.

47. See Applebee, *Tradition* 142.

48. Franklin Bobbitt, "A Correlated Curriculum Evaluated," *English Journal* 26 (1937): 420.

49. Thomas L. Hopkins, "A Correlated Curriculum Evaluated," *English Journal* 26 (1937): 418.

50. J. M. O'Neill, "The Relation of Speech to English: Suggestions for Cooperation," *English Journal* 25 (1936): 40.

51. Franklin Bobbitt, "Questionable Recommendations of the Commission on the Social Studies," *School and Society* 40 (1934): 205.

52. See, for example, Martin James Stormzand, *American History Teaching and Testing: Supervised Study and Scientific Testing in American History, Based on Beard and Bagley's The History of the American People* (New York: Macmillan, 1926).

53. See Hertzberg 66.

54. American Historical Association, *Conclusions and Recommendations of the Commission: Report of the Commission on the Social Studies* (New York: Scribner's, 1934) 98–99.

55. American Historical Association, *Conclusions* 97–100.

56. Grace Wright, *Core Curriculum Development: Problems and Practices*, U.S. Office of Education bull., 1952, no. 5 (Washington, DC: GPO, 1952) 85–89.

57. Quotations are excerpted from Franklin 158–64.

58. See O'Connor 295–311.

59. Neville 371.

60. See Franklin 151.

61. See Cuban 82.

62. Weeks, *Correlated* 10.

63. On the rural origins of curricular reformers and how those origins influenced their theories, see Franklin 14–17, 34–37, 50–51, 98–99.

64. Applebee, *Tradition* 142.

65. Progressive Education Association, *Science in General Education: Suggestions for Teachers in the Secondary Schools and in the Lower Division of Colleges,* Report of the Commission on Secondary School Curriculum (New York: Appleton, 1938); Progressive Education Association, *The Social Sciences in General Education,* Report of the Committee on Secondary School Curriculum (New York: Appleton, 1940); Progressive Education Association, *Language in General Education: A Report of the Committee on the Function of English in General Education* (New York: Appleton, 1940).

66. Bining and Bining, *Teaching* (1952) 147.

67. See Applebee, *Tradition* 175.

68. Burton R. Clark, *The Distinctive College: Antioch, Reed and Swarthmore* (Chicago: Aldine, 1970) 47–52.

69. Barbara Jones, *Bennington College: The Development of an Educational Idea* (New York: Harper, 1946) 67, qtd. in Miller, *Meaning* 86.

70. Jones 86, qtd. in Miller, *Meaning* 89. Examples of assignments in the Bennington curriculum are from Miller, *Meaning* 79–89.

71. Constance Warren, *A New Design for Women's Education* (New York: Frederick A. Stokes, 1940) 25, qtd. in Miller, *Meaning* 92.

72. Cremin, *Transformation* 313.

73. Alexander Meiklejohn, *The Experimental College* (New York: Arno, 1971) 57–58; the following account is drawn from Meiklejohn's report.

74. Bell 14; Miller, *Meaning* 35–37. For a critical view, see Upton Sinclair, *The Goose-Step: A Study of American Education* (Pasadena, CA: [the author] 1923).

75. On the new historians, see Hertzberg 17–19.

76. Qtd. by Buchler in *History* 100.

77. On the organization of the CC course, see Buchler in *History* 53–57.

78. Buchler in *History* 56.

79. See Harry J. Carman, "The Columbia Course in Contemporary Civilization," *Columbia Alumni News* 17 (1925): 143–44; and John J. Coss, "Progress of the New Freshman Course," *Columbia University Quarterly* (Oct. 1919): 332–33.

80. Wood chap. 8.

81. Kandel 99.

82. See Wood 201.

83. Qtd. in Wood 201.

84. Bledstein 327.

85. Veysey 311 and 337–38.

86. See Miller, *Meaning* 17–19; Rudolph, *Curriculum* 249, 273; and Bell 66–68.

87. Buchler in *History* 107.

88. Bell 230–33; Graff 172–73.

8.
The Disciplines Enter the Information Age

1. Clark, *Academic Life* chap. 1.

2. On the current relations between the testing community and composition studies, see Edward M. White, "Language and Reality in Writing Assessment," *College Composition and Communication* 41 (1990): 187–200.

3. On recent developments in writing evaluation, see Edward M. White, *Teaching and Assessing Writing* (San Francisco: Jossey, 1985).

4. See, for example, "Reed College," *Liberal Education* 73 (May/June 1987): 30–31.

5. See D. C. Spriestersbach and Lyell D. Henry, Jr., "The Ph.D. Dissertation: Servant or Master?" *Improving College and University Teaching* 26 (1978): 52–55.

6. "Report of the Committee on Policies in Graduate Education," *Journal of Proceedings and Addresses, Ninth Annual Conference of the Association of Graduate Schools* (New York: AGS, 1957); reprinted in Koefod 189–97.

7. Koefod 4.

8. William James, "The Ph.D. Octopus," *Harvard Monthly* 36 (1903): 1–9.

9. See, for example, Bernard Berelson, *Graduate Education in the United States* (New York: McGraw, 1960) 172–85. (ABD: all but dissertation.)

10. Koefod's 1964 study of writing requirements is a notable exception.

11. See Patricia Sullivan, "From Student to Scholar: A Contextual Study of Graduate Student Writing in English," diss., Ohio State U, 1988, 217–18. See also Carol Berkenkotter, Thomas N. Huckin, and John Ackerman, "Conventions, Conversations, and the Writer: Case Study of a Student in a Rhetoric Ph.D. Program," *Research in the Teaching of English* 22 (1988): 9–43.

12. In the last decade, a few composition specialists have begun to address the problem by offering workshops and support groups for graduate-student writing anxiety. See Lynn Z. Bloom, "Why Graduate Students Can't Write: Implications of Research on Writing Anxiety for Graduate Students," CCCC Convention, Dallas, Mar. 1981 (ED 199 710).

13. Jessamon Dawe, *Writing Business and Economics Papers, Theses and Dissertations* (Totowa, NJ: Littlefield, 1965) 1.

14. See Dawe. Such books often grew out of graduate courses in methods, for example, Jaques Barzun and Henry Graff, *The Modern Researcher* (New York: Harcourt, 1957); for others, see Koefod 255–56.

15. H. R. Struck, "Wanted: More Writing Courses for Graduate Students," *College Composition and Communication* 27 (1976): 192–97.

16. See Alan Golding and John Mascaro, "A Survey of Graduate Writing Courses," *Journal of Advanced Composition* 6 (1986): 167–79.

17. Hurd, *New Directions* 9.

18. See Vincent N. Lunetta and Pinchas Tamri, "Matching Lab Activities with Teaching Goals," *Science Teacher* 46 (1979): 22–24.

19. In *John Dewey: The Later Works, 1925–1933* (vol. 13) 53.

20. Bruner, *Process* 13.

21. Jerome S. Bruner, *Beyond the Information Given: Studies in the Psychology of Knowing*, ed. Jeremy M. Anglin (New York: Norton, 1973) 321.

22. See Jerome S. Bruner, *On Knowing: Essays for the Left Hand* (Cambridge, MA: Harvard U P, 1979) 113–26.

23. Hurd, *New Directions* 30. See also Robert B. Sund, *Teaching Science by Inquiry in the Secondary School* (Columbus, OH: Merrill, 1973).

24. See Bazerman, *Shaping* chap. 6.

25. Lunetta and Tamri 23.

26. For a review of recent literature on laboratory pedagogy in science, see James J. Gallagher, "Summary of Research in Science Education," *Science Education* 71 (1985): 351–55.

27. On recent studies of the effect of writing on science learning, see L. V. Brillhart and M. B. Debs, "Teaching Writing: A Scientist's Responsibility," *Journal of College Science Teaching* 10 (1977): 303–4; and W. E. Davis and Robert Matlock, "Interdisciplinary Teaching of Writing Skills," *Journal of College Science Teaching* 11 (1978): 310–11. Gail W. Hearn's research in biology lab writing is a notable exception: see "Writing in Ecology and the Ecology of Writing," in *Programs That Work: Models and Methods for Writing across the Curriculum*, ed. Toby Fulwiler and Art Young (Portsmouth, NH: Boynton, 1990) 148–54.

28. See, for example, Sypherd.

29. See Connors, "Technical Writing" 342.

30. See Raymond V. Lesikar, "The Meaning and Status of Organizational Communication," *ABCA Bulletin* 44 (1981): 2–5.

31. See, for example, Gordon and Howell 155.

32. Pierson 178; see also Gordon and Howell 156.

33. Lesikar 4.

34. See Souther in Fearing and Sparrow 9–10.

35. See Martin Kaplin's historical analysis, "The Wrong Solution to the Right Problem," in *In Opposition to Core Curriculum: Alternative Models for Undergraduate Education,* ed. James W. Hall and Barbara L. Kevles (Westport, CT: Greenwood, 1982) 2–12.

36. James Bryant Conant, *Education in a Divided World: The Function of Public Schools in Our Unique Society* (Cambridge, MA: Harvard U P, 1945) 108–9, qtd. in Graff 167.

37. Harvard College catalog, 1954–55, 64, 177 (HUA).

38. See syllabi and assignments for Social Science 3 and Natural Science 4, in "The General Education Core, 1953–1954" (HUA).

39. Bell 48.

40. See Harvard College catalog, 1965–66 (HUA).

41. Bell 231.

42. I. A. Richards, *The Philosophy of Rhetoric* (New York: Oxford U P, 1936) 3.

43. Progressive Education Association, *Language in General Education* 32.

44. Objective testing, tracking, cost efficiency, and the like are important themes in the literature of the communications movement; see, for example, descriptions of late 1940s' programs in *Communication in General Education,* ed. Earl J. McGrath (Dubuque, IA: Brown, 1949).

45. Applebee, *Tradition* 157–60.

46. For an excellent overview of the movement as it affected freshman-composition instruction, see Berlin, *Writing* chap. 5.

47. Basic Aims Committee, "Basic Aims for English Instruction in American Schools," *English Journal* 31 (1942): 40.

48. Berlin, *Rhetoric* 96; and Jean Malmstrom, "The Communications Course," *College Composition and Communication* 7 (1956): 21–24.

49. For accounts of the conference, see Nancy K. Bird, "The Conference on College Composition and Communication: A Historical Study of Its Continuing Education and Professionalization Activities, 1947–1975," diss., Virginia Polytechnic Institute, 1977, 31–32.

50. Berlin, *Rhetoric* 96.

51. See Berlin, *Rhetoric* 97–99.

52. On the communications movement, see *Essays on Classical Rhetoric and Modern Discourse,* ed, Robert J. Connors, Lisa S. Ede, and Andrea A. Lunsford (Carbondale: Southern Illinois U P, 1984) 8; and Bird.

53. Jonathan Kistler papers (FWP) 1.

54. Strang Lawson, "The Colgate Plan for Improving Student Writing," *AAUP Bulletin* 39 (1953): 289–90.

55. Jonathan Kistler papers (FWP) 8.

56. Jonathan Kistler, letter to the author, 30 Apr. 1986.

57. Huntington Terrell, personal interview, 31 Mar. 1986.

58. Benjamin H. Lehman, chair, "Report to the Committee on Educational Policy, 1952–53," 5 (PIC).

59. Josephine Miles, *Working Out Ideas: Predication and Other Uses of Language* Curriculum Publications 5 (Berkeley: Bay Area Writing Project, 1979) 11.

60. Josephine Miles, chair, "Report of the Committee for Prose Improvement, 1958" (PIC).

61. Miles, chair, "Report of the Committee for Prose Improvement, 1958," (PIC).

62. Ralph W. Rader, chair, "Report of the Committee on Prose Improvement, 1964–65," 4–5 (PIC).

63. Miles, *Working* 17.

64. Rader 5 (PIC).

65. Agenda for PIC meeting of 28 May 1958 (PIC).

66. Jonathan Kistler papers 11 (FWP).

67. Jonathan Kistler, letter to the author, 30 Apr. 1986.

68. Rader 1 (PIC).

69. Only institutions with highly selective admissions standards had systems of cross-curricular responsibility for writing instruction in the 1960s, usually in the form of general-education freshman seminars (in lieu of freshman composition) with a specific writing requirement. See Thomas W. Wilcox, *Anatomy of Freshman English* (San Francisco: Jossey, 1973) 94–102.

9.
The Writing-Across-the-Curriculum Movement: 1970–1990

1. Two notable exceptions were a pioneering curriculum for the "disadvantaged," Gateway English, at Hunter College, and the Northwestern University curriculum materials, which focused on the process of writing. See Kenneth J. Kantor, "The English Curriculum and the Structure of the Disciplines," *Theory into Practice* 22 (1984): 175.

2. Berlin, *Rhetoric* 122–23.

3. See Myrna J. Smith, "Bruner on Writing," *College Composition and Communication* 28 (1977): 129–33.

4. Bruner, *Process* 31; For Bruner's influence in WAC research in the 1980s, see, for example, Arthur N. Applebee, *Contexts for Learning To Write: Studies of Secondary School Instruction* (Norwood, NJ: Ablex, 1984) esp. 177–78; and Bazerman, *Shaping* 306.

5. Ron Smith, "Composition Requirements: A Report on a Nationwide Survey of Four-Year Colleges and Universities," *College Composition and Communication* 25 (1974): 139.

6. On expressivist writing instruction in composition during the 1960s, see Berlin, *Rhetoric* 145–55.

7. John Dixon, *Growth Through English: A Report Based on the Dartmouth Seminar, 1966* (Reading, UK: National Association for the Teaching of English, 1967), qtd. in Kantor, "English" 176.

8. On the "revival of rhetoric," see Berlin, *Rhetoric* chap. 6; on the MLA, see Donald Stewart, "Status of Composition."

9. On the CUNY experience, see Blanche Skurnick, "Basic Writing at the City University of New York," in *Options for the Teaching of English: Freshman Composition,* ed. Jasper P. Neel (New York: MLA, 1978) 10–15. On Mina Shaughnessy, see Robert Lyons, "Mina Shaughnessy," in *Traditions of Inquiry,* ed. John Brereton (New York: Oxford U P, 1985) 171–89.

10. On the rationalization of university administration, see Clark, *Academic Life* chap. 6; and Clark, *Higher Education System* chap. 4.

11. The National Defense Education Act was belatedly extended to English in 1964 (see Applebee, *Tradition* 198–204).

12. Quotations are from Daniels 138.

13. *Language for Life* (The Bullock Report) (London: HMSO, 1975); James Britton, Tony Burgess, Nancy Martin, Alex McLeod, and Harold Rosen, *The Development of Writing Abilities (11–18)* (London: Macmillan, 1975).

14. *Language for Life* 6.

15. James Britton, *Language and Learning* (London: Penguin, 1970) 214.

16. *Language for Life* 395–96. For Britton's assessment of The Bullock Report, see his essay, "Reflections on the Writing of The Bullock Report," in *Prospect and Retrospect: Selected Essays of James Britton*, ed. Gordon M. Pradl (Montclair, NJ: Boynton, 1982): 185–190.

17. On the Schools Council Project, see Michael Marland, *Language Across the Curriculum: The Implementation of The Bullock Report in the Secondary School* (London: Heineman, 1977).

18. Janet Emig, "Writing as a Mode of Learning," *College Composition and Communication* 28 (1977): 127.

19. See Roy, 1–18.

20. See Applebee, *Tradition* 232–36.

21. For an account of the early years of BAWP, see "Bay Area Writing Project/California Writing Project/National Writing Project: An Overview," University of California at Berkeley, School of Education. Urbana: ERIC, 1978 (ED 184 123).

22. See Applebee, *Writing*.

23. See Clifford and Guthrie 317–18.

24. See Applebee, *Contexts* 187–88; Judith A. Langer and Arthur N. Applebee, *How Writing Shapes Thinking: A Study of Teaching and Writing*, NCTE Research Report no. 22 (Urbana: NCTE, 1987) 138–39; and Deborah Swanson-Owens, "Identifying Natural Sources of Resistance: A Case Study of Implementing Writing Across the Curriculum," *Research in the Teaching of English* 20 (1986): 69–97.

25. Among the university and secondary-school cooperative programs (often associated with the NWP) are those at Beaver College, University of Michigan, University of Washington, Rutgers, Indiana University, George Mason University, and the original at UC Berkeley. See Mary A. Barr and Mary K. Healy, "School and University Articulation: Different Contexts for Writing Across the Curriculum," in McLeod. *Speaking and Writing, K–12: Classroom Strategies and the New Research*, ed. Christopher Thaiss and C. Suhor (Urbana: NCTE, 1984). Christopher Thaiss, *Language Across the Curriculum in the Elementary Grades* (Urbana: NCTE, 1986).

26. In the social studies, see especially Barry Beyer and Anita Brostoff, eds., "Writing to Learn in Social Studies," *Social Education* 43 (1979): 194–97.

27. Recounted in Erling Larsen, "Carleton College," in *Options for the Teaching of English: The Undergraduate Curriculum*, ed. Elizabeth Wooton Cowan (New York: MLA, 1975) 8.

28. See "The Development of the Communication Skills Program at Central College, Pella, Iowa," 1985 (CCA); and Barbara Fassler, "The Interdepartmental Composition Program at Central College," in Neel, *Options* 84–89.

29. Elaine P. Maimon, personal interview, 23 Apr. 1990.

30. Elaine P. Maimon, "Writing, Learning, and Thinking at Beaver College," College English Association Annual Meeting, Savannah, Mar. 1979 (ED 175054).

31. Maimon, "Writing, Learning, and Thinking" 4.

32. On Maimon's experience, see "Writing, Learning and Thinking"; Maimon, "Beaver College," in Fulwiler and Young 142–43; Maimon, "Cinderella to Hercules: Demythologizing Writing Across the Curriculum," *Journal of Basic Writing* 2 (1980): 3–11. On conflicts elsewhere, see Toby Fulwiler, "How Well Does Writing Across the Curriculum Work?" *College English* 46 (1984): 113–25.

33. See Lois Barry, "Eastern Oregon State College," in *New Methods in College Writing Programs: Theories in Practice,* ed. Paul Connolly and Teresa Vilardi (New York: MLA, 1986) 33–39.

34. This account is drawn primarily from Toby Fulwiler, "Writing Across the Curriculum at Michigan Tech," *Journal of the Council of Writing Program Administrators* 4 (1981): 15–20; *Writing Across the Disciplines: Research into Practice,* Art Young and Toby Fulwiler, eds. (Portsmouth, NH: Boynton, 1986); and Toby Fulwiler, personal interview, 24 Mar. 1990.

35. Art Young, "Teaching Writing Across the University: The Michigan Tech Experience," College English Association Convention, Savannah, Mar. 1979 (ED 176 928).

36. Richard Lanham, "Urgency and Opportunity: Implementing Writing Across the Curriculum," address, University of Georgia faculty, Athens, 25 Apr. 1985; reported in *Writing Across the Curriculum* 3 (1985): 5–6.

37. See, for, example Patricia Stock, "University of Michigan, Ann Arbor," in Connolly and Vilardi 117–21; and Milton D. Glick, "Writing Across the Curriculum: A Dean's Perspective," *WPA: Writing Program Administration* 11 (1988): 53–58.

38. On Washington's program, see Joan Graham, "University of Washington," in Connolly and Vilardi 143–48; and Joan Graham, "What Works: The Problems and Rewards of Cross-Curricular Writing Programs," *Current Issues in Higher Education* 3 (1983–84): 16–26.

39. Kenneth A. Bruffee, "The Brooklyn Plan: Attaining Intellectual Growth through Peer-Group Tutoring," *Liberal Education* 64 (1978): 447–68. On California State's program, see Marilyn Sutton, "The Writing Adjunct Program at the Small College of California State College, Dominguez Hills," in Neel, *Options* 104–9.

40. Burton Clark and Martin Trow in *College Peer Groups,* ed. Theodore M. Newcomb and Everett K. Wilson (Chicago: Aldine, 1966) 67, qtd. in Bruffee, "Brooklyn Plan" 449.

41. *A Guide to Writing Programs: Writing Centers, Peer Tutoring Programs, and Writing Across the Curriculum,* ed. Tori Haring-Smith, Nathaniel Hawkins,

Elizabeth, Morrison, Lise Stern, and Robin Tatu (Glenview, IL: Scott Foresman, 1987) 7–27.

42. For community college perspectives on WAC, see Barbara R. Stout and Joyce N. Magnotto, "Writing Across the Curriculum at Community Colleges," in McLeod 21–30; and "Prince George's Community College," in Fulwiler and Young 65–81.

43. National Institute of Education, *Involvement in Learning: Realizing the Potential of American Higher Education* (Washington, DC: NIE, 1984). See also William J. Bennett, *To Reclaim a Legacy: A Report on the Humanities in Higher Education* (Washington, DC: NEH, 1984). For the student-personnel perspective, see, for example *The Freshman Year Experience: Helping Students Survive and Succeed in College,* ed. John M. Lee Upcraft (San Francisco: Jossey, 1989).

44. The term *second stage* was coined by Susan McLeod, "Translating Enthusiasm into Curricular Change," in McLeod. For a range of models and perspectives, see the other essays in McLeod.

45. Susan H. McLeod, "Writing Across the Curriculum: The Second Stage and Beyond," *College Composition and Communication* 40 (1989): 339–41.

46. See Langer and Applebee 146.

47. Kurt Spellmeyer, "A Common Ground: The Essay in the Academy," *College English* 3 (1989): 266.

48. Joan Graham, "Writing Conferences in Disciplinary Contexts: Students Working Out What They Think," CCCC Convention, Chicago, Mar. 1990.

49. See the responses to Spellmeyer's essay by Bazerman and Susan Miller in "Two Comments on 'A Common Ground: The Essay in Academe,'" *College English* 52 (1990): 329–38; and Elaine P. Maimon, "Reexamining False Dichotomies," CCCC Convention, Chicago, Mar. 1990, esp. 6–7.

50. Thaiss, in McLeod (91), notes the prevalence of religious metaphors in discussions of WAC.

51. See Fulwiler, "How Well" 120.

52. For a critique of this approach, see Thaiss in McLeod 91–102.

53. For the 1987 survey, see Susan H. McLeod and Susan Shirley, "National Survey of Writing Across the Curriculum Programs," in McLeod 103–30.

54. See Haring-Smith, "What's Wrong"; and Thaiss in McLeod 94–95. Kitzhaber (*Themes* 102, 153n) noted similar attitudes in 1963.

55. See Thaiss in McLeod 94.

56. Art Young and Toby Fulwiler, "The Enemies of Writing Across the Curriculum," in Fulwiler and Young 293.

57. Thaiss (in McLeod 94–96) lists administrative mandate as one of the three major difficulties that WAC programs must overcome.

58. Rudolph, *Curriculum* 251; see also Bell 25.

59. Steven Weiland, "History Toward Rhetoric," *College English* 49 (1987): 816.

60. Charles Bazerman, "A Relationship between Reading and Writing," *College English* 41 (1980): 656–61; and Charles Bazerman, *The Informed Writer* (Boston: Houghton, 1981).

61. See "Letters," *Physics Today* (May 1989): 9–11; and (Feb. 1990): 11–15, 156.

62. For a useful overview and theoretical discussion of this research, see *Writing in Academic Disciplines,* ed. David A. Jolliffe (Norwood, NJ: Ablex, 1988); and Lucille Parkinson McCarthy and Barbara F. Walvoord, "Models for Collaborative Research in Writing Across the Curriculum," in McLeod 77–90. See also Graham, "Writing Conferences"; Catherine Beyer, "Making Knowledge in Political Economics," CCCC Convention, Chicago, Mar. 1990; David S. Kaufer and Cheryl Geisler, "Novelty in Academic Writing," *Written Communication* 6 (1989): 286–311; Barbara F. Walvoord, ed., *Thinking and Writing in College: A Naturalistic Study of Students Writing in Four Disciplines* (Urbana: NCTE, 1991); Anne Herrington, "Writing in Academic Settings: A Study of the Contexts for Writing in Two College Chemical Engineering Courses," *Research in the Teaching of English* 19 (1985): 331–61; Anderson, et al.; Berkenkotter, et al.

63. Clark, *Higher Education System* 246.

64. See Patrick J. Hill, "Communities of Learners: Curriculum as the Infrastructure of Academic Communities," in Hall and Kevles; and "Swarthmore College," *Liberal Education* 73 (May/June 1987): 32–33.

65. For theoretical perspectives on interdisciplinary study, see Raymond Williams, *Writing in Society* (London: Verso, 1984): 213–26; Sherif and Sherif; and Fish.

66. See Chris M. Anson, "The Classroom and the 'Real World' as Contexts: Re-examining the Goals of Writing Instruction," *MMLA* 20 (1987): 6–9.

67. Elaine P. Maimon, personal interview, 23 Apr. 1990.

68. For critical views of British education in the 1970s and 1980s, see David Bouchier, "Universities and the Government: A Lesson from Britain," *Chronicle of Higher Education* 14 Jan. 1987: 120; and John Carswell, *Government and the Universities in Britain* (Cambridge: Cambridge U P, 1985).

10.
The Writing-Across-the-Curriculum Movement: 1990–2000

1. *Digest of Education Statistics 2000.*

2. These textbooks grew out of early WAC textbooks such as Maimon's *Writing in the Arts and Sciences* and Bazerman's *The Informed Writer,* though often without the epistemological sophistication of these two textbooks.

3. For the distinction, see the 2000 online publication *Writing Across the Curriculum: A Guide to Developing Programs* (ed. Susan H. McLeod and Margot Soven), originally published in print by Sage (Newbury Park, CA), 1992. It's important to note that they see WAC and WID as fundamentally integrated.

4. See, for example, Peshe C. Kuriloff.

5. See, for example, C. W. Knoblauch and Lil Brannon, *Rhetorical Traditions and the Teaching of Writing;* Donna LeCourt; and Daniel Mahala.

6. For the major abolitionist arguments, see Sharon Crowley; and Robert J. Connors.

7. On advantages, see Thomas L. Hilgers et al.;and Martha A. Townsend. On resistance, see Robert Boice.

8. On Cornell's program, see Katherine K. Gottschalk. See also *Cornell Consortium for Writing in the Disciplines.*

9. An excellent collection is Robert W. Barnett and Jacob S. Blumner's *Writing Centers and Writing Across the Curriculum Programs: Building Interdisciplinary Partnerships..* On research, see Jean Kiedaisch and Sue Dinitz; and Judy Gill. On tensions, see Michael A. Pemberton.

10. For articulation, see Loretta Henderson, Emily Jensen, and Bill Stiffler.; and Linda Watkins-Goffman and G. Joyce Dunston. For research, see Gail F. Hughes and Gerald R. Martin; and *Thinking Through Writing: Lord Fairfax Community College, 1990–1992.* For writing fellows, see Timothy J. Dillon. For CAC, see Donna Reiss. TYC WAC collections include Linda C. Stanley and Joanna Ambron, eds., *Writing Across the Curriculum in Community Colleges. New Directions for Community Colleges, Number 73;* and Barbara R. Stout and Joyce N. Magnotto, "Building on Realities: WAC Programs at Community Colleges." On program mergers, see Linda C. Stanley.

11. On Volusha County, NWP, and a range of other programs, see Pamela B. Childers, Anne Ruggles Gere, and Art Young. On Vermont, Kentucky, and other portfolio efforts, see Bonnie S. Sunstein and Jonathan H. Lovell; and David R. Russell and Lizabeth Berryman.

12. On the whole language movement and WAC, see Marilyn L. Chapman; Susan Chambers Cantrell; Barbara H. Davis et al.; and Mary Kay Gibisch et al.

13. On the Primary Learning Record, see Mary A. Barr.

14. Institutions that have very active efforts are North Carolina State University, University of North Carolina Charlotte, University of Dayton, and University of Toledo.

15. Institutions that have very active departmental colloquia are Dickinson College, University of South Dakota, Rice University, and George Mason University. Active college-specific programs include Iowa State University and Clemson University.

16. See, for example, Lee Cuba.

17. For an overview, see Paul Connolly and Teresa Vilardi.

18. On accounting, see Donald A. Nellermoe, Thomas R. Weirich and Alan Reinstein. On law, see James F. Stratman. On ABET, see Rolf Norgaard.

19. Barbara E. Walvoord et al., *In the Long Run.*

20. For a review of early studies, see John M. Ackerman. On new assessment methods, see T. Dary Erwin; Kathleen Blake Yancey and Brian A. Huot; Richard Haswell; and Barbara E. Fassler Walvoord and Virginia Johnson Anderson.

21. Mary McMullen-Light et al.; and *Campus Speaking and Writing Program.*

22. William Condon; on electronic portfolios see *Electronic Writing Portfolio.*

23. Mary A. Barr; Carolyn V. Gipps; Mary A. Barr and Saul Krimsly.

24. On Washington, see Joan Graham et al. On George Mason's program, see Terry Myers Zawacki and Ashley Taliaferro Williams.

25. See Deanna P. Dannels; *Proceedings from the Communication Across the Curriculum Strand.*

26. Donna Reiss, Dickie Selfe, and Art Young.

27. Shaun Slattery; and Joe Essid and Dona J. Hickey.

28. Mike Palmquist, Kate Keifer, and Donald E. Zimmerman; and Peter M. Saunders.

29. *Labwrite.*

30. Mary Hocks and Daniele Bascelli.

31. Scott A. Chadwick and Jon Dorbolo. See also *Electronic Writing Portfolio.*

32. For reviews and analyses, see Gary M. Schumacher and Jane Gradwohl Nash; Ackerman; and Cheryl Geisler.

33. For research summaries, see David R. Russell, "Where Do the Naturalistic Studies of WAC/WID Point?" and "Writing and Genre." For internship studies, see Patrick Dias et al.; and Dorothy A. Winsor.

34. For research reviews, see Russell, "Writing and Genre" and "Where Do." Outstanding WAC guides for faculty published in the 1990s are John C. Bean, *Engaging Ideas: The Professor's Guide to Integrating Writing, Critical Thinking, and Active Learning in the Classroom;* and Rebecca Moore Howard and Sandra Jamieson, *The Bedford Guide to Teaching Writing in the Disciplines: An Instructor's Desk Reference.*

35. *Academic.writing: Interdisciplinary Perspectives on Communication Across the Curriculum.*

36. Barbara Levine and Jay Carson.

37. For a summary of efforts, see the introduction to David Foster and David R. Russell, eds., *Writing and Learning in Cross-National Perspective: Transitions from Secondary to Higher Education.* The book series is *Studies in Writing: International Series on the Research of Learning and Instruction of Writing.*

38. Personal interview, 23 Apr. 1990.

WORKS CITED

Abbott, Andrew. *The System of Professions: An Essay on the Division of Expert Labor.* Chicago: U of Chicago P, 1988.

Academic.writing: Interdisciplinary Perspectives on Communication Across the Curriculum. Ed. Mike Palmquist. Nov. 1999. Colorado State University. 17 Oct. 2001. <http://aw.colostate.edu/>.

Ackerman, John M. "The Promise of Writing to Learn." *Written Communication* 10.3 (1993): 334–70.

Adams, Charles Francis. *Charles Francis Adams, 1835–1915: An Autobiography.* Boston: Massachusetts Historical Society, 1916.

Adams, Katherine H. *A History of Professional Writing Instruction in American Colleges: Years of Acceptance, Growth, and Doubt.* SMU Studies in Composition and Rhetoric Series. Ed. Gary Tate. Dallas: Southern Methodist UP, 1993.

Adler, Mortimer J., ed. *The Great Ideas: A Synopticon of Great Books of the Western World.* Chicago: Encyclopedia Britannica, 1952.

———. *How To Read a Book: The Art of Getting a Liberal Education.* New York: Simon, 1940.

Adler, Mortimer J., and Seymour Cain. *Religion and Theology.* Chicago: Encyclopedia Britannica, 1961.

Ahl, Frances N. "The Technique of the Term Paper." *High School Journal* 14 (1931): 17–19, 53.

Aikin, Wilford M. *The Story of the Eight Year Study.* New York: Harper, 1942.

Ambron, Joanna. "History of WAC and Its Role in Community Colleges." *New Directions for Community Colleges* 19.1 (1991): 3–8.

American Historical Association. *Conclusions and Recommendation of the Commission: Report of the Commission on the Social Studies.* New York: Scribner's, 1934.

Anderson, Worth, Cynthia Best, Alycia Black, John Hurst, Brandt Miller, and Susan Miller. "Cross-Curricular Underlife: A Collaborative Report on Ways with Academic Words." *College Composition and Communication* 41 (1990): 11–36.

Anson, Chris M. "The Classroom and the 'Real World' as Contexts: Re-examining the Goals of Writing Instruction." *MMLA* 20 (1987): 1–16.

Applebee, Arthur N. *Contexts for Learning to Write: Studies of Secondary School Instruction.* Norwood, NJ: Ablex, 1984.

———. *Tradition and Reform in the Teaching of English: A History.* Urbana, IL: NCTE, 1974.

———. *Writing in the Secondary School: English and the Content Areas.* NCTE Research Report No. 21. Urbana, IL: NCTE, 1981.

Arms, George. "The Research Paper." *College English* 5 (1943): 19–26.

Arnold, Horace L., and Fay L. Faurote. *Ford Methods and Ford Shops.* New York: Engineering Magazine, 1919.

Association of Graduate Schools. "Report of the Committee on Policies in Graduate Education." *Journal of Proceedings and Addresses, Ninth Annual Conference of the Association of Graduate Schools.* New York: AGS, 1957.

Association of Teachers of Social Studies of the City of New York. *Handbook for Social Studies Teaching.* New York: Holt, 1941.

Aydelotte, Frank. "Training in Thought as the Aim of Elementary English Course as Taught at MIT," *Engineering Record* 24 Feb. 1917: 300–302.

Bader, A. L. "Independent Thinking and the Long Paper." *English Journal* 25 (1936): 667–72.

Bagg, Lyman H. *Four Years at Yale, by a Graduate of '68.* New Haven: Charles C. Chatfield, 1871.

Bailey, Mathilda, and Bunnar Horn. *English Handbook.* New York: American Book, 1949.

Baker, Ray Palmer. "Problems of Administering English Work in Engineering Colleges." *Society for the Promotion of Engineering Education Bulletin* 23 (1932): 282–91.

Baldwin, Charles Sears. *Composition: Oral and Written.* 1909. New York: Greenwood, 1969.

Barnett, Robert W., and Jacob S. Blumner. *Writing Centers and Writing Across the Curriculum Programs: Building Interdisciplinary Partnerships.* Westport, CT.: Greenwood, 1999.

Barr, Mary A. "Looking at the Learning Record." *Educational Leadership* 57.5 (2000): 20–24.

Barr, Mary A., and Saul Krimsly. *An Analysis of Correlations Between Reading and Writing Scale Placements for the Learning Record and Stanford 9 Reading Battery Total, Language and Spelling National Percentile Scores, 1999.* El Cajon, CA: Center for Language in Learning, 1999.

Barzun, Jaques, and Henry Graff. *The Modern Researcher.* New York: Harcourt, 1957.

Basic Aims Committee. "Basic Aims for English Instruction in American Schools." *English Journal* 31 (1942): 40–55.

"Bay Area Writing Project/California Writing Project/National Writing Project: An Overview." University of California at Berkeley, School of Education. Urbana, IL: ERIC, 1978. ERIC, ED 184123.

Bazerman, Charles. *The Informed Writer.* Boston: Houghton, 1981.

———. "A Relationship Between Reading and Writing." *College English* 41 (1980): 656–69.

———. *Shaping Written Knowledge: The Genre and Activity of the Experimental Article in Science.* Madison: U of Wisconsin P, 1988.

Bean, John C. *Engaging Ideas: The Professor's Guide to Integrating Writing, Critical Thinking, and Active Learning in the Classroom.* San Francisco: Jossey-Bass, 1996.

Bell, Daniel. *The Reforming of General Education: The Columbia Experience in Its National Setting.* New York: Columbia UP, 1966.

Bennett, William J. *To Reclaim a Legacy: A Report on the Humanities in Higher Education.* Washington, DC: NEH, 1984.

Berelson, Bernard. *Graduate Education in the United States.* New York: McGraw, 1960.

Berkenkotter, Carol, Thomas N. Huckin, and John Ackerman. "Conventions, Conversations, and the Writer: Case Study of a Student in a Rhetoric Ph.D. Program." *Research in the Teaching of English* 22 (1988): 9–43.

Berlin, James A. "Contemporary Composition: The Major Pedagogical Theories." *College English* 44 (1982): 765–77.

———. *Rhetoric and Reality: Writing Instruction in American Colleges 1900–1985.* Carbondale: Southern Illinois UP, 1987.

———. *Writing Instruction in Nineteenth-Century American Colleges.* Carbondale: Southern Illinois UP, 1984.

Bestor, Arthur. *Educational Wastelands: The Retreat from Learning in Our Public Schools.* Urbana: U of Illinois P, 1953.

Beyer, Barry, and Anita Brostoff. "The Time It Takes: Evaluating Writing and Social Studies." *Social Education* 43 (1979): 194–97.

Beyer, Catherine. "Making Knowledge in Political Economics." CCCC Convention. Chicago, Mar. 1990.

Bining, Arthur C., and David H. Bining. *Teaching the Social Sciences in Secondary Schools.* New York: McGraw, 1935, 1952.

Binkeley, Harold C. "If the Salt Have Lost Its Savor." *Journal of Higher Education* 11 (1940): 182–88.

Bird, Nancy K. "The Conference on College Composition and Communication: A Historical Study of Its Continuing Education and Professionalization Activities, 1947–1975." Diss. Virginia Polytechnic Institute, 1977.

Birk, Otto. "Interdepartmental Cooperation to Promote the Habitual Use of Correct English." *Society for the Promotion of Engineering Education Bulletin* 16 (1925): 230–36.

Bledstein, Burton J. *The Culture of Professionalism: The Middle Class and the Development of Higher Education in America.* New York: Norton, 1976.

Bloom, Lynn Z. "Why Graduate Students Can't Write: Implications of Research on Writing Anxiety for Graduate Students." CCCC Convention. Dallas, Mar. 1981. ERIC, ED 199710.

Bobbitt, Franklin. "*A Correlated Curriculum* Evaluated." *English Journal* 26 (1937): 417–20.

———. *The Curriculum.* Boston: Houghton, 1918.

———. "Questionable Recommendations of the Commission on the Social Studies." *School and Society* 40 (1934): 201–8.

Boice, Robert. "Faculty Resistance to Writing-Intensive Courses." *Teaching of Psychology* 17.1 (1990): 13–17.

Bossard, James H. S., and J. Frederic Dewhurst. *University Education for Business: A Study of Existing Needs and Practices*. Philadelphia: U of Pennsylvania P, 1931.

Botts, Roderic C. "Influences in the Teaching of English, 1917–1935: An Illusion of Progress." Diss. Northwestern U, 1970.

Boucher, Chauncey S. *The Chicago College Plan*. Chicago: U of Chicago P, 1940.

Bouchier, David. "Universities and the Government: A Lesson from Britain." *Chronicle of Higher Education* 14 Jan. 1987: 120.

Bourne, Randolph S. *The Gary Schools*. New York: Houghton, 1916.

Boyer, Ernest L., and Arthur Levine. *A Quest for Common Learning: The Aims of General Education*. Washington, DC: Carnegie Foundation for the Advancement of Teaching, 1982.

Brereton, John, ed. *Traditions of Inquiry*. New York: Oxford UP, 1985.

Briggs, LeBaron R. *Routine and Ideals*. Boston: Houghton, 1904.

Brillhart, L. V., and M. B. Debs. "Teaching Writing: A Scientist's Responsibility." *Journal of College Science Teaching* 10 (1977): 303–4.

Britton, James. *Language and Learning*. London: Penguin, 1970.

———. *Prospect and Retrospect: Selected Essays of James Britton*. Ed. Gordon M. Pradl. Montclair, NJ: Boynton, 1982.

Britton, James, Tony Burgess, Nancy Martin, Alex McLeod, and Harold Rosen. *The Development of Writing Abilities (11–18)*. London: Macmillan, 1975.

Broadhead, Glenn, and Richard C. Freed. *The Variables of Composition: Process and Product in a Business Setting*. Carbondale: Southern Illinois UP, 1985.

Brockman, John R., ed. *The Case Method in Technical Communication*. Lubbock, TX: Association of Teachers of Technical Writing, 1984.

Brown, Edwin J., and Maxele Baldwin. "The Term Paper in College." *Education Administration and Supervision* 17 (1931): 306–16.

Browne, G. H. "Successful Combination Against the Inert." Leaflet No. 3. Cambridge: New England Association of Teachers of English, 1901.

Bruffee, Kenneth A. "The Brooklyn Plan: Attaining Intellectual Growth Through Peer-Group Tutoring." *Liberal Education* 64 (1978): 447–68.

Bruner, Jerome S. *Actual Minds, Possible Worlds*. Boston: Harvard UP, 1986.

———. *Beyond the Information Given: Studies in the Psychology of Knowing*. New York: Norton, 1973.

———. *On Knowing: Essays for the Left Hand*. Cambridge: Harvard UP, 1979.

———. *The Process of Education*. Westminster, MD: Random, 1963.

Buck, Gertrude. "Recent Tendencies in the Teaching of English Composition." *Educational Review* 22 (1901): 371–83.

Buck, Paul, ed. *Social Sciences at Harvard, 1860–1920: From Inculcation to the Open Mind*. Cambridge: Harvard UP, 1965.

Bureau of the Census. *Historical Atlas of the U.S.* Washington, DC: GPO, 1975.

Caldwell, Robert G. "The Humanities at Technology." *Technology Review* 42 (1941): 210–28.

Callahan, Raymond C. *Education and the Cult of Efficiency.* Chicago: U of Chicago P, 1962.

Campbell, Oscar James. "The Failure of Freshman English." *English Journal* coll. ed. 28 (1939): 177–85.

Campus Speaking and Writing Program. 2000. North Carolina State University. 20 Oct. 2001. <http://www2.chass.ncsu.edu/CWSP>.

Cantrell, Susan Chambers. "The Effects of Literacy Instruction on Primary Students' Reading and Writing Achievement." *Reading Research and Instruction* 39.1 (1999): 3–26.

Carman, Harry J. "The Columbia Course in Contemporary Civilization." *Columbia Alumni News* 17 (1925): 143–44.

Carpenter, George R. "English Composition in Colleges." *Educational Review* 4 (1892): 338–46.

Carswell, John. *Government and the Universities in Britain.* Cambridge: Cambridge UP, 1985.

Century of Engineering Education. Ann Arbor: U of Michigan P, 1954.

Chadwick, Scott A., and Jon Dorbolo. "Interquest: Designing a Communication-Intensive Web-Based Course." *Electronic Communication Across the Curriculum.* Eds. Donna Reiss, Dickie Selfe, and Art Young. Urbana, IL: NCTE, 1998. 117–28.

Chapman, Marilyn L. "Situated, Social, Active: Rewriting Genre in the Elementary Classroom." *Written Communication* 16 (1999): 469–90.

Charters, Werrett Wallace, and Isadore B. Whitley. *Analysis of Secretarial Duties and Traits.* Baltimore: Williams, 1924.

———. "A Spelling Hospital in the High School." *School Review* 18 (1910): 192–94.

Childers, Pamela B., Anne Ruggles Gere, and Art Young, eds. *Programs and Practices: Writing Across the Secondary School Curriculum.* Portsmith, NH: Boynton, 1994.

Clapp, John M. *The Place of English in American Life: Report of an Investigation by a Committee of the National Council of Teachers of English.* Chicago: NCTE, 1926.

Clark, Burton R. *The Academic Life: Small Worlds, Different Worlds.* Princeton: Carnegie Foundation for the Advancement of Teaching, 1987.

———. *The Distinctive College: Antioch, Reed and Swarthmore.* Chicago: Aldine, 1970.

———. *The Higher Education System: Academic Organization in Cross-National Perspective.* Berkeley: U of California P, 1983.

———. "The School and the University: What Went Wrong in America?" Comparative Higher Education Research Group Working Paper No. 8. Urbana, IL: ERIC, 1985. ERIC, ED 265797.

Clark, Donald Lemen. *Rhetoric in Greco-Roman Education.* New York: Columbia UP, 1957.

Clark, John J. "Clearness and Accuracy in Composition." *Society for the Promotion of Engineering Education Proceedings* 18 (1910): 347–57.

Clifford, Geraldine Joncich, and James W. Guthrie. *Ed School: A Brief for Professional Education.* Chicago: U of Chicago P, 1988.

Cohen, Paul E. "Barrett Wendell, A Study in Harvard Culture." Diss. Northwestern U, 1974.

College Entrance Examination Board. *Fifty-Sixth Annual Report of the Executive Secretary.* Princeton, NJ: CEEB, 1956.

———. *Forty-Second Annual Report of the Executive Secretary.* New York: CEEB, 1942.

College Program in Action: A Review of Working Principles at Columbia College by the Committee on Plans. New York: Columbia UP, 1946.

Conant, James Bryant. *Education in a Divided World: The Function of Public Schools in Our Unique Society.* Cambridge: Harvard UP, 1945.

Condon, William. "Accommodating Complexity: WAC Program Evaluation in the Age of Accountability." *WAC for the New Millennium: Strategies for/of Continuing Writing Across the Curriculum.* Ed. Susan McLeod et al. Urbana, IL: NCTE, 2001.

Congdon, R. T. "Some Forms of Cooperation in English Composition Teaching." Bulletin 16. New York: New York City Association of Teachers of English, 1915.

Connolly, Paul, and Teresa Vilardi. *New Methods in College Writing Programs: Theories in Practice.* New York: MLA, 1986.

———, eds. *Writing to Learn Mathematics and Science.* New York: Teachers College P, 1989.

Connors, Robert J. "The Abolition Debate in Composition: A Short History." *Composition in the Twenty-First Century.* Eds. Lynn Z. Bloom, Donald Daiker, and Edward White. Carbondale: Southern Illinois UP, 1996. 47–63.

———. "Personal Writing Assignments" *College Composition and Communication* 38 (1987): 166–83.

———. "The Rise of Technical Writing Instruction in America." *Journal of Technical Writing and Communication* 12 (1982): 329–54.

Connors, Robert J., Lisa S. Ede, and Andrea A. Lunsford, eds. *Essays on Classical Rhetoric and Modern Discourse.* Carbondale: Southern Illinois UP, 1984.

Cooper, Lane. *Louis Agassiz as a Teacher.* Ithaca, NY: Comstock, 1917.

———. "On the Teaching of Written Composition." *Education* 30 (1910): 421–30.

Cornell Consortium for Writing in the Disciplines. 2001. John S. Knight Writing Program, Cornell University. 19 Oct. 2001. <http://www.arts.cornell.edu/knight_institute/consortium/ccwd.html>.

Corson, Hiram. *The Aims of Literary Study.* New York: Macmillan, 1895.

Coss, John J. "Progress of the New Freshman Course." *Columbia University Quarterly* Oct. 1919: 332–33.

Coulter, John Merle. *The Elements of Power.* Chicago: 1894.

Cowan, Elizabeth Wooton, ed. *Options for the Teaching of English: The Undergraduate Curriculum.* New York: MLA, 1975.

Cremin, Lawrence A. *American Education: The Metropolitan Experience.* New York: Harper, 1988.

———. *American Education: The National Experience.* New York: Harper, 1980.

———. *The Transformation of the School: Progressivism in American Education.* New York: Vantage, 1961.

Crowley, Sharon. *Composition in the University: Historical and Polemical Essays.* Pittsburgh: U of Pittsburgh P, 1998.

Cuba, Lee. *A Short Guide to Writing About Social Science.* Short Guide Ser. 4th ed. New York: Harper, 2001.

Cuban, Larry. *How Teachers Taught: Constancy and Change in American Classrooms, 1890–1980.* New York: Longman, 1984.

Curl, Mervin James. *Expository Writing.* New York: Houghton, 1919.

Daniels, Harvey. *Famous Last Words: The American Language Crisis Reconsidered.* Carbondale: Southern Illinois UP, 1983.

Dannels, Deanna P. "Time to Speak Up: A Theoretical Framework of Situated Pedagogy and Practice for Communication Across the Curriculum." *Communication Education* 50.2 (2001): 144–58.

Davis, Barbara H., et al. "Writing-to-Learn in Elementary Social Studies." *Social Education* 56 (1992): 393–97.

Davis, W. E., and Robert Matlock. "Interdisciplinary Teaching of Writing Skills." *Journal of College Science Teaching* 11 (1978): 310–11.

Dawe, Jessamon. *Writing Business and Economics Papers, Theses and Dissertations.* Totowa, NJ: Littlefield, 1965.

Denney, Joseph Villiers. "College Rhetoric." *PMLA* 20 (1894–95): 39–52.

———. *Two Problems in Composition Teaching.* Ann Arbor: Inland, 1897.

Dewey, John. *John Dewey: The Later Works, 1925–1933.* Ed. Jo Ann Boydston. 16 vols. Carbondale: Southern Illinois UP, 1981–1989.

———. *John Dewey: The Middle Works, 1899–1924.* Ed. Jo Ann Boydston. 15 vols. Carbondale: Southern Illinois UP, 1976–1983.

———. *The Public and Its Problems.* New York: Holt, 1927.

———. "The Supreme Intellectual Obligation." *Science Education* 18 (1934): 1–4.

Dewey, John, Albert C. Barnes, Laurence Buermeyer, Mary Mullen, Violette de Mazia. *Art and Education.* 2d ed. Merion, PA: Barnes Foundation, 1947.

Dias, Patrick, et al. *Worlds Apart: Acting and Writing in Academic and Workplace Contexts.* Mahwah, NJ: Erlbaum, 1999.

Diehl, Carl. *Americans and German Scholarship, 1770–1870.* New Haven: Yale UP, 1978.

Digest of Educational Statistics. Washington, DC: GPO, 1989.

Digest of Education Statistics 2000. National Center for Education Statistics. Washington, DC: GPO, 2001. 19 Oct. 2001. <http://nces.ed.gov/pubs2001/digest/dt008.html>.

Dillon, Timothy J. "Writing Across the Curriculum: Annual Report, 1997–98." Monroe County (MI) Community College, 1998. ERIC, ED 423929.

Dixon, John. *Growth Through English: A Report Based on the Dartmouth Seminar, 1966*. Reading, UK: National Association for the Teaching of English, 1967.

Douglas, George H., and Herbert W. Hildebrandt. *Studies in the History of Business Writing*. Urbana, IL: Association for Business Communication, 1985.

Dubofski, Melvyn. *When Workers Organize: New York City in the Progressive Era*. Amherst: U of Massachusetts P, 1968.

Duncan, Carson S. "Rebellious Word on English Composition." *English Journal* 3 (1915): 154–59.

Dunn, Arthur William, comp. *Social Studies in Secondary Education: Report of the Committee on Social Studies of the Commission on the Reorganization of Secondary Education of the National Education Association*. Washington, DC: GPO, 1916.

Dusinberre, William. *Henry Adams: The Myth of Failure*. Charlottesville: UP of Virginia, 1980.

Dwyer, Carol. "Achievement Testing." *Encyclopedia of Educational Research*. New York: Free P, 1982.

Eagleton, Terry. *Literary Theory*. Minneapolis: U of Minnesota P, 1983.

Earle, Samuel. "English at Tufts College." *Society for the Promotion of Engineering Education Bulletin* 2 (1911): 29–43.

———. "English in Engineering Schools." *Society for the Promotion of Engineering Education Bulletin* 3 (1912): 387–88.

Elbow, Peter. *Writing Without Teachers*. New York: Oxford UP, 1973.

Electronic Writing Portfolio. 30 November 2000. Writing Across the Curriculum at Eastern Illinois State University. 20 Oct. 2001. <http://www.eiu.edu/writcurr/ewp.htm>.

Emig, Janet. "Writing as a Mode of Learning." *College Composition and Communication* 28 (1977): 122–28.

"English and Other Teaching." Editorial. *Nation* 19 Mar. 1908: 253–54.

Erskine, James A., Michiel R. Leenders, and Louise A. Mauffette-Leenders. *Teaching with Cases*. London, ON: School of Business Administration, U of Western Ontario, 1981.

Erskine, John. *The Delight of Great Books*. Indianapolis: Bobbs, 1928.

———. *The Memory of Certain Persons*. Philadelphia: Lippincott, 1947.

———. *My Life as a Teacher*. Philadelphia: Lippincott, 1948.

Erwin, T. Dary. *Definitions and Assessment Methods for Critical Thinking, Problem Solving, and Writing*. 1998. U.S. Department of Education, National Center for Education Statistics. Council of the National Postsecondary Education Cooperative Working Group on Student Outcomes, Panel on Cognitive Outcomes. Washington, D.C. 15 Oct. 2001. <http://nces.ed.gov/npec/evaltests/default.asp>.

Essid, Joe, and Dona J. Hickey. "Creating a Community of Teachers and Tutors."

Electronic Communication Across the Curriculum. Eds. Donna Reiss, Dickie Selfe, and Art Young. Urbana, IL: NCTE, 1998. 73–85.

Faigley, Lester. "Competing Theories of Process: A Critique and a Proposal." *College English* 48 (1986): 527–42.

Faules, Don. "Joseph Villiers Denney: English Scholar and Contributor to the Emergence of Speech Theory." *Speech Teacher* 20 (1964): 105–9.

Fearing, Bertie E., and W. Keats Sparrow, eds. *Technical Writing: Theory and Practice.* New York: MLA, 1989.

Feinberg, Walter. *Reason and Rhetoric.* New York: John Wiley, 1975.

Firkins, Oscar W. *Cyrus Northrop: A Memoir.* Minneapolis: U of Minnesota P, 1925.

Fish Stanley, "Being Interdisciplinary Is So Very Hard to Do." *Profession* 1989: 15–22.

Fleck, Ludwig. *Genesis and Development of a Scientific Fact.* Chicago: U of Chicago P, 1979.

Flesch, Rudolph. *Why Johnny Can't Read.* New York: Harper, 1955.

Ford, James E., and Dennis R. Perry. "Research Paper Instruction in the Undergraduate Writing Program." *College English* 44 (1982): 825–31.

Ford, James E., Sharla Rees, and David L. Ward. "Research Paper Instruction: Comprehensive Bibliography of Periodical Sources, 1923–1980." *Bulletin of Bibliography* 39 (1982): 84–98.

Fore, H. F. "Harvard English Plan." *Nation* 29 July 1915: 146–47.

Foster, David, and David R. Russell, eds. *Writing and Learning in Cross-National Perspective: Transitions from Secondary to Higher Education.* Urbana, IL: NCTE, 2002.

Franklin, Barry M. *Building the American Community: The School Curriculum and the Search for Social Control.* London: Falmer, 1986.

Freed, Richard C., and Glenn Broadhead. "Discourse Communities, Sacred Texts, and Institutional Norms." *College Composition and Communication* 38 (1987): 154–65.

Fulwiler, Toby. "How Well Does Writing Across the Curriculum Work?" *College English* 46 (1984): 113–25.

———. "Writing Across the Curriculum at Michigan Tech." *Journal of the Council of Writing Program Administrators* 4 (1981): 15–20.

Fulwiler, Toby, and Art Young, eds. *Programs That Work: Models and Methods for Writing Across the Curriculum.* Portsmouth, NH: Boynton, 1990.

Gallagher, James J. "Summary of Research in Science Education." *Science Education* 71 (1985): 271–457.

Gallagher, O. C. "Cooperation in English." Leaflet No. 67. Cambridge, MA: New England Association of Teachers of English, 1909.

Gardiner, J. H. "Our Infant Critics." *Nation* 19 Mar. 1908: 257–58.

Geertz, Clifford. *Local Knowledge: Further Essays in Interpretive Anthropology.* New York: Basic, 1983.

Geisler, Cheryl. *Academic Literacy and the Nature of Expertise. Reading, Writing, and Knowing in Academic Philosophy.* Hillsdale, NJ: Erlbaum, 1994.

Genung, John Franklin. *The Working Principles of Rhetoric*. Boston: Ginn, 1904.

Gere, Anne Ruggles. *Writing Groups: History, Theory, and Implications*. Carbondale: Southern Illinois UP, 1987.

Gibisch, Mary Kay, et al. "Improving Writing Across the Curriculum." Internal report of Saint Xavier University (IL), 1995. ERIC, ED 386748.

Gill, Judy. "Another Look at WAC and the Writing Center." *Writing Center Journal* 16.2 (1996): 164–78.

Gipps, Carolyn V. *Beyond Testing: Towards a Theory of Educational Assessment*. London: Falmer, 1994.

Glick, Milton D. "Writing Across the Curriculum: A Dean's Perspective." *WPA: Writing Program Administration* 11 (1988): 53–58.

Golding, Alan, and John Mascaro. "A Survey of Graduate Writing Courses." *Journal of Advanced Composition* 6 (1986): 167–79.

Gordon, Robert Aaron, and James Edwin Howell. *Higher Education for Business*. New York: Columbia UP, 1959.

Gorman, T. P., Alan C. Purves, and R. E. Desenhart, eds. *The IEA Study of Written Composition*. New York: Pergamon, 1988.

Gottschalk, Katherine K. "Putting—and Keeping—the Cornell Writing Program in Its Place: Writing in the Disciplines." *Language and Learning Across the Disciplines* 2 (1997): 22–45.

Graff, Gerald. *Professing Literature*. Chicago: U of Chicago P, 1987.

Graham, Joan. "What Works: The Problems and Rewards of Cross-Curricular Writing Programs." *Current Issues in Higher Education* 3 (1983–84): 16–26.

———. "Writing Conferences in Disciplinary Contexts: Students Working Out What They Think." CCCC Convention. Chicago, Mar. 1990.

Graham, Joan, et al. "The Interdisciplinary Writing Program." Internal report of the U of Washington Interdisciplinary Writing Program, 2000.

Greenbaum, Leonard A. "A Tradition of Complaint." *College English* 31 (1969): 174–78.

Greenough, Chester Noyes, and Frank Wilson Cheney Hersey. *English Composition*. New York: Macmillan, 1919.

Griffin, C. Williams, ed. *Teaching Writing in All Disciplines*. New Directions for Teaching and Learning, No. 12. San Francisco: Jossey, 1982.

Griffin, Clifford S. *The University of Kansas: A History*. Lawrence: UP of Kansas, 1974.

Guralnick, Stanley M. *Science and the Antebellum American College*. Philadelphia: American Philosophical Society, 1975.

Hake, Rosemary L., and Joseph M. Williams. "Style and Its Consequences: Do as I Do, Not as I Say." *College English* 43 (1981): 433–51.

Hall, G. Stanley., ed. *Methods of Teaching History*. 2d ed. Boston: Heath, 1883.

Hall, James W., and Barbara L. Kevles, eds. *In Opposition to Core Curriculum: Alternative Models for Undergraduate Education*. Westport, CT: Greenwood, 1982.

Halloran, S. Michael. "John Witherspoon and the Formation of Orators." CCCC Convention. Atlanta, Mar. 1977.

———. "On the End of Rhetoric, Classical and Modern." *College English* 36 (1975): 621–31.

———. "Rhetoric in the American College Curriculum: The Decline of Public Discourse." *PrelText* 3 (1982): 245–69.

Haring-Smith, Tori, ed. *A Guide to Writing Programs: Writing Centers, Peer Tutoring Programs, and Writing Across the Curriculum.* Glenview, IL: Scott Foresman, 1987.

———. "What's Wrong with Writing Across the Curriculum?" CCCC Convention. Atlanta, Mar. 1987.

Hart, Albert Bushnell, and Edward Channing, eds. *American History Leaflets: Colonial and Constitutional.* Nos. 1–36. New York: Lovell, 1892–1913.

Hartog, Philip, et al. *The Marking of English Essays.* London: Macmillan, 1941.

Harvard Committee on General Education. *General Education in a Free Society.* Cambridge: Harvard UP, 1945.

"Harvard Plan." Editorial. *Nation* 22 Apr. 1915: 431.

Haswell, Richard. "Documenting Improvement in College Writing: A Longitudinal Approach." *Written Communication* 17 (2000): 307–52.

Henderson, Loretta, Emily Jensen, and Bill Stiffler. "Adjust the Assignment to the Reader." *Teaching English in the Two-Year College* 25 (1998): 132–38.

Herrington, Anne. "Writing in Academic Settings: A Study of the Contexts for Writing in Two College Chemical Engineering Courses." *Research in the Teaching of English* 19 (1985): 331–61.

Hertzberg, Hazel W. *Social Studies Reform, 1880–1980.* Boulder, CO: Social Science Education Consortium, 1981.

Hilgers, Thomas L., et al. "Doing More Than 'Thinning Out the Herd': How Eighty-Two College Seniors Perceived Writing-Intensive Classes." *Research in the Teaching of English* 29.1 (1995): 59–87.

Hill, Adams Sherman. "An Answer to the Cry for More English." *Good Company* 4 (1879): 234–35.

———. *Foundations of Rhetoric.* New York: Harper, 1892.

———. *Principles of Rhetoric and Their Application.* New York: American Book, 1878.

Hill, Adams Sherman, LeBaron R. Briggs, and B. S. Hurlbut. *Twenty Years of School and College English.* Cambridge: Harvard UP, 1896.

History of Columbia College on Morningside. New York: Columbia UP: 1954.

Hitchcock, Alfred M. "Economy in Teaching Composition." *Education* 24 (1904): 348–55.

Hocks, Mary, and Daniele Bascelli. "Building a Writing-Intensive Multimedia Curriculum." *Electronic Communication Across the Curriculum.* Eds. Donna Reiss, Dickie Selfe, and Art Young. Urbana, IL: NCTE, 1998. 40–56.

Hopkins, Edwin M. "Can Good Composition Teaching Be Done Under Present Conditions?" *English Journal* 1 (1912): 1–8.

———. "The Cost and Labor of English Teaching." *Journal of Proceedings and Addresses, National Education Association* 53 (1915): 114–19.

Hopkins, L. Thomas. "*A Correlated Curriculum* Evaluated." *English Journal* 26 (1937): 417–18.

Horner, Winifred Bryan, ed. *The Present State of Scholarship in Historical and Contemporary Rhetoric.* Columbia: U of Missouri P, 1983.

Hosic, James Fleming. "Effective Ways of Securing Cooperation of All Departments in the Teaching of English Composition." *Journal of Proceedings and Addresses, National Education Association* 51 (1913): 478–85.

———, comp. *Reorganization of English in the Secondary Schools.* Bureau of Education Bulletin No. 2. Washington, DC: GPO, 1917.

Hotchkiss, George Burton. *Business English, Principles and Practice.* New York: Business Training, 1916.

Howard, Rebecca Moore, and Sandra Jamieson. *The Bedford Guide to Teaching Writing in the Disciplines: An Instructor's Desk Reference.* Boston: Bedford, 1995.

Howe, M. A. DeWolfe. *Barrett Wendell and His Letters.* Boston: Atlantic Monthly P, 1924.

Howell, Wilbur Samuel. *Eighteenth-Century British Logic and Rhetoric.* Princeton: Princeton UP, 1971.

Hughes, Gail F., and Gerald R. Martin. "The Relationship Between Instructional Writing Experience and the Quality of Student Writing: Results from a Longitudinal Study in the Minnesota Community College System." 73rd Annual Meeting of the American Educational Research Association. San Francisco, CA, 20–24 Apr. 1992. ERIC, ED 345276.

Hunter, George W. *Science Teaching at Junior and Senior High School Levels.* New York: American Book, 1934.

Hurd, Paul DeHart. *Biological Education in American Secondary Schools 1890–1960.* Washington, DC: American Institute of Biological Sciences, 1961.

———. *New Directions in Teaching Secondary School Science.* Chicago: Rand McNally, 1969.

Hutchins, Robert M., ed. *The Great Conversation: The Substance of a Liberal Education.* Chicago: Encyclopedia Britannica, 1952.

Hutchins, Robert Maynard. *The Higher Learning in America.* New Haven: Yale UP, 1936.

Idea and Practice of General Education: An Account of the College of the University of Chicago, by Present and Former Members of the Faculty. Chicago: U of Chicago P, 1950.

"Instruction in English in Technical Colleges" (The Hammond Report). Appendix in *Society for the Promotion of Engineering Education Bulletin* 31 (1940).

J. M. H. "English in College." *Nation* 1 July 1915: 15–16.

James, Henry. *Charles W. Eliot.* Boston: Houghton, 1930.

———. *The Question of Our Speech.* Boston: Houghton, 1905.

James, William. "The Ph.D. Octopus." *Harvard Monthly* 36 (1903): 1–9.

Jefferson, Bernard Levi, Harvey Houston Peckham, and Hiram Roy Wilson. *Freshman Rhetoric and Practice Book.* Garden City, NJ: Doubleday, 1928.

Jenkins, Philip R. "Is English Going Out?" *English Journal* 31 (1942): 439–44.

Johnson, Loaz W. "The Effect of Integration on Achievement." *English Journal* 25 (1936): 737–44.

Johnson, T. J. "Engineering English." *Society for the Promotion of Engineering Education Proceedings* 11 (1903): 361–71.

Jolliffe, David A. "The Moral Subject in College Composition: A Conceptual Framework and the Case of Harvard, 1865–1900." *College English* 51 (1989): 163–73.

———, ed. *Writing in Academic Disciplines.* Norwood, NJ: Ablex, 1988.

Jones, Barbara. *Bennington College: The Development of an Educational Idea.* New York: Harper, 1946.

Jones, Robert, and Joseph J. Comprone. "Where Do We Go Next in Writing Across the Curriculum?" *College Composition and Communication* 44.1 (1993): 59–68.

Kandel, Issac A. *Examinations and their Substitutes in the United States.* New York: Carnegie Foundation for the Advancement of Teaching, 1936.

Kantor, Kenneth J. "Creative Expression in the English Classroom: An Historical Perspective." *Research in the Teaching of English* 9 (1974): 5–29.

———. "The English Curriculum and the Structure of the Disciplines." *Theory into Practice* 22 (1984): 174–81.

Katz, Michael B. *Class, Bureaucracy, and Schools.* New York: Praeger, 1971.

Kaufer, David S., and Cheryl Geisler. "Novelty in Academic Writing." *Written Communication* 6 (1989): 286–311.

Kennedy, George. *Classical Rhetoric and Its Christian and Secular Tradition from Ancient to Modern Times.* Chapel Hill: U of North Carolina P, 1980.

Kerby-Miller, C. W., and Wilma Anderson Kerby-Miller. "A New Type of Composition Course." *English Journal* coll. ed. 26 (1937): 715–25.

———. "What Is Wrong with Freshman Composition?" *English Journal* coll. ed. 26 (1937): 625–37.

Kerr, Nancy H., and Madeleine Picciotto. "Linked Composition Courses: Effects on Student Performance." *Journal of Teaching Writing* 11 (1992): 105–18.

Kiedaisch, Jean, and Sue Dinitz. ""Look Back and Say 'So What'": The Limitations of the Generalist Tutor." *Writing Center Journal* 14 (1993): 63–74.

Kimball, Bruce A. *Orators and Philosophers: A History of the Idea of Liberal Education.* New York: Teachers College P, 1986.

Kinneavy, James L. *A Theory of Discourse.* Englewood Cliffs, NJ: Prentice Hall, 1971.

Kinney, L. B., and Alvin C. Eurich. "A Summary of Investigations Comparing Different Types of Tests." *School and Society* 36 (1932): 540–44.

Kitzhaber, Albert R. "Rhetoric in American Colleges, 1850–1900." Diss. U of Washington, 1953.

———. *Themes, Theories, and Therapy.* New York: McGraw, 1963.

Kliebard, Herbert M. *The Struggle for the American Curriculum, 1893–1958.* Boston: Routledge, 1986.

Knepper, Edwin K. *History of Business Education in the United States.* Bowling Green, OH: Edwards, 1941.

Knoblauch, C. W., and Lil Brannon. *Rhetorical Traditions and the Teaching of Writing.* Upper Montclair, NJ: Boynton, 1984.

———. "Writing as Learning Through the Curriculum." *College English* 45 (1983): 465–74.

Koefod, Paul E. *The Writing Requirements for Graduate Degrees*. Englewood Cliffs, NJ: Prentice, 1964.

Kuriloff, Peshe C. "What Discourses Have in Common: Teaching the Transaction Between Writer and Reader." *College Composition and Communication* 47.4 (1996): 485–501.

Labwrite. Michael Carter, Eric N. Wiebe, and Miriam Ferzli. Dec. 2000. North Carolina State University. 17 Oct. 2001. <http://www.ncsu.edu/labwrite>.

Langer, Judith A., and Arthur N. Applebee. *How Writing Shapes Thinking: A Study of Teaching and Writing*. NCTE Research Report No. 22. Urbana, IL: NCTE, 1987.

Language for Life. (The Bullock Report). London: HMSO, 1977.

Lanham, Richard. "Urgency and Opportunity: Implementing Writing Across the Curriculum." Address. University of Georgia faculty. Athens, 25 Apr. 1985. Reported in *Writing Across the Curriculum* 3 (1985): 5–6.

Larson, Richard L. "The 'Research Paper' in the Writing Course: A Non-Form of Writing." *College English* 44 (1982): 811–16.

Latour, Bruno. *Science in Action*. Cambridge: Harvard UP, 1987.

Lawson, Strang. "The Colgate Plan for Improving Student Writing." *AAUP Bulletin* 39 (1953): 288–90.

LeCourt, Donna. "WAC as Critical Pedagogy: The Third Stage?" *JAC: A Journal of Composition Theory* 16 (1996): 389–405.

Leonard, Sterling Andrus. *Composition as a Social Problem*. Boston: Houghton, 1917.

Lesikar, Raymond V. "The Meaning and Status of Organizational Communication." *ABCA Bulletin* 44 (1981): 2–5.

"Letters." *Physics Today* Feb. 1990: 11+.

"Letters." *Physics Today* May 1989: 9–11.

Levine, Barbara, and Jay Carson. E-mail to David R. Russell. 15 Oct. 2001.

Lounsbury, Thomas R. "Compulsory Composition in Colleges." *Harper's Monthly* Nov. 1911: 866–80.

Lunetta, Vincent N., and Pinchas Tamri. "Matching Lab Activities with Teaching Goals." *Science Teacher* 46 (1979): 22–24.

Lunsford, Andrea A. "A Historical, Descriptive, and Evaluative Study of Remedial English in American Colleges and Universities." Diss. Ohio State U, 1977.

Lyman, William Rollo. *Summary of Investigations Relating to Grammar, Language, and Composition*. Supplementary Educational Monographs No. 36. Chicago: U of Chicago P, 1925.

MacDougall, Robert. "University Training and the Doctoral Degree." *Education* 24 (1904): 261–76.

MacKenzie, Norman, ed. *The Letters of Sidney and Beatrice Webb*. 3 vols. Cambridge: Cambridge UP, 1978.

Mahala, Daniel. "Writing Utopias: Writing Across the Curriculum and the Promise of Reform." *College English* 53.7 (1991): 773–89.

Maimon, Elaine P. "Cinderella to Hercules: Demythologizing Writing Across the Curriculum." *Journal of Basic Writing* 2 (1980): 3–11.

———. "Reexamining False Dichotomies." CCCC Convention. Chicago, Mar. 1990.

———. *Writing in the Arts and Sciences*. Boston: Little, 1981.

———. "Writing, Learning, and Thinking at Beaver College." College English Association Annual Meeting. Savannah, Mar. 1979. ERIC, ED 175054.

Mallon, Thomas. *Stolen Words: Forays into the Origins and Ravages of Plagiarism*. New York: Ticknor, 1989.

Malmstrom, Jean. "The Communications Course." *College Composition and Communication* 7 (1956): 21–24.

Maloney, John J. "Economy of Time in English." *School and Society* 2 (1915): 96–98.

Mann, Horace. "Boston Grammar and Writing Schools." *The Common School Journal* 1 Oct. 1845: 1–3.

Marland, Michael. *Language Across the Curriculum: The Implementation of the Bullock Report in the Secondary School*. London: Heineman, 1977.

Masoner, Michael. *An Audit of the Case Study Method*. New York: Praeger, 1988.

McCloskey, Donald N. *The Rhetoric of Economics*. Madison: U of Wisconsin P, 1986.

McGrath, Earl J. ed. *Communication in General Education*. Dubuque, IA: Brown, 1949.

McLeod, Susan H., ed. *Strengthening Programs for Writing Across the Curriculum*. San Francisco: Jossey, 1988.

———. "Writing Across the Curriculum: The Second Stage and Beyond." *College Composition and Communication* 40 (1989): 337–43.

McLeod, Susan H., and Elaine P. Maimon. "Clearing the Air: WAC Myths and Realities." *College English* 62 (2000): 573–83.

McMullen-Light, Mary, et al. "A Writing-Intensive Model Closes the Assessment Loop." Writing Across the Curriculum Conference. Bloomington, IN, 2001.

Mearns, Hughes. *Creative Power*. Garden City, NJ: Doubleday, 1929.

Meiklejohn, Alexander. *The Experimental College*. New York: Arno, 1971.

Meister, Morris. "Recent Educational Research in Science Teaching." *School Science and Mathematics* 2 (1932): 875–89.

Mendelson, Michael. "The Historical Case: Its Roman Precedent and the Current Debate." Unpublished manuscript, 1988.

Meyer, George. "An Experimental Study of the Old and New Types of Examination." *Journal of Educational Psychology* 25 (1934): 641–61.

———. "An Experimental Study of the Old and New Types of Examination and Methods of Study." *Journal of Educational Psychology* 26 (1935): 30–40.

Miles, Josephine. *Working Out Ideas: Predication and Other Uses of Language*. Curriculum Publications 5. Berkeley: Bay Area Writing Project, 1979.

Miller, Carolyn R. "Genre as Social Action." *Quarterly Journal of Speech* 70 (1984): 151–67.

Miller, Carolyn R., and David A. Jolliffe, "Discourse Classifications in Nineteenth-Century Rhetorical Pedagogy." *Southern Speech Communication Journal* 51 (1986): 371–84.

Miller, Gary E. *The Meaning of General Education: The Emergence of a Curriculum Paradigm.* New York: Columbia UP, 1988.

Miller, Susan. "An Archeology of English." CCCC Convention. Chicago, Mar.
1990.

———. *Rescuing the Subject: A Critical Introduction to Rhetoric and the Writer.*
Carbondale: Southern Illinois UP, 1989.

Mitchell, Stewart. "Henry Adams and Some of His Students." *Proceedings of
the Massachusetts Historical Society* 66 (1936–41): 294–321.

Monroe, Paul, ed. *Cyclopedia of Education.* 5 vols. New York: Macmillan, 1911.

Montgomery, David. *The Fall of the House of Labor: The Workplace, the State,
and American Labor Activism, 1865–1985.* Cambridge: Cambridge UP, 1987.

Morison, Samuel Eliot, ed. *The Development of Harvard University: Since the
Inauguration of President Eliot, 1869–1929.* Cambridge: Harvard UP, 1930.

Murphy, James J., ed. *The Rhetorical Tradition and Modern Writing.* New York:
MLA, 1982.

Myers, Greg. "Reality, Consensus, and Reform in the Rhetoric of Composition
Teaching." *College English* 48 (1986): 154–73.

———. "The Social Construction of Two Biologists' Proposals." *Written Communication* 2 (1985): 219–45.

Nadworny, Milton J. *Scientific Management and the Unions, 1900–1932: A
Historical Analysis.* Cambridge: Harvard UP, 1955.

National Education Association. *Cardinal Principles of Secondary Education:
A Report of the Commission on the Reorganization of Secondary Education.*
Washington, DC: GPO, 1918.

———. *Involvement in Learning: Realizing the Potential of American Higher
Education.* Washington, DC: NIE, 1984.

Neel, Jasper P., ed. *Options for the Teaching of English: Freshman Composition.*
New York: MLA, 1978.

———. *Plato, Derrida, and Writing.* Carbondale: Southern Illinois UP, 1988.

Nellermoe, Donald A., Thomas R. Weirich, and Alan Reinstein. "Using Practitioners' Viewpoints to Improve Accounting Students' Communications
Skills." *Business Communication Quarterly* 62.2 (1999): 41–60.

Nelson, J. Raleigh. "Letter to the SPEE Board of Investigation and Coordination." *Society for the Promotion of Engineering Education Bulletin* 13 (1922):
251–52.

Neville, Mark. "Sharing Experiences with Farmville." *English Journal* 34 (45):
368–72.

Newcomb, Theodore M., and Everett K. Wilson, eds. *College Peer Groups.*
Chicago: Aldine, 1966.

Newlon, Jesse L. "Stronger Foundation for, and a Better Command of, Spoken
or Written English." *Journal of Proceedings and Addresses, National Education Association* 55 (1917): 694–98.

Nolan, Aretas W. *The Case Method of Teaching Applied to Vocational Agriculture.* Bloomington, IL: Public School Publishing, 1927.

Noll, Victor H. *The Teaching of Science in Elementary and Secondary Schools.* New York: Longmans, 1939.

Norgaard, Rolf. "Negotiating Expertise in Disciplinary "Contact Zones". *Language and Learning Across the Disciplines* 3.2 (1999): 44–63.

O'Connor, Carol A. "Setting a Standard for Suburbia: Innovation in the Scarsdale Schools, 1920–1930." *History of Education Quarterly* 26 (1980): 295–311.

Ohmann, Richard. *English in America: A Radical View of the Profession.* New York: Oxford UP, 1976.

O'Neill, J. M. "The Relation of Speech to English: Suggestions for Cooperation." *English Journal* 25 (1936): 33–41.

Ong, Walter J. *Orality and Literacy.* London: Methuen, 1982.

Osgood, Charles G. "Humanism and the Teaching of English." *English Journal* 11 (1922): 159–66.

"Our Infant Critics." Editorial. *Nation* 27 Feb. 1908: 188–89.

"Our Readers Think: About Integration." *English Journal* 34 (1945): 496–502.

"Our Readers Think: More About Integration." *English Journal* 34 (1945): 555–59.

Palmquist, Mike, Kate Keifer, and Donald E. Zimmerman. "Communication Across the Curriculum and Institutional Culture." *Electronic Communication Across the Curriculum.* Eds. Donna Reiss, Dickie Selfe, and Art Young. Urbana, IL: NCTE, 1998. 57–72.

Parker, William Riley. "Where Do English Departments Come From?" *College English* 28 (1967): 339–51.

Pemberton, Michael A. "Rethinking the WAC/Writing Center Connection." *Writing Center Journal* 15.2 (1995): 116–33.

Perkins, Agnes F. "Cooperation in English." *Nation* 24 Oct. 1907: 371–73.

Perrin, Porter G. "The Teaching of Rhetoric in American Colleges Before 1750." Diss. U of Chicago, 1936.

Phelps, William Lyon. *Teaching in School and College.* New York: Macmillan, 1912.

Piché, Gene L. "Class and Culture in the Development of High School English Curriculum, 1800–1900." *Research in the Teaching of English* 11 (1977): 17–25.

———. *Revision and Reform in the Secondary School English Curriculum, 1870–1900.* Diss. U of Minnesota, 1967.

Pierson, Frank C. *The Education of American Businessmen: A Study of University-College Programs in Business Administration.* New York: McGraw, 1959.

Potter, David. *Debating in the Colonial Chartered Colleges: An Historical Survey, 1642–1900.* New York: Teacher's College P, 1944.

Powers, Ralph S., et al. "A Proposal for Teaching Science." *Thirty-First Yearbook of the National Society for the Study of Education.* Pt. 1. Chicago: U of Chicago P, 1932.

Proceedings from the Communication Across the Curriculum Strand. 2001. NCA Summer Conference, 2001. 25 Sept. 2001. <http://www.natcom.org/Instruction/summerconf/cxc.htm>.

Progressive Education Association. *Language in General Education: A Report of the Committee on the Function of English in General Education.* New York: Appleton, 1940.

———. *Science in General Education: Suggestions for Teachers in the Secondary Schools and in the Lower Division of Colleges.* New York: Appleton, 1938.

———. *The Social Sciences in General Education.* New York: Appleton, 1940.

Purves, Alan C., and Saule Takala, eds. *An International Perspective on the Evaluation of Written Composition.* New York: Pergamon, 1982.

Quandt, Jean B. *From the Small Town to the Great Community: The Social Thought of Progressive Intellectuals.* New Brunswick: Rutgers UP, 1970.

"Reed College." *Liberal Education* May–June 1987: 30–31.

Reid, Ronald F. "The Boylston Professorship of Rhetoric and Oratory, 1806–1904: A Case Study in Changing Concepts of Rhetoric and Pedagogy." *Quarterly Journal of Speech* 45 (1959): 239–57.

Reiss, Donna. "From WAC to CCCAC: Writing Across the Curriculum Becomes Communication, Collaboration, and Critical Thinking (and Computers) Across the Curriculum at Tidewater Community College [VA]." 1996. ERIC, ED 412553.

Reiss, Donna, Dickie Selfe, and Art Young, eds. *Electronic Communication Across the Curriculum.* Urbana, IL: NCTE, 1998.

Reorganization of Science in Secondary Schools: A Report of the Commission on the Reorganization of Secondary Schools. Bureau of Education Bulletin No. 26. Washington, DC: GPO, 1920.

Report of the Committee on Secondary Schools. 1892. New York: Arno, 1969.

"Report of the English Committee." *Society for the Promotion of Engineering Education Bulletin* 12 (1921): 573–74.

Resnick, Daniel P., and Lauren B. Resnick. "The Nature of Literacy: An Historical Exploration." *Harvard Educational Review* 47 (1977): 370–85.

Richards, I. A. *The Philosophy of Rhetoric.* New York: Oxford UP, 1936.

———. *Science and Poetry.* London: Haskell, 1926.

Roach, John. *Public Examinations in England, 1850–1900.* Cambridge: Cambridge UP, 1971.

Robinson, Archer Tyler. "The Teaching of English in a Scientific School." *Science* 30 (1909): 657–64.

Rose, Mike. "The Language of Exclusion: Writing Instruction at the University." *College English* 47 (1985): 341–59.

Roy, Walter. *The New Examination System.* London: Croom, 1986.

Royce, Josiah. *Primer of Logical Analysis: For the Use of Composition Students.* San Francisco: A. L. Bancroft, 1881.

Rudolph, Fredrick. *The American College and University: A History.* New York: Knopf, 1962.

———. *Curriculum: A History of the American Undergraduate Course of Study Since 1636*. San Francisco: Jossey, 1978.

Rugg, Harold, and Anne Shumaker. *The Child-Centered School: An Appraisal of the New Education*. New York: World Book, 1928.

Russell, David R. "Rhetoric Entering the Twentieth Century: Joseph Villiers Denney at Ohio State, 1891–1933." Unpublished essay, 1987.

———. "Romantics on Writing: Liberal Culture and the Abolition of Composition Courses." *Rhetoric Review* 6 (1988): 132–48.

———. "Where Do the Naturalistic Studies of WAC/WID Point? A Research Review." *WAC for the New Millennium: Strategies for Continuing Writing-Across-the-Curriculum Programs*. Eds. Susan McLeod et al. Urbana, IL: NCTE, 2001. 259–298.

———. "Writing and Genre in Higher Education and Workplaces: A Review of Studies That Use Cultural-Historical Activity Theory." *Mind, Culture, and Activity* 4 (1997): 224–37.

Russell, David R., and Lizabeth Berryman. "Portfolios Across the Curriculum: Whole School Assessment in Kentucky." *English Journal* 90 (2001): 76–83.

Samuels, Warren J. "The Teaching of Business Cycles in 1905–6: Insight into the Development of Macroeconomic Theory." *History of Political Economy* 4 (1972): 140–62.

Santayana, George. *Persons and Places*. New York: Scribner's, 1945.

Saunders, Peter M. "From Case to Virtual Case: A Journey in Experiential Learning." *Electronic Communication Across the Curriculum*. Eds. Donna Reiss, Dickie Selfe, and Art Young. Urbana, IL: NCTE, 1998. 86–102.

Schumacher, Gary M., and Jane Gradwohl Nash. "Conceptualizing and Measuring Knowledge Change Due to Writing." *Research in the Teaching of English* 25.1 (1991): 67–96.

Searson, J. W. "Determining a Language Program." *English Journal* 13 (1924): 274–79.

Seaver, Henry Latimer. "English at the Institute of Technology." *Nation* 26 Dec. 1907: 586–87.

Selinker, Larry, and Dan Douglas. "LSP and Interlanguage: Some Empirical Studies." *English for Specific Purposes* 6 (1987): 75–85.

Shelly, Percy V. "English as an Interdisciplinary Subject in the Curriculum." *English Journal* coll. ed. 28 (1939): 349–56.

Sherif, Muzafer, and Carolyn W. Sherif, eds. *Interdisciplinary Relationships in the Social Sciences*. Chicago: Aldine, 1969.

Sinclair, Upton. *The Goose-Step: A Study of American Education*. Pasadena, CA: [the author] 1923.

"Sketch: Robert G. Valentine." *Outlook* 114 (1916): 628–29.

Slattery, Shaun. "Who Is Communicating What to Whom: An Analysis of Communication Across the Curriculum Websites with Annotated Bibliography." Master's thesis. North Carolina State U, 2000.

Sloan, Douglas. *The Scottish Enlightenment and the American College Ideal*. New York: Teachers College P, 1971.

Smallwood, Mary L. *An Historical Study of the Examinations and Grading Systems in Early American Universities; A Critical Study of the Original Records of Harvard, William and Mary, Yale, Mount Holyoke, and Michigan from Their Founding to 1900.* Cambridge: Harvard UP, 1935.

Smith, Eugene R., Ralph Tyler, and the Evaluation Staff. *Appraising and Recording Student Progress.* New York: Harper, 1942.

Smith, J. Winfree. *A Search for the Liberal College: The Beginning of the St. John's Program.* Annapolis, MD: St. John's College P, 1983.

Smith, Myrna J. "Bruner on Writing." *College Composition and Communication* 28 (1977): 129–33.

Smith, Ron. "Composition Requirements: A Report on a Nationwide Survey of Four-Year Colleges and Universities." *College Composition and Communication* 25 (1974): 138–48.

Snedden, David. *What's Wrong with American Education?* Philadelphia: Lippincott, 1927.

Spellmeyer, Kurt. "A Common Ground: The Essay in the Academy." *College English* 3 (1989): 262–76.

Sperle, D. Henryetta. *The Case Method Technique in Professional Training: A Survey of the Use of Case Studies as a Method of Instruction in Selected Fields.* New York: Teachers College P, 1933.

Spriestersbach, D. C., and Lyell D. Henry, Jr. "The Ph.D. Dissertation: Servant or Master?" *Improving College and University Teaching* 26 (1978): 52–55.

"Standards of Efficiency in the Teaching of English." Editorial. *School Review* 23 (1915): 719–20.

Stanley, Linda C. E-mail to David R. Russell. 4 Sept. 2001.

Stanley, Linda C., and Joanna Ambron, eds. *Writing Across the Curriculum in Community Colleges. New Directions for Community Colleges, Number 73.* Los Angeles: ERIC Clearinghouse for Junior Colleges, 1991.

Starbuck, Arthur. "Technical English: A Diagnosis and a Prescription." *Society for the Promotion of Engineering Education Bulletin* 9 (1919): 470–80.

Starch, Daniel, and Eliot C. Elliott. "Reliability of Grading High School Work in English." *School Review* 20 (1912): 442–57.

———. "Reliability of Grading High School Work in History." *School Review* 21 (1913): 676–81.

———. "Reliability of Grading High School Work in Mathematics." *School Review* 21 (1913): 254–59.

Stedman, Carlton H. "An Examination of Science Texts from Early America to the 1900s for Evidence of Inquiry Oriented Presentations." Urbana, IL: ERIC, 1986. ERIC, ED 271291.

Stevenson, Dwight W., ed. *Courses, Components and Exercises in Technical Communication.* Urbana, IL: NCTE, 1981.

Stevenson, John W. "The Illusion of Research." *English Journal* 61 (1972): 1029–32.

Stewart, Donald C. "Rediscovering Fred Newton Scott." *College English* 40 (1979): 539–47.

————. "The Status of Composition and Rhetoric in American Colleges, 1880–1902: An MLA Perspective." *College English* 47 (1975): 734–46.

Stormzand, Martin James. *American History Teaching and Testing: Supervised Study and Scientific Testing in American History, Based on Beard and Bagley's* The History of the American People. New York: Macmillan, 1926.

Storr, Richard J. *The Beginnings of Graduate Education in America.* Chicago: U of Chicago P, 1953.

Stout, Barbara R., and Joyce N. Magnotto. "Building on Realities: WAC Programs at Community Colleges." *New Directions for Teaching and Learning* 19 (1991): 9–13.

Stratman, James F. "The Emergence of Legal Composition as a Field of Inquiry: Evaluating the Prospects." *Review of Educational Research* 60 (1990): 153–235.

Struck, H. R. "Wanted: More Writing Courses for Graduate Students." *College Composition and Communication* 27 (1976): 192–97.

Sullivan, Patricia. "From Student to Scholar: A Contextual Study of Graduate Student Writing in English." Diss. Ohio State U, 1988.

Sund, Robert B. *Teaching Science by Inquiry in the Secondary School.* Columbus, OH: Merrill, 1973.

Sunstein, Bonnie S., and Jonathan H. Lovell, eds. *The Portfolio Standard: How Students Can Show Us What They Know and Are Able to Do.* Portsmith, NH: Heinneman, 2000.

Swanson-Owens, Deborah. "Identifying Natural Sources of Resistance: A Case Study of Implementing Writing Across the Curriculum." *Research in the Teaching of English* 20 (1986): 69–97.

"Swarthmore College." *Liberal Education* May/June 1987: 32–33.

Sypherd, W. O. "Thirty Years of Teaching English to Engineers." *Society for the Promotion of Engineering Education Proceedings* 47 (1939): 162–64.

Taft, Kendall Bernard, John Francis McDermott, and Dana O. Jensen. *The Technique of Composition.* New York: Smith, 1931.

Taylor, Thomas E. "Let's Get Rid of Research Papers." *English Journal* 54 (1965): 126–27.

Taylor, Warner G. *A National Survey of Conditions in Freshman English.* Bulletin No. 11. Madison: U of Wisconsin, 1929.

Tead, Ordway. "Industrial Counselor: A New Profession." *The Independent* 88 (1916): 393–95.

Tellen, J. Martin. "The Course in English in Our Technical Schools." *Society for the Promotion of Engineering Education Proceedings* 16 (1908): 61–73.

Thaiss, Christopher. *Language Across the Curriculum in the Elementary Grades.* Urbana, IL: NCTE, 1986.

Thaiss, Christopher, and C. Suhor, eds. *Speaking and Writing, K–12: Classroom Strategies and the New Research.* Urbana, IL: NCTE, 1984.

"Thinking Through Writing. Lord Fairfax Community College [Middletown, VA], 1990–1992." 1992. ERIC, ED 353016.

Thirty Schools Tell Their Story. New York: Harper, 1942.

Thorndike, Edward L. *Human Nature and the Social Order*. New York: Macmillan, 1940.

Thurber, Edward A. "College Composition." *Nation* 6 Sept. 1915: 328–29.

Thurber, Samuel. "English in the Secondary Schools: Some Considerations as to Its Aims and Needs." *School Review* 2 (1894): 468–78.

Thwig, Charles F. *The College of the Future*. Cleveland: Western Reserve U, 1897.

Ticknor, George. *Remarks on Changes Lately Proposed or Adopted in Harvard College*. Boston: Harvard College, 1825.

Towl, Andrew R. *To Study Administration by Cases*. Boston: Harvard U Graduate School of Business Administration, 1969.

Townsend, Martha A. "Writing Intensive Courses and WAC." *WAC for the New Millennium: Strategies for Continuing Writing-Across-the-Curriculum Programs*. Ed. Susan McLeod et al. Urbana, IL: NCTE, 2001. 233–58.

"Two Comments on 'A Common Ground: The Essay in Academe.'" *College English* 52 (1990): 329–38.

Tyack, David B. *The One Best System: A History of American Urban Education*. Cambridge: Harvard UP, 1974.

United States Immigration Commission. *Reports of the Immigration Commission: Abstracts*. 61st Congress, 1st Session. Washington, DC: GPO, 1911.

Upcraft, M. Lee, ed. *The Freshman Year Experience: Helping Students Survive and Succeed in College*. San Francisco: Jossey, 1989.

Valentine, Robert Grosenver. "Cooperating in Industrial Research." *Survey* 36 (1916): 586–88.

———. "The Human Element in Production." *American Journal of Sociology* 22 (1917): 477–88.

———. "Instruction in English at the Institute." *Technology Review* 1 (1899): 441–65.

———. "On Criticism of Themes by Students." *Technology Review* 4 (1903): 459–78.

Veysey, Laurence R. *The Emergence of the American University*. Chicago: U of Chicago P, 1965.

Viles, Jonas. *The University of Missouri: A Centennial History*. Columbia: U of Missouri P, 1939.

Vose, Ruth M. "Co-operative Teaching of English in the Secondary Schools." Master's thesis. U of Illinois, 1925.

Vygotski, Lev. *Thought and Language*. Cambridge: MIT P, 1962.

Wagner, Daniel A., ed. *The Future of Literacy in a Changing World*. Oxford: Pergamon, 1987.

Wallace, Karl R., ed. *A History of Speech Education in America*. New York: Appleton, 1954.

Walvoord, Barbara E. "The Future of WAC." *College English* 58 (1996): 58–79.

Walvoord, Barbara E., et al. *In the Long Run: A Study of Faculty in Three Writing-Across-the-Curriculum Programs*. Urbana, IL: NCTE, 1997.

———. *Thinking and Writing in College: A Naturalistic Study of Students Writing in Four Disciplines*. Urbana, IL: NCTE, 1991.

Walvoord, Barbara E. Fassler, and Virginia Johnson Anderson. *Effective Grading: A Tool for Learning and Assessment*. San Francisco: Jossey, 1998.

Warren, Constance. *A New Design for Women's Education*. New York: Frederick A. Stokes, 1940.

Watkins-Goffman, Linda, and G. Joyce Dunston. "Writing Across the Curriculum in a Data Processing Class: An Ethnographic Investigation." *Research and Teaching in Developmental Education* 11 (1994): 31–35.

Weeks, Ruth Mary, comp. *A Correlated Curriculum*. NCTE Educational Monograph No. 5. New York: Appleton, 1936.

———. *Making American Industry Safe for Democracy*. Bulletin No. 5. Chicago: Vocational Education Association of the Midwest, 1918.

———. *Socializing the Three R's*. New York: Macmillan, 1920.

———. "Teaching the Whole Child." *English Journal* 20 (1931): 9–17.

Weibe, Robert H. *The Search for Order, 1877–1920*. New York: Hill, 1967.

Weiland, Steven. "History Toward Rhetoric." *College English* 49 (1987): 816–26.

Wells, W. H. "Public High School in Chicago." *American Journal of Education* 3 (1857): 531–37.

Wendell, Barrett. *English Composition*. New York: Scribner's, 1891.

White, Edward M. "Language and Reality in Writing Assessment." *College Composition and Communication* 41 (1990): 187–200.

———. *Teaching and Assessing Writing*. San Francisco: Jossey, 1985.

White, Hayden. *The Content of the Form: Narrative Discourse and Historical Presentation*. Baltimore: Johns Hopkins UP, 1987.

White, James Boyd. *Heracles' Bow: Essays on the Rhetoric and Poetics of the Law*. Madison: U of Wisconsin P, 1986.

"Why Johnny Can't Write." *Newsweek* 9 Dec. 1975: 58–65.

Whyte, William H. *The Organization Man*. New York: Simon, 1956.

Wilcox, Thomas W. *Anatomy of Freshman English*. San Francisco: Jossey, 1973.

Williams, Raymond. *Writing in Society*. London: Verso, 1984.

Wills, Veronica Tischer. "An Investigation of the Use of the Documented Research Paper in College Courses." Diss. United States International U, 1970.

Wilson, Edmund. *The Triple Thinkers: Twelve Essays on Literary Subjects*. New York: McGraw, 1948.

Winsor, Dorothy A. *Writing Like an Engineer: A Rhetorical Education*. Mahwah, NJ: Erlbaum, 1996.

Wolverton, S. F. "Professional Scullery." *Educational Review* 60 (1920): 407–16.

Wood, Ben D. *Measurement in Higher Education*. Yonkers, NY: World Book, 1923.

Woodbridge, Homer E. "Freshman English Course." *Educational Review* 66 (1923): 7–13.

Woods, George Benjamin. *A College Handbook of Writing: A Guide for Use in College Classes in Composition*. Garden City, NJ: Doubleday, 1922.

Woods, Roy C. "The Term Paper: Its Values and Dangers." *Peabody Journal of Education* 11 (1933): 19–26.

Wozniack, John Michael. *English Composition in Eastern Colleges, 1850–1940*. Washington, DC: UP of America, 1978.

Wright, Grace S. *Core Curriculum Development: Problems and Practices*. U.S. Office of Education Bulletin 1952. No. 5. Washington, DC: GPO, 1952.

———. *Core Curriculum in Public High Schools: An Inquiry Into Practices, 1949*. U.S. Office of Education Bulletin 1950. No. 5. Washington, DC: GPO, 1950.

Writing Across the Curriculum: A Guide to Developing Programs. 2000. Susan H. McLeod and Margot Soven. Academic. Writing Landmark Publications in Writing Series. 20 Oct. 2001. <http://aw.colostate.edu/books/mcleod_soven>.

Yancey, Kathleen Blake, and Brian A. Huot. *Assessing Writing Across the Curriculum: Diverse Approaches and Practices*. Greenwich, CN: Ablex, 1997.

Yates, JoAnne. "The Birth of the Memo: A Study in the Evolution of a Genre." Association for Business Communication Annual Meeting. Indianapolis, Oct. 1988.

———. *Control Through Communication: The Rise of System in American Management*. Baltimore: Johns Hopkins UP, 1989.

Young, Art. "Teaching Writing Across the University: The Michigan Tech Experience." College English Association Convention. Savannah, Mar. 1979. ERIC, ED 176928.

Young, Art, and Toby Fulwiler, eds. *Writing Across the Disciplines: Research into Practice*. Portsmouth, NH: Boynton, 1986.

Zaluda, Scott. "Lost Voices of the Harlem Renaissance: Writing Assigned at Howard University, 1919–1931." *College Composition and Communication* 50 (1998): 232–57.

Zawacki, Terry Myers, and Ashley Taliaferro Williams. "Is It Still WAC? Writing Within Interdisciplinary Learning Communities." *WAC for the New Millennium: Strategies for Continuing Writing-Across-the-Curriculum Programs*. Ed. Susan McLeod et al. Urbana, IL: NCTE, 2001. 109–40.

Zuckerman, Harriet. *Scientific Elite*. New York: Free P, 1977.

INDEX

Harvard University, 37, 40, 111, 184;
creative writing courses at, 180;
general education reform at, 252,
255; Redbook reforms at, 252–55;
science instruction at, 94; writing
instruction at, in the eighteenth
century, 37; writing instruction at,
in the nineteenth century, 49–56,
62, 76–77, 80, 83–85, 88. *See also*
Committee on the Use of English
by Students; Lawrence Scientific
School
Harvard University Graduate School
of Business Administration, 126,
129–31
Hayakawa, S. I., 258
Hersey, Frank Wilson Cheney, 90
Hill, Adams Sherman, 49–54, 63, 89,
184
History: departments of, 41, 66; teaching of, 76–78, 84–85, 130, 159,
217
Hopkins, Edwin M., 142
Hosic, James Fleming, 147, 209
Hotchkiss, George Burton, 127
Humanities, 24, 25, 79, 106; case
method of instruction in, 130; and
the communications movement,
268; composition research in, 279;
in engineering colleges, 121, 122,
125; lecture method in, 182, 185;
professionalization of, 168–72,
174, 176, 182; version of general
education, 137, 166–68, 172–74,
185, 197–98, 199; version of general education, at Bennington College, 225; version of general education, at Columbia University,
187–90; version of general education, at Harvard University, 252;
version of general education, at
St. John's College, 195–96; version
of general education, at University
of Chicago, 190, 195; version of
general education and isolation of

from social sciences, 234–35, 252,
255. *See also individual disciplines
by name*
Hurd, Paul DeHart, 98
Hutchins, Robert Maynard, 171, 190–
95

Indiana University, 314, 369n.25
Industry: influence of, on school orga-
nization, 138–40, 210–11; system-
atic management in, 4; writing in,
102–5, 114–15, 250
Ingersoll, Robert, 44
Institute for Propaganda Analysis, 258
International Association for the Im-
provement of Mother Tongue Edu-
cation (IAIMTE), 330
International WAC. *See* Writing-across-
the-curriculum (WAC) movement
InterQuest, 326
Iowa State University, 59–60, 81–83,
124, 320, 325, 329, 373n.15
Isocrates, 171
Ivy League WAC Consortium, xiv

James, Henry, 149
James, William, 80, 84
Jenkins, Philip R., 216, 217
Johns Hopkins University, 86, 184
Jones, Barbara, 225
Jones, Robert, 312
Junior high schools, 215, 362n.38

Kandel, Issac L., 163–64, 232
Kansas, University of, 41, 61, 75, 83,
142
Kansas State Teachers College, 89
Kelly, George, 278
Kentucky schools, 317–18
Kerr, Clark, 264
Kerr, Nancy H., 324
Kilpatrick, William Heard, 201, 203–4
Kimball, Bruce A., 173, 189, 191
Kinneavy, James L., 279
Kinney, L. B., 162

David R. Russell is a professor of English at Iowa State University, where he teaches in the Ph.D. program in rhetoric and professional communication. He has published many articles on writing across the curriculum and coedited *Landmark Essays on Writing Across the Curriculum*, a special issue of *Mind, Culture, and Activity* on writing research, and *Writing and Learning in Cross-National Perspective: Transitions from Secondary to Higher Education.* He has given workshops and lectures on writing across the curriculum, nationally and internationally, and he was the first Knight Visiting Scholar in Writing at Cornell University.